The First Industrial Nation

The First
Industrial Nation

AN ECONOMIC HISTORY OF BRITAIN

1700–1914

Peter Mathias

CHARLES SCRIBNER'S SONS—NEW YORK

Printed in Great Britain
Library of Congress Catalog Card Number 70–85266

In Memoriam
T.S.A.

Contents

Figures

Tables

Preface

The writing of economic history is likely to change over the next years more than most branches of historical scholarship. Any general textbook, such as this, in a field of scholarship where research is active, must suffer attrition more than a monograph. It is not just that the advancing edge of research adds new data and ideas that change traditional perspectives – which it does – but that new methods are bringing a wholly new style into economic history. Perhaps the main single change is going to be the challenge of an historical method based on 'literary' evidence and unsystematic data, with its own tradition of critical evaluation, by systematic quantitative analysis. This is not the place to argue over the issue. Whether a general textbook, attempting to cover all aspects of change in an integrated way, will be possible within the new canon remains to be seen. The search for a unified general theory of economic growth, and future incursions of even less integrated sociological theorizing, suggest that the new demands to measure and to analyse may yield more disparate than unified conclusions. At all events, the general surveys can come only after the monographs and this stream is only now beginning to flow for British economic history.

The inevitable calls for no apology. Any textbook must rest upon past and present scholarship more than it points to the future. I hope I have acknowledged specific references in the text, and indirectly through the bibliographies. But where another party recognizes the turn of a sentence or assumes proprietary rights over an argument I can only ask forbearance (and the chance of a second printing). A general study is more at risk in this way than a monograph. Indeed only the hazards of reforming the Historical Tripos in Cambridge in 1965 (when the lecture course I had been giving was abolished) explains its appearance at all. Such a course of lectures (given between 1960 and 1965) grows like a coral. Virtually any reading in the field, any seminar, any discussion, any supervision or tutorial can throw up a new fact which claims consideration or a new suggestion to alter the balance of an argument. Apart from a lecture course in the history faculty, supported (and not infrequently challenged) in that proving ground of historical argument, college teaching, a few chapters owe their substance to lectures given in the School of Economics at Delhi and the Department of Economics of the University of California at Berkeley in 1967.

Professor C. H. Wilson is responsible for the book containing many fewer errors of fact and judgment than seemed possible when he first saw a draft. For the preparation of statistical material, secretarial assistance and corrections I am grateful to Mrs Ewen (of the economics faculty office in Berkeley), Mrs S. Lawrence, Dr A. Keep and, in particular, to Miss E. N. Bruckner. Mrs N. Anderson showed me how skilled an indexer should be. Mrs K. Plenderleith supplied unfailing enthusiasm and efficiency. I thank them all.

P. M.

Queens' College, Cambridge
27 November 1968

Acknowledgements

The author and publishers would like to thank the following for permission to use figures and tables from the sources given below:

Cambridge University Press for Figs. 1–13, 16–26, and Tables 1–9, 12–18, 20–27, 29–38, from *Abstract of British Historical Statistics* by B. R. Mitchell and P. Deane, for Tables 10, 11, 28, from *British Economic Growth 1688–1959* by P. Deane and W. A. Cole, and for Table V, from *An Economic History of Modern Britain, Vol. II* by J. H. Clapham; Macmillan & Co. Ltd and The Macmillan Co. of Canada Ltd for Fig. 15 and Table 19, from *Impact of Western Man* by W. Woodruff; The Clarendon Press for Table III, from *English Overseas Trade Statistics, 1697–1808* by E. B. Schumpeter; Oxford University Press for Table 39, from *Banking in the Early Stages of Industrialisation* by R. E. Cameron; Harvard University Press for Table VII, from *Economic Elements in the Pax Britannica* by A. H. Imlah; the Editor, *Railway Gazette*, for Table VI, from 'The Railway Mania and its Aftermath, 1845–52', *Railway Gazette*, 1936; E. & F. Spon for Table VI from *Early British Railways* by H. G. Lewin; Liverpool University Press for Fig. 14, from *Studies in British Overseas Trade, 1870–1914* by S. B. Saul; Allen & Unwin Ltd for Table VIII, from *The Development of British Industry and International Competition* by D. H. Aldcroft; Professor E. A. G. Robinson for Table IV, from 'Changing Structure of the British Economy', *Economic Journal*, 1954.

1 Prologue: the industrial revolution—identity and beginning

The term industrial revolution, which is now used so widely in all manner of publications, needs defining. More particularly, the problem is to limit its definition. Emphatically, the expression should not be used just to denote industrial or mechanical innovation, an advance in a technique of production or the mechanization of a process in a single industry, or even the conversion of a single industry onto a mass-production basis with large plants driven by more than human power. If the concept is to mean only this, then the search for its origin would be lost in the remote past. Did it begin with the gig-mill, or the blast-furnace in the fifteenth and sixteenth centuries, the fulling-mill in the thirteenth century or the water- and wind-mill in more remote classical and medieval times? Professor Nef has claimed an industrial revolution in the years 1540–1640. Professor Carus Wilson has attached the term to the fulling-mill. Professor Gordon Child once spoke of 'the industrial revolution of the late Bronze Age'. A typical industrial transformation occurred to urban brewing in London during the seventeenth century, when the structure of the industry was translated from being a handicraft affair where individual families and publicans brewed their own beer to where commercial brewers, producing possibly 10,000 barrels a year in specialized places of manufacture, supplied dependent publicans whose economic function had been reduced to simple retailing. Yet other industries retained their medieval form of production and structure of organization until the later nineteenth century – such as flour-milling, glove-making, shoe-making. The ready-made suit industry was a development of the twentieth century. The present decade is seeing much traditional food-processing leaving the family kitchen and entering the factory and shop. Where can the line be drawn? Clearly, to define the industrial revolution in this way is to universalize the term, to rob it of all limitations as to time and space. A similar semantic problem bedevils the concept of the Renaissance. Innovations in techniques of production, in technical change, although differing as to the pace and scale of change, form a continuum in history.

To be given identity, the concept implies the onset of a fundamental change in the structure of an economy; a fundamental redeployment of resources away from agriculture, becoming self-evident over time. This does not necessarily mean that investment in agriculture, output in agriculture or the labour force in agriculture go down. Indeed all these things may need to increase in absolute terms. But growth in production, investment and the labour force grows more rapidly in other sectors of the economy, which therefore becomes more differentiated. The British economy in 1850 had become structurally more different compared with 1750 than 1750 was with 1650 or compared with structural changes coming in any previous century. One can only see how important this trend is by trying to relate each main sector of the economy, and their relative rates of change, to the whole.

The concept involves also the assumption that industrial production begins to expand at a higher and sustained rate – speaking of output as a whole. The popular phrase is that coined by Professor W. W. Rostow, 'the take-off into self-sustained growth' – in other words the onset of industrialization. Essentially this presumes the idea of measuring the rate of growth of the whole economy (the gross national product or the national income, as the total value of goods and services produced in the economy) or industrial output as a whole. One speaks of a *rate* of growth of production. This has to be so conceptually, even though evidence may be desperately short for certain sectors of the economy, to work out national income and industrial growth rates statistically until after 1800. But if gross national product is to increase by up to 2 per cent per annum – and this is broadly what self-sustained growth meant in Britain – it will have been increasing much faster than in any pre-industrialized economy, which would be growing at less than 1 per cent per annum. And such a rate of growth would involve changes, sooner or later, in every aspect of a country's history and its institutions. Economic 'growth' in this sense of differentiation – structural change, 'deepening' of investment, technical change involving a change in 'production functions' – has to be distinguished from economic 'expansion' – extending a traditional pattern of economic activity without such qualitative changes.

When one asks these questions about the beginning of rapid, cumulative, structural change, with the onset of rates of growth of up to 2 per cent per annum, with all the implications this involved, the industrial revolution can be located in time and place. Britain saw the beginning of such a process between the 1740's and the 1780's. Here came a break with a tradition of economic life, and a pace of change, which had lasted for centuries and which, in certain essential characteristics, had been universal across all countries of the globe up to that time. The actual term industrial revolution was coined in the early nineteenth century in France, in conscious parallel to the French Revolution, but it had also been expressed in other words by contemporaries in Britain like Robert Owen. In 1837 a French economist, Blanqui, explicitly claimed that since the late eighteenth century (he mentioned Watt and Arkwright by name) deep-seated economic changes of this nature were affecting Britain, as fundamental in their effects on the national life, although operating in a less dramatic way, as the political upheavals which had changed the traditional face of France in 1789. The metaphor 'revolution' has one disadvantage: the assumption of very rapid change in a short space of time. In Britain the pace of change has been proved slower than in many subsequent case-histories (for example, the rate of growth of industrial production in Russia in the 1890's), and slower also than literary metaphors like 'revolution' or 'take-off' suggest whenever people have tried to measure that rate of change statistically and to pin-point the take-off point. The metaphor is over-dramatic and implies over-precision in dating. However, judged against the long perspectives of history, the eighteenth century did see pivotal changes of this nature and the development of new trends which may be claimed in retrospect to have changed the entire nature of the economy and to have established the watershed between an essentially medieval and an essentially modernized context in the economic sense.

Britain's was the first industrialization of any national economy in the world. Even more remarkable, it occurred spontaneously, not being the result of conscious government policy sponsoring industrial progress. Although inevitably the results of state policy were significant in legal processes, taxation policies and the like, it derived virtually no momentum directly from public taxation, or public effort, or state-guaranteed loans to raise capital for productive investment. Nor was there imported capital on any scale. Considerable Dutch investment in British government funds during the earlier part of the eighteenth century (which would be releasing indigenous capital for other things) was being repatriated after 1780, exactly when the need for capital investment in Britain was rising. It is worth stressing from the outset that the state had its back turned to the economy, as far as *directly* promoting industrial growth or new industrial skills on any scale were concerned. All later industrializations have been much more involved with public initiative and imported capital, while in the eighteenth century, on the other side of the Channel, much greater efforts were being made to promote new industrial skills by state decree and favour. Even in the United States in the early nineteenth century much of the capital raised for canals, like the famous Erie Canal from the Great Lakes to the Hudson River, was obtained from the sale of state bonds in London, with interest being guaranteed from local tax revenues, if need be; and American railways often prospered, like many of their colleges, on land grants from state governments. In the twentieth century most governments whose countries are not already industrialized have decided that an industrial revolution is something no country can afford to be without, and have set about creating one by state decree. Britain saw an industrial revolution by consent. It owed nothing to planners and nothing to policemen – a phenomenon, as

Professor Chambers has remarked, which grows the more remarkable as it recedes in time.

Increasing interest is now being shown in the British experience by economists and planners wrestling with the problems
of generating economic growth in developing societies in our
own day. In turn, much light has been thrown on the British
experience by the work of scholars with a practical and contemporary orientation to their research. In many senses, all
nations concerned with economic growth at the present time are
treading the path Britain first set foot on in the eighteenth
century. Even though many of the solutions available today are
very different, as are so many aspects of the contexts in which
they are placed, many of the problems are basically the same,
even though differing in scale.

The elemental truth must be stressed that the characteristic
of any country before its industrial revolution and modernization is poverty. Life on the margin of subsistence is an inevitable
condition for the masses of any nation. Doubtless there will be a
ruling class, based on the economic surplus produced from the
land or trade and office, often living in extreme luxury. There
may well be magnificent cultural monuments and very wealthy
religious institutions. But with low productivity, low output per
head, in traditional agriculture, any economy which has agriculture as the main constituent of its national income and its
working force does not produce much of a surplus above the
immediate requirements of consumption from its economic
system as a whole. Most of what is produced beyond these
elemental consumption needs flows into various forms of conspicuous expenditure and construction rather than into productive investment. The population as a whole, whether of medieval
or seventeenth-century England, or nineteenth-century India,
lives close to the tyranny of nature under the threat of harvest
failure or disease, which can bring the death rate up to seventy
to one hundred per thousand in a 'dismal peak' and average it
between thirty and forty per thousand. Increasing numbers in
these circumstances, if there is a shortage of fertile land

cultivatable by traditional methods, without changes in the
economic system will eventually bring checks: diminishing
returns in traditional agriculture and a higher incidence of emigration, famine or disease. Even if population establishes an
equilibrium with resources through various types of social
control, influencing the number of marriages and the number
of children per marriage, thus avoiding Malthusian checks in
their direct form, that equilibrium will be at a very low level of
real income. The graphs which show high real wages and good
purchasing power of wages in some periods tend to reflect conditions in the aftermath of plague and endemic disease, as in the
fifteenth century. If one looks to late fourteenth- and fifteenth-
century England as the golden age of labour as Thorold Rogers
did, it is really the equivalent of advocating the solution of
India's difficulties now by famine and disease – of counting it a
success to raise *per capita* national income by lessening the number of people rather than by expanding the economy.

These problems of poverty, of the threat of mass-starvation,
have been unknown in Britain since the industrial revolution,
and it is well to emphasize such a generalization in advance of
more detailed discussion about movements in the standard of
living during the first century of industrialization after 1750.
Gregory King's evidence of mass poverty reveals a situation
which cannot be solved by the redistribution of income, only by
enlarging the flow of resources being produced by the economy.
And to increase the national income as a whole, and productivity
per head, means changing the nature of the economic system.
This is why the industrial revolution, the start of this rapid
transformation in Britain, becomes the fundamental watershed
in the economic development of this country when seen in the
time-scale of centuries. The last paragraph of Professor Ashton's
book on the industrial revolution, one of the most influential
paragraphs in the writing of economic history in the present
generation, deserves quoting here in full.

... The central problem of the age was how to feed and clothe and
employ generations of children outnumbering by far those of any
earlier time. Ireland was faced by the same problem. Failing to solve
it, she lost in the 'forties about a fifth of her people by emigration or

starvation or disease. If England had remained a nation of cultivators and craftsmen she could hardly have escaped the same fate,
and, at best, the weight of a growing population must have pressed
down the spring of her spirit. She was delivered, not by her rulers,
but by those who, seeking no doubt their own narrow ends, had
the wit and resource to devise new methods of production and
new methods of administering industry. There are today on the
plains of India and China men and women, plague-ridden and
hungry, living lives little better, to outward appearance, than those
of the cattle that toil with them by day and share their places of
sleep by night. Such Asiatic standards, and such unmechanized
horrors, are the lot of those who increase their numbers without
passing through an industrial revolution.[1]

To pose the question of what needs to happen before self-
sustained economic growth can develop is to search for a Holy
Grail of explanation for the secrets of economic growth being
hunted so assiduously in our own day. No single equation, no
single mode of combinations of factors, can provide the answer.
There is no single, general theory of economic growth to which
all case-histories conform. Relationships between factors, the
relative importance of individual factors, have changed dramatically according to their context in time or place. A very deep-
seated instinct exists to look for a pervasive single-cause
explanation for historical phenomena (preferably one which no
one else has yet thought of) in terms of which to seek to explain
everything. In most cases, this tidy assumption is surely misguided in principle and impossible to employ operationally, at
least when one is dealing with such a deep-seated and widespread historical phenomenon like the industrial revolution or
the Renaissance. To search for a single-cause explanation for the
industrial revolution is to pose a false analogy with a simple
equation governing chemical change. It is less tidy, less satisfy-
ing, less simple, but nevertheless more accurate to suppose that
there was no one secret key which undid the lock, no single
operative variable, no one prime relationship which had to be
positive and in terms of which all other aspects of change may
be regarded as dependent variables.

[1] T. S. Ashton, *The Industrial Revolution* (1954 ed.), p. 161.

To create some confusion, which is always a stimulus to thought, it is worth challenging each factor which has been put forward as a single-cause explanation in its own right. The favourable natural resources position existing in Britain had been existing for a very long time before the mid-eighteenth century. Other countries had been equally bountifully endowed by nature. By itself, therefore, a favourable resource position was not a sufficient, though it may have been a necessary, condition for the industrial revolution. The Protestant Non-conformists have also been heralded as the secret weapon of European economic growth, the Calvinists and other sects who became active economic agents of change, the carriers of capitalism. But even though Protestant Nonconformist sects became important activists in the process of growth in Britain, identical basic religious theologies flourished in countries innocent of dramatic industrial change, in Denmark, Sweden, Northern Scotland and other primitive agricultural areas of Europe. A rising population is also said to have created the unique context for growth by expanding the internal market and the labour-force. But Ireland, and subsequently Norway and Sweden and many other non-European countries, have also experienced rapid population growth without concomitant economic development. In turn, such factors as a bourgeois social structure with attitudes orientated towards trade and economic gain, the extent of trade itself or the plentifulness of capital have each been championed as the great unique advantages which put Britain in a class by herself. But were any of these things true by themselves? The rate of interest was consistently lower in Holland and capital more abundant there – seeking investment opportunities abroad which were lacking in industry at home. And wealth from foreign trade, the extent of markets in foreign trade, was greater in Holland than in Britain, relative to the size of her economy. The Dutch social structure was also equally fluid; the 'middling orders' in her society were as important as in England. The economic ethic in that bourgeois, merchant society was equally favourable in this sense as social values in England. Wealth and enterprise, particularly trading enterprise, gave status in Holland equally as in England.

Holland was also a constitutional state with political power reflecting new wealth there as in England. No one could say that in Holland the extravagances of a lavish court robbed the nation of productive resilience, investment resources or the motivations towards business success, which some have posited in the case of France or Prussia. Yet the Dutch economy did not progress from mercantile and shipping supremacy to industrial strength. But Holland had no coal or iron, while high taxation to sustain her world-wide colonial and naval commitments did put a strain on her economy in the eighteenth century.

Nor can industrialization be explained by any sudden outburst of mechanical ingenuity or inventive genius. France had as impressive a record of scientific advance, of high standards of mechanical contrivance in luxury-market industries like watch-making and automata (performing toys) as England. Much greater positive, deliberate help was given by government to acquiring new industrial skills in France and other continental states than in England. The period of main advance in precision skills such as scientific instrument making was in the late seventeenth century, not the mid-eighteenth. Some key inventions, known for many decades, were not actively diffused in the economy until the later eighteenth century, time-lags which suggest that the acquisition of new technical knowledge was not a prime determinant of timing in the development of many new techniques. And if it was just the natural genius of the British people to do these things, there is an onus of proof on explaining just why that genius saw fit to wait until the mid-eighteenth century to throw aside its disguise, and why that natural genius faded in relation to that of other countries a brief century later on. If the natural genius of Protestants, or Anglo-Saxons, or Scotsmen, or any other theologically or racially determined category was so responsive to other criteria in this way, it suggests that those other criteria are the operationally important ones to examine when seeking the explanation for the source and timing of the momentum for economic change, however much that process may have been influenced by these particular groups.

It is much easier methodologically to defend the proposition that, if any *one* prime factor had not been present in eighteenth-century England, if there had developed in any one of half a dozen relationships in the economy absolute resistance, absolute unresponsiveness to change, the whole process of economic growth leading into industrialization might have been held back or slowed down. Setting up the issue in this way sidesteps the precise relationship between variables in the British case, but it is a useful initial analytical tool. What prime relationships can be identified? Causation must be divided into factors which operated on a long time scale and those generating change in the shorter run: slowly generating forces and 'trigger-mechanisms'. This division is useful provided the analogy does not mislead by exaggerating the stability before the changes which came during the eighteenth century and implying too sudden a change thereafter. Compared with the experience of later case-histories of industrialization, such as Japan, and twentieth-century growth rates of leading industrial nations, the main characteristic of growth in eighteenth-century and early nineteenth-century Britain was moderation.

Arthur Lewis, when referring to the contemporary world, gave top priority to what he called 'the will to industrialize'. He meant that there must be a social system and a government which has not got its face turned against economic change, or at least has not got effective power and influence to prevent spontaneous forces for change from acting. Where the momentum for change is mainly spontaneous and the mechanisms and institutions promoting economic growth mainly private, rather than state-inspired or organized, the social context, its structure and attitudes, becomes strategic. The values of the whole society are not necessarily orientated to economic growth (although momentum will be maximized if these are permissive, responsive to change) but certainly the values of activist minorities must be positive. Social prejudice against enterprise or status won by new wealth, may not prove very significant unless it is institutionalized in law and given sanctions by the state and the judicial system. This generalization may be more applicable to the 'supply side' of the process of growth, looking at inputs of factors of production such as entrepreneurship, capital and so forth. The social structure and prevailing social attitudes were probably of greater generalized significance on the 'demand side', affecting market structures and the patterns of demand. In many of these relationships, Britain proved to be fortunately endowed by the early eighteenth century. Government, in terms of aggressive economic nationalism, actively underwrote the development of trade, bound up with imperial expansion and naval potential. The revenue demands of war, even more than deliberate protectionism, created high tariff walls round the economy in the late seventeenth century, which gave considerable shelter to domestic industry. The social structure in England had become more flexible (particularly considering mobility over one or two generations) than any in Europe except, perhaps, Holland. An economy already much differentiated with trade and commerce had become associated with a much differentiated social structure, known throughout Europe for the importance of its 'middling orders', and a political structure giving much influence to commercial and professional interests. The social differentiation was also marked by an increasing religious heterodoxy with the various groupings, particularly of the Protestant Nonconformists, associating their different theological bases with differing social ethics and economic roles. The peerage was 'open-ended', with noble status confined to the eldest son (unlike many continental parallels), and strong pressures existed to create a flow of new recruits and capital to land ownership and a complementary flow away from land. For all these reasons, Britain possessed one of the most active land markets in Europe, and associated with this, a most commercially orientated attitude to land and agriculture.

A second prerequisite for economic growth was sufficient economic resources to develop new sides to the economy. When a country has become industrialized, in the circumstances of the late nineteenth or twentieth centuries, with modern methods of ocean and inland transport and modern energy resources, it is extraordinary to consider how much of its vital raw materials and energy requirements can be imported rather than being indigenous. Incalculable natural advantages still remain, such as an equable climate and sufficient water (the most important

raw material of all), but coal is now the only major natural
resource Britain possesses in abundance, with low-grade iron
ore. However, at the beginning of the process a favourable
resource position was vital, particularly in energy resources and
particularly in relation to existing methods of transport. Favourable local mineral fuel supplies close to navigable water was, in
fact, a key locational advantage for developing a mass-output,
low-cost heavy industry. The logistics of energy inputs based
upon coal, translated against available transport in a pre-railway
age, precluded any major industrial complex in heavy industry
from developing *except* where coal and ore were plentiful and
adjacent to one another and to water carriage. Here Britain
enjoyed very considerable advantages when her natural resource
position was matched to the technology upon which the early
stages of industrialization were based. Plentiful coal and iron ore
were conveniently placed with regard to water carriage in many
regions of the island; a strategic river system, in particular the
Trent and the Severn, stretched into the heart of industrial
England. These natural advantages cannot be related to the
precise timing of the industrial revolution, having existed long
before the mid-eighteenth century. But technological change
and extending river navigation was gradually making more of
these potential advantages, a geological and climatic endowment,
into active economic assets.

To economic resources must be added inventiveness, applied
science or, from some source or other (even if it means importing other people's ideas and skills), a flow of technical innovations through which production and productivity can be increased. Applied science does not seem to have been particularly
prominent in this process during the eighteenth century, save in
a minority of strategic points in its latter decades. But of the
general energetic questing for experiment, innovation, trying
new ways of doing things, there is no doubt. It was expressed,
however, largely in an empirical tradition of shrewd heads and
clever fingers, the emerging scientific experimental tradition
being one aspect of this general context. Certainly the flow of
innovations from applied science was in no wise comparable to
that which came after 1850. Technical innovation and business

development also have a human dimension. Economic growth, on the land as well as at sea, in the factory or the mine, meant the appearance and growth of an entrepreneurial group, the men under whose charge new sectors of the economy could be developed and innovations brought into productive use. Such men were the shock troops of economic change.

A collateral requirement to effect technical change is always the demand for capital embodied in such investment. Innovation in industry or agriculture meant, in the circumstances of eighteenth-century England or any underdeveloped country today, investing capital in the productive process, whether for enclosure, drainage and improvement in agriculture, expensive fixed capitals in industry or in new methods of transport – roads, canals and then railways – to cope with the new flows of materials. The largest investments of all were probably outside the direct context of industry, in transport and then in increasing investment in social capital (not directly productive in the same way as factories or machines) to meet the social implications of the new changes in production. For example, urbanization, changes in the local distribution of population and increases in total numbers multiplied severalfold the impact of demand for new housing. When economic growth involved the agglomeration of population into industrial towns – urbanization as well as industrialization – new forms of capital investment in social overheads appeared – sanitation, water supplies, paving, lighting, hospitals – all virtually unknown in village England. Increasing output per head meant directly more capital equipment per man of the labour force in industry and agriculture, as well as greater capital investment in the necessary services to sustain these sectors, such as transport.

The industrial revolution implied an increase in the rate of growth of industrial production, which meant in turn increasing the rate of investment to sustain it. This increase in the aggregate national rates of investment is now not thought to have been as high or as rapid as Professor Rostow once suggested (taking his figure from Professor Arthur Lewis), from below 5 per cent to above 10 per cent of G.N.P. But sectionally, in those areas of the economy which were expanding rapidly, rates of investment had to be greatly increased. Few people would now think that England was short of aggregate savings for this necessary increase in investment, which rose gradually, it seems, from about 5 per cent of G.N.P. in the mid-eighteenth century to 7 per cent by 1800 and to 10 per cent of G.N.P. only in the 1840's, under the impact of railway construction. War was very much more expensive than the demands of the economy in its claims on loanable funds, and massive sums were raised for war. Government loans totalled £500 million from 1793 to 1815, whereas only £20 million was invested in the canal system between 1750 and 1815. The capital problem remained much more an institutional one of creating legal procedures, instruments and channels along which savings could flow from those groups receiving them in society to those other groups who needed credit and capital. The problems involved in raising the rate of investment, the process by which this was done and the purposes for which savings were invested provide one key to industrial progress in eighteenth-century England. 'It is the habit of productive investment that distinguishes rich from poor nations,' Arthur Lewis has written, 'rather than differences in equality of income or differences in the respect accorded to wealthy men . . . The really significant turning point in the life of a society is not when it begins to respect wealth, as such, but when it places in the forefront productive investment and the wealth associated therewith.' Possibly this will not be an attitude typical of the entire society, but it will certainly be characteristic of those social enclaves which provide the active agencies of economic change.

The responsiveness of two sectors in the economy in generations before the decades of the eighteenth century, with which the term industrial revolution is usually associated, also proved vital conditioning factors to industrialization in Britain: agriculture and foreign trade. Agricultural progress needs to match industrial development or problems will intensify. This is potentially vital for food supplies, conditions of demand, the supply of savings and the creation of an industrial labour force. Agriculture was not a leading sector in England's industrialization destined for the same strategic role as in the case of

Denmark. But even without being a main source of momentum, agricultural development proved a crucial enabling condition – perhaps a precondition – for industrialization. The critical innovations, new crops and rotation techniques, antedated the mid-eighteenth century – one even speaks of an agricultural revolution of the seventeenth century[1] – and agricultural output was growing markedly in the first half of the eighteenth century, if the movement of prices and agricultural exports are a guide. But the main pace of development in enclosure and drainage came after 1750, with rising population and prices. That is to say, agriculture continued to respond when industrialization got under way and did not become a source of constraint. It gave rising production, to cope with rising population, and rising productivity, to cope with changes in the structure of the labour force in the country as a whole, as a declining proportion of the population remained involved in growing food.

Foreign trade also proved a vital sector which did see dramatic changes and expansion coming in the century before industrialization. One can also speak of a commercial revolution from 1650 to 1750.[2] Foreign trade proved an important generating source for economic momentum in different ways long before the mid-eighteenth century, affecting levels of wealth, the size of markets available to the industry of a relatively small country, sources of savings, the differentiation of the economy and society (that is to say, the higher percentage of G.N.P. and occupational groups associated with trade and services, compared with agriculture) in England in relation to other countries. When new production techniques enabled British industrialists to undercut the handicraft industries of the rest of the world in price and quality, very great opportunities resulted.

In a sense, the roots of many of these changes go back into the remote past, long before the eighteenth century. Obviously there was no sudden appearance in the mid-decades of the eighteenth century of such things as a favourable natural resource endowment or a social structure favourable to economic growth or new Protestant sects, such as Quakers and Unitarians,

---

[1] E. Kerridge, *The Agricultural Revolution* (1968).
[2] R. Davis, *The Commercial Revolution* (Historical Association Pamphlet).

to provide the enterprise groups in industrialization or new social attitudes to provide a catalyst for change. The same is probably true for the existence of capital; there does not seem to have been evidence of great capital scarcity in Restoration England. The development of these long-run relationships is on a longer time-scale and certainly not responsive just to economic relationships. Developments in Europe between 1500 and 1700 (including foreign trade and agricultural change) were, in many ways, the crucial differentiating themes when considering the mysteries of why industrialization should spring from the British or European context in the eighteenth century, and not from the Asian. However, change in most sectors of the economy (apart from agriculture and foreign trade) up to the mid-eighteenth century occurred slowly, piecemeal, and in aggregate – relative to the total national income – did not develop much spontaneous momentum to drag other sectors of the economy forward in harness with them. Population as a whole, it seems, rose very slowly, if at all, in the preceding century. Certainly no violent redeployment of numbers took place from countryside to town, from agriculture to non-agriculture, from south-east to north-west in population density, before the mid-eighteenth century, to compare with the sustained movement after the mid-eighteenth century. London and some west-coast towns, such as Bristol, grew in response to growing foreign trade, and some important regional increases in the first part of the eighteenth century may be disguised under a national average of stable numbers.

Nor did any major break-through in industrial productivity occur before the mid-eighteenth century, at least in strategic industries like metals and textiles. This awaited massive machinery, made of iron, and the massive water-powered textile mills of the 1770's; then Watt's rotary steam engine of the 1780's. Technical progress had been proceeding in various branches of industry before this, but as significant is the fact that some major technical innovations, such as smelting iron with mineral fuel and steam power, had been pioneered, but not brought into general use or adopted by entrepreneurs in the industries as a whole. Invention did not produce cumulative innovation on the same scale as it did after the mid-eighteenth century.

Greater differentiation also came to the economy, developing at about the same time. Before the mid-eighteenth century no major changes had come to the economic range of traditional methods of transport for shifting bulk goods, to sustain the deployment of the increased flows of material coming with industrialization and rising population. Turnpikes had been improving the road approaches to London, and some river navigations were being extended, but the canal age began in the 1750's, with improvements before that time being piecemeal with no great capital investment taking place in transport. The major development of financial institutions on a national scale needed to service the vastly increased transactions and credit involved with industrialization, again came after 1750, with the rise of a linked national network of country banks, London bankers, bill brokers and other specialized intermediaries handling the transfer of credit between different regions of the country. Although great wealth from land and foreign trade was available, potentially, for mobilization long before 1750, the institutional development which accompanied the changes in economic structure came primarily after the mid-century.

These new beginnings sprang in necessary response to the more rapid rate of industrial change and rise in population, and may be summarized under the definition of structural change and differentiation in the economy. If one defines the industrial revolution by a break in the rate of change in series measured quantitatively, there are reasons for putting the 'take-off' at the end of the American War in 1783 when foreign trade values began to rise very steeply. Certainly the 1780's saw a sharply increased rate of growth in many new developments, such as transport investment and the spread of banking, and crucial technical innovations in cotton, iron and steam power. The 1750's and 1760's saw the onset of many structural changes and important trends in industrial innovation in key industries. Apart from the longer-run conditions which favoured economic growth in eighteenth-century England, which have sometimes been given the name of 'pre-conditions', shorter-run influences conditioned the timing of new growth during the eighteenth century. Low farm and food prices in the agricultural depression 1730–50 probably gave a boost to internal consumer demand. Foreign trade values showed a great leap, particularly in the 1740's, which was strategic for the expansion of markets in certain industries, even though the total level of internal trade was several times greater than that of external commerce. The maintenance of money wages, and a rise in money wages in some areas, then gave a strong boost to internal markets with rising population after 1750. During the generation from 1750 to 1780, foreign trade does not appear to have been as important a trigger-mechanism relative at least to the internal market. Rising demand, high wages, the shortage and inflexibility of skilled labour then created a great stimulus in the mid-decades of the century to innovation, mechanical advance and an eventual break-through to new forms of power, materials, machines and factory production. After 1783 foreign trade once again provided a strong boost to industrial expansion on the demand side. Once innovations had allowed cost-reducing techniques and rising productivity to become established, then the circle became a self-reinforcing process with strong forces built in to diffuse and institutionalize further innovation. All these issues now have to be explored in more detail in separate chapters covering the different sectors of the economy and the various main relationships involved in industrialization in the British case.

Reading list

GENERAL READING AND TEXTBOOKS FOR PART I

ASHTON, T. S. *An Economic History of England: the 18th Century*, London, 1955.
ASHTON, T. S. *The Industrial Revolution, 1760–1830*, London, 1948.
BEALES, H. L. *The Industrial Revolution, 1750–1850*, London, 1928.
BRIGGS, A. *The Age of Improvement*, London, 1959.
CLARK, G. N. *The Wealth of England from 1496 to 1760*, London, 1946.

COURT, W. H. B. *A Concise Economic History of Britain from 1750 to Recent Times*, Cambridge, 1954.

DEANE, P. *The First Industrial Revolution*, Cambridge, 1965.

DEANE, P. & COLE, W. A. *British Economic Growth, 1688–1959: Trends and Structure*, 2nd ed., Cambridge, 1967.

DOBB, M. H. *Studies in the Development of Capitalism*, rev. ed., London, 1963.

HOBSBAWM, E. J. *Age of Revolution: Europe, 1789–1848*, London, 1962.

HOBSBAWM, E. J. *Industry and Empire*, London, 1968.

KITSON CLARK, G. S. R. *The Making of Victorian England: being the Ford Lectures delivered before the University of Oxford*, London, 1962.

MANTOUX, P. *The Industrial Revolution of the 18th Century*, London, 1961.

MITCHELL, B. R. & DEANE, P. *Abstract of British Historical Statistics*, Cambridge, 1962 [for reference].

IN A DIFFERENT TRADITION:

MEIER, G. M. & BALDWIN, R. E. *Economic Development: theory, history, policy*, New York, 1957.

ROSTOW, W. W. *The Stages of Economic Growth: a non-communist manifesto*, Cambridge, 1960.

THE INDUSTRIAL REVOLUTION: IDENTITY AND BEGINNING
[*See also under General Works, p. 18.*]

CLARK, G. N. *The Idea of the Industrial Revolution*, Glasgow, 1953 (Murray Lecture, 1952) (Glasgow University Publications, no. 95).

COLEMAN, D. C. 'Industrial growth and industrial revolutions', *Economica*, 1956, **23**, no. 89. Reprinted in E. M. Carus-Wilson (ed.), *Essays in Economic History*, vol. 2, London, 1962.

DEANE, P. & COLE, W. A. *British Economic Growth, 1688–1959: trends and structure*, 2nd ed., Cambridge, 1967, chs. 1–2.

FONG, H. D. *The Triumph of the Factory System in England*, Tientsin, 1930.

FLINN, M. W. *Readings in Economic and Social History*, London, 1964.

FLINN, M. W. *Origins of the Industrial Revolution*, London, 1966.

HABAKKUK, H. J. 'Historical conditions of economic growth', in L. H. Dupriez (ed.), *Economic Growth*, New York, 1951.

HAMILTON, E. J. 'Profit inflation and the industrial revolution, 1751–1800', *Quarterly Journal of Economics*, 1942, **56.**

HARTWELL, R. M. (ed.) *Causes of the Industrial Revolution*, London, 1967.

HARTWELL, R. M. *Industrial Revolution*, London, 1965 (Historical Association: General Series, no. 58).

JOHN, A. H. 'Aspects of economic growth in the first half of the 18th century', *Economica*, new series, 1961, **28,** no. 110.

NEF, J. U. 'The industrial revolution reconsidered', *Journal of Economic History*, 1943, **3,** no. 1.

Past and Present, 1960, no. 17, 'The origins of the industrial revolution'.

ROSTOW, W. W. (ed.) *The Economics of Take-off into Sustained Growth*, Proceedings of a conference held by the International Economic Association, London–New York, 1963, particularly papers by H. J. Habakkuk and P. Deane, and W. W. Rostow, S. Kuznets, A. K. Cairncross. [See also reports of discussion of papers at end of book.]

PART I

The industrial economy is born: 1700 to the early nineteenth century

2 Gregory King's England—the pre-industrial economy

The most precise picture of the British economy and social structure just before the industrial revolution is given by the work of Gregory King. His project sprang typically from the intellectual world of the later seventeenth century, manifesting above all an intense curiosity, parallel to Newton's quest about the physical world or Locke's about human nature. There is also a scientific concern with discovery, experimentation and reducing things to rule, and – as in much seventeenth-century science – a lot of guesswork and crazy assumption-making thrown in. But at least it gives us a cross-section of English society and the national income on the eve of industrialization more reliable than any between Domesday and Victorian England. Such a flurry of interest in national strength and wealth, enumerating national resources, was a side issue, in part, of the power struggle against the Dutch and the French. It can thus be seen as one aspect of mercantilist problems. The interesting thing, however, was the underlying assumption and conviction that 'exact scientific study, if possible on the basis of figures' was the best approach to such investigations. This rational, empirical approach to problems was enshrined in the newly founded Royal Society. Quite clearly Gregory King realized the importance of sample surveys, as we should now call them. Moreover, his work was accepted by contemporaries and later investigators as of high repute. Modern investigations have broadly confirmed his opinions on the size of total population, and on that of London. Gregory King also had access to what official statistics there were, notably the Hearth Tax Returns, but also excise taxation (for estimates of such things as beer consumption) as well as his own local surveys, which became

23

TABLE I: *Gregory King's estimate of the population and wealth of England and Wales, calculated for 1688*

Rank	Number of families	Heads per family	Persons	Yearly income per family £	Yearly expenditure per family £	Total income of group £
Temporal Lords	160	40	6,400	2,800	2,400	448,000
Spiritual Lords	26	20	520	1,300	1,100	33,800
Baronets	800	16	12,800	880	816	704,000
Knights	600	13	7,800	650	498	39,000
Esquires	3,000	10	30,000	450	420	1,350,000
Gentlemen	12,000	8	96,000	280	268	3,360,000
Clergy, superior	2,000	6	12,000	60	54	120,000
Clergy, inferior	8,000	5	40,000	45	40	360,000
Persons in the Law	10,000	7	70,000	140	119	1,400,000
Sciences and Liberal Arts	16,000	5	80,000	60	57.10s.	960,000
Persons in Offices	5,000	8	40,000	240	216	1,200,000
Persons in Offices	5,000	6	30,000	120	108	600,000
Naval Officers	5,000	4	20,000	80	72	400,000
Military Officers	4,000	4	16,000	60	56	240,000
Common Soldiers	35,000	2	70,000	14	15	490,000
Freeholders (better sort)	40,000	7	280,000	84	77	3,360,000
Freeholders (lesser)	140,000	5	700,000	50	45.10s.	7,000,000
Farmers	150,000	5	750,000	44	42.15s.	6,600,000
Labouring people and servants	364,000	3½	1,275,000	15	15.7s.	5,460,000
Cottagers and Paupers	400,000	3¼	1,300,000	6.10s.	7.6s. 3d.	2,600,000
Artisans, Handicrafts	60,000	4	240,000	40	38	2,400,000
Merchants by sea	2,000	8	16,000	400	320	800,000
Merchants by land	8,000	6	48,000	200	170	1,600,000
Shopkeepers, Tradesmen	40,000	4½	180,000	45	42.15s.	1,800,000
Common Seamen	50,000	3	150,000	20	21.10s.	1,000,000
Vagrants			30,000	2	3	60,000

Persons increasing the wealth of the country 2,675,520
Persons decreasing the wealth of the country 2,825,000 (underlined in the table)
Total income of persons in the country £44,394,800
Total expenditure of persons in the country £42,205,400

true sampling techniques. He became secretary to the Commissioners for the Public Accounts.

Problems remain about interpreting his work in the light of present-day national income accounts. Much of the tables remain guess-work, of course, without basis in calculation. (He thought there were 1 million rabbits and 24,000 hares and leverets in England and Wales.) No modern standards of accuracy can, therefore, be imposed on his efforts. Some of the groups in society have the 'number of persons in a family' ratio probably calculated on too low a multiplier, such as the cottagers and paupers. Vital information remains concealed by the categories he used. For Gregory King, as for many other investigators, the national unit of social accounting was the household, not individuals or families. 'Family' in this context included domestic servants, apprentices, 'living-in' journeymen and labourers. No indication results about the size of the natural family for upper social groups. The household was a natural unit of calculation for the seventeenth century, being an important unit of 'domestic economy' in the great house, on the farm with living-in servants, in much handicraft industry with apprentices living under the same roof as their master. But one of the main occupational groups is thereby concealed – the servants. Possibly 12–16 per cent of the population comes under this heading of 'living-in' employees. Not all of them were domestic servants, but this was the largest group (and it was not a marrying group in general either). In a prosperous London parish 25 per cent of the inhabitants could be servants.

This makes calculations of income per head within groups meaningless. These calculations being just incomes of households, no corporate revenue is considered. No corporate (nondistributed) income is recorded for the Crown, the Church, royal estates, trading companies, charities, colleges, trusts, etc. A large underestimate of national income therefore results; but the short-fall is not nearly as much as it would have been in other European countries, or in England a century or more before, with a much greater stake in the national wealth in land belonging to the Crown or to the Church.

Some other problems emerge when we look at his conclusions.

Gregory King assumed that the total population of England and Wales was about five and a half million. About half a million persons lived in the built-up area of London, or about a tenth of the nation. London remained, therefore, very much the largest market in the land, concentrated in a small area. This affected the structure of industry there (particularly the food processing industries and such workshop trades as furniture making) while demand from London affected land use and trade in agricultural products throughout the Home Counties and East Anglia. London's fires provided the main market for coal, from the greatest coalfield in the country, on the north-east coast, and in more specialized markets the 'magnetic field' created by London dominated the economy. For example, being a main centre for naval purchasing, London was a key market for the iron industry and the timber trade.

Looked at in aggregate, however, the town dweller was a quite unrepresentative inhabitant of seventeenth-century England. Apart from London, and the older provincial cities such as Bristol and Norwich, no towns were of great importance demographically. Three-quarters of the population were living in villages and hamlets; as high a percentage of the employed population earned their living in agriculture, many with some secondary employment. In this, England is similar to a present-day developing country. The same is true of the dimensions of poverty revealed by Gregory King's calculations. Over half the total population were not able to live by their income (these groups are underlined in the table). Their expenditure totals were being supplemented by charity and poor relief. Whole classes – a total of 2·8 million – had this fate: labouring people, outservants, cottagers, paupers, common soldiers and seamen. To Charles Davenant, moreover, this was a conservative estimate: 'very judiciously computed'. These were the classes known in the eighteenth century as the 'labouring poor'. They include the 'deserving' as well as the 'undeserving' poor. 'Cottagers' in this context were evidently squatters without land, 'housed beggars' according to Bacon, or those with not enough land to support a family. Such a statistic, of course, raises doubts about the definition of 'decreasing the wealth of the nation', when these masses, working on whatever lay to hand, could not make ends meet. The frightening scale of the problem of poverty, revealed by Gregory King, is paralleled only by non-industrial, underdeveloped countries today. The redistribution of income cannot do very much to solve poverty so deeply structured into society. The real curse of the underdeveloped country today, its economy dominated by fairly primitive agriculture and construction, lies in underemployment and seasonal unemployment, as well as in the low productivity of basic techniques. Only a change in the nature of the economic system with increasing output per head can increase output enough to pull up average standards for the broad masses of the nation. Much of the problem in seventeenth-century England came from underemployment. Technology in agriculture, industry or transport remained much subjected to the interruptions of nature: in frost, flood, gale or calm the wheels did not turn. Not much shipping put out of port between October and March. There was not much work available on the land in bad weather in some of the winter months. Building activity declined in the winter.

From Gregory King's work, England and Wales are also shown to have a very mixed or differentiated economy and society. Already the fact that this was a long-standing commercial nation had left its mark on social structure: 50,000 families were merchants, tradesmen or shopkeepers; 60,000 were artisans and handicraftsmen; a further 55,000 made up the professional classes (the Church, navy, army, office holders, and so forth) *excluding* landowners. All other countries in Europe, except Holland, would have their social structure much more heavily weighted to cultivators of the soil and landowners. England, being a much more commercial economy, possessed a much more complex society, much more so than an underdeveloped country today such as Nigeria or Burma.

There was also a large spread of class status and income among the landed classes. The leading group of 'landed society' proper comprised the 'temporal lords' down to 'gentlemen', followed by the class of 'freeholders (better sort)', 'freeholders (lesser)'. The 'lesser-freeholders', yeomen and peasants (owning or tilling their own land), form a substantial group of 140,000 families. Their income level is almost as low as that of the artisans and handicraftsmen (such as blacksmiths). This was really a prosperous peasantry, not an 'esquire' class. But already there were 150,000 farmers' families; that is, the men who were tenants renting land and employing labour. These formed the middle class, the employing class, of rural England. They prospered on income from the profits of agriculture, being a rent-paying and wage-paying group. Thus, a three-deck structure of rural society was already significant, even though many owner-cultivators still remained. As will be shown, this was important in considering the ways in which rural society influenced industrial and agricultural progress.

High differentiation existed with respect to wealth, as well as classes, in this society. Landed classes' income totalled £6 million (mostly, in aggregate, from the 'gentlemen'); the professional classes', nearly £4 million; the freeholders' and farmers' (the rural middle classes), nearly £17 million; and trading groups', £4·2 million. This is patently an underestimate for groups classified here as non-landed. Much wealth from trade would be counted under the heading of 'knights' and 'esquires' in landed groups. On the whole, however, Gregory King thought landed incomes still larger than commercial incomes.

One should also consider the sources of savings in Gregory King's England, for upon the savings of society depend its investment, its material progress. The total savings of persons he thought to be £2·2 million, distributed between freeholders, £560,000; merchants, £400,000; landed classes, £400,000; farmers, nearly £200,000; persons in the law, £210,000. No savings were possible, of course, from the depressed half of the population dependent on charity. Thus, the main source of savings was rural society – the landowners, farmers and freeholders who supplied over half of the total. A serious weakness exists in these figures in that the spending total may very well include what we would now call investment, rather than spending just on consumption. Spending on productive investment, such as improving agriculture, or extending capitals in trade and industry, would be adding to the capital stock of a nation and would have more important economic effects than spending on consumption needs such as increasing the number of one's servants, indulging in a more splendid Grand Tour or building a more magnificent country house.

Gregory King's tables do not distinguish between the agricultural and non-agricultural labour force. He has some excuse for this. The 'domestic' or 'putting out' system in textiles, nailing and a lot of finishing trades in metals, leather working, etc., did distribute industrial work to the underemployed agricultural population. They were underemployed of necessity on the land. Apart from certain times, particularly harvest time, there may be long stretches when one cannot work the land, while some have too little land to occupy all their energies even at the busier times. In some regions in England, as in the Low Countries long before, the loom or the stocking frame had become the only refuge for families not able to get access to land. But the clear division of the labour force into different sectors: agriculture, industry, transport, trade was itself a consequence of industrialization. Similarly, the seamen in the navy, and seamen in merchant fleets were not separately listed by Gregory King. This labour force was very much intermixed depending on whether it was war or peace. 'Manufacturers' (with the meaning 'industrialists') are also absent. 'Manufacturer' was usually found in the expression 'poor manufacturers'. They are, in fact, artisans and cloth workers, the lowest groups in the manufacturing sector of the economy. The wealthy men, the organizers of manufacturing and industry in this structure of production were the merchants. Manufacturers *qua* industrialists were a product of the factory system, of large-scale industry.

Another very important conclusion of King's is that the subsistence sector of the economy was very small. A very tiny percentage of the population and national income was derived from those who grew and consumed their own food, largely insulated from the market in buying and selling. The very poor peasants 'cottagers and paupers' must have done so. But almost all groups of society were committed to the market in some way; producing for sale, working for a wage, receiving rents and profits, investing, lending to some degree. Most other European

countries, Ireland, Scandinavia, and those east of the Rhine –
even more the Elbe – had a much larger percentage of the
population as peasantry or serfs, with a greater degree of 'subsistence' to them.

The landed classes in England were not an economic category
strictly speaking. Wealth made in any occupation bought land –
a traditional movement in English society. Apart from hereditary
landowners, this group becomes a club of those successfully
graduating from office, from farming, from trade, from the professions, as they acquired status with wealth. What remains true
is that the greatest single flywheel of the economy was the land,
the greatest source of wealth in rents, profits and wages, and
the greatest single employer. Directly and indirectly much of
industry depended upon the domestic harvest for its raw
materials. The brewer, miller, leatherworker, chandler, weaver,
even the blacksmith in village England were supporting and
being supported by agriculture. As in the labour force, so in
the economy more generally, there was no dichotomy between
industry and agriculture.

As far as foreign trade can be quantified in relation to national
income, its importance matches the indications suggested by the
social structure. Imports totalled, perhaps, 10 per cent of a net
national product of £50 million, with exports about the same
level, an unusually high figure for any country, save Holland,
at the time. On the same basis, national income *per capita* in late
seventeenth-century England may well have been more than
double that of a present-day underdeveloped country, such as
Nigeria, with a very large subsistence peasantry – in so far as
these comparisons over such a long span of time have any meaning. Capital formation in seventeenth-century England appears
to have been less than 5 per cent of national income; with
government expenditure a roughly similar proportion.

Reading list

BARNETT, G. E. (ed.) *Two Tracts by Gregory King*, Baltimore (Md.), 1936.

CLARK, G. N. *The Wealth of England from 1496 to 1760*, London, 1946 (Home University Library).

COOPER, J. P. 'The social distribution of land and men in England, 1436–1700', *Economic History Review*, 1967, **20**.

GEORGE, M. D. *England in Transition: life and work in the 18th century*, London, 1953 (Pelican Books, no. A 248). [These two works print King's tables.]

GLASS, D. V. [two papers on Gregory King printed in] D. V. Glass and D. E. C. Eversley (eds.), *Population in history; essays in historical demography*, London, 1965.

LASLETT, T. P. R. *The World We have Lost*, London, 1965.

MARSHALL, D. *England in Transition*, London, 1967.

WILSON, C. H. *England's Apprenticeship, 1603–1763*, London, 1965.

WRIGLEY, E. A. 'London's importance, 1650–1750', *Past and Present*, 1967, no. 37.

3 The state, rural society and the land

Industrialization in Britain, from at least the mid-eighteenth century onwards, is usually taken, rightly, as the classical case of spontaneous growth, responsive primarily to market influences and underlying social, institutional forms, not shaped consciously by government design, in the interests of promoting industrial growth. In so far as the state was important, its main role was to institutionalize these underlying social and economic forces, to provide security at home and abroad within which market and economic forces, social and cultural drives would operate. It did not aim to provide a central momentum to the process of industrial growth, to shape development, to act as a counter to economic and social forces which might be inhibitory to industrialization. It was concerned more with the context than with the process; with regulating the external conditions rather than the actual internal productive forces; with trade more than industry. Compared with countries like France, Prussia, or even Russia in the eighteenth century, and with the process of industrialization in all other countries in later times (including the United States), this may stand as a relative truth, and an important one. Industrialization in Britain after the mid-eighteenth century, as distinct from the expansion of trade, was not the result of deliberate government policy sponsoring industrial progress. The state did very little indeed to promote industrial innovation as an act of policy, to stimulate productive investment (except via its military expenditures), to mobilize capital for productive investment, whether directly by way of taxation or indirectly by guaranteeing the return on capital

32

raised on the market (by a promise to mortgage tax receipts for dividends) or offsetting risks in different ways. It did not conduct enterprise itself on any scale, certainly not in strategic areas of industrial growth and innovation, limiting its direct commitments to a handful of naval dockyards (producing specialized warships and very active only when new fleets were in commission) and ordnance works such as Woolwich Arsenal. The state did not set out energetically to attract foreign capital or foreign skills. It was reluctant even to accept responsibility on a national scale for meeting the social investment consequent upon industrialization and urbanization (at least until the 1840's) – either the social investment needed to aid economic growth or to cope with its consequences: effective local government, city improvement, health, sanitation, education. It did not even concern itself much with establishing the usual infrastructure of planning, financing, or organizing the financing of roads, canals, railways or public utilities like docks.

The most important exception to these several generalizations relates to protection. Here the state did set a context which favoured the growth of new and rising industries, such as linen, silk, paper, cotton and shipbuilding. Although the fact that England became a high tariff country at the end of the seventeenth century owed more to revenue demands than to 'protectionism', the results were still influential. State intervention may thus be considered in a more favourable light in the pre-industrial revolution period. Many of the features of the policy of other European states, encouraging new skills and indigenous enterprise, were characteristic of government policy in England in the seventeenth century, though scarcely promoted very vigorously by committing large resources to these ends. By the mid-eighteenth century, the momentum to be derived from such interventions in the market place was probably more than counterbalanced by their disadvantages.

Indeed one can argue a case that Britain had the worst of both worlds from the positive and negative responses of the state. Where the state acted its impact was often to increase the obstacles to transition. There was virtual prohibition of company floatation and publicly raised capital in the manufacturing industry after the Bubble Act of 1720; banking legislation, extracted under pressure of the Bank of England, restricted the size of individual banks in England and Wales; the Corn Laws (particularly between 1815 and 1842) encouraged instability in the corn trade with wider price swings and probably maximized economic dislocation by the harvest cycle. The Settlement Laws, in so far as they had any influence, discouraged the migration of labour away from agriculture. Taxation sapped working class purchasing power, and a key imported raw material, timber, suffered very high import duties from 1800 to 1840. And so on . . . while, on the negative side, the absence of public control over growing towns, the lags in the development of essential public services ranging from small denomination currency, to sanitation legislation, to an effective police force and local government, certainly increased the social costs of the transition to an increasingly industrial, urbanized economy. At all events, the phenomenon of British industrialization, with the state playing virtually no part in organizing innovation, mobilizing capital (even for social overheads such as transport) or conducting enterprise itself, becomes historically more unusual as it becomes judged in the perspective of a growing number of other case histories.

The issue of analysing the impact of the state upon the process of economic growth still exists, however, judging by results even more than by intention. Politics can never be ignored when looking at any wide issue in economic history: indirectly the state and the legal framework were of great importance in shaping the context within which the process of growth occurred and in influencing the process itself.

Law making (and enforcing) processes are always instrumental. The decision to allow free-market forces to condition a country's economic development – or the extent not to allow this – the attempts to create competitive conditions by statute – or block market tendencies which are reducing competition – remain always positive political decisions. One cannot opt out of politics. At the most elemental, a market always implies the acceptance of common rules, a special institutional, legal, and hence, political context (as Britain has been discovering afresh since 1961 in seeking to join the Common Market). At the most basic level, the fact that Britain enjoyed internal peace, subject to very occasional local interruptions, such as food riots in towns or the irruption of the Scots in 1715 and 1745, was of elemental importance. Constitutional processes allowed the forces for change to be accommodated. Even corruption in parliamentary representation, with pocket boroughs, enabled new wealth to buy political representation. A high level of internal security produced an incalculable effect on business risks and incentives for long-term projects. Within the political process, too, it is worth mentioning that a key mechanism for implementing a local productive or social purpose was the private Act of Parliament, sponsored by private initiative and the local M.P.s, to enclose, or drain, or promote a canal, a turn-pike or a railway, or urban improvement. This became the main legal vehicle for coercing a reluctant minority who opposed such projects. On balance, such private Acts affected economic change more importantly than general statutes. This did bring the state into the centre of the processes of economic change.

More particularly we must look at the areas of the economy subject to positive legislative or administrative controls; then at the economic consequences of state action in other fields. One begins with the fact that the context within which the two main sectors of the pre-industrial economy (agriculture and foreign trade) operated, were subject to such constraints. Foreign trade was shaped by legislation in its direction and in its structure, by differential duties, the regulation of shipping, colonial economies and the attempted exclusion of rival trading nations like the Dutch and the French. In the century 1650–1750 these political forces were probably of great influence in stimulating and shaping the fortunes of overseas trade; although after that they were increasingly neutralized by compromise or rejection (as with the American War of Independence). The most important markets for exports and raw materials, America and north Europe, lay outside the mercantilist fence and were not controlled by any monopolist trading companies. For a generation before the free trade legislation of the 1840's the protective system had probably acted, on balance, as a drag to expansion. Given that foreign trade was of such great importance in the process of growth for Britain, state initiative here should be acknowledged. The British Empire was the largest free-trade area in the world in the eighteenth century. One of the main arguments for the Scots in accepting the Union in 1707 was to get in on it – particularly the colonial trades. Naval protection supported commercial expansion, with consular services overseas and other provisions making the world safe for British trade. All this performed a vital public role.

Agriculture remained a specific object of attention by the legislature through export bounties and import duties from 1689 to 1846, designed to protect the industry from being fully exposed to market forces – though more in the interest of landowners than farmers. Deliberate attempts to promote agricultural improvement were marginal, typified by the temporary and amateur efforts of the Board of Agriculture during the Napoleonic Wars. In the agricultural case the impact of legislation was probably very small, relative to economic and commercial determinants. The bounties operated to encourage the development of exports in the period 1710-50, but did not prevent a fall in price and depression for farmers. The stringent import controls from 1815 to 1828 also did not prevent depression. The intention here was of more importance than the results. In its turn, free trade did not bring low prices for a generation after 1846. Until this time tariffs proved of very small effect on prices in comparison with the impress of market forces.

Formal restrictions in law on price and wage controls, controls against combination, the Settlement Laws, controls against the emigration of skilled artisans, and controls against the exports of certain technology such as textile machinery, were all important enough to produce agitations and political reactions on occasion. Businessmen spent time and money in seeking to invoke the law on their side. However, there is overwhelming evidence to suggest that they were very largely ineffective in the long run in economic terms; and their removal did not immediately produce any noticeable changes of trend. On all these issues other, non-legal, criteria were the prime determinants of change.

Patent laws are rather different, but have proved particularly intractable to analyse or to assess. There are so many unknowns that it is impossible to quantify. Were the inducements to inventors which they provided *ex ante* greater than the obstacles they put in the way of diffusion of inventions *ex post facto*? Patents did, of course, describe inventions exactly and fully publicized them as a condition of their existence thus helping to create a general awareness of new knowledge. Watt's and Arkwright's patents do appear to have held back the diffusion of innovation for some time. Nation-wide petitioning took place against the attempt to renew Arkwright's patent in 1781. In the face of much piracy Boulton and Watt took energetic legal action to hold their patents effectively to 1800. But the side of the patent law system which is too often ignored lies in its effects upon the inducement to invest rather than the inducement to invent. It created incentives for persons to back an inventor with risk capital in the riskiest of all ventures by offering them monopoly returns in the case of success. Often backers took their rewards in licences to operate a patent themselves without fee.

There was also virtual prohibition of incorporation in manufacturing business between 1720 and the early nineteenth century. All attempts to incorporate a firm by letters patent, royal charter or private Act of Parliament had to run the gauntlet of a Parliament hostile to anything thought productive of speculation and open to challenge by all rivals with friends at Westminster. But it remains doubtful how important a blockage to enterprise this hostility by the law created. No great pressure was put on Parliament by frustrated manufacturers or an industrial lobby. Very little institutional pressure built up and no great flood of applications for incorporation resulted after the repeal of the Bubble Act in 1825. Furthermore, legal devices were developed in the early nineteenth century to allow *de lege* partnerships the *de facto* advantages of incorporation, by use of a common seal, under the form of the equitable trust or through specific limitation of liability on all contractual obligations incurred. Had great pressure built up from business interests for such advantages in the eighteenth century, or before, such legal devices might well have been evolved long before. Forms of enterprise demanding incorporation in order to share risks and to assemble very large and pre-mobilized capitals developed their own appropriate legal forms allowing such investment as transport undertakings, insurance companies, shipping, mining and land improvement. Conditions of high risk and poor communications demanded personal management for the effective control of manufacturing industry, so that the identification of ownership and managerial control was related to much more deep-seated conditions in the context of enterprise. Law remained relatively responsive to demands for change in eighteenth-century England. It could well be argued that the state of the law prevented more waste than it did enterprise. A very high rate of failure of business occurred for firms launched as corporations under the general limited liability statutes of the mid-nineteenth century. In the absence of an effectively administered code of company law – which was inconceivable in the circumstances of the time – open access to incorporation could have brought chaos.

Banking statutes do appear to have maximized instability, if a comparison with the Scottish banking scene is valid. The legal position represented a dangerous balance of control over structure, with freedom over operation. English banks remained small with six partners or fewer and unincorporate. Yet, in their operation (in great contrast with most continental states) no public control was exerted on the extent of their note issues, their cash ratios, their reserves, cheque transactions or expansionist credit policies. Thus, instability was maximized. But such instability has itself to be judged in the long run. It fed expansion, while encouraging economic fluctuations; it maximized the loss of confidence and the collapse of credit in bad years but did nothing to curb the vigour of booms.

One may say, in conclusion, that the attitude of the judiciary in the late seventeenth century, cutting down the legal status of guilds, exclusive charters and other internal monopolies, remained much more important for opening up the British economy to the free play of market forces than other legal restraints imposed against those forces. The law freed internal trade and industry effectively, while the external context of the economy remained much influenced by fiscal and administrative incursions into the free play of the market.

Public finance

Undoubtedly government financial policy, reflecting the balance of political pressures, administrative possibilities and economic objectives, was the most important single influence of the state upon economic activity. The table gives the broad picture of the public revenue from taxation and public expenditure for selected years. The rising total of the national debt shows the gap between these levels met by borrowing. This was almost exclusively a phenomenon of war finance: over 40 per cent of war expenditure on average was met by borrowing on permanent funded debt. Finally, a tentative figure is suggested for the scale of public expenditure in relation to the national income at these different dates. The *per capita* figures are better founded.

Various conclusions follow from these figures. The main revenue producers were the indirect taxes, of customs and excise, producing over two-thirds of total revenue from taxation in peacetime; falling in proportion (though sharply increased in total yield) in war when Parliament reluctantly agreed to increase direct taxation. The land tax was, it appeared, effectively levied at the end of the seventeenth century, but its yield rapidly atrophied as the assessments became standardized, not reflecting the actual increase in property values. Other assessed taxes levied on wealth during the eighteenth century – falling on carriages, cards, windows, servants, hair powder, watches and the like – although looking like symbols of social justice from the French side of the channel, really symbolized the failure of Parliament to face the issue of taxing wealth and capital efficiently, or even to maintain the efficiency of the land tax. This was only modified by the levy of an effective income tax between 1799 and 1816, reimposed in 1842 at a very low level.

Thus the real burden of taxation was highly regressive, for the greater part of the yield of indirect taxes came from commodities in mass demand – beer, spirits, malt and hops, bricks, salt, glass (printed calicoes were an exception) in excise taxation; tea, sugar, tobacco, spirits, corn (in certain years) and timber in customs (wine was an exception there). Virtually no taxation fell upon business profits or business capitals and relatively little upon landed capital or farming profits. Increments to national capital were not effectively tapped, and particularly capitals in trade, business and industry. In consequence, the impact of taxation fell upon the level of internal demand in the industries facing the mass markets, rather than upon the sources of savings. Hence, taxation did not prejudice capital accumulation or investment levels by competing for investment funds or reducing incentives. The main sources of investment capital – the savings of businessmen, merchants, farmers and landowners – were relatively unscathed.

Contemporaries thought this an advantage on the whole (despite its acknowledged social injustice) because they tended to give the difficulties of capital accumulation in the economy higher priority than the problems of the level of internal demand. The lower masses of society in Britain, as elsewhere, could not be a significant source of savings, in any case. If beer or tea and sugar had been lower in price, they would have consumed more, or more of other things (including other foodstuffs), or maximized leisure, perhaps, rather than increased their savings. They remained much too close to the margins of subsistence to be able to afford the middle-class virtues of thrift and saving. It is doubtful if many modern scholars would see a potential shortage of savings, of capital for productive investment, as a prime issue for the eighteenth-century economy – at least in the aggregate.[1]

The expenditure side of the public revenue accounts reinforces this conclusion. In peacetime, typically, more than 50 per cent of expenditure went into paying the interest on the national debt – a transfer operation that is to say, back into the same sort of pockets in society from which the direct taxes on land,

[1] See below, pp. 144–6.

TABLE II: *Public finances of Great Britain, 1715–1850*

I. PUBLIC REVENUE FROM TAXATION (£m.)

Date	Customs and Excise		Land and assessed taxes		Post Office and Stamp duties		Total	
	£m.	(%)	£m.	(%)	£m.	(%)	£m.	(%)
1715	4·0	(71)	1·1	(20)	0·4	(9)	5·5	(100)
1750	5·0	(67)	2·2	(39)	0·2	(3)	7·5	(100)
1783	8·5	(67)	2·6	(20)	1·6	(13)	12·7	(100)
1801	19·3	(58)	9·9	(30)	3·8	(12)	33·0	(100)
1820	41·4	(70)	8·0	(14)	9·6	(16)	59·0	(100)
1850	37·6	(67)	11·9	(21)	8·9	(12)	56·3	(100)

II. PUBLIC EXPENDITURE BY CENTRAL GOVERNMENT (£m.)

Date	Interest charges		Military expenditure		All other expenditure		Total expenditure		National Debt (cumulative total: £m.)
	£m.	(%)	£m.	(%)	£m.	(%)	£m.	(%)	
1715	3·3	(53)	2·2	(37)	0·7	(10)	6·2	(100)	37·4
1750	3·2	(44)	3·0	(42)	1·0	(14)	7·2	(100)	78
1783	8·1	(34)	13·7	(58)	1·8	(8)	23·6	(100)	231·8
1801	19·9	(32)	37·2	(60)	4·2	(8)	61·3	(100)	456·1
1820	31·2	(59)	16·2	(30)	6·9	(11)	54·3	(100)	840·1
1850	28.0	(57)	14·5	(31)	7·0	(12)	49·5	(100)	793·5

III. PUBLIC EXPENDITURE RELATIVE TO NATIONAL INCOME APPROXIMATIONS AND PER CAPITA

Date	% G.N.P.	Per Capita (£ current prices)
1715	c. 7 (post-war)	1·0
1750	c. 6 (peace)	1·0
1783	c. 16 (immediately post-war)	3·0
1801	c. 27 (wartime economy)	5·8
1820	c. 20 (post-war)	3·3
1850	c. 10 (peace)	2·4

Local government income and expenditure not included.

property, assessed taxes, and income tax had been taken. This was a shift of income from the mass with the higher propensity to spend towards the few with a higher propensity to save or to spend on services. These flows are on a large scale, equivalent to about half the value of total exports, for example, up to 1820, or to more than the entire wage bill of the cotton industry in 1850, and much greater than the receipts from direct taxation. The tax system was thus doubly regressive.

The next largest item was consistently military expenditure – one-third approximately of the whole in peacetime and rising to almost two-thirds in war. Apart from these two items, the total remainder was very small, and this includes grants to the Crown and royal family (the civil list) and holders of civil office. There is thus absolutely minimal expenditure, or investment, on public account save under the heading of military expenditure. No momentum was given to economic growth by investing capital or creating demand from resources brought in by taxation or loans. This represents the 'minimum' state in financial terms, at least, which reflected issues of profound constitutional importance: the political imperative of low taxes, the hatred of a professional civil service, of direct assessments of income and property values, of a standing army in time of peace, of a lavish court supported by public revenue. One has to search to find individual items outside the military budget: some marginal help for strategic transport routes; the Holyhead Road, General Wade's military roads in Scotland after 1745, a few bridges, the Caledonian Canal (even the Brighton Military Canal, which had supposedly strategic uses in war); some subsidizing of early nineteenth-century steamship routes, as mail carriers; the very occasional state pension to a poverty-stricken inventor. An occasional grant of short-term credit was made to create liquidity in a depression – as in 1793 and 1826–7. But all these are quite unrepresentative, quite exceptional, quite marginal.

These expenditure figures, coupled with the creation of the national debt, indicate that as far as its financial demands affected the economy, the entry of the government into the loan market, making demands on the flow of loanable funds, was more important than its tax revenue, mainly wrung out of the lower orders of society through indirect taxes. And the national debt was a function of war finance, to be considered under that heading, together with the economic impact of military expenditure.

The most important general conclusion from these aggregates is that taxation and public expenditure in relation to national income was lower than in other European countries which accepted greater public commitments. Natural, spontaneous economic flows were less distorted; less private capital was siphoned off. In particular, lags in social overhead investment by the state in the first half of the nineteenth century affected the process of growth. While not making demands upon investment resources, they increased the social costs of the transition to an industrial, urbanized society. Compared with Holland, the impact of taxation on the level of demand (or on interest rates) was significantly less.

War

War is a wide topic on its own, wider than just the role of the state. Moreover, it is impossible to generalize about the impact of wars upon the economy in the abstract. Different wars had different results. However, where national rivalries and war were endemic in eighteenth-century Europe, absorbing very great demands in resources and finances, campaigns were not fought over British soil and were not directly destructive of productive strength, apart from shipping losses. Not being committed to much heavy land campaigning on the continent between the generalships of Marlborough and Wellington, war did not prove a great drain on man-power either, as it did for Prussia or Sweden. Colonial wars in the seventeenth and eighteenth centuries became, in effect, an essential part of the process of an expanding overseas trade. Hence, even if trade figures suffered during the actual years of war, in the long run such military effort was integral with one of the most aggressively expanding aspects of the economy. In point of fact, different wars had greatly contrasting effects upon foreign trade. The Seven Years' War 1756–63 brought no great interruption to trade values. The War of American Independence, when command of the sea was lost for some time, imposed a sharp interruption and a decline in the values of foreign trade as a whole in the decade 1775–84. The long French Wars, 1793–1815, saw a stimulus on trend to foreign trade, with exports expanding at 3·8 per cent per annum, faster than before or subsequently. French and continental commerce was very much disrupted by blockade and destruction, as the pivot of European Atlantic commerce swung to centre on Britain. Relatively also, these wars proved disastrous for the trading strength of France. Heavy payments in loans and subsidies to allied powers were taken up in large part by the supply of British goods.

The sharpest economic impact of war derived from military expenditure and the impact of government borrowing on the money markets. One of the few constancies in history is that the scale of commitment on military spending has always risen. It was running at a rate of about £5–6 million per year of war in the early eighteenth century; £15 million per year of war in the mid-eighteenth century and no less than £40 million per year of war between 1793 and 1815. The Napoleonic Wars cost Britain £1,000 million directly in military expenditure. When these figures are judged against investment rates in industry or values in foreign trade, military finance is seen to be big enough to become an important factor in influencing productive effort. But it is still difficult to obtain a quantitative analysis.[1] Nor can we quantify the distortions (both expansions and contractions) in other sectors of the economy consequent upon the increased claims by the government on loanable funds and military spending. One cannot derive a net figure. There is no doubt, however, that government spending, considered alone, was inflationary at these times: spending was in excess of income from taxes to the tune of £9 million in 1711; £11 million in 1761; £15 million in 1782; and £36 million in the desperate year of 1797 (which was, perhaps, one-sixth of G.N.P.). Equally certainly, the effects of Sinking Funds to reduce the national debt, coupled with

[1] The effect of military spending depends upon the proportion of the total which was dispensed overseas rather than at home or used for purchasing manufactured goods, and what productive capacity was created for this. The multiplier effects of such spending are obviously determined by the answers to such questions.

contractions in spending relative to government income, were deflationary in the years after war.

The economic stimulus proved most marked in a few industries. War often brought an acute shortage of shipping, even though foreign trade could be depressed. Private yards were active with admiralty contracts as well as the five naval dockyards, even though hampered by reduced timber imports from the Baltic. Probably neutral carriers and ship-builders in Europe benefited more than belligerents. Professor Davis sees war reducing the peacetime rate of expansion of shipping on the whole (at least until 1793). Timber merchants and naval contractors in foodstuffs, iron and other supplies expanded business in the south of England, in the hinterlands of the naval ports and London. This regional transference of purchasing power remained very important for certain national markets. The dying iron industry of Sussex had life kept in its embers during the first half of the eighteenth century almost solely by cannon contracts. The number of beasts coming to Smithfield market increased in wartime also because of naval purchasing there. Undoubtedly, a great sectional benefit accrued through military spending but it is impossible to determine precisely to what extent this was balanced by contractions elsewhere in the economy. Net gain resulted nationally for the iron industry as well as ship-building. War boosted total production, probably stimulated the timing of innovations, and imports of Baltic iron were interrupted. Wartime expansion, in fact, usually created excess capacity in the iron industry which took some years of peace to absorb. It also induced a desperate search for new markets and new uses for iron to employ the extra capacity laid down for military contracts in the casting shops. Thus, the distortions of wartime demand accelerated the extension of capacity but created problems of fluctuations. The same was true of the copper and lead industries. In less quantifiable ways, the Birmingham and Sheffield industries gained in capacity and skills from small-weapon contracts, which were fed into their range of precision metal-working operations.

War brought sectional distortions to other trades more than clearly defined net expansion. In textiles, canvas, cheaper shirtings and woollens gained from government contracts; fine cloths for particular export markets could suffer. This meant local benefit and local distress in different areas because of the extreme localization and specialization of the textile industry. The same was true of branches of foreign trade, in particular the re-export trades to Europe. Very great dislocation was produced in the short run from blockade. During the Continental System in 1807–8 British exports to Europe were running at £9 million per annum. When the ports opened again in 1814 £28 million, much of it derived from re-exports of colonial goods, was sold. The blockade had also induced a desperate search for substitute markets in South America and elsewhere. Government expenditure in war, and other effects of war were certainly at the expense of general standards of consumption. Living standards came under pressure from increased taxation which sapped purchasing power, and food prices went up when imports were prejudiced in years of scarcity. Employment could be prejudiced by distortions in trade but also stimulated by military recruiting. War finance also increased inflationary pressures through the monetary system, with government borrowing, particularly with the 'paper pound' in some years during the Napoleonic Wars, when the Bank of England went off gold.

Government borrowing

The effect of government borrowing is clearest in its impact upon the level of activity in some sectors of the economy. With great political resistance to increasing direct taxation and limits on the inelasticity of demand for articles under indirect taxation, inevitably, much recourse was had to the loan market. The burden of interest payments, which were deflationary on the whole, upon following generations was increased by inefficient marketing of loans and Sinking Funds. When the government was plunging heavily in the loan market in order to increase its rate of spending interest rates were driven up. In so far as funds were tempted out of hoards and idle balances, this would produce a net gain if resources were lying idle from want of demand. But an element of inflation was also present, particularly during the Napoleonic Wars. Diverting the flow of loanable funds towards the government also prejudiced investment in certain fields, particularly the construction industry. In building and public utilities, projection of turnpike trusts and canal companies where capital charges were an important element in total costs, plentiful credit and a low rate of interest much influenced the timing of activity. Mortgage rates moved in harmony with the going rate of interest on government stock. Construction fell away at these times of high rates induced by government wartime borrowing. The building industry was also prejudiced when Baltic timber supplies were threatened.

The operation of the Usury Laws put a specific cut-off point on much private investment. Commercial interest rates above 6 per cent were prohibited from 1700 to 1714 and above 5 per cent from 1714 to 1832, a restraint which did not apply in practice to government borrowing. Consequently, when market rates of interest, induced by government borrowing, rose beyond this point, the flow of funds was abruptly diverted. Bankers and other intermediaries handling credit flows switched their custom away from discounting or mortgages into funded or floating government paper. War finance in conjunction with the Usury Laws substantially increased the instability of the economy by creating fluctuation in the money market and in the main investment industries. Because of this great diversion of funds and economic activity, it is difficult to say whether, overall, the increase in government spending allowed by this privileged access to the loan market increased the sum total of activity in the country. The distortions were favourable to growth by extending capacity under forced draft in the iron industry, unfavourable by producing lags in construction investment. And the other general problem about war production always is that so much of it consists of expendable assets of strictly military use or designed to be destroyed. What calculations of general rates of growth there are suggests that they were reduced by the effects of war, at least during the years while the war was being fought.

War and military spending were also not very productive in innovations during this period, at least compared with the twentieth-century example, where wartime emergency and peacetime defence spending have proved the forcing ground for key innovations laying the basis for a whole range of growth industries. In the eighteenth century new swords did not produce such important ploughshares. Nor were there many strikingly new swords either. A large number of innovations of a second order of importance can be identified. The most well known is probably John Wilkinson's cannon-boring device which enabled him to make a true cylinder for steam engines.[1] From admiralty spending came improved cartography, exploration, some improvement in the design of ships, an extension of the use of iron in construction, copper sheathing, the famous chronometers (invented in connection with the attempt to find a means of establishing exact longitude at sea), certain medical and dietary innovations, and the like. Many other examples can be quoted but they are of a similar level of importance.

Beyond making a subjective judgment, the diversity of relationships summed up in the general catch-all concept 'the role of the state' precludes striking a net balance or drawing up a precise profit and loss account.

The first conclusion to be drawn is that the net result was to maximize instability in the economy. This came partly from the absence of controls designed to limit the instabilities inherent in natural market processes (for example, an effective company law, banking controls, counter-cyclical action against depression and speculation, or in urbanization problems). Positive state actions also had the effect of increasing instability (for example, the techniques of raising money for war finance, war itself and the like).

More fundamentally, the role of the state in Britain, compared with other European countries, minimized the distortion of natural flows, in the sense of diverting resources through public channels. Given the state of administrative efficiency in most branches of the public service in eighteenth-century England this had its advantages. Alternative courses of action have to be measured not against a theoretical norm of the potential advantages to be gained from increased state action, but against the actual political context of the times. Any institution falling

[1] This type of boring machine was well known in France long before.

under state control in that context was not apt to be administered with a view to its functional efficiency. The demands of political cohesion at Westminster received transcendent priority. The institution concerned, whether the Royal Mint, the Bench, the army or the Anglican Church became drawn into the patronage system to provide the spoils of office essential for buttressing a ministry's majority, placating the magnate families and their clients, and in general securing that informal cohesion of the British political *élite* which was the wonder of Europe. Functional efficiency, it might be remarked in passing, had a higher premium in the case of the navy, partly because the importance of the navy's role received more general recognition at Westminster; partly because a stupid naval captain was less likely to survive at sea than a stupid general in a land campaign (at least by the end of the eighteenth century).

In relation to the internal and international context, the processes of diffusing skills and the sources of innovation, this absence of direct state controls over the greater part of productive processes reaped an economic gain. The constructive results in other countries during the eighteenth century, where the government showed much greater initiative in economic control or in the development of new skills, were not impressive. But such a context was changing by the mid-nineteenth century where the springs of economic growth were coming to depend more and more upon an increasingly active participation by the state in those fields which it had chosen to neglect in Britain, particularly education. A discussion of the role of the state in the century after 1850 would not, therefore, lead to such a clear-cut conclusion.

Detail is altered, but the broad proportions are scarcely changed when local government is brought into the picture. Despite very incomplete figures of county and borough expenditures these were too small to affect the pattern significantly – at the end of the eighteenth century aggregated county rates totalled under £300,000, the major part of which went to sustain gaols, prisoners, constables and prosecution procedures. A small fraction was devoted to the construction and repair of bridges. Much the greater part of local expenditure consisted of poor relief

payments, levied on a parish basis. Here receipts were considerable compared with central government totals for civil expenditure – being just under £·75 million in the mid-eighteenth century, rising steadily to £5·3 million in 1803, and over £8 million
in 1813, at about which level they continued until after 1834.[1]
This transfer payment to the poorest groups in society at the
local level must temper the judgment made about regressive
indirect taxation at the national level.

Looking more broadly at the contributions of local government to economic change is to see contrasting detail. Local
bodies often reflected the dynamic of their constituency interests. Liverpool Corporation, in particular, provided a focus
for much mercantile and business initiative which led to extensive 'pump-priming' activities. The eighteenth-century Liverpool Corporation engineers surveyed many of the rivers in the
Mersey area for navigation improvement schemes, with parliamentary bills also supported with local government finance.[2]
The influence of government, at the periphery as well as at the
centre, cannot be judged simply according to the extent of the
financial resources engaged.

LANDOWNERSHIP AND CHANGE IN RURAL SOCIETY

Changes in landownership and rural society in the eighteenth
century affected agricultural development and economic growth
in several important ways. Three main groups were directly
concerned with the land. Landowners were interested in land
primarily as units of ownership, income-yielding units with
rent-paying occupants, not directly as units of production. Few
of the larger landowners farmed for a profit themselves as
employers of labour. They ran the home farms on their estates
mainly to supply their households with fresh produce, not so
much to augment their cash income by selling on the market.
Aristocratic model farms in the late eighteenth century were not,
by and large, commercial propositions. Magnates wanted the

[1] Expenditures on actual poor relief were running at about four-fifths of
this income.
[2] See T. C. Barker, 'The beginning of the Canal Age . . .' in *Studies in
the Industrial Revolution* (1960), ed. L. S. Pressnell.

technically best animals and seeds – just as they wanted the fastest horses – not so much for profit as for prestige (which is not to say that the landowners were unconcerned with techniques of land use and improvement by their tenants). The second group in rural society were those further down the social structure having rights over the cultivation of land. These formed a mixed group including the small freeholders, owner-cultivators who enjoyed the title to some land (thus not paying rent), the rent-paying peasantry not employing labour (the family-worked farm), the farmer who paid rents and employed labour, the smallholders and squatters, possessing no legal title to land as owners but rights of customary usage over common land. All these groups were mainly concerned with land as a unit of production as much as ownership. The terms upon which they could use the land formed their main concern. The pattern of landownership and its evolution remained largely distinct from changes in land use or in the techniques of farming. Both were closely related but were far from being identical. For example, the accumulation of great estates could and did take place over the heads of the farmers (who simply changed landlords) and their farm labourers without any great change in agricultural technology, without much change in the number or size of farms and without much change in output or productivity in agriculture. On the other hand the development of a great estate, when its owner was active and efficient like the Cokes or the Bedfords, could lead to the consolidation of farms, improvement, rising productivity, rising farm profits and, eventually, rising rents. The third group, at the base of the pyramid of rural society in England, were the farm labourers, without ownership or rights of use over land, a rural proletariat working for wages.

No sharp divisions existed here between rural groups. A characteristic of English society as a whole was exactly the lack of sharp frontiers between classes. No formal boundaries existed: landowners did not form a caste. They shaded down from the great magnates to the squires and landed gentry to the lesser freeholders. Dukes and earls such as the Talbots, the Wentworths or the Bedfords in the eighteenth century might

possess rent-rolls of £10,000–£30,000 per annum.[1] The squirearchy, from whose ranks were drawn the knights and Members
of Parliament for the counties, such as the Isham family of
Northamptonshire, would have their estates and influence
primarily limited to within their counties, as would the landed
gentry, those of J.P. status, commoners with influence localized
to their own neighbourhoods. Similar differentiation occurred in
the other groups in English rural society. The farmer might own
some patches of land and rent much more from different landlords. The word 'farmer' covered a great range of enterprise, as
it still does, from men controlling hundreds, occasionally more
than a thousand, acres in East Anglia to the small peasant in
Wales or Cornwall. The records of the single estate, which show
an impoverished yeoman owning three or five acres of land, can
be deceptive. This could be true, but the man might be renting
much more land from other landlords. The view of the farm
from the estate book of a single country house or the tax assess-
ment lists does not reveal this complexity. In income, if not in
status, a prosperous farmer might rival a landed gentleman,
particularly in eastern England. The man who worked for a
wage might also have some income from a patch of land or a
garden and a cow. Cobbett almost presumed that a prosperous
farm labourer would keep a pig in the 1820's. There was also the
question of some family income derived from spinning, weaving,
gloving or other out-work, and some income in kind.

Social flexibility was reinforced by mobility in the social
hierarchy over one or two generations. The class structure was
a little like the rooms in an hotel with occupants passing fairly
quickly up and down the hierarchy of status, however firm the
graduations of categories at any one time. A spendthrift family
or a string of daughters, each of whom had to receive part of the
estate (or its income) as a dowry, or the absence of any children
at all could wreck a family's fortunes and undo the work of
several generations of accumulating a landed estate. By contrast,
a conscientious farmer might save and buy land so that his son
could find that he was as interested at the end of his life in the

---

[1] The Duke of Bedford enjoyed a gross income from rents of £31,000 in
1732.

movements of his own rents as in the movement of corn prices. He had become a landed gentleman as well as a farmer. In the church at Fenstanton, near Huntingdon, is the marble tomb of Lancelot Brown, Esquire. He died as a landed gentleman, being lord of two manors and the owner of a prosperous small estate. Capability Brown began as a jobbing gardener, but a gardener with genius. He received the gift of his manors from a financially embarrassed lord who could not pay his bill. Capability Brown's son became an admiral. Opportunities for mobility in the course of one or two generations were probably much greater outside rural society in eighteenth-century England because trade and industry were expanding at a faster rate than agriculture.

A very important characteristic of the English aristocracy and society in general was that of its 'open-endedness'. Because primogeniture kept titles with the eldest son, the younger sons were pushed out of noble status, out of the family estate and into the professions or even into trade. On the other hand, wealth easily bought knighthoods, rotten boroughs and a parliamentary career, very occasionally a peerage, when translated into enough land. Moreover, the translation of commercial wealth into landed estates was characteristic of English society and it greatly enhanced the economic efficiency of using the land. Adam Smith commented, 'Merchants are commonly ambitious of becoming country gentlemen, and when they do they are generally the best of all improvers.' He spoke in contrast of 'mere landed gentry', who did not improve, as we might speak today of gentlemen farmers who raise nothing except their hats. In the 1720's Defoe found one country seat after another which had passed into the possession of a great merchant, or which had been maintained by the foresight of its noble owner marrying into trade. 'It is observable', he wrote, 'that in this part of the country [the Home Counties] there are several very considerable estates purchased and now enjoyed by citizens of London, merchants and tradesmen. I mention this to observe how the present increase of wealth in the City of London spreads itself into the country, and plants families and fortunes who in another age will equal the families of the ancient gentry.'

Commercial instincts brought to the land habits of accounting

and profit calculation learned in trade, habits of ploughing back
capital into a business to expand it. The flow of capital back to
the land by merchants in later life was especially marked. Agriculture received as much as it gave. Investment in land brought
status, a good investment (with rising capital values and rising
rents following improvement) and remained a much safer investment for merchants' families than anything else, particularly
if their sons were young or if they had only daughters. Josiah
Child, one of the greatest merchants in the country, wrote, 'If
a merchant in England arrives at any considerable estate, he
commonly withdraws his estate from trade before he comes near
the confines of old age; reckoning that if God should call him
out of the world while the main part of his estate is engaged in
trade, he must lose one-third of it, through the inexperience and
ineptness of his wife to such affairs; and so it usually falls out.'
Dr Johnson said roundly in 1780: 'Lands are fitter for daughters
than trade.'

Professor Habakkuk has shown that the period 1680–1740
saw an increase in the large estates at the expense of smaller
proprietors, the smaller gentry as well as the freeholders. At the
same time the squirearchy and gentry class was changing its
composition. 'Mere' landed gentry, living on rents from one
generation to another, were being squeezed out. Recruits to the
smaller landowning class were coming mainly from successful
tradesmen and professional classes. Above them in the hierarchy,
the squirearchy with rentals of about £1,000 per annum remained very stable, with lower groups more hard pressed.
Estates with rentals of above £2,000–£3,000 per annum gained.
The trend of the times was running against the small estates, at
least for the central counties of England, such as Northamptonshire and Bedfordshire. The peers probably enjoyed the fruits
of office more than lesser men whose horizons were more confined to their counties where local office did not tend to be so
lucrative. Probably the peers had a better chance of sustaining
their fortunes by marrying heiresses. The larger estates also
employed professional stewards, secretaries and accountants.
Being larger, they could afford the overheads of a professional
staff which in turn could impose higher standards on tenants.

High land taxation in the war years 1690–1715, running at a
level of 4s. in the pound, sapped the profits of smaller, less
efficient estates, whose owners had no income from other sources.
Taxation proved a heavy burden, particularly on estates in
central England which were efficiently valued and assessed.
This had lightened by the mid-eighteenth century, when the
rate of tax fell in peacetime to 2s. in the pound and became
compounded by less efficient valuations which did not reflect
the rising capital values of land. The land tax suffered the
traditional fate of assessments in English direct taxation which,
because of lags in re-assessment, became fixed and traditional
while actual values rose. The period of low agricultural prices,
1730–50, when rents fell into arrears, put added pressure on
smaller landowners, without the reserves of the larger owners,
who could ride out these stringencies more comfortably.

Two legal devices, strict entail and new legal terms for raising
a mortgage, also played into the hands of the more powerful
landed families. Strict settlement and entail was an arrangement
seeking to prevent the head of the family from selling any part
of the estate, short of outright bankruptcy. Its effect was to make
the son of a landed family a life tenant of the estate, enjoying
its revenue but not possessing power to sell any capital. Integral
with strict entail were the better mortgage terms also gained.
Legal refinements created the ruling that, provided the annual
interest continued to be paid on the loan, a creditor could not
demand sale of land (with the developing market a creditor
could pass on the loan to another seeking an investment). This
ruling made mortgage a much more long-term loan, the interest
being a burden only on the income of the estate. Provided that
remained secure estates could now carry permanently a very
high load of debt on mortgage from one generation to another
quite safely. For the creditor, a mortgage on a sound estate was
the best and safest security available – as good as investment in
the 'funds' after the 1690's. Landed families could now raise
capital more easily on mortgage, to provide dowries for
daughters and capital for younger sons who could not get their
portions in land because of the strict settlement. Husbands also
settled land on their wives to give them an income in case of

widowhood. Hence a double movement developed of families getting indebted to provide dowries for daughters, those dowries being used to extend the landed estates of their husbands. Increased pressure was added from merchants' daughters seeking noble – or at least landed – husbands, which was bidding up the price of dowries. So, upon the financial basis of the mortgage and the strict settlement, landed estates accumulated more land and became more indebted at the same time. By the mid-eighteenth century about half the land of England was estimated to be under strict settlement. Add to this picture rising standards of expenditure as the magnates sought to build more magnificently, live more lavishly, stock their houses more grandly and travel more expensively.

Several important conclusions followed. Primogeniture and entail encouraged younger sons to take their inheritance as capital sums, often into the Church, the army or into commerce, because they could not get their inheritance in land and were not encouraged to cling to landownership on the traditional family lands. Strict entail also encouraged a shift in role away from landownership. The peerage and landowner groups were therefore open-ended in a double sense. A stream of persons from titled and landed families were leaving this occupational group at one end while a stream of recruits were arriving at the other. Smaller estates were being absorbed into the larger as the process of dynastic alliances accumulated estates consolidated under strict entail. By the later eighteenth century the land market seemed to be drying up. The landed magnate was in duty bound allowed to marry an actress only after he had done his duty to the family by marrying an heiress first. As lands were accumulating, so the search intensified for efficient tenant farmers to occupy them. They became an expanding and strategic group on the land as smaller owners and occupiers were squeezed out, tenanting lands previously held by smaller landed gentry, freeholders and commoners.

By the mid-eighteenth century, the burden of debt was creating great pressure upon the landed classes for increasing the income from their estates to cope with interest charges and increasing expenditure. Both these circumstances helped to create a drive from the landlords for the improvement of land, increasing the yield of land to result eventually in increased rents. Salvation might be possible through the exploitation of minerals underneath one's land (which in Great Britain belonged to the landlord) or from opportunities for investing in turnpikes and canals which might be instrumental in improving the access of one's estates or mineral leases to urban markets. The Pagets and Fitzwilliams at Wentworth Woodhouse had coal worked almost up to the shadow of their mansions. Enclosure, 'the talisman for all ambitious or impoverished squires', might double rents in a generation. The rise in the price of grain after 1750, as the rising population increased the demand for food supplies, came to the rescue of the landed classes. Enclosure became more worth while; agricultural improvement a key to solvency. Thus great incentives were developing from within the social context of rural society for productive investment in land and minerals. An important direct flow of savings from the land, being created from farming profits and agricultural rents, fertilized agricultural improvement, mining, transport improvements in turnpike trusts and canals. At the same time other flows of capital came back to the land with new recruits to the landed classes, from commerce, industry and the professions. It is impossible to say if the net flow was towards or away from the land. This theme is discussed in more detail elsewhere, but it must find its place in any discussion about the economic consequences of English rural society, in particular because of Gregory King's assumption that more than half the available savings of the nation were accruing to the landed classes.

English landowners had a particular interest in agricultural improvement, with the transcendent object of increasing their rent rolls eventually. Improvement assumed that technical innovations were extant, that markets existed for extended production, that transport improvements could make all other changes possible and profitable. To improve meant enclosing. It also often meant short-term leases of seven, fourteen or twenty-one years, not the old customary rents with variable entry fines, although much improvement also took place without such leases. It meant ploughing capital back into the land, investing in turnpikes and canals. It meant writing improvement clauses into one's leases, choosing good tenants, encouraging the more efficient kinds of farming, getting one's steward to keep the tenants up to scratch. Usually the choice of good tenants and an efficient bailiff were the twin keys to success. As well as being potentially profitable, agricultural improvement subsequently became a passion. Lord Townshend was christened Turnip as a bit of a joke in the first half of the century, but increasingly the aristocracy followed his lead after 1750. Improvement subsequently became a status-giving practice when adopted by leading members in agricultural society. Not accidentally, George III, a Hanoverian determined to be English by adopting the social conventions of his aristocracy, established model farms at Windsor, writing anonymously (but not too anonymously) as Mr Robinson for Arthur Young's *Annals of Agriculture*. George Stubbs, the most fashionable portrait painter of his day, painted cattle for noble patrons to hang on the walls of their mansions on equal terms with his paintings of their horses or their families. In the libraries of country houses were the well-thumbed copies of twenty to thirty commentators on agricultural improvement. The best writers on improvement were men like Nathaniel Kent and William Marshall, stewards of large estates. Arthur Young took an introduction from the Marquis of Rockingham when he first called to see Robert Bakewell's improved strains of sheep at Dishley Grange.

The force of example of the few improving magnates was more influential than their numbers in rural society. The main improvers and innovators were not in general, however, the great landed proprietors, with the few very notable exceptions. The landed gentry, the large owner-occupiers and the tenants on substantial farms (the men Arthur Young called 'great farmers') controlling between 200 and 500 acres, proved the key groups. These were men with risk-capital able to back their ambition. It was not usual for landlords to provide farm stock. The key role of the landlord lay in establishing the conditions under which improved farming could develop by providing security of tenure, by effective leasehold or, quite commonly, simply by verbal promise and convention with annual tenancies. Landlord capital would help with fixed capital, improvements such as new buildings and drainage but not with movable stock. Even the high rents demanded by landlords could prove a stimulus to improvement in so far as they forced farmers to produce larger cash crops for the market and organize their lands more efficiently.

Leasehold, the main form of land tenure in England, itself had certain technical economic advantages. The larger landowner had better access to the capital markets for mortgages than smaller cultivators and peasants. Some forms of improvement in agriculture demanded decisions being made which covered a large area – such as enclosure or drainage – for which it would be very difficult to obtain collective agreement amongst a large number of peasants, without state pressure. Landowners could take such decisions over the heads of their tenants. Leasehold also allowed a change of cultivator without a change of owner, so that the inefficient farmer could be removed more easily. Where landlords provided the fixed capital, the tenant put his own savings into stock and equipment, farmers not being as tempted as peasants to use all their profits for buying land, particularly where adjacent land was not available. This led to greater incentives to improve stock and invest capital in productive ways on the farm. Leasehold allowed the consolidation of farms to occur more easily, without bankruptcy, and other responses necessary for increasing efficiency and raising rents.

Even though the agricultural innovations – particularly the new implements – spread over the country very slowly, the connection between the diffusion of new agricultural techniques and large-scale landownership was also fundamental. The Cokes of Holkham, later Earls of Leicester, the most famous improving landlords in Norfolk, ploughed over 20 per cent of their rents back into improving the land. This was exceptional: the Bedfords, almost equally famous as improvers, invested at less than half this rate. The greatest social occasions and meeting-points of rural society in Norfolk and Bedford became the annual sheep-shearings of the Cokes at Holkham and the Bedfords at Woburn, the greatest agricultural shows in Europe, attracting several thousand guests, with dukes rubbing shoulders with broadclothed tenant farmers.

The improvements in agriculture with which the fortunes of the landed classes became associated, put great pressure on the small proprietors of land, the peasantry and those lower down the social structure in the countryside. Enclosures of open fields, engrossing of smaller plots and holdings into larger agricultural units (units of production and tenure rather than units of ownership) established the basis of improvement. Smaller farms were becoming less economic as far as the production of crops was concerned, just as the smaller estate was becoming less viable as a unit of ownership. No exact computation is possible of the extent of the decline of the small proprietors, the independent peasantry. Colquhoun in 1803 put them at 160,000, only 20,000 less than Gregory King more than a century earlier, but considered them more depressed in income, now falling below the farmers. Judging by literary evidence, which can be deceptive, this is an understatement. The decline in numbers ran on from the mid-seventeenth to the late eighteenth century, reversed only by very high wartime prices until 1815, when any proprietor, however small, could make money from selling corn.

Much more ruthless elimination occurred of persons without ownership of land sufficient to support a family, but who had made ends meet by their rights of common over fens, commons, wastes, woods, heaths and moors. Enclosure, by breaking up these wastes and commons, destroyed the user rights of these marginal people. Even where their rights of common were converted into the offer of a small plot of land of which they had legal title, the expense of setting up as a smallholder in enclosing the land was more than they could usually bear, and the plots were very often too small to be economic. Much social tragedy came with enclosure, as a long literature has documented, but there was no large outbreak of rural violence against it and no peasants' revolts. It was a break-up of a traditional way of life, of cultural values. Economic change always hurts some people, however beneficial it may be to society at large in the long run. The break-up of the peasantry was the price

England paid for the increased supplies of corn and meat to feed her growing population. This process had been continuing since the sixteenth century (possibly half the land in England had been enclosed before 1750). Cottagers, squatters and many smallholders faced the choice of becoming farm labourers or leaving agriculture. A stream of pamphlets and literary commentators mourned, as Goldsmith did, the times 'where wealth accumulates and men decay'. This might mean leaving the village for the towns or the mines. But many agricultural villages were transformed by the invasion of textile employment and other out-work. In the West Riding cloth areas, for example, and in Nottinghamshire the loom and the stocking frame sometimes took the place of the smallholding and the rights of common to keep the family intact in the village without the man of the house becoming a farm labourer. Or both might happen.

By the mid-eighteenth century a three-deck structure of rural society had become characteristic in England. A two-deck rural society, composed of landlords and rent-paying family cultivators – a peasantry – remained characteristic of many parts of Ireland, parts of central Wales, the North-West Highlands of Scotland and the islands (as opposed to east Scotland, a region of large farms and advanced agriculture). Smallholders also increased in certain other localities where specialized crops were flourishing, Kent with hop-gardens, orchards, market-gardens and market-gardening areas adjacent to growing towns. The economic effects of the break-up of the English peasantry were manifold but certain earlier assumptions cannot now be sustained. No rural depopulation occurred in eighteenth-century England, which denies the old analysis of the expropriation of the peasantry in its simple form being the necessary condition for the creation of an industrial labour-force. If social tragedy there was, it came from a change of status more than anything else. The fenland of Holland (Lincolnshire) saw almost all parishes increase their numbers during this period, as did Lincolnshire as a whole, a county untouched by much industry or town building. Between 1563 and 1801 its population increased by 66 per cent. Sir Frederick Eden, who made the most detailed enquiries into the state of the poor at the end of the

eighteenth century, summed it up by saying: 'Deserted villages
in Great Britain now are only to be found in the fictions of
poetry. Our agricultural parishes are better stocked now than
they were one hundred years ago when industry had not purged
the country of its superfluous mouths and the visionary evils
ascribed to the existence of commercial and agricultural
capitalists did not exist.' Numbers employed in agriculture went
on rising during the first half of the nineteenth century, and no
English county declined in population in the period 1750–1850.
Local migration from the rural areas to industrial, mining
centres and ports came from increments in population being
born in the countryside, not from the effects of enclosure in
driving people off the land. It should also be said that the worst
examples of agricultural poverty and destitution were to be
found exactly in the peasant areas of Ireland, Wales and Scotland rather than in farm-labourer villages, low though those standards were. Social protest did spring from changes in status.

The reasons for this are clear. Enclosure, the cultivation of
wastes and fenland, woods, moors and commons brought much
new land under regular crops for the first time, quite apart from
the labour demanded by the actual work of enclosures. A vast
extension of the cultivated area, more particularly after 1750,
took place, and previously cultivated land became farmed more
intensively. The agricultural innovations following enclosure
increased the value of output per acre more than the output
per head of the labour force. No dramatic break-through took
place in the mechanization of agriculture comparable to that
of the later nineteenth century with mechanical reaping and
the general diffusion of eighteenth-century inventions.[1] Much
enclosure was undertaken to produce more arable crops – the
most labour-intensive – to feed the expanding nation with its
bread and beer. The new 'mixed farming', particularly root
crops like turnips, required more labour. All this meant a need
for a greater labour-force on the land to cope with the great rise
in agricultural production. Numbers in agriculture only declined

---

[1] The high cost of labour during the Napoleonic Wars encouraged the
spread of thrashing machines, which reduced winter employment on the
farm.

relative to numbers employed in other industries, which were expanding more rapidly than agriculture after 1750.

But the effects of the creation of a rural proletariat were still very important in other ways. In England universal access to land no longer existed, as in Ireland or the Scottish Highlands. Landlords and farmers refused to agree to sub-divide holdings when population increased and the numbers of families in English villages were growing rapidly. A population increase in Ireland and the Highlands did mean sub-division of holdings (the potato enabling families to exist on smaller plots) and a multiplication of peasantry. A rise in population in these contexts took place without significant change in economic structure. In England, unless employment opportunities expanded in agriculture, the extra children in the villages had to seek non-agricultural work when they grew up. Either industrial work came to the villages, or they migrated locally to neighbouring towns, ports or coalfields. Only a relatively small proportion of the natural increase in numbers in the villages could stay to work completely in agriculture where expansion brought an increase in the demand for labour at a lower rate. Migration away from agriculture was thus very much induced by the nature of rural society, a pattern of society established before the great rise in population began in the 1740's.

The subsistence sector in England at the beginning of the eighteenth century was already very small indeed. The masses of rural society – the cultivators – were already working for money wages. Farmers were paying rents and paying wages, receiving income from profits, and landowners were receiving money rents. The reactions to a rise in income, or swings in income, of the agrarian sector and reactions to an increase in population, with the general dynamics of a population increase, are different where the landed context has a rural structure dominated by a two-deck pattern of landowners, or those receiving income from land but not themselves cultivating, and a mass of peasantry working holdings without employing labour beneath them. In the peasant context a fall in agricultural prices can lead to a contraction of the income of most families on the land. A diversion of the circular flow of the economy develops away from the agricultural sector. In the English context the majority of poor families in rural society (as well as in the towns) were wage labourers whose real income was maximized when prices fell. Moreover prices usually fell as a result of an abundant harvest which maximized the volume of work in both collecting and processing that harvest. Consumers' demand on elemental commodities – in food, drink, clothes and household goods – was maximized. In the short run the farmers bore all the losses from falling farm income, and doubtless their levels of consumption and investment decisions were lessened at these times. Further incentives to improve and cut costs were thereupon created.

Farming being a business in England more than a subsistence pursuit to support a peasantry meant that output per head in agriculture was maintained and increased at a time of increasing population. Underemployed marginal labour on the land was being squeezed out as numbers rose. Social pressure on the land thus brought economic advantage to the country, particularly where the rising industries had higher output per man than agriculture. The expansion of national wealth created in this way brought, eventually, a long-run social advantage to everyone, compared at least with the social devastation that came with famine to the peasant societies in Ireland and the Highlands in the 1840's.

AGRICULTURAL CHANGE

In the early stages of industrialization sustained economic change coming to the non-agricultural sectors of an economy depends very intimately on changes in agriculture. A paradox facing countries such as India at the present time is that the success of five-year plans in industry can be – and have been – quite frustrated by what happens in agriculture. The industrialist depends upon the peasant, upon the farmer. In twentieth-century Britain, it may be more excusable, though still false, to assume that agriculture and industry live in separate boxes, with very few links between their fortunes. But to understand the connections between agricultural change and economic growth generally in eighteenth-century England is to put the progress in English farming in new perspective. Agriculture may be seen as a 'matrix' for industry as much as being a separate sector of the economy in the eighteenth century. It provided many raw materials for industry; the labour-force, in many regions of the 'putting out' system, was really a joint labour-force with agriculture. Capital and credit flows between the land and non-farming activities were intimately linked. Agriculture was by far the largest sector of the economy, as it is in all underdeveloped societies before industrialization. In 1800 more than one-third of the occupied population in Britain were employed in agriculture. Probably one-third of the national income derived from agriculture directly and even more if indirect linkages are also included. Perhaps two-thirds of the weekly family budget of the labouring masses was spent on food and drink. One should therefore expect changes in agriculture to be very influential in the fortunes of the economy as a whole.

The connections were four-fold. With the agricultural sector providing the largest single contribution, directly and indirectly, to the savings produced by the economy before the industrial revolution, capital flows from the land were crucial. Landlords' rents and farmers' profits contributed capital for investment outside agriculture (particularly in transport) as well as for investment in agriculture itself. The greater willingness of the English landed classes to invest in these economically productive ways, the greater ability of English farmers to invest, and the greater opportunities for such profitable investment in England than in many continental countries proved very important indeed. Direct investment by groups in the landed sector became supplemented by a much more widespread connection once the country banking system began to tap the savings of agricultural districts more widely, and when farmers and landowners began to bank their balances rather than keeping them hoarded at home. The fact that the land also received capital from other sectors does not deny the importance of these flows. Both are evidence of a resilient economy.

In essence, the problem with labour is simple. Industrialization means the growth of a large non-agricultural labour-force.

At the beginning of the process the bulk of the population were employed in agriculture in one way or another. Even though the natural rate of increase of population in the industrializing regions may be high (much higher than the national average), a flow of labour away from the land needs to take place at the same time as food production is increased to feed those who depart. A smaller proportion of the population will exist as growers of food, which always creates a problem of rising productivity in agriculture as industrialization proceeds, unless circumstances favour a growing import of food. The problem of creating an industrial labour-force is much eased if industrialization is proceeding at a time of rising population. Extra numbers tend to flood off the land. But in this case the problem of feeding the growing total numbers increases the strain on farming, adding a problem of increasing total agricultural production, and hence investment in agriculture, as well as increasing agricultural productivity. If industrialization is proceeding in a context of fairly stable population, the demands made on total investment and increased output in agriculture are less, but the problem of getting labour off the land into non-agricultural employment may be intensified. It must be remembered, however, that during the eighteenth century much agricultural labour was at the same time employed part-time in domestic industry.

Food supplies remain a critical factor. The progress in trade and industry, the changes in the structure of an economy occurring with industrialization, mean a rapid rise in the numbers of people in society, and their proportion in relation to total numbers, who do not grow their own food. Unless food production rises in step with these extra numbers consuming food, prices will rise. This can create food riots and political problems in the towns. It can also have serious economic effects. With very low standards of living and food prices absorbing a high proportion of the wage bill, higher food prices can cause a cessation in spending by those not receiving the extra income from the sale of food, on everything else except food. A crisis in demand can therefore result for the products of industry in non-farming markets. If a way out of the trap is sought through the mass imports of food, then exports will have to be mortgaged to pay for them and the economy may run into a foreign exchange crisis. Importing food may have to be at the expense of importing raw materials or capital equipment for industry.

At the present time, underdeveloped countries face much graver international effects from the consequences of a failure of agricultural development than eighteenth- and nineteenth-century Britain. Much more strain falls on the debit side of the balance of payments from heavy import programmes of capital equipment, and the annual burden of interest to be paid on imported capital. They find it difficult to pick up mass exports in manufactured goods in an international economy so blockaded by quota restrictions and tariffs. The linchpin of their foreign exchange earnings therefore tends to be primary produce, either minerals and oil or agricultural produce. The failure of productivity of agriculture to rise, particularly if population is rising, will therefore mean mortgaging more land to growing food-crops for internal use or importing foodstuffs, both of which will be to the detriment of their balance of payments. Being first in the field, eighteenth-century England was not importing capital equipment or capital on any scale. Her leading sectors in industry were export-orientated, textiles expanding on export demand as much as, if not more than, home demand after 1780, and hence earning their own foreign exchange for imports of raw materials. Conditions in the world economy were then highly favourable to expanding industrial exports. Indeed, in the early nineteenth century the problem was reversed to some extent. Buying more from the primary producers abroad by abolishing import tariffs meant creating purchasing power abroad which could stimulate export purchases from Britain.

However, in the first half of the eighteenth century corn exports became a welcome earner of foreign exchange, and until the second half of the nineteenth century only a small proportion of the population became dependent upon imported food supplies. Those left on the land, a declining proportion of the labour-force, produced enough to feed both the rising total numbers of the population and the rising proportion of that population not growing their own food. That is to say, productivity per man, output per head and total output rose in agriculture, and the industrial and trading sectors of the economy were not subject to strain from this source. Only in years of bad harvest were mass food imports necessary. No crisis of famine food prices occurred, except during the special circumstances of the Napoleonic Wars. In fact the farmers were complaining of low food prices from 1730 to 1750, and 1815 to 1835. Cobbett spoke of the 'dreadful evils of abundance'. Depression in agriculture in Britain, when induced by abundant harvest and low prices, was beneficial for everyone except farmers and landowners by the early nineteenth century.

Connected with this were income conditions in the agricultural sector – the spending of families depending on farming incomes as a market for industrial and other goods. Swings in agrarian incomes are the net result of a complicated balance depending upon what proportion of demand came from agricultural labourers, whose incomes expanded with good harvests maximizing employment on the farm and reducing their food bills, and what proportion from those whose incomes and demand varied directly with agricultural prices in the short run, as discussed above.[1] Low agricultural prices, as from 1730 to 1750 and 1815 to 1835, did reduce demand from farmers, but not from farm labourers, and reduced the savings going to landowners because rent payments fell into arrears. The rise in farm incomes after 1760 stimulated savings from rising agricultural incomes, stimulated demand from farmers, while at the same time rising money wages, even for agricultural labourers in the developing regions of the economy, kept up their demand also. This gave perhaps the most favourable balance of conditions possible for increases in the demand for industrial goods from the farm sector, both consumer goods such as textiles and capital goods.

The pattern of imports and exports of corn in relation to changing prices creates suspicion about the traditional dating of the agricultural revolution, as does the dating of innovations. A growing agricultural surplus developed in the first half of the eighteenth century, when population was not growing rapidly. After high wartime prices, the price trend was downwards from

[1] Pp. 61–3; see also below, pp. 229–31.

1713 to the 1740's, while a considerable surplus was exported. Nearly 400,000 quarters of wheat per annum went abroad in the

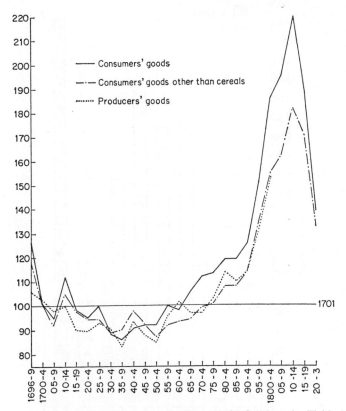

Fig. 1. Schumpeter-Gilboy price indices, 1696–1823 (see also Table 6, p. 454). After Mitchell & Deane, 1962, pp. 468–9.

decade 1740-50, culminating in the peak year of 1750, when almost one million quarters were exported.[1] All these outflows

[1] In comparison with wheat, little barley featured in the export trade, with less than a quarter of a million quarters exported in the same peak year. Malt exports remained rather larger than barley, encouraged by a slight fiscal advantage in the bounty system.

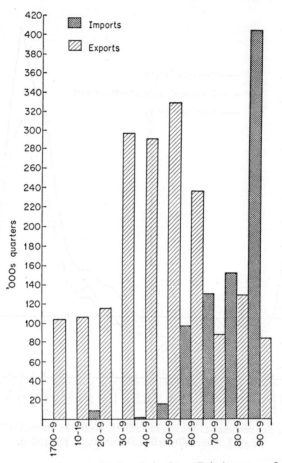

Fig. 2. Wheat and wheat flour trade in Great Britain, 1700–1800 (see also Table 20, p. 471). Annual average per decade. After Mitchell and Deane, 1962, pp. 94–5.

of grain died away during the second half of the eighteenth century, so that by 1800 there were net inflows of all grains (mainly wheat and oats), particularly in years of short harvest. The surplus capacity relative to internal needs developed in agriculture during the first half of the eighteenth century provided a cushion which was available when rising population increased total demands for food after 1750. This took some of the strain off the need to expand agriculture and relieved pressures upon prices to some extent. However, the importance of export and import figures is only assessable relative to total production and home demand, which are not accurately known until after 1866. Certainly imports and exports did not represent any great percentage of home demands. Total corn output rose from about 13 million quarters in 1700 to nearly 15 million in 1750, to 19 million in 1800, and 25 million in 1820. In the generation after 1820 probably under 5 per cent of home demand was supplied by imports, and in the 1840's only 2 million out of a population of 17 million were fed by foreign wheat. There was even more complete reliance upon home-grown barley. In meat, increases in output derived mainly from the rise in the numbers of sheep, which increased from 11 million in 1688 (a guess by Gregory King) to 26 million by 1800 (another guess). The rise in the number of cattle does not appear to have been nearly as great, but the weight of the individual beasts rose somewhat, perhaps by over one-quarter. The roast beef of Old England was always a myth, as far as the labouring masses of the nation were concerned, except on feast days. The English labourer was a granivorous animal rather than a carnivorous animal, as Professor Ashton has reminded us. Bacon and mutton remained, however, much more common than beef.

Agriculture was a protected industry throughout the eighteenth century. The export surplus was encouraged by bounties, imposed by statute in 1689, while import duties also came into effect when British prices were low. But both bounties and import duties came off when home prices rose beyond a certain point, so that foreign corn might enter the ports without fiscal restraint and home-grown grain not be encouraged abroad when bread prices were high at home. The bounties and duties were not as important in their economic effects as the political battles over them implied.[1]

British agriculture increased its output in this period through a combination of several factors. New land was brought into cultivation and previously cultivated land farmed more intensively. The advances in productivity proved insufficient to cope with the extra cultivation without a continuing increase in the labour-force. More capital was needed to bring these first two inputs to economic effect, and finally technical innovations, improvements in technique, which translated the other inputs onto a greater scale of expansion. Output per acre rose with more intensive land use; output per head rose too (but not dramatically) particularly from a fall in underemployment on the land, as the marginal producer was squeezed out. The extension of cultivation and changes in agricultural techniques were closely connected. Gregory King thought that a quarter of the country – 10 million acres – was uncultivated in 1688. The Board of Agriculture claimed that 8 million acres were still wasteland in 1795. By 1815, after the period of high wartime prices, most of the wastes and moors left were uncultivatable, but much remained to be drained. Cobbett called Surrey at this time 'devilish, horrid desert'. Much of this extension of the cultivated area and the change in land use from rough, un-improved grazing land to mixed farming depended upon tech-nical innovations and, above all, on enclosure. Enclosure was the necessary prerequisite. Every agriculturalist concerned with good husbandry from Thomas Tusser in the sixteenth century to Arthur Young and even Cobbett (who was very much on the side of the poor) cursed the open fields, where custom, tradi-tional methods, the standards of the poorest cultivator, held sway, where innovations could come only with difficulty, whether innovations in land use with new crops and rotations or innovations in animal breeding. The old system was only defended upon social, cultural grounds, although recent research suggests that it was more flexible than was commonly supposed in earlier times, particularly on lighter soils. Enclosure also did

[1] Printed in Ernle, *English Farming Past and Present*, appendix.

not always, or automatically, result in technical improvements. But it was still the most important single development.

Enclosure increased the cultivated area by eliminating commons and wastes that had occupied a traditional and necessary place in the old rotation patterns as rough grazing areas. It brought them into a regular sequence of cultivation in the new rotation patterns. Enclosure was quantitatively the most important single movement affecting land use because it made all other innovations possible. The extent of enclosure still defies measurement. Perhaps half of England was enclosed before 1750. Open fields had never existed in some areas and had been outmoded for a long time in others; in the south-west (Cornwall, Devon, Somerset), the marches (Monmouth, Hereford, Shropshire), the south-east (Suffolk, Essex, Kent, Sussex) and also the north (Cheshire, Lancashire, Westmorland, Cumberland, Northumberland and Durham). Over half of Lincolnshire land and Leicestershire land was enclosed before 1750.

Seven million acres were covered by parliamentary enclosure awards between 1760 and 1815, with over 1,000 acts passed between 1760 and 1800, and a further 800 between 1800 and 1815. Only 130 parliamentary enclosure awards were on the statute book before 1760. This does not reveal very much. The acreage was inclusive of older enclosures within the total area covered by a parliamentary award. Nothing is known of the considerable areas enclosed by agreement or under the authority of a single landlord, which did not leave a parliamentary record. And the figure of 7 million acres covered by parliamentary enclosures does not reveal what the net addition was to the cultivated area, nor the increase in productivity per acre wrought by more intensive farming. But the bulk of eighteenth-century enclosures seems to have come under the stimulus of rising prices, which puts them after 1750 and primarily by parliamentary process. The distribution of parliamentary enclosures shows a high concentration in the corn-growing districts of the east midlands, the east and the north-east. Previous enclosures were most profitable in the pastoral, mixed-farming and cattle-fattening counties, like Leicestershire and the Vale of Aylesbury. Defoe remarked of the latter place, 'All the gentlemen hereabouts are graziers, though all the graziers are not gentlemen.' Enclosures of the later eighteenth century, by contrast, were directly linked to rising grain prices in the grain belt of England.

The fens posed a special problem. The most dramatic attack on the Cambridgeshire and Lincolnshire fens had come long before in the 1630's and 1640's with the band of Stuart adventurers, king, nobles and magnates in profitable conspiracy. The adventurers engaged the famous Dutch engineer, Cornelius Vermuyden, who brought over skilled dykers from Holland. The Bedford family became the leading financiers in the drainage of the Bedford Level. Every scheme faced the hostility of fen communities, who lived by using much of the fen for summer grazing and the permanent marsh for geese, fishing and fowling. The King took one-third of the recovered 'commons', the drainers took another third, leaving only one-third for those with rights of common. The object of the drainers was to turn land under the plough, establishing much more intensive cultivation, a much greater value per acre, more profitable as rentable land and, incidentally, demanding a greater labour-force to work. New crops of flax and hemp, cole-seed (for oil), oats and wheat came in with the drainers – all the innovations from Holland. Dutch influences in East Anglia remained strong, whether Dutch gables in fen villages or Dutch crops.

During the Civil War, the work stopped and fen villagers took over much of the land of the drainers in Lincolnshire. From this time, very little was done for almost a century: the end of rising corn prices meant an end to the incentive for investing new capital. Then some local drainage began in a piecemeal way again in the early eighteenth century. The first private drainage act was taken out for Haddenham Level in 1727. This meant windmill drainage, the portent for a long series of local acts. Such drainage required the adoption of another standard Dutch technique – and the mills were also mainly Dutch-type tower-mills rather than English post-mills. Little was done on improving the main drains and the outfalls until after 1750, when rising profitability once more tempted greater capitals into improvement. Then piecemeal drainage accelerated, with the Crown no longer taking one-third of the land and local communities not protesting as violently as before. Drainage acts were the equivalent in the fens to enclosure acts elsewhere and had similar results. If four-fifths, or sometimes a smaller proportion, by numbers and extent of property, were agreed in support of a project with landowner and tithe-owner, parliamentary sanction was assured for the private bill. Only in the early eighteenth century did such legislation become the usual method of procedure.

It is very important to stress that the technical innovations coming to English agriculture were not the only aspects of agrarian development governing the progress in farming, although most of the books on farming history take everything else for granted except the innovations. Innovations giving rising output will not be taken up unless there are rising markets for agricultural products, and rising demand itself cannot be exploited in many cases until improved transport brings lower freight charges to urban markets. First in innovation came the new crops, and here the seventeenth century saw the innovations and the eighteenth and nineteenth centuries their diffusion. These were Dutch innovations, too, in the main, like the drainage skills: artificial grasses, clover, lucernes, sainfoin, which could be sowed instead of the fallow year, and 'fixed' nitrogen in the soil. These and other crops, notably the famous turnips, but also swedes and mangels, increased winter feed for animals. On this basis 'convertible husbandry' set a new pattern. Short 'leys' of grass took the place of much permanent pasture and much greater flexibility, as well as more intensive cropping, came to land use. 'Floating' water meadows by flooding flat fields adjacent to streams also brought in an earlier 'bite' of spring grass for stock. Only increased fodder for stock enabled arable cultivation – straw crops – to be grown regularly on many light sandy soils for the first time. In the days before the mass import of fertilizers and the home production of artificial fertilizers, dung from animals was the only main source of fertility on the farm. Land under straw crops in regular rotations thus became a function, almost a dependent variable, of manuring,

and the number of beasts kept was a function of the amount of
winter feed. This remained broadly true despite the search for
other methods of fertilizing land. Seaweed, rotting rags, pil-
chards in Cornwall, were all flung on the land, with lime, marl
and sand where they could help. Night-soil from the towns
was usually allowed free of toll on the canals to the country
districts.

Turnips were probably the most important single new feed
crop which increased the number of sheep, in particular, that
could be kept on light land. Theirs was the golden hoof which
made it possible to grow barley regularly on light sandy soils.
Much of Suffolk and Norfolk turned from barren heaths into
rich barley land on the famous Norfolk rotation of turnips,
barley, lucernes and spring wheat. Turnips were being planted
as a field crop in High Suffolk (i.e. east Suffolk) by 1646–56,
when references begin to 'turnip-fed stock'. They were popu-
larized by Sir Richard Weston in a treatise *Discourse of the
Husbandrie used in Brabant and Flanders*, written in 1645 and
pirated in 1651. He had been in exile there during the Civil War.
Lord Townshend also learned about turnips and clover when
Ambassador at the Hague. He publicized them well in the
1690's and became an important practitioner and publicist of
the new farming, already long established in the region, when
he retired to his country seat at Raynham, Norfolk, in 1730.
Other writers took up the advocacy of roots, clover and artificial
grasses in the 1680's (John Houghton's series, *Letters for the
Improvement of Husbandry and Trade*, began to appear in 1681).
Already by 1720 Defoe could remark that High Suffolk was an
historic spot: 'remarkable for being the first where the feeding
and fattening of cattle, both sheep as well as black cattle, with
turnips, was first practised in England, which is made a very
great part of the improvements of their lands to this day and
from whence the practice is spread over most of the east and
south parts of England to the great enriching of the farms
and increase of fat cattle'. Defoe had encountered some farmers
with £1,000 of capital tied up in cattle alone, and when he described the gentry towns of Bury St Edmunds and Newmarket
(of which he disapproved) he remarked, 'The pleasure of

West Suffolk . . . is much of it supported by the wealth of High Suffolk.'

Jethro Tull (1674–1741) added a much more equivocal contribution to the new farming, being typical of the experimental and scientific tradition of his day: a mixture of brilliant observations and false hypotheses. Tull was undoubtedly a crank who believed that thoroughly pulverizing ground with a hoe was a much better substitute for all manurings. But he was also an innovator in rational ways. He measured and controlled his experiments, establishing a tradition of experiment and observation in implements as well as in technique. He always questioned tradition upon the test of improved efficiency. In particular, he advocated the use of efficient light iron implements – harrows, rakes and hoes – drawn by a single horse, publicizing this in his famous book, *Horse-hoeing Husbandry* (1733). To this goes back a widening field of innovation in the eighteenth century. Horses were becoming increasingly the motive power in the fields rather than oxen, more expensive in feed but stronger and faster. And with the horses came an increasing range of iron implements, ploughs, harrows, hoes and rollers. The Norfolk plough became the most widespread of these innovations, drawn by two horses. Not accidentally, the range of implements was particularly utilizable on the light soils that formed the basis of the new farming techniques. Most of them remained quite impracticable for heavy land. Tull also drilled in seed by implement rather than scattering it broadcast by hand, a much more efficient technique because it provided an even distribution at a uniform depth. But this device, in particular, proved very slow in spreading to affect a significant proportion of crops sown before the mid-nineteenth century. When inspecting farming practice in Hertfordshire, one of the most advanced counties, in 1805, Arthur Young commented that he neither saw nor heard any evidence of drilling crops in the county.

The first main innovations were mainly improving rotations and crops, seed-yields and strains in plants. Advances in animal breeding and the widespread substitution of the horse for the ox on the farm followed mainly in the wake of these improvements.

This also was not accidental. The new animals demanded more efficient, better feeding. The old styles of unimproved stock remained a natural and appropriate response to poor pasture, waterlogged fields in the winter and scanty winter feed. Neither sheep nor draught-animals could serve a specialized function: the ox was eaten when it could no longer draw. As with new crops and rotations innovations long preceded the famous names of farming history. The most famous breeder of improved stock was Robert Bakewell (1725-95), who created the new Leicester and three other breeds of sheep – all designed for fertile lowland pastures. Less dramatic, anonymous improvers preceded him, using very similar methods. Bakewell measured increase in weight against the weight of feed, breeding completely for meat (sometimes, it was said, fat), not for wool. He was less successful in improving the Longhorn breed of cattle, again for meat rather than milk. His farm at Dishley Grange, Leicestershire, was right in the middle of the cattle-fattening country, and although he achieved great fame in his own lifetime, he had become only the most famous of a large tribe of anonymous improvers working on all the farm animals. Contemporary breeding techniques remained unscientific. Animals with the best points were selected and their progeny inbred to develop them further. It was a matter of knowing what was wanted, having a shrewd eye for a beast, travelling a great deal to see as wide a range of animals as possible and then luck, with exact observations and recording on the progeny.

The actual effects of the eighteenth-century breeders were probably not very widespread. Bakewell wanted always to keep his prices up and restrict his sales, letting his best Leicestershire rams for a season's fee of 6,000 guineas. The Colling brothers, who became the master-breeders in cattle with the development of the Durham Shorthorn, sold their best bull for 1,000 guineas and their best cow for 500 guineas. At the sale of stock after Charles Colling's death, the *average* price totalled £130 per beast. The improved stock thus remained confined to a fairly small coterie of aristocratic and substantial commoner farmers, all impressed by the need to maintain exclusive pedigrees and prices. The herdbook population remained very small indeed in relation to the numbers of sheep, cattle and pigs in the country. However the new stock, which became famous, was symptomatic of changing attitudes and characteristic of a much more widespread anonymous movement proceeding at humbler levels in the farming hierarchy, which did not get into the textbooks but which perhaps did affect a significant proportion of total numbers of sheep and cattle in time.

The time perspective of agrarian change needs emphasis. In an important sense, the agricultural revolution is a misnomer, for change on the land proved a slow, protracted diffusion of innovations, essentially a gradual process. During the seventeenth and eighteenth centuries it was much more a Norfolk revolution, or at least an eastern and central England revolution, rather than a national one. The key counties were Northumberland, Suffolk, Leicestershire, Northamptonshire, the east Scottish counties and, above all, Norfolk. Progress remained fastest on the lighter soils, slowest on the stiff, wet, cold, heavy clays, which suffered the shortest growing season, the heaviest costs in horses, the least flexibility in cropping, the highest risk of failure in a wet harvest or a cold spring. Considerable changes in land use followed on the innovations. Convertible husbandry brought much light land, sandy and chalk soils, under the plough; while heavy clay lands, previously corn country, went down to grass. Progress was faster on the larger farm, slowest on the small farm; more widespread on the eastern side of the country than in the west. Enormous gaps in technical standards existed as one moved across the country from Norfolk to Cornwall. William Marshall wrote of Devon in 1794 that there was not a pair of wheels to be seen in the county on a farm.

One final point. Breeding became as much of a passion in the later eighteenth century as land improvement or gambling. It possessed very close links with the latter. Breeding techniques undoubtedly were pioneered upon racehorses (particularly the new Arab stock), greyhounds and foxhounds in the seventeenth century. Newmarket, the centre of so much fashionable pleasure in Restoration England, was not far from Norfolk. Knowing how to breed for speed in the sporting animals meant also knowing how to breed for other qualities in a farm animal. Robert Bakewell began by breeding horses. One of his neighbours, Hugo Meynel, the first Master of the Quorn Hunt, was breeding foxhounds 6 miles away from Dishley Grange before Bakewell began on sheep. That passion for hunting and gambling, noticed by every continental visitor to England, thus had a direct bearing on economic history. The economic world is always drawing sustenance from the non-economic.

Reading list

THE STATE AND ECONOMIC DEVELOPMENT IN BRITAIN, 1750–1850

(i) *National finances and the state*

BINNEY, J. E. D. *British Public Finance and Administration, 1774–1792*, Oxford, 1958.

BUXTON, S. C. *Finance and Politics: a historical study, 1783–1885*, 2 vols, London, 1888.

DICKSON, P. G. M. *The Financial Revolution in England: a study in the development of public credit, 1688–1756*, London–New York, 1967.

HOPE-JONES, A. *Income Tax in the Napoleonic Wars*, Cambridge, 1939.

KENNEDY, W. *English Taxation 1740–1799*, London, 1913 and 1964.

PEACOCK, A. T. & WISEMAN, J., assisted by J. VEVERKA. *The Growth of Public Expenditure in the UK*, Princeton–London, 1961 (National Bureau of Economic Research: General Series, no. 72).

SCHUMPETER, E. B. 'English prices and government finance, 1660–1822', *Review of Economic Statistics*, 1938, **20**.

WARD, W. R. *The English Land Tax in the 18th Century*, London, 1953.

(ii) *The state, war and economic growth*

ASHTON, T. S. *Economic Fluctuations in England, 1700–1800*, Oxford, 1959, chs 3–4.

CROUZET, F. 'Wars, blockade and economic change in Europe, 1792–1815', *Journal of Economic History*, 1964, **24**, no. 4.

JOHN, A. H. 'War and the English economy, 1700–1763', *Economic History Review*, 2nd series, 1955, **7**, no. 3.

JOSLIN, D. M. 'The London bankers in wartime, 1739–1784', in L. S. Pressnell (ed.), *Studies in the Industrial Revolution*, London, 1960.

LANDOWNERSHIP AND CHANGE IN RURAL SOCIETY

CHAMBERS, J. D. 'Enclosures and labour supply', *Economic History Review*, 2nd series, 1953, **5**, no. 3; reprinted in D. V. Glass & D. E. C. Eversley (eds.), *Population in History: essays in historical demography*, London, 1965.

DAVIES, E. 'The small landowner, 1780–1832, in the light of the land tax assessments', *Economic History Review*, 1927–8, **1**, no. 1; reprinted in E. M. Carus-Wilson (ed.), *Essays in Economic History*, vol. 1, London, 1954.

GONNER, E. C. K. *Common Land and Inclosure*, London, 1912.

HABAKKUK, H. J. 'Economic functions of English landowners in the 17th and 18th centuries', *Explorations in Entrepreneurial History*, 1953.

HABAKKUK, H. J. 'English landownership, 1680–1740', *Economic History Review*, 1940, **10**, no. 1.

HABAKKUK, H. J. 'Marriage settlements in the 18th century', *Transactions of the Royal Historical Society*, 4th series, 1950, **32**.

HUGHES, E. 'The 18th-century estate agent', *Essays in British and Irish History in Honour of James Eadie Todd*, ed. H. A. Cronne, T. W. Moody & D. B. Quinn, London, 1949.

MINGAY, G. E. *English landed Society in the 18th Century*, London–Toronto, 1963.

MINGAY, G. E. 'The large estate in 18th-century England', *Papers of the 1st International Economic History Conference*, Stockholm, 1960.

SMOUT, T. C. 'Scottish landowners and economic growth, 1650–1850', *Scottish Journal of Political Economy*, 1964, **11**, 3.

THIRSK, J. *English Peasant Farming: the agrarian history of Lincolnshire from Tudor to recent times*, London, 1957.

AGRICULTURAL CHANGE

BOSERUP, E. *The Conditions of Agricultural Growth: the economics of agrarian change under population pressure*, London, 1965.

CHAMBERS, J. D. *The Vale of Trent, 1670-1800; a regional study of economic change*, London–New York, 1957 (*Economic History Review*, Supplement no. 3).

CHAMBERS, J. D. & MINGAY, G. E. *The Agricultural Revolution, 1750-1880*, London, 1966.

ERNLE, LORD. *English Farming Past and Present*, 6th ed., London, 1961.

HENDERSON, H. C. K. 'Agriculture in England and Wales in 1801', *Geographical Journal*, 1952, **118**, pt. 3.

JOHN, A. H. 'The course of agricultural change, 1660-1760', in L. S. Pressnell (ed.), *Studies in the Industrial Revolution*, London, 1960.

JONES, E. L. 'The agricultural labour market in England, 1793-1872', *Economic History Review*, 2nd series, 1964-5, **17**, no. 2.

JONES, E. L. 'Agriculture and economic growth in England, 1660-1750', *Journal of Economic History*, 1965, **25**, no. 1.

JONES, E. L. (ed.) *Agriculture and Economic Growth in England, 1650-1815*, New York–London, 1967.

JONES, E. L. '18th-century changes in Hampshire chalk farming', *Agricultural History Review*, 1960, **8**, pt. 1.

JONES, E. L. & MINGAY, G. E. (eds.) *Land, Labour and Population in the Industrial Revolution* [articles by E. L. Jones and A. H. John], London, 1967; New York, 1968.

KERRIDGE, E. 'Turnip husbandry in High Suffolk', *Economic History Review*, 2nd series, 1956, **8**, no. 3.

MINGAY, G. E. *Enclosure and the Small Farmer in the Age of the Industrial Revolution*, London, 1968.

MINGAY, G. E. 'The agricultural depression, 1730-1750', *Economic History Review*, 2nd series, 1956, **8**, no. 3; reprinted in *Essays in Economic History*, vol. 2.

MINGAY, G. E. 'The "agricultural revolution" in English history: a reconsideration', *Agricultural History*, 1963, **37**, no. 3.

MITCHISON, R. 'The old Board of Agriculture, 1793-1822', *English Historical Review*, 1959, **74**, no. 290.

OJALA, E. M. *Agriculture and Economic Progress*, London, 1952.

PARKER, R. A. C. 'Coke of Norfolk and the agrarian revolution', *Economic History Review*, 2nd series, 1955, **8**, no. 2; reprinted in E. M. Carus-Wilson (ed.), *Essays in Economic History*, vol. 2, London, 1962.

TROW SMITH, R. *English Husbandry from the Earliest Times to the Present Day*, London, 1951.

4 Trade, policy and transport

THE REGULATION OF FOREIGN TRADE AND SHIPPING

From the sixteenth to the mid-eighteenth century a general assumption prevailed that government had a necessary role in attempting to ease the problems afflicting the economy by interfering with natural market mechanisms. There was no real champion of *laissez-faire* before Adam Smith, however much contemporary commentators disagreed on what the correct policy was, or however much they acknowledged that particular aspects of policy were frustrated by inefficient administration, fiscalism and corruption.

The greatest stimulus to legislation was 'an attempted defence against the vagaries of economic dislocation' – the immediate pressing problem in the actual world of foreign markets, shipping, domestic industry rather than legislation in the service of an abstract, total idea of some economic dogma called mercantilism. Speculation about general ideas in economic relationships can usually be tracked down to an actual real problem. Very often, even if the general hypothesis is absurd or illogical as a piece of abstract reasoning, it may make sense when related to a short-run or structural problem facing contemporaries.

Underlying much of the legislation was a great fear of unemployment, particularly in the textile districts, with its attendant political problems. Certain areas, particularly East Anglia, were so dominated by textile employment, dependent on success in foreign markets, that they had become much the most sensitive regions for governments worried about disaffection, at a time when the local police system was at its most ramshackle and poor relief ineffectual. Areas with large congregations of poor workers were usually textile districts, and often much dependent upon exports to maintain local levels of employment.

Much contemporary debate in economic policy, to the days of Hume and Adam Smith, made the assumption that bullion inflows were desirable, so that a favourable balance of trade was to be encouraged even after the export of bullion itself was permitted by statute in 1663. Bullion was needed for trade – it was the lubricant of commerce – for a war-chest, for reserves. War increased foreign spending sharply: for naval supplies, loans to allies, purchasing by armies abroad, and for fleets on foreign stations. 'Invisible' exports were lost to neutral shippers. At the same time certain foreign markets could be disturbed, and, in any case, exports were unlikely to expand quickly enough to absorb these strains in the balance of payments. Cash reserves were vital for these emergencies. All contemporaries also knew that a business depression meant an acute shortage of cash, which disappeared from circulation. By encouraging a favourable balance of trade by legislation there would naturally be an inflow of bullion, to the value that sales to other nations exceeded their sales to us (ignoring the question of capital movements). This would achieve the same advantages in aggregate that the bullionists had desired, but particular trades would not suffer as they would if no bullion at all could be exported. The East Indies trade, the Levant trade and the Baltic trade all needed the export of bullion from England directly or indirectly, if they were to survive.

Reducing all the circumstances of policy to this single overall rule was tautologous – it avoided the problems of how you could achieve, and even more maintain, a favourable balance of trade. It avoided the very real truths that Britain's balance of trade could be upset by foreign governments changing the relative advantages of trade by manipulating their currencies and their internal price levels. As they depreciated and inflated so their exports became more competitive and English sales to them more difficult. But the balance of trade argument was much more relevant to policy and to the actual state of things than previous legislation attempting to ban bullion exports, which dealt only with the results of the problem, not its causes, and ineffectively at that. Britain's pattern of foreign trade contained several chronic 'deficit areas'. Keynes deduced a further advantage in a favourable balance of payments. He saw an increasing quantity of precious metals in circulation as likely to reduce the rate of interest. And this in turn would induce more investment, more activity, more employment. He realized that this might well lead into a boom where prices would rise and so frustrate exports; and he also thought interest rates might get so low compared with those prevailing in other countries that investors might move capital abroad to get these higher returns – which would frustrate the original objective.

Industrial protection of home industry became another object of legislation; together with the denial of advantages to industrial competitors, where it lay in the power of British law to do so. The woollen industry undoubtedly lay at the centre of this series of enactments. 'The clothiers . . .', wrote Adam Smith, 'succeeded in convincing the wisdom of the nation that the safety of the commonwealth depends upon the prosperity of their particular manufacture.' Broadly speaking this was true: the woollen industry was the largest single occupation outside of agriculture, and the clothing areas, being dependent for employment on the state of trade, particularly foreign trade, were very much more volatile socially than the purely agrarian areas. Laws prohibiting the export of raw wool, sheep and rams, continued through the eighteenth century, despite much 'owling' on the south coast, as smuggling of wool was called. Between 1719 and 1825 the emigration of artisans and artificers was forbidden; the export of textile machinery and some other devices was not allowed until 1843.

With this went periodic attempts to widen the home market by statute in favour of the woollen industry and to protect it from the invasion of rival products from abroad.[1] In 1700 the import of silks and printed calicoes was prohibited, a blow struck against the East India Company ostensibly for the wool trade, but with the effect of giving a stimulus to the infant English cotton and silk industries (and thus also to the Levant Company which prospered largely on the import of raw silk). In 1721 came another, strictly enforced, act against the import of printed calicoes.

Associated with the intention of protecting home industry

[1] Anglican clergy are still supposedly prohibited from wearing pyjamas because Canon Law enforcing 'nightgowns of woollen cloth' is unrepealed.

was another general aim of the regulatory system, the control
of colonial economies. The official rules intended that the
economies of territories over which Westminster had political
control should be regulated in the interests of the metropolitan
economy to secure and maintain complementarity between
them. These were the laws that Adam Smith called 'impertinent
badges of slavery'.

One aspect of this affected rival industrial activity in the
colonies. There was an attempt to ban the woollen industry in
the colonies in 1699; to limit the export of Irish wool textiles
only to Britain, and to outlaw any inter-colony trade in woollens.
Their currencies were also controlled. At another time the
colonists were forbidden to export beaver hats, in deference to
English hatters. In 1750 the making of steel, the refining of iron
and manufacture of finished articles from iron was prohibited
in the North American colonies. This latter act, very much
hated in America, emphasized the economic role of the colonies.
They were to act as protected markets for the export industries
of the mother country; hence their own spontaneous economic
development and foreign trade had to be checked when it ran
counter to these principles. The obverse to this was the encouragement of colonial economies as primary produce suppliers to
the metropolitan economy. Sugar, tobacco, rice, cotton and
pepper were products which fitted into this framework har-
moniously. The New England colonies were thought of as
suppliers of timber, naval stores and pig-iron: the production
of pig-iron had been encouraged there, though not very successfully, to end dependence on Swedish and Russian iron, which
was not under British political control. But furnaces to produce
pig-iron must not be followed by forges and slitting mills to
refine the metal, and thus block lucrative markets for Birmingham and Sheffield. In compensation colonial pig-iron was
allowed into Britain duty free. It was the same with timber and
naval stores – although colonial ships were allowed to be built
freely, and this industry profited very greatly at the expense of
British shipbuilding. One-third of the ships under British
merchant marine colours were said to be colonial built in the
mid-eighteenth century.

This relates to another general aim of the regulatory system – strategic planning. The hope was that in strategic materials such as naval stores – hemp, pitch, turpentine, tar, timber (mainmasts and soft wood more than oak) – the mother country and her satellite colonial economies could be self-sufficient in war. 'Imperial autarky' was the aim. The Baltic had long been a danger spot. States there were likely to be involved in hostile coalitions; and the Sound might be effectively closed to commerce. If this happened, once the stocks in the mast-ponds at naval dockyards had been used up, all British naval strategy might be threatened.

In pursuit of this strategic end, there was always anxiety in peacetime to maintain military potential. War proved as prevalent as peace in the seventeenth and eighteenth centuries, determining the consciousness of kings and politicians. The two most important single features of peacetime strategy were therefore to encourage shipping capacity and the numbers of seamen. Here was a standing argument for keeping the Dutch and the French out of all trade between Britain and the colonies, and out of the British coasting trade. Where political authority existed it should be used to encourage self-sufficiency in trade and in shipping. In the mid-seventeenth century British shipping could not stand up to Dutch competition without political advantage. If imperial trade was to provide a forcing house for shipping capacity and a nursery for seamen, it had to exclude the Dutch, and subsequently the French by legislation.

The fisheries had an important role in these strategic arguments. One prime basis of Dutch prosperity was the distribution of Baltic grain and North Sea smoked and salted herring to the rest of Europe. All efforts to oust the Dutch from their control of the European fish trade failed. The reasons for the British failure are still unrevealed. One of the minor mysteries of economic history is why the British kipper only triumphed in the nineteenth century.

Many inconsistencies and irrationalities are revealed if this legislation is construed as an articulate, systematic, logically-

organized system. Its principles were always being broken for
political expediency. This had advantages because a grasping
Crown could always hope to make money by selling licences to
break the law. Sometimes the laws really became pretexts for
levying taxes on merchants. The acute shortages of shipping in
wartime meant that the shipping provisions of the Navigation
Acts usually had to be relaxed at these times. Political pressures,
too, could break economic principles. The political antagonisms
produced in large part by attempts to manipulate the colonial
economies in North America had brought the whole system into
disrepute by 1776. The American War proved the dangers of
the system – although other colonies, like the West Indies, relied
on the same laws to prevent non-Empire sugar from cutting off
their markets in Great Britain. In countries like the West
Indies, where a natural complementarity existed between
Britain and the products and trade of the colony, or where most
of the colonists repatriated their wealth, and eventually themselves, to Britain, the system could work tolerably. In continental
America it created more political problems than the economic
gains justified – as was proved after independence.

There were also inconsistencies within the actual economic
provisions; not only by way of their adverse political effects.
The Corn Laws sought to protect agriculture and the landed
interest; yet the ban on the export of sheep and wool reduced
the farmers' markets. The brewer (and through him the farmer)
was encouraged by a bounty on the export of beer; he was discouraged by a ban on the import of malt, and a bounty on the
export of malt. If shipping was too scanty in relation to the
needs of the economy, provisions to encourage shipping might
operate to the disadvantage of industry – making exports more
expensive in foreign markets – or Dutch ships might have to be
licensed on a large scale. One object might be to keep foreign
luxuries out; to keep imports down as much as possible. Once
those foreign luxuries began to figure in the re-export trades
then this reversed the arguments previously put up against them.
Protecting British shipbuilding meant greater reliance on the
Baltic for its raw materials – to the detriment of the balance of
trade in that market.

Adam Smith's main argument was that all these regulations were in the interests of merchants and manufacturers or the government to the detriment of all consumers in the land.[1] This was true of consumption – in its effects upon citizens as consumers – but conceivably some benefits reached the humble masses of the nation in so far as employment in the woollen industry or in shipping and fishing was protected by these laws.

A further irony concerns the actual level of import duties imposed on British foreign trade, apart from the other forms of discrimination embodied in the Navigation Code. Despite the consolidation of this formidable apparatus in the mid-seventeenth century, average levels of duty remained low until the Marlborough Wars at its end. England emerged from these wars a high tariff economy (with import duties of *c.* 30 per cent or more), duties having tripled or quadrupled in the meanwhile. The main explanation for this increase was the demands of the government for extra revenue to pay for the wars (in particular to service the new permanent funded debt) rather than a specific aim of protecting British industry. Vested interests quickly built up in defence of the high duties, of course, and the Navigation Code gave greater emphasis to industrial protection during the eighteenth century. The levels of duty, however, did not greatly alter again until the renewed emergencies of the Napoleonic Wars once more increased the burdens laid upon foreign trade.

Two widespread assumptions of the mercantilist arguments, which are irrational in strict logic, can be interpreted more rationally when related to actual circumstances of commerce. The bullionist desire to go on importing bullion as a set policy, and the sophisticated version of this that the balance of trade must always be favourable, were self-defeating, in the absolute sense, as Hume and Adam Smith argued. As bullion flooded into a country, its internal price level would rise and the export industries would find it correspondingly more difficult to compete in foreign markets. This would reverse the balance of trade and so lead to an outflow of bullion. David Hume first demon-

---

[1] See below, pp. 290–2.

strated this truth and classical economists wrote off mercantile aspirations on this assumption. This conclusion is subject to qualification about what is happening to the 'invisible items' in the balance of payments, business services and the movement of capital between countries (not shown up in figures of commodity trade, which was all contemporaries were able to count), but its general truth remained. As it stands the mercantilist thesis is irrational. Quite apart from the effects of war, in fact and in expectation, upon the balance of payments, it related to a particular business problem in the context of the day, and became more intelligible when related to that problem. There were some trading areas where it was commercially impossible to sell as much by value as was imported from the area. These were areas of chronic deficit, or of 'hard currency' as is now said. The Baltic was one such place. It was a national necessity for several European countries to bring timber and naval stores from the Baltic on an increasing scale. British efforts to find a substitute trade from North America did not pay off on any scale until the Napoleonic Wars. Yet the Baltic was sparsely populated. The inhabitants did not use British goods on a large scale. The Dutch had the main import trades in herring, salt and wine and cloth, and even they needed to send in bullion. There was too primitive a trading system east of Dantzig, before the end of the seventeenth century at least, to use credit instruments enough to offset the need for cash. The exchanges were often so depressed that it was cheaper to use bullion than depreciated bills of exchange. In the mid-eighteenth century over a million pounds sterling was known to pass into the Baltic during some years in bullion and coin. However, the bullion normally acceptable in the Baltic was Dutch rix-dollars; little bullion appears to have been exported direct to the Baltic from Britain after 1700 but a great deal flowed to Holland, and a complementary stream flowed from there into the Sound.

It was equally the case with the East Indies, only here the imports were not a strategic necessity such as naval stores – but luxuries like silks, cottons, tea and spices of various kinds. The Eastern market would not take European goods in exchange. Only silver could create trade, and 22·5 million oz of silver

(£5·73 million) were shipped by the East India Company in the years 1700–17. A much lesser and more sporadic drain nourished the Turkey trade. If areas of chronic deficit existed then it was highly important to encourage other areas of a favourable balance to get inflows of silver sufficient to satisfy these demands. In the post-1945 world hard-currency areas have been seen to defy any self-regulating system without political controls. Freedom from such controls could lead to national bankruptcy, regional unemployment, or strategic weakness in the short run – before the market economy brought adjustments in the long run. The regulations after 1945 prohibiting the export of gold or dollars, the feverish anxiety about the bullion reserves and the exchange control regulations all make the mercantilist problems appear only too familiar. A real problem existed of getting enough bullion flowing into the country to satisfy these commercial needs. A second argument then became more powerful. The East India Company also claimed that when they had re-exported a large proportion of the coffee, tea, pepper and spices, which they had originally imported, to the continent this earned more bullion than their original consignments needed to buy the commodities in the East. The prices paid for pepper in Europe were several times that paid for it in the East. The re-export trades had become of great significance in the pattern of trade in the second half of the seventeenth century with the rise of colonial trade, particularly that of the West Indies and Virginia.

The other misconception current was that there was a fixed quantity of trade, that trade was 'war', so that successful commerce could only be at the expense of the other party. In absolute terms this was also patently false. Colonial trade in general was expanding very rapidly and *direct* trade between two parties is *mutually* beneficial. Considering bi-lateral economic relationships, for A to buy the goods of B, purchasing power has to be created by country B buying goods from country A and thus creating the necessary foreign exchange (unless there are compensating transfers of capital or services). Britain had to import from others to create sterling credits for buying British exports. But when one considered trade to third party markets, the assumption is not so stupid. The most rapidly rising trades in the late seventeenth and eighteenth centuries were exactly the new colonial staples: sugar, tobacco, pepper, coffee, tea. The prize was the European market as a whole. Were British merchants or the Dutch or the French to be the main distributors of these goods to the Baltic, to Germany, Poland, Russia and the Mediterranean basin? Most other European countries did not have large distant-water fleets or the colonial possessions to be serious competitors. The Dutch, the French and Britain became the main contenders as imperial powers and as shipping rivals. The capacity of Sweden or Germany to buy sugar or tobacco at any one time was limited (it might change over time) so that, broadly, the more sugar the Dutch sold in Sweden the less we sold there.

The main commercial battles in the period were exactly related to the new colonial trades, to the siting of the European entrepôt in these trades and the development of re-exports in these commodities.

THE COURSE OF FOREIGN TRADE

The prize sought by the Navigation Acts reserving inter-Empire trade to British and colonial merchants and ships was more than just the direct trade in the goods concerned, or whether tobacco or sugar were carried across the Atlantic to British ports in Dutch or English ships. Much other wealth followed in the wake of the ship that carried the cargo. Shipping initiative carried so many other implications with it in the colonial re-export trades. If a foreign ship loaded tobacco in Chesapeake bay, it would go to Amsterdam and not England; the cargo would be insured in Amsterdam, the bills of exchange discounted in Amsterdam, the profits of warehousing and the employment at the ports would be Dutch. The processing industries – arising from the colonial trades – sugar refining, rum distilling, tobacco-chopping, snuff grinding, packaging, were all located at the entrepôt. The final distribution to the ultimate markets would be by Dutch ships with Dutch profits. All these opportunities for employment, for profit, were reserved for Glasgow, Whitehaven, Liverpool, Bristol and London – the most rapidly growing trading cities in Britain in the later seventeenth and eighteenth centuries. Enormous wealth and capitals were piling up there exactly in response to the redirection of trade encouraged by the operation of the Navigation Acts.

The effects of this in the remaining years of the seventeenth century revealed a startling development in the pattern of British overseas trade. Total exports had risen from £4·1 million in the 1660's to £6·4 million in 1700. More than half of this rise (over £1 million) came from re-exports, which were then £2 million out of £6 million. Almost all these were re-exports to Europe. Woollens had fallen relatively from having an 80–90 per cent share of our exports to about 50 per cent. Colonial and Eastern goods as re-exports now formed 30 per cent of total exports. Two-thirds of these re-exports in 1700 were made up of tobacco (£420,000); linens and calicoes (£522,000) and sugar (£287,000). The tobacco trade was more an outport than a London traffic, a portent for the great rise of the Atlantic ports on sugar, tobacco, slaves. The eighteenth century saw a diversification of trade with the rise of these west-coast ports on trans-Atlantic commerce. In 1700 London had over four-fifths of the nation's imports; 70 per cent of exports and no less than 86 per cent of re-exports. Defoe remarked that London 'sucked the vitals of trade in this island to itself'. London's share fell below two-thirds after 1730 (but remained above half of the total volume of trade).

The new trades brought dramatic growth to Liverpool. Defoe in 1720 thought its expansion 'one of the wonders of Britain . . . what it may grow to in time I know not'. At the end of the sixteenth century there were fewer than 200 houses there. In 1700 the population lay between 5,000 and 7,000. There were 10,000 inhabitants by 1720, and 30,000 in 1750. Bristol also doubled its population in the first half of the eighteenth century, to reach 90,000 by 1750. It was a similar story with Glasgow. This came at a time when the total population of the country was not thought to be rising and it happened before the momentum of industrialization built up in the hinterlands of Liverpool and Glasgow.

Much of the activities of these rising ports was associated

with the effects of colonial commerce upon shipping. Most of the new trades were very distant ones: of one voyage per season usually. In the case of the East Indies a ship sometimes took two years to go out and back. Shipping in north European markets (save for far distant Baltic ports) did at least two trips per season, sometimes more. The new trans-oceanic trades therefore made heavier demands on shipping capacity. Moreover, the colonial staples were bulk trades in fairly cheap products – and hence became very large users of shipping. Half a million hundredweight of sugar were imported in 1700 and 32 million lb weight of tobacco. In 1800 – 3 million cwt of sugar; over ½ million cwt coffee; over 50 million lb of tobacco and over 50 million lb of cotton. In the 1740's over 200 ships were engaged in the tobacco trade. In 1700 although 15 per cent by value of foreign trade was engaged in the Atlantic trades, over one-third of the total of shipping in foreign trade was needed to carry it.

The new trades were considerable users of shipping space outwards in re-exports – but this was usually in neighbouring markets. The only other major user of shipping space in the export trades was grain in the first half of the eighteenth century. Cloth exports did not use up much shipping. In fact most ships cleared outwards with some ballast aboard – they were half empty.[1] The size of the merchant fleet was determined by the volume of imports, and thus responded very directly to the new commodities which came under the 'staple' policy.

The rise of the Baltic trade, which was concerned above all in supplying shipbuilding and maintenance materials should therefore be seen as the consequence, in large part, of the increase in the demand for shipping being created by the rise in other trades, particularly the trans-Atlantic trades and the London coal trade. One of the most important areas of investment in the century after 1650, in fact, flowed from this great increase in shipping capacity, probably the greatest demand on investment resources created by the expansion in overseas trade. The East

[1] This explains the presence of cheap bulk cargoes such as bricks and beer to such distant markets as Petersburg and the West Indies – they were 'quasi-ballast'.

Indies trade was not a great user of shipping, importing high-priced articles of small bulk. Though the ships themselves were large and splendid (looking like ships of the line and very often painted in protective fashion like a man-of-war with black and white chequers along the gun-ports) there were seldom more than 30–40 of them. The sugar and tobacco fleets on the other hand were numbered in hundreds.

Throughout the eighteenth century, in peacetime, over four-fifths of the shipping using British ports was British – much of it protected by the navigation system. So the tonnage of ships broadly followed the increase in volume of trade – save that American-built ships had a large share in British foreign trade before 1776. In wartime the navy drew off many merchant ships for use as supply vessels for the fleets. Others were sunk or captured. Hence licensed neutral ships took much cargo which would normally have travelled in British ships. One-quarter to one-third of the shipping using British ports in wartime was foreign. The most important single contributor to the expansion of shipping was the coal trade, essentially the London coal trade from the north-east coast. That, with the export of grain in the mid-eighteenth century, the Irish trades and the fisheries, gave the greatest 'bulk' freights (even though these ships were fairly small and made so many voyages per season). Thus, coastal trade was probably a greater creator of freights for determining the capacity of the shipping industry than foreign trade. Peacetime proved more favourable for expansion here than war; but, as a whole, the eighteenth century saw formidable growth. British-owned shipping tonnage rose from 323,000 tons when the century opened to over 1 million tons by 1788.

The tables showing the values of English overseas trade in the eighteenth century reveal many important conclusions about the growth and changing currents of international trade that affected British industrial growth. However, the figures must be used with particular care. All are 'Official Value' figures, based on unchanging prices, mainly decided on when the returns were started in 1696 or when new commodities first entered the Customs House books. The figures therefore reflect changes in the volume of trade (at constant prices) not changes in the

TABLE III: (a) *English overseas trade values*
(Figures in £m. Official values)

	Exports	(Including re-exports)	Bullion Exports	Imports
1700	6·47	(2·13)	·83	5·97
1710	6·3	(1·57)	·4	4·01
1720	6·91	(2·3)	1·03	6·09
1730	8·55	(3·22)	3·43	7·78
1740	8·2	(3·09)	·67	6·70
1750	12·7	(3·23)	2·43	7·77
1760	14·7	(3·71)	·88	9·83
1770	14·3	(4·76)	·64	12·22
1780	12·55	(4·32)	·9	10·76
1790	18·9	(4·83)	–	17·44
1800	40·81	(18·4)	–	28·36

(b) *Destinations of exports and sources of imports: England and Wales, 1700–1800*

(Figures in £m. Official values. Annual Average for each 5-year period)

Area		1701–1705	1726–1730	1751–1755	1776–1780	1796–1800
North Europe	Exports	3·12	3·53	5·13	3·9	11·77
	Imports	1·35	1·53	1·22	1·6	2·68
Baltic	Exports	·3	·2	·29	·37	1·34
	Imports	·48	·61	·97	1·61	3·19
Portugal and Spain	Exports	·63	1·55	2·14	1·25	·92
	Imports	·41	·79	·68	·75	1·22
Mediterranean countries	Exports	·6	·85	1·00	·75	·74
	Imports	·56	·93	·91	·64	·39
Africa	Exports	·1	·2	·23	·24	1·00
	Imports	·02	·04	·04	·06	·07
East Indies	Exports	·11	·11	·79	·91	2·21
	Imports	·55	1·00	1·12	1·30	4·83
British West Indies	Exports	·31	·47	·71	1·24	4·38
	Imports	·61	1·36	1·63	2·75	5·90
North America	Exports	·27	·53	1·30	1·30	6·79
	Imports	·29	·63	1·00	·16	1·96

(c) *Percentage of total imports and exports: England and Wales*

	1700	1750	1772	1790	1800
Imports					
Groceries	16·9	27·6	35·8	28·9	34·9
Raw cotton	–	·9	1·2	5·0	6·0
Linens	15·6	14·8	10·4	8·5	5·6
Textile materials	16·2	16·4	21·8	19·6	15·4
Exports					
Woollens	57·3	45·9	42·2	34·8	28·5
Cotton goods	·5	–	2·3	10·0	24·2
Other textiles	2·4	6·2	10·6	7·4	6·1
Grain	3·7	19·6	8·0	0·8	–
Iron	1·6	4·4	8·0	6·3	6·1

After E. B. Schumpeter, op. cit., 1960.

current values in trade, dependent on the changing price of articles, as well as changes in the quantities of them entering into trade. The index is very useful for estimating changes in the structure of trade: not so good for trying to find out about such things as the balance of payments, which are affected very much by changing prices.

In the table listing the areas of trade re-exports are not separately shown; areas with an unfavourable balance, like the British West Indies, or the East Indies, may be highly favourable in the end because of the large re-exports of sugar, pepper, coffee, calicoes, etc. to north Europe, where very large surpluses were running.

Only the values in the *direct* trade between Britain and other areas are shown, and totalled in the first table, which understates the true importance of some trades, such as the trade to Africa and the West Indies. Large values were involved in the traffic in negroes from Africa to the West Indies, which was not recorded by British customs officials. The same is true of the 'country trade' in south-east Asia, based on India, conducted by the East India Company. This is an integral part of the strategy of trade, producing shipping revenues and profits which were returned to Britain, but not recorded in British trading statistics.

More generally these figures do not show the total gain from trade by any means, being just the record of the actual goods passing through British ports. Most of the commercial initiative went with the shipping. The bulk of British trade was conducted under the enterprise of British merchants, the cargoes and the ships insured and the bills of exchange discounted in London. Profits were earned by operating the ships. The profits of business earned overseas, the capital piling up in planters' estates in the West Indies or amongst the nabobs in the East Indies was often repatriated to Britain, and must certainly be counted in the total gain from trade. Yet they are not shown in the totals of physical goods recorded by customs officials. And all these things affect the balance of payments position.

The figures are accurate enough to be interesting, but there was a lot of smuggling in the eighteenth century. It was a well-organized trade, but confined mainly to commodities like tea, silks and brandy from France, where the traffic was favoured by a short sea trip and very high rates of duty. There are many other weaknesses: merchants did not record their cargoes accurately in the absence of customs duties; they exaggerated them where export bounties could be earned – but the broad trends of the figures, save in the case of imports from France, are probably not in doubt. Most smuggling remained on the import side and most smuggled cargoes were not a question of muffled oars on a moonless night but the less energetic business of bribing or deceiving customs officials on the quay side.

From Table III (a) the fact of expansion in trade is at once obvious: the volume doubled between 1700 and 1780. Exports showed rapid expansion in 1700–15, then no great trend rise until after 1730. Then came recovery with spectacular growth in 1745–60. Decline and stagnation followed from 1760 to 1783; then very rapid growth to unprecedented heights at an unprecedented pace. This latter surge was very clearly linked with factory production in textiles. Thus there were two main spurts in exports: one lift in the 1740's from £8 million to £12 million per annum (not reflected in imports so much); then the much greater expansion after 1780. Imports rose in the third quarter from the 1740's until the 1770's (particularly in 1745–60). The disastrous effects of American war upon British foreign trade 1774–83 are also made clear. Re-exports played a declining role on trend by the end of the century in normal years. The decennial figures happen to mask this movement to some extent because re-exports were very swollen in war years. From being a third of total exports at the beginning of the eighteenth century, however, they had declined to usually below a quarter by 1800. Re-export values rose rapidly between 1780 and 1800, but some exaggeration was given to these figures by the official value index. The price of these re-export commodities, sugar, tea, tobacco, etc. had fallen markedly during the course of the century, which is not shown up in these figures. There was not so much of a change in the general structure of prices in other commodities. A very high proportion of the tobacco and coffee went abroad again (usually over four-fifths) but tea had become a commodity in mass demand by 1800. This showed one of the clearest ways in which expanding population, changing taste – and probably rising incomes too – were reflected in foreign trade. Only 70,000 lb weight of tea were imported in 1700 – and most of that went out again. 15 million lb were coming in by 1800 – of which 12 million were drunk at home. The habit of tea drinking, in fact, had progressed steadily down the social scale. As always, the luxuries of the rich became in time the necessities of the poor. 'It is the curse of this nation,' wrote Jonas Hanway in 1756, 'that the labourer and mechanic will ape the lord ... you will see labourers who are mending the road drinking their tea.'[1] Sugar, too, became primarily dependent on the home market as the eighteenth century progressed. By the end of the century five-sixths of the sugar imported was usually consumed in Britain. Here again, a rise in population and a change in social habits had re-orientated the fortunes of the sugar trade.

The two lower tables show the breakdown of the aggregate totals in Table III (a) into trading areas and commodities. They reveal that these increases came about with a profound re-orientation of trade, which the movement of the totals hides to a large extent. For most of the eighteenth century, as for the

---

[1] This attitude was duly pulverized by that great tea drinker and supporter of the poor, Samuel Johnson.

latter part of the seventeenth century, the older trading areas of northern Europe and the Mediterranean were lagging behind the others, until the enormous leap under wartime conditions and the momentum of the industrial revolution in 1796–1800. The Baltic, too, was lagging in exports. The great expanding areas were North America, the West Indies, the East Indies and Africa (although the two latter countries did not take very much in relation to the total, still under 10 per cent in 1800, despite their rapid rates of growth). When the eighteenth century opened 78 per cent of British exports were going to Europe; in 1800 only 45 per cent. On the import side the same is true: over 50 per cent of imports came from Europe in 1700; by 1800 this had fallen to 31 per cent.

Trade with Portugal and Spain – dominated by Portuguese rather than Spanish trade – also developed rapidly in response to the famous Methuen Treaty of 1703, which opened Portugal for British cloth and allowed Portuguese wines to be imported into England at one-third less duty than French. Port was the mercantilist drink, not claret. Political reasons led to discrimination against France at the time; but the Portuguese trade also had the 'mercantilist' economic asset of being very 'favourable' – and brought in much bullion. It was only seriously curtailed in the 1770's when King Pombal tried to nationalize the port-trade and exclude English merchants from their factory in Oporto. The development of Spanish and Portuguese trade also reflected, at one stage removed, the increasing importance of the trans-Atlantic commerce to their colonies. In a similar way, the Africa total does not reveal its true importance in the multi-angular trades between Britain, Africa, the West Indies and North America. In fact not much bullion, if any, was exported to the West Indies, despite the very heavy adverse balance suggested by these figures. An adverse balance continued to the East Indies and to the Baltic.

The most important expansion of all came to the North American market (more the colonies that became the United States than the Canadian area) apart from the war period, 1776–80.[1] The astonishing thing to contemporaries was its

[1] In fact this period saw much trade re-routed to Canada.

Official values (£'000)

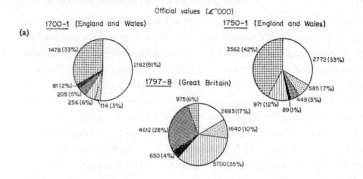

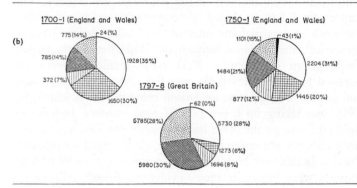

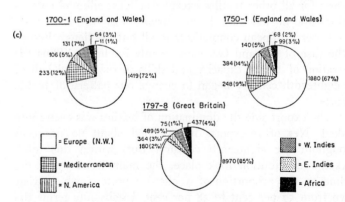

Fig. 3. (a) Direction of exports. (b) Direction of imports. (c) Direction of re-exports (see also Fig. 23, p. 414). After Mitchell and Deane, 1962, p. 312.

recovery, when the United States had broken free from the restrictions of the Navigation Code. By 1785 trading values had fully recovered their pre-war totals and the period 1786–90 saw exports to the U.S.A. above £2 million per annum and the next period 1791–5 above £2·5 million. This is the period when the United States was becoming Britain's most important supplier of raw cotton to feed the growing textile mills.

Changes in world markets were also linked to changes in commodities, as Table III (c) indicates. At once the dominance of textiles in overseas trade is apparent and the changes that came within the textile markets in the course of the century. The import total here included all commodities that were subsequently re-exported and most of these fall under the head of 'groceries': sugar, spices, tobacco, etc. They formed the largest single group consistently. Next came textile materials (as opposed to finished textiles) – raw flax, silk, wool, some yarn and cotton. The greatest expansion came in cotton which, by 1800, was taking up 6 per cent of total imports. Imports of finished linen, on the other hand, steadily declined, as a native linen industry got under way and cut out the need for imports. Previously this very high total percentage – 15 per cent of total imports were linens in 1700 – evidenced British reliance on imports for all other textiles except woollens: silk and cottons at this time no less than linens. Britain was still very much behind her European competitors in all but woollens – France in the case of silk and Germany mainly for linens. Thus the generation of textile capacity and skills in the second half of the eighteenth century began to change our pattern of textile imports.

On the export side the domination of textiles was even more marked. Net of re-exports it remained about 60 per cent throughout the eighteenth century. But, within this total, marked redistribution took place, the main trend being the decline in the proportion of woollens exported – which went down from 57 per cent to 28 per cent. In absolute terms the value of these woollens had grown from about £3·5 million per annum in the early part of the century to above £5 million at its end. This was not at all as dramatic a rise as in other fabrics, but even within woollens came significant change. The second half of the seventeenth century had seen the stagnation of the older markets in north Europe, and with this the stagnation of the older textile areas in Britain and their traditional products – the heavy broadcloths. The rising cloths were the bays and says of Essex and the serges of Exeter – lighter cloths of the worsted variety destined for the warmer climates of Portugal, Spain and the Mediterranean. As the eighteenth century advanced so the East Anglian worsted industry in Norwich and its hinterland progressed at the expense of other areas, and even more so the Leeds and Bradford areas of Yorkshire. Radical reorientation, the rise in new markets and new products thus underlay the comparative stability of the total values in the traditional industry of woollen cloth.

The changing pattern of textile exports was more changed by the relative advance of the cotton industry – which already formed about a quarter of the volume of exports by 1800. Giant strides had been taken in the last twenty years of the century with the onset of factory productivity in spinning. Retained imports of raw cotton averaged about 3 million lb a year up to 1770, 30 million lb per annum by the 1790's; above 50 million in the decade after 1800. Grain died out of the export trade completely during the second half of the century from being 20 per cent of total exports in the peak year of 1750. Iron exports advanced (but never became very significant in relation to textiles), mainly nails to the colonies, hollow ware and wrought iron.

Is it possible to sum up the effects of the 'commercial revolution' and 'shipping revolution' which preceded industrialization by a century? In general terms the process of industrialization in Britain was to become more integral with international trade than in virtually all other countries. In the eighteenth century internal and Irish commerce remained in aggregate much higher than foreign trade values. However, index numbers of industrial output show the connection: on a base of 100 for 1700 for all industries, by 1800 the export industries had reached 544 (thus expanding by over five times); home industries 152 and agriculture 143.[1]

The link is clear in the case of textiles. Probably more than 50 per cent of total production was exported. Nor is it accidental that some of the most rapidly advancing sectors of the new industrial economy were those most committed to foreign trade, which was true of Yorkshire woollens as well as Lancashire and Cheshire cotton. The main markets of the iron industry were at home, providing the fixed capital for economic growth. Nevertheless, export markets were important to some iron manufacturers. One report – exaggerated – of 1760, spoke of £500,000 out of a total of £600,000 annual production of Birmingham ware (in other metals as well as iron) being destined for export. The same is true of Sheffield – over half its production was said to have been exported in the early nineteenth century.

The commitment to foreign trade meant that the size of the market was not limited by the extent of home demand; nor was the rate of expansion limited to the rate of expansion in home demand. A large and expanding volume of production encouraged division of labour and innovations in productive processes under Adam Smith's famous rule: 'The division of labour is limited by the extent of the market.' If an industry could get innovations which allowed it to undercut costs in the world market the scope for expansion was very much wider than that available in Britain. Tapping world demand can be easier and it can have greater scope if local markets are poor, or with a high degree of rural self-sufficiency. A very poor standard of living of the masses will limit the scope of home market often, even if the population is very large. The smaller an economy and its home market, the more unbalanced its resource pattern, then the greater the role of international trade is likely to be in the process of industrialization. The strategic industry in the British industrial revolution was undoubtedly cotton, even if its contribution to the national income was at first small. It had major dependence on foreign trade, and these international

[1] Deane and Cole, p. 78, Table 19. This does not specify the proportion of total output of the 'export' industries which was exported.

marketing systems were built up before the beginning of the industrial revolution. Commercial (and imperial) expansion prepared the way. This is particularly the case after 1783 but not so true for the expansion of demand in 1760-83, when exports were not rising very much.

The process may be complicated. One cannot just leave the analysis at the stage of saying that Britain had an export boom and this was the wave upon which industry expanded. Export booms were not just the effect of changes going on outside Britain, having nothing to do with the internal position. In many markets a boom in British exports to them implied an increasing ability in these countries to buy from Britain, just because their exports were expanding and giving them more sterling purchasing power. That is to say an increase in imports to Britain could pay off in a further stimulus to exports, given the right circumstances. And such an increase in imports to Britain, which had these echoes and re-echoes in the world economy, could be a response to increasing internal purchasing power, a rise in incomes at home.

The second question which relates foreign trade to industrialization is that of capital. Much capital accumulated as a result of this trade, particularly in the west coast ports, Glasgow, Liverpool, Bristol, which long antedated the surge of capital investment in industry in their hinterlands. Some direct connection developed between commercial wealth in Glasgow and Liverpool and industrial investment in the textile industries that sprang up in the hinterlands of these two great ports. Merchants were in the partnerships of some mills; considerable mercantile credit flowed to the manufacturer from the merchant (not only, of course, the merchant in foreign trade). The Coalbrookdale iron works were largely financed from mercantile capital in Bristol from the Quaker families of Champion and Goldney who were partners with Abraham Darby. The same point is demonstrated by the industrial development of south Wales. With little local capital available, the main south Wales industries, coal mining, tin-plate and iron making, were already operating on quite a large scale, demanding expensive capital equipment. Non-local capital had to flow into this region: much of it was

capital from the profits of foreign trade. Anthony Bacon, a London merchant and naval contractor set up the famous Cyfartha
iron works at Merthyr Tydfil in 1765, and was joined by Richard
Crawshay, another London merchant interested in Admiralty
cannon contracts. They were moving their capital back from
trade to industry, investing in the products that brought them
profits as merchants. Usually a Bristol or a London merchant
was to be found in the partnerships of Welsh iron works in the
late eighteenth century.

INLAND TRANSPORT IN THE INDUSTRIAL REVOLUTION

Industrialization could proceed only with the development of
investment and innovation in transport keeping pace with
investment and innovation in production. The size of the market
– a vital condition for industrial growth – according to the
degree that goods are bulky relative to their value, becomes a
function of transport costs. The cheaper transport costs become
the larger the area over which such cheap and bulky goods can
get marketed. Areas with special advantages in processing costs –
cheap coal, cheap power, cheap raw materials, good local labour
supplies – can thus expand their markets as 'transfer costs'
decline. And this chance of expanding markets makes possible
and encourages more division of labour, innovation, all the
economies of larger-scale production. Rising output and productivity will lower the average costs of the commodity – but
only if the goods can be cleared to a widening market. Cheap
transport thus becomes economically important according to the
degree of its effects upon total costs.

When this happens local high-cost production areas, often
handicraft industries, which were previously sheltered from
competition with the products of lower-cost manufacturing
areas facing high transport costs, are invaded. Local monopolies
get protected far more effectively by high transport costs than
by any other device. Cheaper transport cracks them open.
Economic gain and social hardships result from this, as from so
many other aspects of economic change. New specializations
are forced upon the invaded high-cost production areas or, at

worst, migration of people if the level of locally available employment falls. In the industrial areas favoured with special advantage in production costs, localization and concentration of industry intensifies as their markets widen and production expands.

The first gain was, in principle, a question of relocating production at more economic sites. But the greatest effect of improved transport proved a creative one. Resources hitherto completely sterilized by their location away from water carriage or away from a market were mobilized for production. Again this was particularly important for the cheap bulky materials – stone, brick, ores, timber – coal above all – exactly the materials needing to be deployed in vast quantities during industrialization. J. Phillips, in his book, *A Treatise on Inland Navigation*, 1785, remarked that canals 'highly benefit the manufactures where they have taken place and they occasion the establishment of many new ones'. Quarries, mines, manufacturing plants sprang into life along the lines of the new canals and railways. Phillips commented on the Bridgewater navigation opening up the ducal coal mine: 'This mine had lain dormant in the bowels of the earth from time immemorial without the least profit to the noble owner, on account of the price of land carriage which was so excessive that they could not be sold at a reasonable price.' Once canals and later railways were seen to have this effect they were projected and built in advance of traffic – on faith. Their creative effects proved of much greater dimensions than their substitution effects, a parallel with the effect of steam power. Over-estimates of eventual demand in this way led to over-investment. Many unprofitable canals were built, particularly in agricultural areas and subsequently many uneconomic railways.

The development of a transport system also had a stimulating economic effect as an industry in its own right, quite apart from promoting economic activity generally by lowering transport costs. A very high proportion of the capital invested in transport projects involved extra demand on the construction industries – bricks above all, stone, timber and iron. They also generated much purchasing power through the wages of the 'navvy' gangs in construction and then maintenance and operating staff. Towns like Stourport or St Helens were also a product of improved transport. Canals made them important transit centres and manufacturing centres because they allowed economic activity generally to be expanded.

Before the railways, water carriage inland, as overseas, was the only means of transport able to cope with the scale of mobilizing and distributing raw materials, food stuffs and finished products involved with industrialization. Here was another parallel with the development of power. Factory production also began on water power, but the momentum of expansion was such that, after a short time, further increase could be supported only by steam power. Within two generations, the momentum of growth in transport that had been sustained by the canals and turnpikes could only be continued by the application of steam power to transport, in the railways. In Adam Smith's world, however, water carriage was the key to advance. He observed:

> ... by means of water carriage a more extensive market is opened to every sort of industry than what land carriage alone can afford it, so it is upon the sea coast and along the banks of navigable rivers that industry of every kind naturally begins to subdivide and improve itself, and it is frequently not till a long time after that those improvements extend themselves to the inland parts of the country.

He then calculated, slightly optimistically perhaps, that 6 or 8 men sailing one ship between Leith and London could carry the same quantity of goods as '50 broad-wheeled waggons, attended by 100 men and drawn by 400 horses' would take overland. The difference in costs was clearly enormous, much greater than subsequent differences between canals and railways.

As long as these conditions existed a fairly small country with a long coastline and deeply penetrating river systems was much more favourable for economic growth than a large land-locked mass like the United States or Russia, particularly where fuel and raw materials were separated by vast distances. Even before man-made improvements were effected, therefore, English resources were much more accessible to water carriage than many other places. No point in England is farther than 70 miles from the sea and very few were more than 30 miles from navigable water. The greatest coalfield in Northumberland and Durham was virtually on the coast; the Lancashire coalfield was within half a dozen miles of the Mersey estuary at its nearest point. The south Wales coalfield was also not far away from the coast. In particular the river systems of the Severn and the Trent brought water carriage to the industrial Midlands – with the Severn navigable up into Shropshire, and the Trent into Staffordshire. Coal here was also very close to water carriage. The main river systems of the Thames and the Wash equally gave outlets to the produce of some of the main agricultural areas of the country. There was navigable water from 13 counties into the Wash, which gave Stourbridge Fair its great importance; 'In a word,' remarked Defoe, 'all the water of the middle part of England which does not run into the Thames or the Trent comes down into these Fenns.'

But rivers were not kept navigable, or improved for navigation, without deliberate efforts and capital invested for the purpose. Indeed, medieval England was more concerned to exploit the smaller rivers as sources of power than as highways, so that conflicts abounded between millers defending their weirs and water rights against bargees and merchants demanding a 'flash' of water through the weirs to get boats past the obstruction. No double locks were built to solve this difficulty. The demands to improve navigation on the waterways built up steadily in the late seventeenth century. By 1724 there were over 1,000 miles of river navigation, which had been doubled within the previous century, but without vast investment on the scale needed to make artificial cuts. Observers like Andrew Yarranton in the 1680's and Defoe a little later canvassed the merits of canals, pointed to the example of the Canal du Midi in France, joining the Atlantic with the Mediterranean, financed by the state.

The canal age did not spring suddenly to life in the 1750's, but was rather the conclusion of a mounting momentum of effort improving river navigations in the previous hundred years. Local committees of merchants at places too far upstream on navigable rivers pressed for 'pound' locks (double locks) and artificial cuts to by-pass meanders in their rivers. Their example was the Exeter lighter canal cut in 1564, which first used the double lock in England and was, in fact, a mainly artificial channel. However, it was only four miles long and was un-economic compared with the land journey for most goods because of trans-shipment at both ends of the very short water-way. 'Breaking bulk' is always exceedingly important in the economics of transport. Important improvements were in pro-gress after 1710, particularly in the Liverpool region, centring on the Lancashire and Cheshire basin. A dock was built there under the initiative of the local council (which meant mainly the merchants). In 1712 they ordered surveys of the rivers of south Lancashire and Cheshire with a view to improvement schemes – to get to the coalfield at Wigan from the Ribble; to get to the coalfield from the Mersey up the Irwell, and to get to the salt-field in Cheshire at Winsford up the Weaver south from the Mersey. In 1734 the latter navigation was extended to Nantwich – involving pound locks and artificial cuts round meanders. By the mid-eighteenth century further improvement of navigation in the rising industrial districts depended on still-water navigation, and the first projects were carried out after a score or more schemes had been promoted. The first canal proper in the British Isles (apart from the Exeter Canal) was the Newry Canal from Lough Neagh south to Newry opened in 1742 to get coal cheaply to Dublin. This project had been mooted since 1703 but its construction depended, significantly, on funds made available from taxation revenue in Ireland: sufficient spontaneous momentum did not exist for self-financing. The Newry Canal had 15 locks and was about 35 miles long. It had been built by the engineer who was the main adviser to Liverpool Corporation, Thomas Steers.

Then followed the first industrial canal in England cut from the Mersey to St Helens in 1757 to bring Cheshire salt to Lancashire coal, essentially complementary to the Weaver navigation south of the Mersey. This also was designed by a Liverpool Corporation Docks engineer, Henry Berry, and had

Liverpool initiative behind it. The Corporation again sponsored the survey, and lent £300 towards the parliamentary
expenses. This project was one of a number, and the period
from 1750 to 1755 was one of low interest rates, which clearly
influenced the projection of such schemes. Finally, in 1761,
comes the famous textbook date as the canal age opened, with
a blare of publicity, when the Duke of Bridgewater's canal, built
by James Brindley, was opened. This ran from the Duke's
colliery at Worsley almost to Manchester, and had dramatic
features such as an aqueduct over a valley and a tunnel through
a hill. These were unprecedented but the canal itself was
not.

The major potential of the canals was not realized, however,
until the trunk lines began to be built in the 1770's. These
created interior lines of communication by water carriage across
the heads of the river systems, breaking the economic watershed
which ran down the spine of the country. All previous canals
had been feeders to rivers and estuaries facing outwards to the
sea. For trunk canals, again, England had great natural advantages because the cuts joining the river systems across the
middle needed to be relatively short compared with other
countries to have all the advantages of creating interior lines of
communication.

The stages whereby the cross links were established are as
follows: the Mersey was linked to the Severn at Stourport in
1772; the Trent was linked to the Mersey in 1777; the Severn
was joined to the Thames in 1789; finally the Mersey was joined
to the Trent and the Thames in 1790. By the latter date London,
Bristol, Birmingham, Liverpool and Hull were all joined. The
links between Lancashire, the Potteries and the Birmingham
area with London were still poor, however, because the canal
from Coventry went to the Thames at Oxford and was a narrow-
boat canal. The main link from the Midlands to London was
launched in 1793 – the Grand Junction Canal, which was
completed for large traffic finally in 1805, feeding London
direct from the industrial regions, just at a time when French
privateers were making insurance rates very heavy for the trip
round the south coast from Lancashire ports. A strategic need

persuaded the government to finance the Caledonian Canal to save an equally exposed journey round the north of Scotland. The central pivot of the canal system, thus created, lay between Birmingham, Coventry and Stafford – known as 'the cross' – with almost 160 miles of canals in the immediate vicinity of Birmingham. This local canal system was the most important single step in opening up the central industrial region and the Midland coalfield to the major ports on all sides of the island; and the curb imposed upon the development of Birmingham as an urban giant was removed. By 1815 about 2,200 miles of still water and 2,000 miles of river navigation were open. Three routes had been driven over the Pennines by the time of the railways, all reading heights of 500 ft or more. The Huddersfield Canal even had a 5,400 yd tunnel at 637 ft above sea level. Three routes also operated between London and the west coast: the Thames and Severn, the Kennet and Avon, the Wiltshire and Berkshire.

From this sequence of development, and from the study of canal projects which did not come to fruition, it is clear that the initiative of industrialists and merchants, frustrated with existing transport facilities, lay behind the launching of canals and that the problems of moving industrial raw materials and products were creating the incentives, in a marked way 50 years before the mid-eighteenth century, but with irrepressible force thereafter. Much the most important material behind the Canal Acts was coal. A contemporary calculated that 90 out of the 165 passed between 1758 and 1802 had coal as their main prospective traffic. The Duke of Bridgewater's own canal had halved the price of coal in Manchester and he made himself a fortune from a previously uneconomic pit. His comment was that 'a navigation should have coals at the heel of it'. This truth was proved by default in the failure of the Cambridge Canal from Bedford, and the poor record of dividends and financial struggles over the promotion of canals in several agricultural districts. None of the canals across the watershed in southern England was profitable. When they had been cut they were often important for the economic development of their districts, but scarcely profitable for the proprietors. Again, a similar

sequence ensued a century later with many unprofitable railways.

Turnpikes and roads

The economic functions of roads remained largely complementary to water carriage – as Adam Smith's illustration
showed. People, mail, grain, other food produce and animals
who walked themselves to market provided their main traffic
rather than the heavy bulk staples (although these travelled
shorter distances by road). Official attitudes to the roads were
curious but constitutionally significant. Highways were in a
terrible state, some have said as the Romans left them (save for
a few strategic highways), dependent on ineffectual parish
obligations for maintenance. But good roads, as in France, were
a symbol of the *corvée* – forced labour – and an autocratic state.[1]
An efficient road system might also be used to mobilize troops
to overawe London – and was to be considered constitutionally
complementary to a standing army after 1660. This attitude only
changed when the absence of highways impeded the mobilization of troops against the 1745 rebellion. But even after that
most public efforts were confined to road-building in the Highlands, exactly on the French example to deploy a standing
army rapidly, and on strategic routes such as the Holyhead
road.

Very little public effort and public capital went into road
improvements, as into river and canal schemes. A characteristic
of legislation until the 1780's was to preserve the road by putting
restrictions on the vehicles using it rather than building the road
to suit the vehicles. Laws enforced a minimum width of wheel
(9 in. for all goods wagons in 1753) to preserve the surfaces at the
expense of speed. The main agency of road improvement was
the turnpikes – a comparable instrument to that used to extend
water carriage. The initiative was purely local. Parliamentary
authority was given through a private act to local *ad hoc* bodies
of trustees empowered to raise capital at fixed rates of interest

---

[1] This was a little similar to the accusation in pre-war Italy that Musso-
lini made the trains run on time, implying that a police state was needed to
achieve the feat.

and administer it in improving a stretch of road, for which the users paid a toll.

Turnpike Acts thus followed the same sort of incentives as river improvement schemes. But the main urgency of road improvement was occasioned by the breaking down of the main roads handling London traffic in the Home Counties, caused by the expansion of London in the seventeenth century, with food wagons and cattle droving as the main agents of destruction. The first turnpike toll-gates were put up at Wadesmill, Herts, in 1663, and Defoe gave 16 pages in his *Tour of the Whole Island* to listing the turnpikes in 1720. 'It must be acknowledged,' he concluded, 'that they are very great things and very great things are done by them, and 'tis well worth recording for the Honour of the present age that this work has begun . . .'

Arthur Young's strictures on the Lancashire roads in the 1770's are also really evidence of the steep rise in traffic with industrialization which the older techniques of road making could not sustain. The new techniques which came with the work of Macadam and Thomas Telford during the construction boom of 1788–95 largely solved these problems. But the agency of maintaining the roads was still largely public authority devolved onto private initiative, private capital and payment by users. High-speed mail coaches developed only in the decades after 1784, when the time taken on trunk routes to Scotland and the north was more than halved. Startling evidence for the revolutionary increase in the speed of specialized road freights can be seen in the timetable for the London to Edinburgh coach. In 1754 this was being advertised as '10 days in summer; 12 days in winter'. By 1832 the journey was billed as taking '42 hours 33 minutes'. The famous Independent Tallyho coach from London to Birmingham covered the 109 miles at an average speed of 15 m.p.h. in the 1830's. But, however good the road system, given the economics of freight transport by horse and wagon, the canals were the only medium which could sustain the impact of industrialization and urbanization before the railways.

A great penalty of local initiative determining the evolution of new transport investment in Britain – canals, turnpikes and railways – was the absence of national planning. The economic potential of these transport media was, therefore, never fully realized. The turnpikes were piecemeal, with many gaps, and their management bedevilled by corruption (particularly before the Consolidation Act of 1773). The canals came into existence without a national strategy, with different widths and depths and much inefficient routeing, which caused considerable delays and trans-shipment. All this was to be duplicated on an even larger scale with the railways, including the liability of over-investment, when capital was cheap and the expectations of potential shareholders uncritically optimistic.

The high capital costs of investment in transport make transport improvements one of the potential blockages to the progress of industrialization in many countries. Investment in an inland transport system, shipping and ports is one of the prerequisites for industrial growth; yet to create such a system there must be extensive prior mobilization of capital and the agencies to effect it. A large transport project needs to be complete before its benefits accrue to the economy or before any income can be created from tolls to pay for it. One cannot begin the venture in a small way, like many manufacturing concerns, and allow it to grow by re-investing profits, pulling itself up by its own boot straps. The minimum scale of initial investment in a project is extremely high: capital is 'lumpy'. The Duke of Bridgewater calculated that the rough 'rule of thumb' guide for capital outlays on a canal was '10,000 guineas a mile'. The scale of investment in transport was unrivalled in the decades which saw the canal booms and the railway booms – the latter became the major economic events of their years. £8 million was raised for canals in the boom between 1788 and 1795; and possibly £20 million had been invested in the system by 1815. This was very small, however, in comparison with the sums raised by government in the national debt. Railway construction had a much greater impact in its turn.[1] It was not accidental that transport projects had already begun to cluster at certain times,

[1] See below, pp. 282–3, 287, and Table 36, p. 488.

before the canal age began: times which were marked by a surge of business activity and cheap credit. The booms in business increased demands on existing capacity and efficiency in transport and proved the need for expansion. A low rate of interest implied that capital was available and the financing of large projects would be more economical. With the pre-canal river-improvement schemes, there were three main bursts of activity: 1662–5; 1699–1705; 1718–20. Six companies were projected in the latter boom before the South Sea Company's bubble burst.

A similar phasing characterized the canal age: the years 1750–1755 were a time of low interest rates; and also the years of the great canal boom 1788–94 (when £8 million was raised). An even more marked periodicity in the projection of railway investment occurred in its first twenty years. In the construction industries, where the cost of paying interest on capital was one of the most important elements in costs, low rates of interest did prove important. These periods were usually years of peace (or of very early war years before active campaigning had brought marked economic effects). The government were not plunging heavily in the loan markets, diverting the flow of loanable funds into their own pockets by higher rates of interest. Nor had war sapped incomes by higher taxation or disturbed trade.

The mechanism of the private Act of Parliament was devised for raising capital for these improvements, similar to that devised for improving agriculture, the other main sector of investment needing to mobilize capital on a large scale. It shows a complete contrast between the ways of financing transport investment and manufacturing industry. In both, however, there was very little public money or public guarantees. Some state initiative is to be found in strategic routes – such as the Great North Road and some highways to Holyhead and Scotland after the 1745 rebellions. The same is true of the canals – the Forth and Clyde (1784), the Caledonian Canal (1799), the Brighton Canal. A little local government initiative encouraged docks, harbours, river improvements and canals in places like Liverpool and Dublin. But the vast majority of projects were raised by private capital and, therefore, the system had to be self-sustaining, with users of both improved roads and rivers and canals paying tolls to provide the dividends for the investors who had put up the money.

The parliamentary process was still essential. An act gave compulsory powers to acquire land. It allowed capital to be raised publicly, without the liability of investors being responsible for the debts of the concern. It gave all the benefits of incorporation. Canal shares became freely negotiable and were quoted on the Stock Exchange like government securities at the end of the eighteenth century. Most launchings of shares were still done by the company at its local headquarters, however, and transfers arranged by the secretary, rather than through the Stock Exchange. Companies were usually empowered to raise more capital by loans or by selling annuities. This allowed canal projects and turnpikes to tap a national market for capital – uncommitted, 'anonymous' capital, often quite 'blind' – not from persons who had a hope of profiting commercially from the canal, but who were simply investors. Usually the treasurers of canals and turnpikes were bankers, and through them banking capital often went into the project, if the company was pressed for funds during construction. Financing transport investment thus required a different institutional basis from the pattern of investment of long-term capital in manufacturing industry.

Parliamentary permission gave monopoly powers: the company was therefore usually limited to a maximum dividend, while it sometimes had to seek parliamentary permission to raise toll rates or more capital. It usually had to carry certain goods like lime and manure free of toll. This was clear recognition that, where ordinary competitive restraints did not apply, then public restrictions were justified. The principle was carried forward to railway legislation in the hey-day of *laissez-faire*.

Financing canals and turnpikes showed how plentiful capital was in eighteenth-century England, and how favourable the social context was for investment. Lists of trustees of navigation companies and investors read like catalogues of the county families and the commercial men hoping to profit from the canal. The Grand Junction Canal of 1793, for example, had its promotion led by the Marquis of Buckingham (his arms were on the Company Seal), the Duke of Grafton, the Earl of Clarendon, the Earl of Exeter, the Earl Spencer. Five M.P.s were on its board in 1812. In many midland and northern canals a body of investors listed as London residents were to be found amongst the shareholders, even if most of the capital came from the counties through which the canal ran. The strong support of the landed classes, particularly those with riparian estates, often came from the hope of augmenting the capital values of their land, or in the hope of exploiting minerals underneath their estates, apart from local patriotism or the chance of *rentier* income. Some were undoubtedly bribed with shares when the projectors needed the support of all persons with parliamentary influence to get their Act through, against the opposition of a rival interest whose position was threatened by the new venture. The scale of parliamentary corruption – or 'expenses' – with canals was on a very modest level compared with the railway bills of the 1830's and 1840's.

Reading list

THE REGULATION OF FOREIGN TRADE AND SHIPPING

ALBION, R. G. *Forests and Sea Power: the timber problem of the Royal Navy, 1652–1862*, Cambridge (Mass.), 1926 (Harvard Economic Studies, vol. 29).

BEER, G. L. *The Old Colonial System, 1660–1754*, 2 vols, Part I: *The Establishment of the System, 1660–1688*, New York, 1912.

COLEMAN, D. C. Review of HECKSCHER, E. 'Mercantilism', in *Scandinavian Economic History Review*, 1957, **5**, no. 1.

HARPER, L. A. *The English Navigation Laws: a 17th-century experiment in social engineering*, New York, 1939.

LIPSON, E. *Economic History of England*, vol. 3, 6th ed., London, 1956.

MUN, T. *England's Treasure by Foreign Trade*, London, 1664, reprinted Oxford, 1949.

SMITH, A. *Wealth of Nations* (1776), bk 4, 2 vols, London–New York, 1954.

SPERLING, J. 'The international payments mechanism in the 17th and 18th centuries', *Economic History Review*, 2nd series, 1962, **14**, no. 3.

WILSON, C. H. *Mercantilism*, London, 1958 (Historical Association: General Series, no. 37).

WILSON, C. H. *Profit and Power: a study of England and the Dutch Wars*, London, 1957.

WILSON, C. H. 'Treasure and the trade balance: the mercantilist problem', *Economic History Review*, 2nd series, 1949, **2,** no. 2.

THE COURSE OF FOREIGN TRADE

BERRILL, K. E. 'International trade and the rate of economic growth', *Economic History Review*, 2nd series, 1960, **12,** no. 3.

DAVIS, R. *A Commercial Revolution*, London, 1967.

DAVIS, R. 'English foreign trade, 1660–1700', *Economic History Review*, 2nd series, 1954, **7,** no. 2; reprinted in E. M. Carus-Wilson (ed.), *Essays in Economic History*, vol. 2, London, 1962.

DAVIS, R. 'English foreign trade, 1700–1774', *Economic History Review*, 2nd series, 1962, **15,** no. 2.

DAVIS, R. *The Rise of the English Shipping Industry in the 17th and 18th Centuries*, London–New York, 1962.

DEFOE, D. *A Plan of the English Commerce, being a compleat prospect of the trade of this nation, as well the home trade as the foreign*, London, 1728, reprinted Oxford, 1928.

FISHER, H. E. S. 'Anglo-Portuguese trade, 1700–1770', *Economic History Review*, 2nd series, 1963, **16,** no. 2.

MINCHINTON, W. E. 'Bristol: metropolis of the West in the 18th century', *Transactions of the Royal Historical Society*, 5th series, 1954, 4.

MINCHINTON, W. E. (ed.) *The Trade of Bristol in the 18th Century*, Bristol, 1957.

PARES, R. *A West-India Fortune*, London, 1950.

PARKINSON, C. N. *The Rise of the Port of Liverpool*, Liverpool, 1952.

PARKINSON, C. N. (ed.) *The Trade Winds: a study of British overseas trade during the French Wars, 1793–1815*, by C. E. Fayle, London, 1948.

PRICE, J. M. 'The economic growth of the Chesapeake and the European market, 1697–1775', *Journal of Economic History*, 1964, **24,** no. 4.

PRICE, J. M. 'The rise of Glasgow in the Chesapeake tobacco trade, 1707–1775', *William and Mary Quarterly*, 3rd series, 1954, **11,** no. 2.

SCHLOTE, W. *British Overseas Trade from 1700 to the 1930s*, translated by W. O. Henderson and W. H. Chaloner, Oxford, 1952.

SCHUMPETER, E. B. *English Overseas Trade Statistics, 1697–1800*, with an introduction by T. S. Ashton, Oxford, 1960 [for reference].

SUTHERLAND, L. S. *A London Merchant, 1695–1774*, Oxford, 1962.

WILLAN, T. S. *The English Coasting Trade, 1600–1750*, Manchester, 1967.

WILLIAMS, J. E. 'Whitehaven in the 18th century', *Economic History Review*, 2nd series, 1956, **8,** no. 3.

WILSON, C. H. *Anglo-Dutch Commerce and Finance in the 18th Century*, Cambridge, 1941.

INLAND TRANSPORT IN THE INDUSTRIAL REVOLUTION

[ASHTON, T. S.]. *Studies in the Industrial Revolution Presented to T. S. Ashton* . . . ed. L. S. Pressnell, London, 1960.

BARKER, T. C. 'The beginnings of the canal age', in L. S. Pressnell (ed.), *Studies in the Industrial Revolution*, London, 1960.

HADFIELD, E. C. R. *British Canals*, 2nd ed., 3rd impression, Newton Abbot, 1966 [and regional volumes].

JACKMAN, W. T. *Development of Transportation in Modern England*, 2nd rev. ed., London, 1962 [for reference].

SAVAGE, C. I. *An Economic History of Transport*, London, 1961.

SKEMPTON, A. W. 'Canals and river navigations before 1750', in C. Singer (ed.), *History of Technology*, Oxford, 1957, vol. 3.

WILLAN, T. S. *River Navigation in England, 1600–1750*, new impression, London, 1964.

5 Industrial growth and finance

INDUSTRIAL ORGANIZATION AND CHANGE

Before the industrial changes of the eighteenth century an extension of production in the consumer goods industries did not involve much investment demand on the capital goods industries. Equipment was simple, of the size of handicraft looms and spinning wheels in the main. The numbers of workers had to be increased with the number of their tools. But not many specialized buildings or massive plant were needed. Expansion of output therefore involved little investment problem in industry in the modern sense and no increases in productivity occurred with the expansion of capacity in traditional, or very slowly changing technology. When expansion in textiles meant also cumulative innovations in the technique of production – culminating in the rise of the factory system – it did create large demands directly and indirectly on these capital goods industries. The capital goods industries have special problems. The rhythms of their expansion and depression are more violent. The problems of capital investment for them, even the problems of locating and marketing, are all very much influenced by this distinction. Evolving structural differences of this new sort lay behind the enormous increases in total production and in productivity per man which the new technology made possible.

Many capital goods industries were already being conducted on a substantial scale in 1700 and had quite a lot in common with what they became under the stimulus of industrialization. The biggest manufacturing units in the country in the seventeenth century and perhaps in the eighteenth century also, were the naval dockyards, comprising an enormous capital and labour force. And the technology here remained a traditional handicraft affair in the main, as it was in most of the construction industries.

The primary side of the metal industries, making refined metal from fuel and ores, was already significantly larger in scale than the final-product metal industries of the Black Country and Lancashire villages and Sheffield. Non-ferrous metal industries – lead, tin, copper – were already using mineral fuel on a large scale in reverberatory furnaces long before the industrial revolution and were sited on coalfields. The early eighteenth century saw them pulling away from Bristol and its neighbourhood, which was suitable for location because of markets (and a base for foreign trade) and skills, to south Wales where fuel was cheap. Similarly, smelting works for copper were being closed down next to the mines in Cornwall to be re-sited near Swansea in the 1720's because coal was half the price in Wales. In the process of smelting many times more the weight of fuel was consumed than of ore. Hence it was much cheaper in shipping space and costs to locate smelting at the site of the fuel and carry the ore than to locate processing at the ore and carry the fuel. The technicalities of smelting also often required that ores from different lodes be mixed, which added to the incentives to locate smelting industries on the coalfields. It so happened that the main ores for non-ferrous metals, unlike many of the iron-ore deposits, were not located close to coal. Cornwall and – later in the century – Anglesey were the main sites for copper; Cornwall for tin; Derbyshire and north Wales for lead. Most Anglesey copper, when mining developed after 1768, was smelted on the Lancashire coalfield. Some was brought round to south Wales because fuel was even cheaper there. Already in 1750 over half the British copper was being smelted on the south Wales coalfield near Swansea and it was a similar story with lead.

These concerns rapidly became integrated so that partnerships would have an interest in ore-mining in one area of the country, smelting (and often colliery owning) in south Wales, and sometimes a stake in a refining shop, or a rolling mill, or a plant using copper or lead in the final-product manufacturing areas, such as Birmingham. The views of these industrialists were already nation-wide, capitals were extensive and they were already doing cost-accounting calculations to see whether it was cheaper to locate smelting works in Lancashire or south Wales. Copper production rose from *c.* 2,000 tons per annum in 1700 to *c.* 7,000 tons at the end of the century.

The iron industry was also located, and changing its location, because of fuel and power needs – but in 1700 still searching for untapped woods and water power to work bellows at the blast furnace and tilt hammers at the forges – not yet seeking cheap coal for smelting. The old Wealden industry of Sussex was dying from scarcity of fuel and raw material so that iron masters were being driven to more remote sites in the border country up the Severn, in Wales, Cumberland and Scotland. Only after 1709 did coal begin to exercise its influence on the location of the iron industry, as it had done for some time in the non-ferrous metal industries. Shropshire was perhaps chosen by Abraham Darby for his iron works because it gave access to the Severn, immediately adjacent, and water carriage from there to the sea. There was good 'sweet' coal and iron ore in the vicinity (he smelted with coke from his first year at Coalbrookdale in 1709) and a good stream ran by to work his bellows. Canals were soon to give greater mobility to water carriage, and thus encourage siting at coal and ore more completely. Darby's innovation was not taken up widely by other iron masters, however, until after 1760 – a very significant time-lag.

Until the two inventions of Henry Cort in 1784, the puddling furnace – a reverberatory furnace – and the rolling mill, refining the pig-iron, which had been made in the blast furnace, into a malleable bar-iron was usually done at a separate site from the furnace. Forges needed much water power and also charcoal fuel – so that they were often driven away from the site of the iron ore where smelting occurred. Henry Cort's innovations allowed coal to be the main fuel used in refining; and the rolling mill allowed a steam engine to be the main prime mover for producing refined bar-iron and rolled iron. The 1709 innovation of Darby released the blast furnace from charcoal (but not from water power for its bellows). The 1784 innovations of Cort released the second stage of manufacture from charcoal and water power. After this the iron industry came together in integrated concerns at sites determined by coal and ore. Watt's steam engine by then had made its main power-source mobile. Soon after this Staffordshire, Yorkshire and south Wales began to dominate the location of iron manufacture. Great increases in the size of blast furnaces developed with the use of coke, giving important economies of scale and then, with Cort's invention, in forging and rolling. On these two primary innovations, coke-smelted pig-iron and puddled, rolled bar-iron – both blast and forge-hammer and roller being operated by the engine – most capacity in the iron industry was laid down until the mid-nineteenth century. Capitals expanded, production from the single plant increased enormously, as in the factories in textiles.

Before then the industry was still operating with fairly large technology – blast furnaces, even though small ones, water-tilt hammers, etc. – which prevented workers from any sort of independent ownership. They could not buy the tools of their trade easily, like a spinner or a weaver or a nailer, and work was always in a specialized industrial site – not a cottage. In this the iron industry was on a level with other mill industries – such as paper-making, also located by water for power, and water as a raw material used on a large scale in production.

Businessmen had to have large horizons in the iron industry. Ambrose Crowley was the largest ironmonger in Europe in 1700. He made bar-iron (he did not manufacture pig-iron) in Sunderland, and had a nearby slitting mill and forges, where he made chains, anchors and fulfilled admiralty contract work. He ran a nail factory there rather than in the Black Country because coal was cheaper and victuals a third cheaper than in the midlands (coal and coke being used by blacksmiths and makers of products from the refined metal long before it was used in producing the refined metal). Crowley bought rod and bar-iron from Sussex, Kent, Sweden and the midlands, and owned four ships to ply between these depots. He had established warehouses at his main markets: London, Blackwall, Greenwich, Ware, Wolverhampton, Walsall, Stourbridge. More remarkable, he ran the whole sprawling enterprise from his house at Greenwich by correspondence through the very primitive postal system of the day. He was an exceedingly remarkable man (by origin a Quaker, subsequently a Knight, a high-Tory M.P. and an

Anglican) and so were his letters; reflecting a personality which was iron-willed – even iron-hearted – like his product.[1]

The Darby iron works at Coalbrookdale cost about £3,500 to set up as an operating concern. The Walker brothers set up an iron foundry near Sheffield on the smallest scale possible in 1741, with indeterminate capital, possibly as little as £10. Capital in 1746 was £600. By 1750 it was £2,500; by 1760 £11,000. When the famous Carron works (smelting iron from coke) were set up on a large scale in Scotland in 1759 the partnership had £12,000 capital, and £50,000 in 1764. In 1770 it totalled £130,000.

The largest iron works were casting shops. Cast iron was one of the great materials of the industrial revolution. Casting direct from the blast furnace into the moulds, or from reheated pig iron into the moulds, enabled the iron masters to produce final products themselves, not just bar-iron for the Birmingham trades. They therefore were able to face their own markets directly. Hence the warehouses set up in London, Bristol, Cornwall, by such iron works as Coalbrookdale and Carron. The castings market was one of the most rapidly expanding as the range of iron products diversified: castings for domestic ware like cooking pots, for traditional uses like the bushes on cart-wheel axles and windmill bearings, but also for the new uses of the industrial revolution: steam engine parts, canal ironmongery, structural members, like the pillars and beams in warehouses after 1795, railings, balconies, manhole covers, street furniture, bridge castings after the famous cast-iron bridge put over the Severn in 1779, military castings.

A quite opposite sort of industrial structure survived into the mid-nineteenth century, and later, in the consumer goods, and final product sides of the metal industries. The characteristic unit in the secondary metal industries of the Black Country, Birmingham, Sheffield and Lancashire, was very small in comparison to the large casting shops and blast furnaces, being

---

[1] One ended: 'I would have you all know that the orders I have made . . . are built upon such a rock that while I have my understanding it shall be out of the power of Satan and all his disciples to destroy them.' Invoking Satan as the enemy to worldly success was not an insignificant or accidental image for such a man.

composed of cottage workshops and forges. Even the 'primary' side of the steel industry was composed of a large number of very small plants. It was still very much a 'domestic industry', despite the occasional large business; a workshop-trade dominated by the skilled handicraftsmen. In such a context division of labour amongst skilled artisans remained the essence of productivity in these trades, not massive fixed plant power driven.

Before industrialization began, the woollen textile industry was, of course, very widespread in the land. International specialization had already become marked between the different production areas. Each was already operating on a world-wide market within a sophisticated commercial system before the factory system put its vast momentum behind the increase in output and the decline in costs and prices. Units of production everywhere were small and scattered. The main processes took place in cottages. Only fulling, which was a very minor process in the serges and worsted trades, was 'mechanized' with mill machinery, and the finishing processes such as dyeing conducted on a fairly large scale. Up to Arkwright's patents for roller spinning by the 'water frame' of 1769 and Crompton's patents for mule spinning of 1779, all the innovations had been compatible with cottage industry: the stocking frame in the sixteenth century, the complicated Jacquard loom for weaving figured cloth, the flying shuttle by Kay in 1733, even the spinning-jenny by Hargreaves of 1766 (which did increase output per head very much). All could be worked by hand by the single worker and his helpers. All fitted into a traditional family economy. In technology, in productivity, in the place of work and the social relations of manufacture this was still part of the medieval world.

But, as far as the ownership of the means of production was concerned, the development of a proletariat in many textile regions antedated the coming of the factories. In all the clothing areas except the West Riding, the actual manufacturers had little independence, little commercial initiative, and less capital in their hands. In the west of England clothing areas (Wiltshire, Somerset and Exeter); in the Norwich clothing area; in the

Bradford (Yorks) worsted areas; in the Nottinghamshire stocking and lace manufacturing districts, the man who organized production, and who owned the capital in production was the clothier or 'putter out', the cloth merchant, the hosier. The stocking frame and the Jacquard loom increased the cost of capital equipment (in a modest way); hence they encouraged the dominance of the merchant-capitalist machine-renter over the 'manufacturer'. Markets were often very specialized and very distant – only the merchant aware of the needs of these markets could effectively organize production. Raw materials needed to be bought in from many sources, possibly a long time in advance, sorted and graded and stored. This, again, needed to be done on a fairly large scale by someone whose commercial horizons were wide and whose access to capital and credit secure. Most capital was owned in the stocks of raw material, finished goods and goods 'in the pipe-line'. There was little in equipment. Most costs would therefore be costs of materials and costs of labour, with very little embodied in 'overhead' costs to keep plant, machinery and buildings in operation. In all these ways the merchant controlled the capital needed for production throughout its course. He owned the raw materials, often right through the sequence of processes, paying the spinners and weavers for their labour rather than buying yarn or cloth from them as independent businessmen. He would rent out the looms and stocking frames, sometimes to many hundreds of dependent families. In this way the structure of ownership which characterized the factory system in fact existed in certain regions of the country long before the development of modern technology.

In the Halifax region of the West Riding of Yorkshire weavers and spinners do seem to have been largely independent masters in their own right, owning their spinning wheels and looms, buying wool and yarn, taking their pieces of cloth to the Cloth Hall every week for sale to the merchants, whom they faced as persons owning the cloth they sold. In a sense the Cloth Halls erected in the West Riding towns were symbols of this structure of production based on the small masters, even if they were also an employing class. This sort of structure of production was not at all characteristic of the cotton industry in Lancashire. But even in the Halifax area the small masters were employing labour in their little manufactories and the fulling, dyeing and finishing processes were organized on a more capitalistic basis, usually being controlled by the merchants who sold the finished cloth. Again, this is a question of the men with capital and the commercial initiative controlling production processes which needed to be conducted on a large scale with expensive equipment and expensive materials.

Changes in the structure of production came first on the spinning side of the cotton industry. But it was preceded by the first genuine factory, which was a silk throwing mill (which prepared yarn for weaving) put up on the river Derwent in Derby in 1719 by Thomas Lombe, who had brought back the secrets from Italy. A single wide paddle wheel above the powerful river worked over 25,000 movements. The mill was six storeys high, the building 500 ft long, and 300 were employed – mainly women and children – to reknot the threads when they broke; light work in terms of physical exertion but demanding very high standards of attention. This context was exactly characteristic of that which developed after 1769 in the cotton industry. Why then did not the silk industry stand in the forefront of industrial progress in textiles? Raw silk was still inelastic in supply and expensive; the silk market was a luxury market and very narrow. No ready export markets existed in silk, for continental and eastern countries were more competitive with higher quality cheaper silks (kept out of Britain by high tariffs). Moreover, acute technical problems prevented the weaving side of the industry from being hitched to power and semi-automatic machines in the same way.

Cotton had many advantages on all these counts. The raw material supply proved so elastic that in response to demand production soared and the price fell steeply once the plantation system was organized in the American south. Secondly, cotton was an attractive alternative fibre to wool – lighter, more washable, potentially cheaper because of the raw material position. Thus an enormous substitute market was waiting in Britain, as well as increasing demand from a rising population and exports once innovation could lead to a fall in costs and prices. And then, with this enormous potential, cotton proved to be the most tractable fibre technically. One could adapt it to machinery at every process more readily than wool – a more delicate, more complicated fibre – and more easily than flax and jute which were too stiff. Finally cotton was a new industry founded in Lancashire in the seventeenth century (where it provided yarn for use in mainly mixed fabrics with wool). Hence it grew up in areas without guild control, where the provisions of the 1563 Statute of Apprentices were judged not to apply, in a later industrial world where older traditions of restrictions on production were inoperative. When equivalent innovations were pioneered in cotton, therefore, they did not run into the difficulties which put restraints on the expansion of capacity in silk.

In the 1770's Arkwright's mill at Cromford employed 300. His labour-force had increased to 727 by 1816. Jedediah Strutt was employing over 300 at his mills in Belper. The largest spinning mills increased in size to employ over 1,500 by 1816. This signifies that technology had at once caused a revolution in the mode of manufacture, given that all other circumstances were favourable. Only the spinning side of the industry underwent this transformation in textiles in the eighteenth century, despite the desperate search for an effective steam loom. The first successful steam loom patents were taken out by Horrocks of Stockport in 1813, but little impact was made on hand weaving until after 1825. By then the basic spinning process, and the preparatory processes to spinning like carding had been adapted to machinery in flax (William Marshall took out patents in 1790), worsted spinning after 1790; wool spinning after 1810 (Benjamin Gott of Leeds leading the way), as well as cotton and silk. By 1820 there were 110,000 operatives in spinning mills; but only 10,000 in weaving factories. Over 250,000 weavers still toiled at hand looms, and their long-drawn-out tragedy had only just begun.

The capital demands made by Arkwright's massive machinery were also of a different order of magnitude from those made by any previous innovation in the industry; just as were their

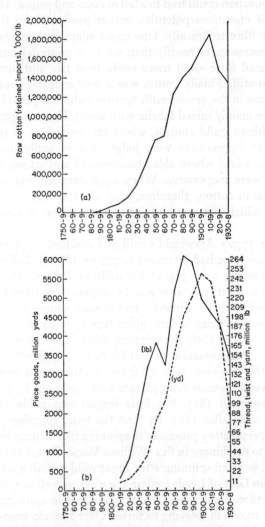

Fig. 4. Cotton: (a) retained imports of raw cotton; (b) exports (see also Table 34, p. 486). Annual average per decade. After Mitchell and Deane, 1962, pp. 177–81.

effects on productivity, on the whole world of the worker in the
textile industry and on location. Lombe's mills at Derby, and
another at Stockport, cost between £15,000 and £20,000 to
build and stock. Jedediah Strutt's mill at Belper in 1793 cost
£5,000 in building, as much again to stock with machinery, and
then possibly as much again for materials to start production.

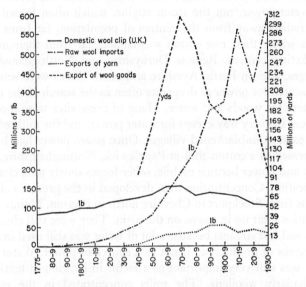

Fig. 5. Woollens (see also Table 35, p. 487). Annual average per decade.
After Mitchell and Deane, 1962, pp. 190–1, 195–7.

William Marshall's first flax spinning mill at Leeds in 1793 was
valued at £5,000 for the fixed plant; £3,000 for the machines
and £6,000 for stock. If an industrialist had to begin with
accumulated capital of this order the strong likelihood existed
that he would have to borrow capital on a large scale, or come
himself from the ranks of those in the textile industry with
capital – that is to say from being himself a merchant or a
hosier, or form a partnership with mercantile wealth. The stocks

of raw materials he might hope to acquire on credit from his suppliers.

Arkwright's spinning innovations also caused a problem of location. From 1770 to 1785 the new technology meant that location was determined mainly by the existence of water power, massive water power at that. The factory system was pioneered on water power, not the steam engine, which often forced industrialists away from the centres of population, far from the ports where their raw cotton was landed, far from their main marketing centres. Remote Derbyshire and Nottinghamshire villages, sites in Perth, Ayrshire and north Wales were sought in a search for power as desperate often as the search of the iron masters for woods and water. Many of these sites were inconvenient in every way except for water power, and the mills often still exist in unblackened villages. Once steam power had been harnessed to a cotton mill at Papplewick, Nottinghamshire, in 1785 and power became mobile, other forces slowly took charge of location. Concentration then developed in the present cotton towns from Stockport in Cheshire north to Preston. Mainly the factories went up in towns on the plain. They were still close to hills and fast streams because a lot of water was still used in the processes of production, if not as a source of power. Water, in fact, was still very important as a factor in location in textiles, particularly woollens. The mills concentrated in the more populated regions, in places where communications were easier and cheaper for getting in raw materials from Liverpool. The pull of Liverpool and Manchester also became important as marketing centres, the first for cotton buying, the other for sales. Very shortly other 'external economies' developed. Once a pool of skilled labour grew up in a mill town that added to the 'inertia' of location. It made it more worth while for expansion to occur in the same locality. A factory-trained labour force, of semi-skilled women and adolescents, was also an immense local advantage by the second generation. Another very important external economy was the convenience of specialized service industries – such as the bleaching firms, the machine-making shops, machine-servicing facilities which grew up in the shadow of the mills. All these things exercised a 'centripetal' pull on the cotton industry, as did similar pressures on other branches of textiles that still preserve their traditional associations.

Unlike the metal industries, however, it may be doubtful how much cheap coal had to do directly with this movement of cotton mills away from remote country districts to the Lancashire coalfield. It helped of course. But power and fuel costs in textiles were never an important item in total costs of production which is what counts in estimating how important any particular factor was in explaining innovation or a change in location. It was very much more important to have some good local firms to repair the machines when they got out of adjustment, or a good supply of fitters for hiring. And the specialization of engineering firms could only come in places when factories could concentrate in numbers – not in narrow remote Derbyshire valleys.

In fact, although relatively the cotton industry concentrated in the towns of the north-west and capacity expanded mainly by steam power, the demand was such, the opportunities so great, that even water-powered country mills increased in numbers up to 1830 – although very much more slowly. Four-fifths of cotton mills were steam powered in 1838; nine-tenths in 1850. Then each depression squeezed out more country mills. By 1838 out of a total of 1,600 mills in England, 1,200 were in Lancashire. A similar concentration was taking place, for similar reasons, in Scotland, where the little towns around Glasgow like Paisley became manufacturing satellites for the main commercial centre of Glasgow in much the same way as the Lancashire towns were satellites for Liverpool and Manchester. One-seventh of British cotton capacity centred on the Glasgow area, but technically Manchester was always in the lead.[1]

[1] For further reading on industries see below, pp. 178–82.

INDUSTRY AND INNOVATION

Steam power was the greatest of the technical innovations developed in the course of the industrial revolution because it became the agent and instrument for applying basic innovations in so many industries and transport. By 1800' the continued momentum of advance in strategic industries like cotton spinning and iron was dependent on enlarging the uses of the steam engine, even though only a small proportion of productive effort in the economy then depended on the engine. Everyone knew that the greatest strides in technical progress lay in applying the steam engine and iron machinery to more and more processes in more and more industries. A contagion was in progress. The supremacy Britain had achieved in technology in Europe by 1800 was also based upon a combination of cheap iron and coal, skills of accurate metal working and the skills of mechanical engineering – in machine building and steam power in particular. Each of these was growing more dependent on the others. But the gap between Britain and the most advanced other economies in this field was quite unprecedented, and unrepeatable.

By what stages did the advance of technique in certain industries on the leading edge of advancing technology come to depend on the steam engine? The device came out of an international struggle in the seventeenth century amongst amateur aristocratic inventors. Capt. Thomas Savery 'Gent.' of London had demonstrated an 'atmospheric' fire engine before the King and the Royal Society before 1700. When he collaborated with a Dartmouth blacksmith, Thomas Newcomen (who had developed a steam engine independently) they soon had a commercially useful device, which was at work in a colliery in 1712. The engine at this point had profound limitations. It was not very powerful – steam was condensed inside a cylinder and the atmospheric pressure outside pressed down a piston. It was very slow, it consumed large amounts of fuel, it was very large and expensive. Savery had called it the 'Miners' Friend', proposing that it be used for supplying the cisterns and fountains at the houses of noblemen and gentlemen, for water works, fen drainage, raising water into a mill pool to work water wheels in the dry season, and – above all – for pumping out mines. It had only reciprocating motion and could only pump gently, slowly and expensively – but not as expensively as keeping horses to work a pump in a gin. Horses had to be fed when they were not working. Steam engines abroad remained almost confined to the laboratories of aristocrats. But, by 1775, when James Watt arrived in Birmingham, perhaps 40 Newcomen engines had been erected in Cornwall and 60 on the Northumberland coalfield.

Watt's separate condenser quadrupled the efficiency of Newcomen's engine, a model of which he had used in the laboratories at Glasgow University. At the same time he had the great advantages of the best precision metal-working skills available in England outside the Royal Arsenal at Woolwich, in Boulton's workshops at Solo, Birmingham. Part of the improved efficiency came from them. One needed accurate steam-proof valves. They depended on accurate plane surfaces. Then he had the benefit of John Wilkinson's device for boring cannon accurately, invented to fulfil ordnance contracts in 1774. This made possible an accurately bored large cylinder – the most important part of all. Steam-engine technology was bedevilled by inaccurate cylinders. Standards of precision in gun-making had become the highest known for large metal objects in the eighteenth century. And swords are always being beaten into ploughshares. Until 1781 Watt converted many Newcomen engines in Cornwall – the mine owners there demanded improved efficiency more than colliery owners, because fuel was dear in Cornwall. Boulton urged Watt to take out patents to convert the engine for rotary motion in 1781 – he said there was only one Cornwall and manufacturers elsewhere were 'steam-mill mad'. By 1795, 150 Watt engines had been erected – the four main trades taking them being coal mining, canals (in both these they were still used for pumping mainly), cotton – the greatest number of all – and breweries. In these latter two industries they were used for turning shafts. Watt's patents were defended by Parliament until 1800, when the field was thrown open.

The important conclusion to draw from the record by 1800 is that the diffusion of steam power in the economy was being held up by Watt's patents and by Watt's own cautiousness. He became increasingly conservative with success, as did Robert Stephenson two generations later in the development of the steam locomotive. Boulton, it appears, pushed Watt into rotary motion. Watt was reluctant to experiment with road traction or rail traction, or engines for boats. He set his face against the development of high-pressure steam engines. By 1790 a score of engineers in Cornwall, Lancashire, Northumberland, Birmingham, Scotland and London – every major industrial region – were developing high-pressure engines, locomotives, boat engines, bench engines, steam carriages. Richard Trevithick was only the most famous of these in Cornwall. None of these innovations, none of these engineers, was in the same scientifically literate, scientifically trained tradition as Watt himself. Watt's engine, although now rather old-fashioned, was still the most reliable, but this was mainly because of the very high metal-working standards available to his business.

The history of the application of steam power to the economy illustrates some general truths about innovation. It was far from being the work of brilliant individual inventors. The names that have reached the textbooks are those few out of a large crowd who were feverishly working on every one of the major inventions developed. The actual progress of every major innovation depended not only on basic advances made by the famous but on innumerable smaller developments made by the unknown. An innovation evolves almost 'biologically' as a species slowly advances. This showed also in the high rate of simultaneous inventing by different people: making constructive reactions to similar problems. Each person was responding to the demand created by businessmen anxious to adopt a machine to solve a problem or make a fortune. Innovation, as opposed to invention, is the relating of individual genius to the economic and commercial context of the age. The successful realization of these inventions often depended upon the advance in techniques in other fields, for example, on the rising level of workmanship in the metal industries in the eighteenth century, much as advances in aeronautics now depend on the skills of the metallurgists. Progress is always impossible at a speed greater than that at which the economy creates demand for new techniques, and at a speed greater than technical standards allow.

By and large innovations were not the result of the formal application of applied science, nor a product of the formal educational system of the country. Great determination, intense curiosity, quick wits, clever fingers, luck, capital, or employment and a backer to survive the period of experimenting, testing, improving were more important in almost all fields than a scientific training. Most innovations were the products of inspired amateurs, or brilliant artisans trained as clock-makers, wheelwrights, blacksmiths or in the Birmingham trades. William Murdock, Boulton's greatest mechanic, was more representative than James Watt. They were mainly local men, empirically trained, with local horizons, often very interested in things scientific, aware men, responding directly to a particular problem. Up to the mid-nineteenth century this tradition was still dominant in British manufacturing industry. It was no accident that the Crystal Palace in 1851 was the conception of the head gardener of the Duke of Devonshire. He knew about greenhouses. Richard Arkwright was a barber. After the mid-nineteenth century increasingly the stimulus behind innovation changed. Then it did become largely a matter of applied science in one industry after another. But the chemistry of iron making was unknown before that; none of the great London porter brewers of the eighteenth century, or anyone in their businesses, knew the scientific nature of fermentation.

There are one or two exceptions to this, but not many. James Watt was a superb product of the Scottish university world. He had listened to Joseph Black's lectures on latent heat at Glasgow University.[1] He undertook specific experiments on the elasticity of steam and the conductivity of metals. But the dozen and more inventors and improvers of techniques in steam power, and the entire pioneering of high-pressure engines, was in the amateur, and the blacksmith tradition. Some of the industrialists and

---

[1] This had no direct bearing on his inventions. See D. S. L. Cardwell, *Steampower in the Eighteenth Century.*

innovators in the bleaching industry, where sulphuric acid became the basis of the process, and in other branches of chemicals were chemists, trained as such, like the famous Dr Roebuck, who had a hand in so many ventures. But his doctorate was actually in medicine. Usually this meant Scottish universities or continental ones. Industrialists did begin increasingly to use scientific measuring devices like thermometers and hydrometers to reduce their empirical practices to rule where possible. Scientific attitudes, with experimentation, observation, testing were much more widespread than scientific knowledge. But the individual examples of trained chemists pioneering innovations, or industrialists using trained chemists to advise them, do not form a representative selection. This was certainly proved after the mid-nineteenth century when the government realized that almost no trained chemists existed in the country to produce a flow of innovations from applied science. A national crisis was discovered here in the 1870's exactly parallel to the one going on now.

The skills that underlay innovations can scarcely be ascribed to an increase in mechanical ingenuity. There was no new burst of inventive genius in the British race to explain the burst of mechanical innovation that took place in the eighteenth century. The highest standards of precision and ingenuity known in the mechanical world belonged not to the industrial context at all in strategic industries like iron and textiles. They existed in scientific instrument making, in watch- and clock-making, in mechanical toys. They developed most markedly in Restoration England, with navigation instruments, astronomical studies, microscopes. This was partly the world of the Royal Society; partly that of the Admiralty; partly that of the luxury market for watches and performing dolls. High standards of mechanical ingenuity had existed long before this. Some medieval cathedral clocks involved the gyrations of figures – almost in miracle play-lets – as well as time keeping. Queen Elizabeth I sent as a present to the Sultan of Turkey in 1596 an automatic organ built by a Lancashire clock-maker, Thomas Dallam. Birds flapped their wings and sang, bells chimed, trumpets sounded, little figures gyrated and performed. It played a whole sequence

of madrigals, in four-part settings, automatically, as a complete
Tudor juke-box – an extraordinary monument to precision building and mechanical ingenuity. A windmill showed ingenuity on
a much larger scale, even if condemned to rather elephantine
precision through the use of mainly wooden machinery. A more
sophisticated example from the eighteenth century was the
silver repeating watch given to George III on his birthday in
1764. It struck the hours and was perfectly accurate. But it
weighed less than a sixpenny piece and was less than $\frac{1}{2}$ in. in
diameter. Its maker had designed special tools to make its
manufacture possible.

The existence of these very high standards of mechanical
precision, long antedating the industrial revolution, make the
problem of innovation highly intriguing. Watch-making had
become a large trade in eighteenth-century England. 120,000
watches per year were made in London at the end of the
eighteenth century; perhaps almost as many in Lancashire.
There was extreme division of labour, much more so than in
Adam Smith's famous example of pin-making. It was a world
of rationalized production and interchangeable parts, which had
induced all sorts of specialist tools – slide rests, screw cutting
lathes, pre-set lathes. The French led Europe in these devices,
and they existed long before 1750. Here was a complete pre-
cision-engineering workshop, with many of the machines of the
later machine tool industry already documented, and published
in the *Encyclopaedia*. In fact, many of them were described and
illustrated in Leonardo da Vinci's notebooks, over 200 years
before this. Why was this not translated long before into machine
building for the textile industry?

It was a world in miniature and a world for the luxury market
in many cases. All these tools fitted into a vice on a bench. The
material used was mostly brass, an easily worked metal (which
could be worked cold) but not strong enough for large machines.
The maximum motive power for these instruments (the organ
as well as the watches) was clockwork, the steel-spring. Human
muscle power worked all the watch-making tools. There was no
mass production of parts by automatic machinery. Each unit
produced was therefore expensive, and the market was a luxury

market only. Productivity per head was low, even though production was rationalized by division of labour.

Innovations which revolutionized productivity in textiles needed large machinery made of iron, not brass. This was a very much more difficult metal to work on a large scale. They needed a massive source of power. It was a question therefore of translating the precision standards existing in working brass on a miniature scale into the large-scale working of iron, and then putting power to the machines. The engineering industry of the late eighteenth century thus saw a meeting between two widespread older sorts of skills: the skills of the blacksmith, carpenter, and millwright taken up to the standards of accuracy known by the watch-maker. It was the work of organizers of workshops like Boulton and Watt in Birmingham and Henry Maudslay later in London to take in millwrights and carpenters and clock-makers and turn them into fitters. But this did not begin to take place until the development of momentum in strategic industries such as iron and textiles, created the inducements for businessmen to demand these skills in producing iron machinery and new forms of power. The actual mechanical skills and the ingenuity predated this development. Indeed, one of the astonishing things is the extent of the gap which sometimes extended between knowledge and action, between invention and innovation, between innovation, as 'best practice' technique and the diffusion of innovation to become 'representative' technique. Coke-smelted iron had a time-lag between innovation and diffusion from 1709 to 1760 and later; steam power in rotative form even longer, pound locks in canals longer still.

There were certain common features about the effects of the basic innovations in the eighteenth century. Expensive machinery and large plant increase fixed costs or 'overhead costs', which are incurred whether goods are being produced or not. The works must be maintained and the depreciation in capital values allowed for. Industrialists with expensive machinery therefore had rising incentives to keep their plant running at as near full capacity as they could. The increased output from the machines increased the flood of goods; but so also did this new commercial incentive. Both led to the need to extend the market, and to cut prices to sell more. With the chances of increasing production industrialists began to take narrower profit margins, and to extend these over greater output. When prices went down there was then an added inducement to seek new innovations to cut one's costs. In a competitive situation, this was a self-reinforcing circle, provided two essential conditions existed: that there were good opportunities for further innovation and that demand kept up. One cotton spinner remarked to a Parliamentary Committee in 1833, 'Our profits are extremely low and I do not see any prospect that we have of improving it except by reducing the price still further and extending production.' He was actually complaining that low profit margins forced him to spend money on the latest machinery.

These are commercial incentives which help to make innovation a cumulative process. Cutting prices did lead to an extension of demand, as both population and national income were rising; and there were boundless opportunities of adapting the engine and iron machinery to new processes, enlarging machinery and cutting costs. At this period there were virtually no *effective* combinations by industrialists to cut down production and maintain prices (although groups in several industries often tried to do so). In the circumstances of the time, therefore, the new technology created massive production and rising fixed costs. Both of these effects tended to force a further expansion of production, lower prices, lower profit margins, more cost-reducing innovations – a competitive response to falling prices in conditions where further innovation was possible and a major force generating expansion and innovation.

For other reasons, too, once an economy is on the move innovations become cumulative. One innovation breaks an equilibrium in a traditional sequence of processes, creating a distortion with the others. The flying shuttle created such a demand for yarn by increasing the productivity of weavers that it created great incentives to develop an innovation to increase productivity there. Hargreaves' spinning-jenny was born in a flurry of activity to do just this. On a larger scale factory-spinning created the same incentive to develop power-weaving.

The 'distortion', the bottleneck, or the problem created by an innovation could be one of material as well as of the flow of production. When a steam engine was attached to wooden machinery it shook it to pieces and required the innovation of iron machinery. That innovation allowed more complicated, heavier machinery to be built, which created an incentive for a more powerful engine. This lay directly behind Watt's development of the double-acting low-pressure engine. One can multiply such examples without end. The disequilibrium created by one innovation inducing another operated also between manufacturing processes and the forms of power needed to sustain them; between production and forms of transport needed to clear the goods and supply the materials. It operated between one industry and its subsidiary industries. The conversion of bleaching from being a cottage affair using the sun as its agent and taking a matter of months became a great blockage to the flow of textile production once this had started speeding up. The modern chemical industry was born in Britain in the wake of the mechanization of cotton production, producing bleaching agents to do the job in factory production style in a matter of hours. The disequilibrium could be one of speed, or of scale of production, of costs, of efficiency, of materials.

In circumstances where techniques are fairly stable, when demand is fairly constant and the general momentum of change in an economy low, such problems are likely to bring the original innovation to a halt. A disequilibrium can then be a brake on innovation. The circle is then a vicious one. When the general momentum for change is high, when the economy is on the move with self-sustained growth in progress – for a combination of many reasons – then challenge can invoke the response of more innovation. The chain reaction then converts the whole sequence of processes onto the new rhythms, the new standards, the new materials.

Between 1700 and the later nineteenth century this self-sustaining process of innovation led back again and again to steam power, coal, iron machinery, engineering skills, and emphasized the advantages of locating industry near cheap coal. Disequilibria were continually being solved by innovations which increased the reliance on this new matrix of industries, materials and skills. The most important example of this truth came from the incentives to innovation developed between mining, steam power, the iron industry and the railways. Steam power was pioneered through the demands for draining mines; the increasing demand for coal and iron ore was the greatest stimulus for applying steam power to transport. By 1850 the railways were the biggest single market for the iron industry and through that for coal. It was exactly in this combination of accessible coal, iron ore – the strategic new materials – that Britain's natural resource position was ideal. It was exactly in the skills associated with the strategic new industries of iron and engineering that her lead over other countries was most marked.

The new matrix gave increasing freedom from the old traditional limitations of nature, which had been imposed upon the economy in all previous ages. There was freedom from the limitation of strength in animal power or human muscle; there was a new freedom from the old interruptions to production dependent on water and wind power: in flood, or drought, or frost, or gale, or calm, the wheels could not turn or the ships sail. These new industries were not dependent upon the seasonal rhythm imposed on them by the harvest, as were so many of the older ones whose raw materials came from the yield of beast or crop. In the new precision engineering workshops of the early nineteenth century the machine-tools were freeing the machine and tool-making trades from the inaccuracies of the human hand and eye – creating the most 'unnatural' standards of measurement and tolerances.

It is accurate to call the main innovations capital saving and cost-reducing if by this one is referring to the costs of a unit of output. By themselves they vastly increased the capital behind production. One can call them labour-saving, too, if by this is meant the costs of labour, or the cost of skilled labour, in a unit of production. But in absolute terms, again, industries were expanding their total output so tremendously that, even with the great increase in productivity per man, and productivity per pound of capital employed, the most rapidly growing labour force in the country was forming exactly in the new industrial towns and mining areas. Industrialization, coupled with urbanization, became the greatest creator of the need for capital; the greatest creator of employment the world had known. The generalization that the industrial revolution was a destroyer of skills is also scarcely accurate. Some skills it did destroy, such as hand-loom weaving (though the great expansion of hand-loom weavers in the cotton industry was a *consequence* of mechanized spinning); and there were great social problems created when a traditional handicraft skill was undermined by machine production. But industrialization bred the need for new skills much faster than it destroyed old ones. The pace of diffusion of the new techniques was limited by the scarcity of skills as much as by scarcity of capital or problems of transport.

CAPITAL ACCUMULATION

The process of capital accumulation, and its problems, may be looked at in aggregate from the national viewpoint or from the viewpoint of the individual firm. In aggregate it seems clear that no absolute shortage of savings relative to the demand for productive investment threatened to constrain the process of economic growth in eighteenth-century Britain. The country possessed a rich agriculture and rising, lucrative foreign trade. As the chapter[1] on landowning and agriculture has suggested, many direct conduits existed whereby landowning and farming wealth flowed to investment for improving land and transport, while commercial wealth flowed to industry, whether by way of merchants in foreign trade financing industrial ventures with capital and credit or merchants in inland trade moving themselves into manufacturing. A banking system began to mobilize savings more widely after 1750. The alternative demands made on savings and successfully implemented reinforce this conclusion. Compared with war, the demands for productive investment were slight. With taxation and loans combined, the total cost of the French wars between 1793 and 1815 of £1,000 million created a financial burden borne at the expense of growth-rates and

[1] Above, pp. 54–7, 65, 117–18.

living standards to some extent. Inflation developed (although by some twentieth-century standards at a modest rate), a modest slackening in the overall rates of the construction industries occurred. However, much of the inflation which sapped living standards came from food shortages not directly connected with the burden of financing war. A generation later, by far the biggest single lump of capital to be found for productive investment was needed for the railways, which absorbed £250 million in nominal capital between 1830 and 1850. This occurred without noticeable inflationary pressure, but by this time the economy was over any hump which might have been created by a capital blockage derived from a shortage of savings at the onset of sustained growth.

Apart from war, one must consider the great flow of wealth in the mid-eighteenth century and before being poured into pleasure, travel, luxury, ostentatious building, the cultural looting of Europe on the Grand Tour and so on. Even the occasional waves of speculation, culminating in the South Sea Bubble, suggest that no shortage of savings existed. Eighteenth-century England, in fact, was not at all in a position comparable to some underdeveloped countries today, where the economic surplus is so small that the absolute shortage of savings can make the necessary increase in investment for economic growth difficult to achieve. Investment demands in the eighteenth century, given the scale of the economy and the nature of technology, proved much more modest and less 'lumpy' than for underdeveloped economies facing a twentieth-century scale of technology. The problem of capital accumulation in eighteenth-century England was therefore primarily one of establishing the conduits by which capital could get from those groups in society who were making the savings to those who needed the credit; to allow thrift to support enterprise. Even if aggregate savings were sufficient, social, political or institutional constraints could block their diversion to productive ends. Such an institutional gap could prevent, or slow up, the necessary flows. One should therefore look for the institutions, the professional intermediaries, the procedures and mechanisms which allowed such a gap to be filled both on an inter-regional scale and locally. In part, the problem was geographical, in part sociological; between the farming savings of East Anglia and the credit demands of Lancashire; between the entrepreneur in a fairly humble station in life and a landed magnate.

Much the most efficiently organized – and much the largest – capital market in the country serviced the issue and subsequent jobbing of government stock, which provided almost all the business of the Stock Exchange in the last quarter of the eighteenth century. Productive demands for investment were not excessive. The total capital accumulated in the canal system over sixty or seventy years after 1750 totalled only c. £20 million, and transport was one of the lumpiest forms of investment. Moreover the industries requiring very high rates of capital accumulation and rapidly expanding credit were a relatively small enclave in the total economy. Because of this, when Miss Phyllis Deane set out to measure the accumulation of capital, she did not find that there was a *sudden* need to double the rate of investment from below 5 per cent to above 10 per cent, but rather that the rate of investment in England rose very slowly from about 5 per cent of G.N.P. to perhaps 7 per cent during the latter half of the eighteenth century, and reached 10 per cent of G.N.P. only under the great stimulus of railway investment in the 1840's. At the peak of the railway investment boom during this decade, transport demands for investment perhaps claimed 7 per cent of the national income, but this was exceptional.

The long-term rate of interest was falling on trend during the eighteenth century, seen in the mortgage market and in the yield of government stocks, both of which were very sensitive indicators in the best organized credit markets of the land. Rates fell from 6 per cent per annum in 1700 to about $3\frac{1}{2}$ per cent per annum in the mid-eighteenth century. From 1714 to 1832 the usury laws prevented legal commercial interest rates from going above 5 per cent per annum, but these did not apply in practice to fixed interest securities, such as government stocks. In wartime, but only occasionally, 'natural' rates of interest reached 5 per cent and a little beyond. Low interest rates were very important in encouraging projects where large capitals had to be mobilized in advance and where loan charges formed a high proportion of the annual costs that had to be covered – in the construction industries above all, building, public utilities such as warehouses, docks, canals and land improvement.[1] Booms here clustered in times of plentiful and cheap credit (as in the late 1780's or early 1790's), and these sorts of investment suffered when government borrowing in wartime drove interest rates up to 5 per cent or above and the operation of the usury laws sharply diverted the flow of loanable funds away from commercial projects, as in the late 1790's. London's house-building was very severely affected by these wartime stringencies of credit. These sorts of investment were also much involved in institutional ways of mobilizing capital for investment, either through mortgages or in corporate ventures, such as canal companies or turnpike trusts, appealing directly to the public for funds.[2]

Movements in interest rates were not so clearly important with loans to manufacturing industry, at least in long-term lending and personal lending. Short-term lending in the discount market covering bills of exchange did have rates of interest moving in parallel with government stock and mortgage rates. But most personal loans and long-term loans to businessmen tended to run on regularly at 5 per cent per annum. And the difference of a point or two points in the cost of credit was not a matter of such great moment to an entrepreneur in manufacturing industry. The difference in the cost of credit did not usually make up a significant figure relative to his total costs (as it might have done for a canal company) – which was particularly true of periods where prices, and profits, were rising. The availability of credit, not small fluctuations in its price, and the condition of his market was the key here.

Before looking into the processes of capital investment in industry, the capital structure of eighteenth-century business needs a mention, because this was very influential in showing

[1] The 'real' rate of interest was affected by price movements. When prices were rising borrowing at fixed interest rates was less costly in real terms.
[2] See section on transport, pp. 115–18.

which kinds of credit were instrumental. In the pre-factory, domestic system, as has been mentioned, almost all capital lay in stocks of materials, with a very small fraction indeed in fixed assets such as buildings or machinery. Even in the early factories, in textiles, breweries and the like, amongst the most heavily capitalized less than one-seventh or one-eighth of total assets typically were in buildings and plant; six-sevenths to seven-eighths and more still being absorbed by 'movables' or 'circulating capital' – raw materials, goods in the pipeline, goods being sold but not yet paid for. Many 'capital economizing' devices were used to escape large outgoings in fixed capital – such as renting buildings or adapting older premises to new uses. In the initial years the fixed assets of the industrial revolution were so often improvised. Even the most heavily capitalized enterprises of all – a large iron-works or a deep coal-mine – usually had less than half of its assets in fixed capital. To take one example: Truman, Hanbury and Buxton's brewery in Spitalfields in 1760, which was among the largest factory plants in the land, had total assets of £130,000. Of this sum, £74,000 was in good trade debts owed to the brewery for beer sent out but not yet paid for. A further £24,000 was absorbed by stocks of materials and beer being matured in vat. The total value of the brewhouse, utensils, casks and leaseholds of public houses (all of which were revalued annually) was only £30,000 – less than one-tenth of the whole. Such a distribution of assets was typical for a manufacturing business in the early factory system.

The importance of such an asset structure is at once apparent when one considers the sources of credit for eighteenth-century industry. Short-term credit requirements were by far the greatest need quantitatively: financing raw material purchases, stocks, discounting the bills of exchange arising from sales to get back into cash before the customary credit period was up. This was, above all, the sort of credit that local bankers supplied or which mercantile credit provided through the industrialist buying materials 'on tick' (and then often his merchant creditor being helped by bankers). By the end of the eighteenth century inter-regional flows of short-term credit were mounting between country banks in different parts of the country, particularly in the discount market of bills of exchange. The generalization about British banks only lending short and not supplying long-term loans for capital investment in fixed assets – even if true – meant that banks were still financing by far the largest credit needs of industry. The banker's role as a professional inter-mediary, standing between the savings of those receiving sur-pluses and those needing credit, could be as important within a locality as with such national flows. Such an institutional development meant that the inadequacies of depending on per-sonal, face-to-face contacts to equate saving and borrowing were being overcome, so that savings ceased to be largely hoarded, sterilized from productive use, and became activated, if only because bankers had to make greater profits by using the funds which their customers deposited with them than the interest they had to pay on these deposits themselves.

Long-term credit could still be a problem. The greatest single source undoubtedly was the 'plough-back' of retained profits – as it still is. As Professor Ashton summed up: 'The records of firm after firm tell the same story . . . the proprietors agreed to pay themselves small salaries, restrict their household expenses and put their profits to reserve.' In a sense, 'plough-back' implies the wrong concept – the profits were never taken out of the business in the first place. But this is far from being the end of the story. Some capital had to exist in the first place, so that a business could be established. After that, at certain times entrepreneurs might want to invest capital for expansion at a faster rate than profits were accumulating. Any expansion at all could require investing a larger lump of capital in a single throw than accrued annually; so that this large 'lump' of capital might need to be borrowed and then repaid gradually over the next few years. In a time of business depression, also, if a liquidity crisis overtook a business, it might need cash urgently to pay creditors which could only be paid off over some ensuing years. Although such instances may not prove typical of the ordinary times in which business operated, these occasions are neverthe-less crucial for a business, whether for its establishment, its growth or its survival.

Where did industrialists turn in such circumstances, remembering that almost no manufacturing enterprise was able to seek public capital as a company appealing for funds by issuing shares on the Stock Exchange before the mid-decades of the nineteenth century? Mercantile credit from merchant suppliers could be very important here, much more so than has been commonly suggested. Apart from this, if an industrialist, his wife or either of their families had freehold land or houses in their possession, then raising a mortgage was often a key instrument for getting a long-term loan. Freehold property remained the best security extant in eighteenth-century England, and the mortgage market was one of the most efficiently organized sides of the capital market. Apart from London acting as the main cross-roads for larger transactions in the mortgage market, flourishing local lending also existed, with the local attorney often being the key figure or at least the key intermediary in such transactions. Considerable balances of money often lay in his hands, and much more passed through his hands, in trust funds and the like.

Where relatively small capitals were involved, as they so often were – and depending upon the family groups in question – kinship contacts were usually the first to be exploited. Eighteenth-century business flourished as a face-to-face society of friends, cousins and business associates. This world of personal contact by kinship and friendship was often the first resource for cash. The resources which could be drawn in through this network remained very limited in scale, except for businessmen lucky enough to find themselves members of very wealthy and extensive kinship groups such as the Quaker bankers. The diary of Mrs Thrale, describing how her husband's firm survived the depression of 1772, reveals the operation of such a personal, non-institutionalized world of business. 'First we made free with our mother's money,' she wrote, '. . . about three thousand pounds 'twas all she had; and big as I was with child, I drove down to Brighton to beg of Mr Scrase . . . six thousand pounds more: dear Mr Scrase was an old gouty solicitor, friend and contemporary of my husband's father. Lady Lade [Henry Thrale's sister] lent us five thousand pounds

more.' Mrs Thrale herself prepared to mortgage her own estates
in north Wales, and to cut the timber on them, always the landowner's first line of financial reserves. But, in the end, the main
creditors of the brewery were the malt and hop merchants, by
default rather than by design. Their bills of £130,000 remained
unpaid for some years.

Bankers were also involved in long-term lending more than
the books on banking have suggested. As the number of business
histories accumulates, so it is being revealed that businesses
not uncommonly got over the hump of a great decision to
expand or survived a depression with bank capital. This did not
become a regular, permanent feature of capital formation, but
was still crucial at certain times. It is further discussed below,
with banking.[1]

THE ENTREPRENEURS

The entrepreneurs (particularly the Protestant Nonconformists)
were not the long-lost cause of the industrial revolution. They
sprang from economic opportunity as much as they created it.
They depended everywhere upon a necessary creative environment. They join the circle of other factors in economic growth
as part cause and part effect, a dependent attribute and a
creative part of industrial progress. But they are important.
Latent resources can lie unused until 'men of wit and resource'
organize them for a market they have promoted. Once formed
attitudes, often consolidated within social groups, exert an
inertia of their own, like institutions, for good or ill. Samuel
Smiles, who wrote the biographies of some of these men, was
right to see them as a unique phenomenon in British society.
The industrial revolution was not merely consequential upon
the economic logic of geography or geology.

Pre-eminently the entrepreneurs were known as organizers.
Relatively few were the pioneers of major innovations or inventors in their own right. In *some* industries they needed to be

[1] See below, pp. 175-7.

highly skilled themselves (in chemicals, or iron-works or brew-ing). Always they needed to know enough about technical problems to be able to bring new inventions into commercial production, to control managers, take decisions, not to be fooled. But their skills were more diverse than this. To develop massive production needed many talents.

Of these one of the most important for the new industrialists remained merchanting skills and the ability to be able to organize the commercial problems surrounding production. To be successful manufacturers they needed to hold the initiative in the purchase of raw materials, to maintain uniform standards of quality at the same time as the consignments into their factories grew into a flood. With large-scale production under the control of single men the centre of gravity of power and decision-making began to swing away from the merchant, the organizer of outwork, to the factory owners. They often began to bypass the independent merchants who owned and distributed raw materials to small manufacturers, buying themselves direct from the importers and laying down their own specifications. Fieldens, the cotton spinners who became the economic masters of Todmorden, sent their own buying agents to America in the early nineteenth century. The great London porter brewers bought little malt in the open market at Mark Lane or Bear Quay. They appointed their own agents or employed factors to buy from the maltsters in east Anglian barley regions, set up their own maltings to ensure standards of quality and bought direct from the farmers. Their demand for regularity of supply and uniformity of quality conditioned these arrangements. In particular there was a change in the structure of merchanting induced by the assumption of control over raw material supplies by the industrialists – the rise of commissioned brokers or factors. They organized the flow of supplies, sending samples to the industrialist who kept all the initiative of timing and pricing of buying in his hands. A sentence from a letter of Sampson Hanbury, a London brewer, to his main malt factor reveals this fact, 'I have sent you by the coach a sample of the last pale malt you sent in,' he stormed, 'it is so infamously bad . . . that I will not receive another sack of it into my brewhouse . . . Should I have occasion ever to write such another letter I shall entirely alter my plan of buying.'

The same held for control of marketing of finished goods. Industrialists needed to control and change the techniques of production to ensure that their goods suited changing markets at uniform quality, a vitally important consideration if their mills were to run efficiently to capacity with such vast outputs. The market decided the nature of production. The textbooks often conceal that one of the basic skills of the entrepreneurs remained, in Charles Wilson's words, the possession of 'a sense of market opportunity combined with the capacity needed to exploit it'. Cloth and iron were not just homogeneous commodities – they existed in bewildering varieties for a bewildering range of customers. Adapting problems of production to problems of sale was the central concern of industrialists spanning both functions. In pursuit of this objective, mass production in brewing in London led to the industrialists gaining control of almost half the public houses in the capital and setting up their own agents in Dublin to control distribution there.

Usually the entrepreneurs whose names are well known arose by pioneering a new technical innovation which led to factory production. This led to great problems in the actual control of the new methods of production. The sheer control of a large labour force was perhaps their major difficulty in the eighteenth century. There was a self-imposed family discipline in cottage industry, the hours of work and intensity of work decided by the master of the family. Men commonly worked furiously at the end of the week to finish the piece of cloth or their stint in nailing by Saturday when the merchant collected it. They were then idle or drunk until the following Tuesday, having kept 'Saint Monday'. By contrast, in the factory regularity was the prerequisite. All the machines were geared to the engine, and the entire sequence of production demanded that each worker subordinate his own will to that of the whole working unit. The extraordinary codes of discipline, with fines and sanctions, imposed by large-scale industrialists like Ambrose Crowley, Richard Arkwright and Wedgwood are understandable in the light of the great problem of imposing standards of discipline and regularity on an untrained labour force. It partly accounts for their preference for young people and women, more amenable to accepting harsher restrictions on traditional self-imposed standards, as well as having lower wages. They made contracts for 3 months or a year to try to cut down labour turnover. Any entrepreneur needed to be a tough resilient man to impose his own will in these circumstances. He demanded absolute control over production, as he demanded absolute control over buying and merchanting. The nature of the problems of production varied enormously, of course, according to the industry. With Wedgwood and Boulton they were very much the efficient control of labour, the maximum exploitation of division of labour and scarce skills. In other industries the crucial task lay in the application of steam power to as many processes of production as possible. The more entrepreneurs depended on a large labour force, or the higher their wage costs were in proportion to the total costs of production, the more their success depended on efficient control of labour.

In the building industry, significantly, typical entrepreneurs appeared without any technical innovations of note. Technology there remained medieval and the new men arose purely as reorganizers of traditional relationships between craftsmen. Thomas Cubitt emerged after 1817 as the organizer and permanent employer of over 1,000 skilled and unskilled labourers, keeping centralized stores and workshops and leading the industry by his efficient control of men and materials. He was able to do this by ensuring a steady flow of large contracts, in barrack-building in the Napoleonic Wars and in West End squares and public institutions in the great revival of city building after 1815. He himself arranged the financing of his projects on mortgages. These crucial organizational changes enabled Cubitt to make a fortune and revolutionize the economics of building without a technical innovation. Characteristically, the difficulty that induced him to abolish subcontracting and employ men directly and permanently was labour trouble with subcontractors which prevented him from finishing a time contract erecting the London Institution at the appointed date.

Many of the problems and responsibilities facing the first and second generation industrialists were of a new sort, not usually faced by industrialists now save in underdeveloped countries. Many of the new enterprises grew up in isolated sites, on cheap coal or water power. Their massive technology involved a large labour force. Where only small local communities existed the extra families had to be housed by the industrialist creating the employment and bringing labour to the site. He had to provide shops and schools very often, because these communities were growing much more rapidly than normal social and commercial facilities were developing spontaneously. Samuel Oldknow in Stockport was faced with the problem that his cotton mill provided employment for women and adolescents, with no local employment available for men. He therefore had to go into farming to provide outlets for the men to hold his labour force in the factory in being. Many of these expedients were forced on industrialists by the absence of public provision of services.

One of the most annoying problems of all was the failure of the Mint to supply the provinces with enough silver and small change, just at the time when industrialization was generating unprecedented demands for increased supplies of money to pay wages and for retail transactions in the shops of growing industrial and mining regions. Industrialists were therefore led to economize in money – by paying wages at fewer times, often fortnightly or less; paying wages in credit slips which were really titles to purchase supplies in tommy shops; paying groups of men with large denomination notes or coin which they had to get changed in public houses, and by coining their own token money. If the momentum of expansion was to be maintained, industrialists had inducements to adopt such expedients, in the absence of public provision or independent social provision of these services. All of them increased the power which employers could exercise over labour. In the hands of unscrupulous men, therefore, company housing, the tommy shops, truck payments, lightweight tokens, long pay, could and did become instruments which increased the exploitation of labour. In origin many of them are evidence for the extraordinary difficulties facing entrepreneurs in the logic of the new industrial context, the extraordinary responsibilities they had to accept as the total architects or engineers of the communities their works created, in circumstances of neglect or corruption in public authority, rather than being just evidence that industrialists were born with double doses of original sin. The Factory Acts in the early nineteenth century forced the standards of the worst employers to be kept up to the standards already accepted by the best employers and, with the rise of the industrial towns round the mines and mills, the excuse for most of these things died a natural death before 1850.

It is difficult at first glance to make any valid generalizations about the social origins of the entrepreneurs. They arrived from every social class and from all parts of the country. One can say that the entrepreneurs did not form a *class*, but a *type*. The Earls of Leicester (previously the Cokes of Holkham) merited the title in agriculture; Earl Fitzwilliam, even the Bishops of Durham, and their stewards were very active in developing coal mining. The Duke of Bridgewater provided the capital (some of it loaned from his banker) and a good deal of the decision-making and responsibility for cutting his famous canal. He must be called an entrepreneur just as much as his engineer, James Brindley. At the other end of the scale, many of the first engineers and machine builders – Joseph Clements, Bramah, Henry Maudslay – were sons of peasants or humble weavers, and they began life as carpenters and blacksmiths.

The first fundamental is to relate the sort of person who controlled the destinies of the new industries to the scale of production concerned, and the kind of capital needed. When a new trade had units of production which were still very small, entry into it could come from the humblest levels in society – as with the machine-makers. They had the essential skills and were usually financed to start with by the wealthy cotton-masters who provided their orders. When the scale of enterprise was larger, bigger capitals were needed and wealthier men, or the younger sons of landed families, often became industrialists in these trades. Entrepreneurs in the cotton industry in 1760 and 1800 were very different because of the increase in scale and capital engaged. Very few first generation entrepreneurs sprang from labouring groups – from the humblest levels of society without savings or schooling. Most came from families with some savings, even if modest; many married wives with some savings – or access to savings. Most enjoyed positions of respectability in local society, being of good local repute, which enabled them to borrow money, or get credit enough to start up in business. Samuel Whitbread came to London in 1742 with a patrimony of £2,000, as the youngest son of a wealthy nonconformist freeholding family in Bedfordshire, being apprenticed to the best brewer in London for £300. He had an uncle who was something in the City. His establishment independently in trade owed a lot to this middle-class background and his family's capital. He needed also to take a sleeping partner. But his subsequent success depended on his personal qualities. And in this he is one of a type rather than a class. His great rival was Henry Thrale, a high church Tory who had been sent to Oxford by his father on an allowance of £1,000 a year. The third contender in the race to be the greatest brewer in London was Benjamin Truman, a Quaker.

When adoption of innovations for massive production depended on capital, many of the new industrialists came from related branches of the industry where capital had been accumulated. Many grain merchants or maltsters became brewers; the characteristic industrialist in the woollen industry had set up a factory from being a woollen merchant. A typical instance of this sequence was Benjamin Gott of Leeds, who went into woollen production to fulfil the demands of regularity of supplies and consistency of quality which he needed as a merchant. In the metal industries most of the iron masters had been in the secondary-metal trades – making final products from refined metal – and they then moved back to making iron. Other capital flowed in from partners who were merchants handling the trade in iron products. Apart from capital, such links gave knowledge of the trade, help with orders and friends in useful places.

Society in Britain was so flexible, the economy was growing at many different points and the need for capital and enterprise proved so widespread after 1760 that all sectors of society supplied the men of enterprise. That said, the next main generalization must be that a very large proportion of enterprise lay in the hands of the Protestant Nonconformists, essentially middle-class groups, certainly a much greater proportion than their numerical presence in the total population would indicate. In 1800 Quakers were well established in grain merchanting, milling, brewing (Barclay, Perkins, Trumans, Hanburys), in iron making and merchanting (Lloyds, Darbys, Ambrose Crowley had begun life as a Quaker), in banking (Barclays, Bevans, Lloyds, Gurney and others). Unitarian cotton spinners were another important group. No trade was exclusively controlled by these sectarian groups. Agriculture and mining in particular were not much influenced by them – being very much more intimately connected with landowning.

It is not at all straightforward to explain what encouraged and strengthened the hold of these groups, very often family clans in the case of the Quakers, on rising sectors of the economy. But the answer lies very close to the secrets of enterprise in eighteenth-century England. In the first place certain legal restrictions affected Nonconformist families who were strict in their faith. They were excluded from civil and military office; they could not go to Oxford or Cambridge (although they could go to Scottish universities). This blocked certain careers which might dissipate capital and ambition from business enterprise. They were thus denied access to certain collateral activities which were the preserve of the ruling groups in landowning – the magistracy, lieutenancies of counties, a parliamentary career. A sense of social alienation accompanied the legal restraints. Many of the attendant social attitudes prevalent in landowning circles, inculcated at Oxford and Cambridge and major schools such as Eton, encouraged by a career at Westminster, could also prove prejudicial to success in business. The goals in life were different, and habits of leisure, pleasure and ostentatious personal spending. Given the institutional context of business, the predominant pattern of family ownership, this could be vital. The Nonconformists developed their own schools – the Dissenting Academies – which provided the best education for a commercial career available in eighteenth-century England, having a very practical emphasis (with foreign languages, mathematics, accounting and often some 'experimental philosophy', as science was called). Richer families often employed private tutors following the dictates of a family tradition and role already established in business, or sent their sons to Scottish universities. Instead of a Grand Tour they often went abroad for a year or two living with a cousin or a fellow sectarian who was a merchant, as part of their business training. Thus the private educational pattern established by the Nonconformists, and business groups generally, tended to be inward-looking in its values, orientated to the general values of the minority group – including the values associated with their economic role in society – fostering and consolidating them. Next to the family context itself education is probably the most powerful moulding influence upon values and motivations.

The individual religious convictions held by Nonconformist groups reinforced some of these values, particularly the social and individual virtues which characterized these religious convictions. They maintained a strict insistence on personal probity and honesty. Luxury and idleness were the twin evils of these faiths, vices that presided, not only over damnation in the next world, but so often over bankruptcy in this one. Many Quaker diaries, like private confessionals, poured out details of the prices of the Funds and business deals interspersed with urgent warnings to their writers to remember the parables of the talents and the wise and foolish virgins. This is not just a question of thrift, of the peasant virtue of hoarding, but of enterprise and energy, of personal thrift and abstention in order to plough more capital back into the business and allow it to expand more rapidly. In these circumstances abstinence became a buttress of industrial expansion because what was not spent on personal account stayed in the business. Personal abstinence is one of the qualities most universally attributed to the entrepreneurs – not least in their own recollections of responses evoked by pressing problems. The same idea underlies Adam Smith's conception of capital being the result of parsimony – of saving from consumption. Most of the capital for long-term expansion of industry and trade came out of the profits; from plough-back. Where industrialists both owned and managed their own businesses less personal spending meant more investment.

Too much of the debate on the relationship between Protestantism, or Nonconformist Protestantism in the English context, and business has been focused on the issue of these faiths, or theologies, providing an *individual* religious consciousness ideologically favourable to success and expansion in business. In parts of Scotland and parts of Scandinavia and northern Europe Calvinist and other Protestant sects flourished in primitive agricultural societies. But given the context of expanding business opportunities such sects often developed a set of social values and a social nexus which were both highly favourable for business success. Their faith was nourished in a social context.

Legal restraints, the sense of social separateness and a common faith made the Meeting House and the Chapel the focus for a communal life of great resilience and tenacity. Here was a bond of confidence, of mutual trust within the charmed circle, which is a characteristic of minority groups everywhere. Moreover they were widely scattered, mainly in trading towns all over the country: in the Quaker case, as with the Jewish communities, internationally.

Less capital, ambition and energy flowed out into land holding or *rentier*-status from these 'enclaves' within society. Capital available for investment was as likely to rest in the business of a fellow Quaker as be put in the Funds. When the Quakers, Robert Barclay, Sylvanus Bevan and John Perkins bought Henry Thrale's brewery in 1781 the price was £135,000. They paid it off by borrowing £50,000 from Quaker bankers (their cousins), £20,000 from other Quakers and relatives and £40,000 from other personal friends and connections. One of these investors wrote with her draft of £6,000, 'I had rather it lay in your House than in the Stocks, for I may then have it when I please without difficulty . . . you will give me better interest and it may be convenient to both you and myself.'

Quaker meetings were under the obligation of helping any member in difficulties. They boasted that no Quaker received poor relief. They also expelled members for a lapse in personal probity, or for bankruptcy which came from a moral fault. Consequently Quaker communities were virtually, in Dr L. S. Pressnell's words: 'schools for the inculcation of business virtues and clubs for encouraging the practice of them'.

A bond of confidence in business was very commonly reinforced by kinship: marriage partners were chosen from the same charmed circle. Recruits for partnerships were also to be found from the cadets of other families in the clan. Ownership, capital, succession to partnerships, extensions of enterprise all tended to run within the same social and religious enclave and often be sealed by a kinship link. This could become self-reinforcing, particularly when the values protected in these enclaves encouraged a higher propensity to work and invest than in the echelons of society above these groups and below them in the social structure. By such a mechanism a high rate of investment and expansion could be achieved in such firms.

Daniel Defoe, himself a dissenter from exactly this enclave of society from which so many entrepreneurs sprang, author of the *Essay on Projects*, the *Complete Tradesman*, the *Plan of English Commerce*, and the keenest observer of economic growth of his time in the *Tour of the Whole Island*, expressed part of this personal, individual motivation of work, accumulation and enterprise in one of the best economic myths of the age, *Robinson Crusoe*. This was the characteristic response of minority groups who became key agents of economic growth in eighteenth-century England.

The context within which business had to be conducted in eighteenth-century England heightens the relevance of the role of dissenting minorities. The eighteenth century was a time of high risk and uncertainty in business, compared with later periods. The institutional structure within which business operated was weak and uncertain compared with our own day. Communications were slow. It was difficult to keep close control of agents at a distance. Legal processes for recovering debt were expensive, protracted, less certain than today. The institutional ways of raising capital were very limited; so were institutional techniques for owning and managing enterprise. As a result of the shock given to the country by the speculative fever of the

South Sea Bubble (before the crash) the Bubble Act was passed in 1720, which virtually outlawed the company form of enterprise in manufacturing industry. Because transferable shares, publicly-raised capital on the Stock Exchange, limitation of liability, were all prohibited, each partner in an enterprise was fully responsible in his private estate for the debts of the partnership to the last guinea, to the last acre. Anyone investing money in an enterprise and receiving profits as reward for that investment, as opposed to making a personal loan to one of the partners at a fixed rate of interest, was deemed to be a partner in law and thus fully committed as responsible for any debts the concern made. No concept of a sleeping partner who was not responsible for the debts of the firm, and whose stake in it was just limited to the amount of his investment, existed in English law. The benefits of incorporation and limitation of liability were available to individual firms only by Royal Charter, Letters Patent or a special Act of Parliament, which were very seldom granted for a manufacturing industry. Adam Smith defended this opinion, believing that company floatation encouraged speculation and was proper only to public utilities like water works and canal companies, and to insurance companies. Legal prohibitions survived until after the repeal of the Bubble Act in 1825.

Business was therefore organized in partnerships or the family firm except for the great trading companies and a few mining companies which had been incorporated before 1719. One or two other quite unrepresentative examples existed. The banking system which grew up only after 1750 did not usually facilitate long-term lending (regularly at least) for industrial investment either. So, without capital being mobilized nationally for investment through a banking system and without publicly-raised capital being available through the Stock Exchange, where was long-term capital to come from, except through ploughed-back profits once a firm was under way?

One answer was usually clear: from one's family and friends. Business operated in as uninstitutional a way as eighteenth-century politics. Kinship was the organizing principle of most business – as it usually is wherever the institutional structure is weak in a country. One could trust one's cousin; blood is thicker than water. The larger one's kin and the personally known group of friends that trust one another, in these circumstances the safer one might be in a business depression.[1] Kinship was equally important for providing the succession to ownership in business. The story of the industrious clerk who married his master's daughter came true remarkably often. It was sometimes even better to marry your master's widow. But this is not really the traditional success story of the eighteenth century, but the typical tragedy of the family firm without a male heir to carry on the trade. Just as in landownership the genealogical fortunes of a family were vital: its ability to produce male heirs and not a string of daughters; to produce sons who would husband the family's resources and marry well to buy more land – so also the fortunes of eighteenth-century businesses remained intimately bound up with kinship. It was a personal world above all. This is one reason which explains how the Quaker and Non-conformist communities had such tremendous resilience in business at this time.

Quaker groups manifested astonishing fecundity, living careful, responsible, regular lives, with a great propensity for widows and widowers to take second partners. For example, David Barclay, one of the greatest Quaker merchants of the mid-eighteenth century, had 14 children by two wives, and through their marriages was related to the powerful Quaker merchant and banking families of Barclay, Kett, Freame, Gurney, Lloyd, Bevan and Willett. This gave them great resilience in business with self-reinforcing advantages.

The same sort of advantages were enjoyed by the little groups of Scotsmen who became important in British trading colonies all over the world and in certain special industries in Britain, such as engineering. They joined that club of all Scotsmen who were allies together when living and working outside Scotland. Coutts the banker had the custom of almost all the Scots in London for that reason. An astonishing amount of enterprise in England in the new skills of mining and engineering came from north of the Trent, and north of the Tweed.

<hr />

[1] See above, pp. 150–1.

Kinship and the sect, the minority enclave in society, have been very important in finance and commerce for many centuries. The role of religion here is probably more important as the organizing principle for a sectarian group than a particular theology is for its actual motive power. Jewish communities have been important all over western Europe in these particular economic functions; Arab minorities have become main trading groups in west Africa and parts of east Africa; the Indians in South Africa; the Chinese in south-east Asia; the Armenians in the eastern Mediterranean; the Parsees and the Gujeratis in India. And kinship has been one main institutional advantage they have used, once established in the economy as traders, money lenders, bankers, industrialists; and also the mainspring of their own control and ownership of enterprise. So many different theologies, Christian and non-Christian, have become associated with value systems favourable to enterprise, when the economic context has been favourable and the communal context of the group with the particular religious faith has nurtured such an economic role. This fact alone casts doubt on the importance of any single theology as the prime initiating factor in the constellation of related variables.

With great wealth, in the second and third generations, a lapse in the strict tenets of the sect commonly matched a slide towards the establishment. Very often it began with educating one's children at a famous school, the choice of a marriage partner, the accumulation of landed estates and with this the temptation to be pressed into a magistracy or a knighthood. Emerson remarked that no Quaker family rode in a coach for more than two generations (not implying that the family ceased to ride in coaches). Sometimes the business suffered by such a change in values, particularly when ownership and control were the responsibility of the single man. Samuel Whitbread II committed suicide in 1815 as a near-bankrupt after letting his business slide into inefficiency while pursuing a parliamentary career with the great Whigs, an ambition to which he was introduced when he met the sister of Charles Grey as an undergraduate at St John's College, Cambridge. But often the business did not suffer, if the heroic days of urgent demand for capital in the early stages of its growth were past and the profits were large enough to sustain both expansion and a princely style of personal expenditure.

The large-scale manufacturers thrown up in cotton spinning, the handful of great iron masters and a very few large-scale Birmingham industrialists like Boulton, a few London brewers, Wedgwood in pottery, are quite untypical of the industrial economy as a whole in the eighteenth century. They are the first of a growing tribe as massive technology changed the structure of more and more sectors of industry but at a fairly slow pace. The merchant, the putter out – and the farmer – remained the pivotal figures of most branches of production in the eighteenth century; and as a corollary to this the domestic system, the cottage workshop or the small urban workshop remained the typical unit of employment for most workers.

BANKING AND INVESTMENT

Three main groups emerged in the banking system that grew up in eighteenth-century England: the Bank of England, the London private banks and the country bankers. Right at the end of the century a fourth specialist appeared on the scene, not a banker but an important intermediary between bankers – the bill-broker.

The foundation of the Bank of England in 1694 was part of a deal made between the Crown, desperately short of finance in wartime, and a group of the leading London merchants and financiers. A great shortage of silver and confusion in the metallic currency aided the launching of the scheme. They provided the Crown first with a loan of £1·2 million at 8 per cent, of which £·5 million was in paper – virtually bank-notes issued on their credit. During the rest of the war years to 1713, and in the early eighteenth century, the most important business of the Bank lay in lending to the government. Successive renewals of its charter in the eighteenth century became the occasions for large interest-free loans to the government.

In return the financiers were able to bargain their way into a very strong position by 1710. Statutes had given them a monopoly of joint-stock banking in England, while other banks were limited to not more than six partners without any of the advantages of incorporation. This position lasted until 1826 but did not apply to Scotland, where joint-stock banks did develop in the eighteenth century. The Bank of England also profited by acting as the government's banker in other ways: holding balances of cash, acting as the issuers of government stock and the receivers of subscriptions for loans and Treasury Bills, purchasing gold and silver for the government and the Mint, handling the government's overseas business in finance. Quite a lot of capital lay with the Bank on occasion from these balances, providing quite remunerative banking business. Bank of England notes escaped into circulation in London through loans to government, which were paid by the Bank in printed paper 'promises to pay'. Until 1793 the lowest denomination of these notes was £10 – so they did not become important as a mass circulating medium for wages, or ordinary individual purchasing. Even their circulation was mainly confined to London, although they became popular in Lancashire at the latter end of the century. Until 1797 Bank of England notes were convertible on demand into cash, so the Bank had to keep bullion in reserve to face a possible 'run' on its notes in a panic, when they would be presented by those who had lost faith in them, or who felt that their creditors would not accept them as cash. This threat of convertibility acted as a check against over-issues.

Apart from its note issue and government business the Bank of England acted as a private banker in its own right to the great trading companies and to some of the larger merchants in London, discounting bills of exchange for them, making short-term loans and the like. Here again, it created credit and allowed merchants to draw on accounts held at the Bank to a much greater extent than it covered all these loans and credit facilities with bullion, so its reserves also had to face a run from the private banking side of its business in a panic. The Bank had no branches and the operations of its banking activities, as well as the circulation of its notes, was mainly confined to the London business community. It was really, as Clapham maintained, the Bank of London.

The London private bankers included the oldest and most honourable names in banking in Britain; some, such as Hoare's and Child's, with their pedigrees flourishing since being gold-smith bankers in Restoration England. Illiquidity or bankruptcy amongst them was very rare (their status remained very different from that of many country bankers in the late eighteenth century). They usually issued notes in the early eighteenth century, but note issue never formed an important part of their business and had died away almost completely by 1770, so that Bank of England notes and coin monopolized the circulating media of London. Thus they were not engaged in the creation of currency, one of the greatest contrasts between them and the country banks and the Bank of England.

Quite a marked specialization came to the business of London bankers in the course of the eighteenth century. Banks in the West End, such as Hoare's (still in Fleet Street) and Coutts' did not act very much in commercial discounting of trade-bills for merchants; nor did they become the agents of country banks, also prospering on this kind of business. In fact they rather looked down on soiling their hands with commerce. Close association with it might have prejudiced their custom with their main clients – the aristocracy, gentry and wealthy gentlemen. Those West End bankers who did both kinds of business some-times had different rooms for gentry and merchants. Very often their buildings were not located in the merchanting districts of London, and they did not join the London clearing house of bankers set up in the City. Their main business lay in lending to the wealthy not in trade, handling transfers for them when up in London from their country estates, investing in govern-ment stock. In addition they were drawn into the mortgage business – inevitable with this class of client – which meant lending long however much they might dislike it.[1]

Most London bankers were in the City, and doing a very

---

[1] There is the classic reply of Coutts to George IV at a dinner, after the King had toasted his banker: 'Your Royal Highness has done me the honour of keeping my money for thirty years.'

different class of business. Their numbers rose rapidly in the
second half of the eighteenth century, from under 30 in 1750 to
50 in 1770 and 70 in 1800 – most of the increase being in the
non-West End bankers. Their main business lay in discounting
bills of exchange for merchants and industrialists, making short-
term loans to stockbrokers, and lending on 'call', on the understanding that the loan could be called in at once if the banker
needed cash. This formed the general business of English banks
– lending short, rather than long, on instruments such as bills
of exchange which were self-liquidating in a matter of months
(12 months at a maximum usually), so that their cash position
was always fairly good or could become so fairly quickly in an
emergency. This meant financing trade as a general rule rather
than long-term investments like buildings, machinery or land
improvements. The classic rule of English banking is said to
have been, 'Always know a bill from a mortgage'. Some of the
rules listed by a partner in Martin's Bank in 1746 emphasized
caution and keeping one's assets fluid; 'to have the Investiture
of that money in Effects that are easy to convert into money',
and 'Not to boast of great surplus or plenty of money'. To what
extent the banks fulfilled only these short-term lending functions is a question touched on in considering the processes of
capital formation and considered below.[1]

The other rapidly expanding source of business for the City
banks after 1770 was agency-business for the country bankers.
Country bankers needed a London correspondent to handle
their business with the capital – sending down supplies of gold
and silver, and later Bank of England notes, keeping balances
or providing them with overdrafts and, particularly, handling
the great flows of bills of exchange being transferred between
the provinces and London, which the country banks were discounting. A large proportion of the nation's business dealing in
the eighteenth century was being financed by the 'bill of London', which took the place of later cheque transactions for
transfers larger than coin could conveniently settle. Sometimes
the London banker handled commercial deals, or deals in
government stock, for his client-banks. When there was a crisis

[1] See above, p. 151 and below, pp. 175–7.

of confidence in the provinces, the local bankers therefore looked to their London correspondent for cash.

This agency business brought in a great deal of activity and profit, particularly before many specialized intermediaries like the bill-brokers provided other links between country bankers and the London money market after 1800, and before the Bank of England set up branches in the provinces after 1826 to handle the distribution of cash and notes from London and accept some discounting and rediscounting business. Their function was also dependent upon the existence of independent local banks, before single large banks with a London head office spread their network of branches across the country. Agency-business in the second half of the eighteenth century thus became the main institutional link in the financial structure of the country between the provinces and London. It exposed the London bankers most deeply committed to it to the risk of being involved in a provincial panic, and needing themselves to turn to a source for cash to be rescued when they were paying out to their country clients. In the great panic of 1825, when 80 country bankers closed their doors, it severely hit just the London bankers doing most agency work. Pole, Thornton and Co. who went bankrupt then (a rare event for a London bank) had 43 correspondent banks. The same was true of the panic of 1793.

Thirdly came the country bankers – a clear instance of the momentum of economic expansion inducing in its wake the requisite financial institutions. There was a bank in Bristol by 1716, one of the first provincial banks and in the leading provincial business community. Burke thought not more than a dozen were in existence in 1750 (which Dr Pressnell's work has confirmed). But there were about 120 outside London in 1784, 290 by 1797, 370 by 1800, and by 1810 at least 650. Some estimates give 780 in 1810. The general expansion can be phased correctly, even if every actual figure is doubtful. Growth in numbers became marked first in the 1780's. Numbers also expanded fast in easy credit conditions, as might be expected: in the early 1750's, 1789–93, and in the wartime expansion of credit, when the Bank was off gold, from 1797 to 1815.

Certainly, therefore, the establishment of country banks fed the surges of economic activity that these periods experienced.

Country bankers specialized out from every dominant business activity in every region of the country: wealth made in trade, manufacturing, the law, spawned banking. Often it was difficult to tell to what extent a man was a specialized banker (which accounts in part for the uncertain statistics) – he had added dealing in money and in credit to his other business activities which still continued, often closely associated with his new activity. The bank was often just a separate counter in his office. The Fosters in Cambridge (a bank which became absorbed into Lloyds Bank) were millers and corn merchants – the dominant local trades – who moved into banking in 1804; the Mortlocks, prosperous cloth merchants and drapers, became bankers in the 1750's – quite informally. Most of the Liverpool banks grew out of merchant houses established in foreign trade. Lloyds in Birmingham came from the iron trade, Smiths in Nottingham from being hosiers, the Gurneys in Norwich from being yarn merchants and worsted manufacturers. Most Cornish bankers were partners in mines; most Southwark bankers hop merchants. In little Hertfordshire and Essex towns the malt merchant often turned to banking; 50 brewers became bankers. Drapers and mercers, as the leading local shopkeepers, probably provided the largest number of recruits of all. Receivers of taxation in the counties, and the treasurers of turnpike trusts also often became bankers.

In many small towns the opportunities for the largest draper or brewer or grain merchant expanding his trade from profits were limited. Beyond a certain point capital accumulated and he was tempted to make a profit on it by lending it, and trading with it. This is probably the general case with the brewer-bankers and the drapers. Tax receivers and solicitors used the stock of money passing through their hands as their original capital. Others had banking as a natural collateral activity to trading. Welsh cattle drovers who returned from London markets with cash were naturally drawn into the remittance business, also Scottish cattle drovers. Country merchants dealing with bills of exchange themselves were willing to supply bills,

acceptable to their London connections, for other people needing facilities to make payments in London or to get payments
made from London. When they had cash, they were willing to
accept bills themselves for discounting – and many brewers
profited in this way. When they needed coin or notes for their
own dealings, they could act as agents for obtaining cash for
other people. Manufacturers were much involved in dealings in
bills – both from the purchase of their raw materials and in their
sales of goods. They also had a further incentive for dealing in
currency – through their needs for cash for wages. Capital and
profits from business gave them the wealth to set up as bankers;
the commercial functioning of their business often gave them
the incentives to extend the offer of these services for other
customers.

Apart from the remittance business in bills, the country
bankers provided the main provincial circulating medium with
their notes. Much the greater number of them profited by note
issue. They therefore created currency as well as extending
credit, or extended credit by creating currency. Where farmers
wanted accommodation, or merchants discounting facilities, the
cash their banker provided was usually in the form of his own
notes. Hence where there was a local demand for accommodation the banker's notes got drawn naturally into circulation. He
was then under an obligation to pay cash for them when presented back across his counter. Like the Bank of England, he
kept a certain amount of gold in reserve to cover his note issue;
but this cash reserve varied with the prudence of the banker and
the demand on it with the state of local confidence in him and
the general prosperity of business. In a panic he might well not
be able to liquidate all his own investments rapidly enough to
protect his reserves, and would then send off post-haste to his
fellow bankers and to London for cash, while his clerks paid out
as slowly as they could (often in sixpences) to delay the hour of
bankruptcy. Even the Bank of England paid out in sixpences in
the crisis of 1745.

From being note-issuers, through providing accommodation
and discounts, the country bankers, like the London bankers,
gradually grew into being deposit bankers. This was naturally

a later evolution, because only when a banker was trusted in a local community would someone entrust their savings to him, rather than seeking credit from him. The first functions of the country bankers, creating credit by issuing notes to those who wished to borrow from them, was one of the ways in which the development of a banking system buttressed economic expansion. Deposit banking was the second way. This mobilized the savings of the nation, hitherto sterilized in hoards, into the banks, which then put them to active use by lending and at profit.

When deposit banking spread, there was increased opportunity for rash industrialist and mining bankers to tie this capital up in their own business, or for banks in agricultural areas to lend to farmers and landowners on mortgage. Such a move so often proved the first step to bankruptcy when loans could not be realized in a crisis. But the banker still had to profit by lending this capital (he was having to pay interest on it, sometimes on current accounts) and so he sought bills of exchange to discount, or sent capital to his London agent for investment, where local short-term investments were not available. Here was a mounting pressure in some areas for a national traffic in short-term credit, which added to the other links between regions being established by the country banks and their London agents.

These different elements combined into a nationally-linked financial system – loosely-jointed, vulnerable in a money panic, easily interrupted in war conditions, but fairly serviceable in normal times. As a note issuer the Bank of England became securely placed after the panic of 1745 – when an influential body of merchants declared their faith in its paper. In subsequent crises the notes were accepted as cash and did not flood back to the Bank in return for gold. The panic in 1763, and every subsequent panic, also revealed that the Bank of England was becoming the lender of last resort. Merchants who could find no accommodation from their private bankers sought discounts from the Bank of England – and it did lend down to the limit of its reserves on these occasions. By the end of the century the Bank was also acting as lender of last resort to the

London bankers. They began to keep accounts with the Bank and to use rediscount facilities in a crisis – handing on bills which they had accepted for discounting to the Bank for cash. They often began to let their reserves of gold lie with the Bank at a profit.

The Bank therefore became the holder of the only major gold reserve in the banking system, and thus bore the brunt of a liquidity crisis, whether it came from a balance of payments crisis, with bullion pouring abroad in an external drain, or into the provinces with an internal lapse in the confidence of country bank notes and credit. The Bank kept its discount rate (bank rate) at 5 per cent, imposing high standards upon the bills it agreed to accept for discount, which meant that in normal times (though not when rates of interest were high in wartime) most discount business stayed with other bankers.

This happened even though there was no change in the formal policy of the Bank, and no admission by its Directors that they had accepted the public responsibilities of a central bank. But the volume of circulation of its notes was twice that of the country bankers, the status of its reserves, and its position in relation to government finances, made the logic of this position inevitable. Then, after 1797, the Bank was released from its obligations to exchange its notes for gold. Bank of England paper consequently became the anchor for the other local paper currencies. Taxes and legal obligations could be settled in Bank of England notes. The notes of local banks were then presented to their issuers for Bank of England notes rather than for gold. Convertibility into Bank of England notes after 1797 and until 1821 thus acted as the only external check on over-issues of paper in the provinces, in the same way as the right to demand convertibility into gold normally acted as the check on the over-issue of Bank of England notes. After 1821, when convertibility returned to Bank of England notes, other bankers in London and the provinces usually held their main reserves in Bank of England notes. Only the Bank held large quantities of gold covering its note issue and its banking operations.

The country banks were almost all local. Some very few, like Smith, Payne and Smith of Nottingham or Lloyds of

Birmingham had come to London as well as keeping their local headquarters, drawn there by the flow of business with the metropolis. Where others had set up branches, like the Gurneys in East Anglia or Vincent Stuckey in Somerset, their groups of banks lay in neighbouring towns in the same region. They could not therefore handle inter-regional transfers of bills or credit and cash (bills creating much the greatest traffic) within their own businesses, as the national joint-stock banks do today. Local banking or unit banking demanded specialized intermediaries when the traffic grew to a flood. Thomas Richardson, a Quaker who was a clerk with the Gurneys' London agent, became the first bill-broker. He offered to supply any banker wanting good bills to discount – that is a banker with spare cash looking for good short-term investments. He charged the owners of the bills his fee, a commission of $\frac{1}{8}$ per cent, not their discounters. The flow of bills derived mainly from other bankers, which made Richardson primarily an agent between banker and banker. The timing of the move was much influenced by the London bankers moving away from discounting into government securities during the years of high interest rates in the 1790's.

The direction of the flow of bills through Richardson's hands was significant. The demand for them from bankers with investible surpluses came mainly from the agricultural regions – from East Anglia above all, from the south and west of England. Gurneys in East Anglia and Stuckey's banks in Somerset were his main customers. In these areas of the country local demands for credit were not mounting as rapidly as income, particularly landowners' and farmers' income was accumulating. This was true in the war years, when prices and farm incomes were high, and much investment in agriculture was going on; it remained true when peace brought depression in agriculture and large-scale investment on the land stopped for a generation. The rising manufacturing and commercial areas of the country needed all the short-term capital they could get for financing the transactions resulting from industrial and urban expansion. London became the great junction for this flow of bills from Lancashire and the other industrial counties being fed out to the agricultural areas with surpluses by the bill-brokers. These flows probably varied much between the seasons: in the months just before harvest farmers themselves needed credit. Brokers stood between merchants and industrialists (and their bankers) seeking discounts, and farmers and landowners (and their bankers) offering credit. In Professor Ashton's words, 'The thrift of the south and west supported the enterprise of the midlands and north.' This is another way in which agricultural wealth helped to finance industrial expansion. In 1809 the Gurney Bank in Norwich was holding $£1\frac{1}{2}$ million portfolio in bills organized for them by Richardson. By 1813, Richardson's turnover in bills had reached $£13\frac{1}{2}$ million, by 1823 £20 million, and his firm was now leading a considerable group of other bill-brokers. So important did Richardson become to the Gurneys in Norwich, and so lucrative a traffic was being opened up by these transfers, that they sent one of their cadets, Samuel Gurney, to take up a partnership with his fellow Quaker in 1807.

What evidence was there of participation of the banks in industrial and agricultural long-term investment? Indirectly, of course, discounting bills of exchange by banks released mercantile and industrial capital for fixed investment. If businessmen had had to finance the expansion of their trade as well as their plant – with most of this capital coming out of profits – the rate of expansion would have been cut down. This is particularly true where an important proportion of this short-term capital came from agricultural regions. Banking credit was also involved indirectly in ways not immediately apparent from the books of the bank or the industrial enterprise. Merchants giving extended credit to a business might well be receiving credit themselves from bankers, and private creditors to industrialists could be similarly placed. Many of the individual firms in textiles and metals which have been investigated do show some instances of direct loans from bankers. Boulton borrowed heavily from the Hopes of Amsterdam. The Carron Ironworks had £13,750 loaned to Samuel Garbett, one of its partners, by Glyns, who had accepted £40,000 more in bills of exchange – which subsequently became locked up as permanent investments. The debts became 'funded' as permanent capital loans to the firm in 1772 and run on to 1819. Other instances known include

Arkwright, Strutt, Samuel Oldknow and John Wilkinson. One of the most famous paper makers of the early nineteenth century, William Balston, raised £20,000 from Maidstone bankers. The Duke of Bridgewater owed £25,000 to his bankers while his canal project was stretching the family resources. These were often fairly isolated instances, coming at a time of great need or very rapid expansion of enterprise and they could be paid off within a few years. Few of the firms mentioned seem to have depended on bank capital for a high proportion of their invested capital or to have taken very long loans, save where a banker became a partner and put in his personal estate rather than the capital he was trading on as a banker. But nevertheless occasional loans could be crucial and they could come at a crucial time for the firm, whether for expansion or for survival. There is other evidence on the banking side. Banking crises – such as that in 1793 and that in 1816 – brought down many mining banks and many banks in agricultural districts. Bankruptcy, more than short-term loss of liquidity, provides good evidence that these bankers were making long-term loans. The same is true when industrialist-bankers accepting deposits went bankrupt: the bank had usually been mortgaged to the firm. Such instability may have been beneficial to the economy in the long run by maximizing the expansionary trends in booms more than it wasted capital through bankruptcy and panic in depression years. In banking practices, as with other forces making for economic instability, the process of growth received benefits at a certain social cost.

Sometimes, too, the device of the short-term loan became an instrument of long-term investment, although appearing in the books of both banker and industrialist as credit for a few months. The bankers were lending short, sure enough, but historians may have been deceived about the firm borrowing short. The point was that these loans were often renewed for a further period, if the banker did not wish to redeem the cash when he had the option to do so every few months. Loans on bond to partners in Quaker breweries from their cousins in Quaker banks sometimes ran on undisturbed for ten or more years. It was a profitable and safe transaction for both parties and if the

banker did run into trouble he could demand his cash quickly.
This also happened in defiance of the bankers' wishes. A banker
lent short for three or six months, but then found at the end of
the period that he could not get his money back from the
debtor. If the business remained sound, it was not worth the
creditor's while, be he banker or merchant supplier, to sell up
the debtor to retrieve his cash. Only the lawyers would benefit.
It was much better to convert the loan onto a longer-term basis
at 5 per cent per annum and maintain the commercial connection. In other circumstances short-term loans became the instrument of long-term finance by agreement between the banker
and the industrialist, who borrowed with the intention of
renewing the loan if it was mutually convenient.

Bankers became wealthy men in their own right from the
profits of their trade. Sometimes they put their personal wealth
into business as partners or as personal creditors, even where
they did not put their customers' deposits at risk in this way.

As more case histories reveal the number of instances in
which this generalization about the banks not financing industrial investment was broken, the generalization may itself
come under some suspicion. One has to distinguish between
judging by results and judging by the affirmations leading
bankers made to parliamentary committees or committed to
paper as the 'rules of country banking'. Possibly only among
conservative London city bankers in the eighteenth century was
this golden rule fully operable; and as the banking system grew
more sophisticated in the nineteenth century, and amalgamated
itself into the few national banks, so these conservative banking
principles were implemented nationally. By the 1870's the
British banking system was divorced from long-term industrial
investment, in great contrast to France and Germany. In the
eighteenth and early nineteenth centuries there were probably
more links than the textbooks acknowledge.

In Lancashire and the West Riding of Yorkshire few country
bankers issued notes (in general it was the agricultural district
bankers who were the greatest note issuers rather than the
industrial area bankers). The circulating media of Lancashire,
apart from coin, were mainly made up of bills of exchange,

which circulated as currency being endorsed on the back by
everyone through whose hands they passed. Bank of England
notes also circulated on a much smaller scale in Lancashire in
the eighteenth century until they drove the bill-currency out of
circulation in the 1820's.

Coin was short and Bank of England notes were £10 and
upwards in value and not locally issued – as elsewhere. But the
first centre of large-scale industry produced a flood of bills in
the course of its daily transactions. Bills were well known and
familiar to most groups concerned with remittance needs above
those of ordinary retail needs – for which coin sufficed. Moreover, as currency, bills became safer the more they circulated
and the more names of backers appeared endorsed on them.
Where an endorsement was that of a well-known firm of
established reputation then it was as safe as a Bank of England
note and safer than many local bank-notes. The 'currency' so
created was in awkward amounts – balances needed to be made
in coin – but it served. Decline started to some extent during
the long French wars when Bank of England notes of £1 and £2
began to circulate, but it became rapid only after 1820. Stamp
duties were increased on bills of exchange, at the same time as
rates of interest came down, which gave greater incentives to
discount bills and get into cash, rather than holding them in
circulation. Then, in 1826, the Bank of England opened a branch
in Manchester, followed by one in Liverpool in 1827, to distribute notes and sovereigns, which drove out the small bills
circulating as currency. By this time, too, payments by cheque
were becoming more common.

Reading list

INDUSTRIAL ORGANIZATION AND CHANGE; INDUSTRY AND
INNOVATION
[Deane & Cole; Mitchell]

(i) *Non-ferrous metals*

ALLEN, G. C. 'An 18th-century combination in the copper-mining
    industry', *Economic Journal*, 1923, **33**, no. 129.

CHALONER, W. H. 'Charles Roe of Macclesfield, 1715–1781: an 18th-century industrialist', *Transactions of the Lancashire and Cheshire Antiquarian Society*, 1952–3, **63,** pt. 2.

DODD, A. H. *The Industrial Revolution in North Wales.* 2nd ed., Cardiff, 1951, ch. 5.

HAMILTON, H. *The English Brass and Copper Industries to 1800*, 2nd ed., London, 1967.

HARRIS, J. R. 'Copper sheathing of ships', *Economic History Review*, 2nd series, 1966, **19,** no. 3.

HARRIS, J. R. *The Copper King: a biography of Thomas Williams of Llanidan*, Liverpool, 1964.

MINCHINTON, W. E. *The British Tin-plate Industry: a history*, Oxford, 1957.

ROWE, J. *Cornwall in the Age of the Industrial Revolution*, with an introduction by A. L. Rowse, Liverpool, 1953.

(ii) *Coal*

ASHTON, T. S. & SYKES, J. *The Coal Industry in the 18th Century*, 2nd ed., Manchester, 1964.

LEVY, H. *Monopoly and Competition: a study in English industrial organization* [translation], London, 1911.

SMITH, R. *Sea Coal for London*, London, 1963.

SWEEZY, P. M. *Monopoly and Competition in the English Coal Trade, 1550–1850*, Cambridge (Mass.), 1938 (Harvard Economic Studies, vol. 63).

(iii) *Iron Industry*

ADDIS, J. P. *The Crawshay Dynasty: a study in industrial organization and development, 1765–1867*, Cardiff, 1957.

ASHTON, T. S. *An 18th-century Industrialist: Peter Stubs of Warrington, 1756–1806*, Manchester, 1939.

ASHTON, T. S. *Iron and Steel in the Industrial Revolution*, 2nd ed., Manchester, 1951 (Publications of the University of Manchester: Economic History Series, no. 2).

CAMPBELL, R. H. *Carron Company*, Edinburgh–London, 1961.

COURT, W. H. B. *The Rise of Midland Industries, 1600–1838*, London, 1953.

ELSAS, M. (ed.) *Iron in the Making. Dowlais Iron Company letters, 1782–1860*, Cardiff, 1960.

JOHN, A. H. *The Economic Development of South Wales, 1750–1850: an essay*, Cardiff, 1950.

JOHN, A. H. *The Walker Family, Ironfounders and Lead Manufacturers, 1741–1893*, London, 1951.

RAISTRICK, A. *Dynasty of Ironfounders: the Darbys and Coalbrookdale*, London, 1953.

SCHUBERT, H. R. *History of the British Iron and Steel Industry from c. 450 BC to AD 1775*, London, 1957.

(iv) *Textiles*

CHAPMAN, S. D. *The Early Factory Masters: the transition to the factory system in the Midland textile industry*, Newton Abbot, 1967.

CHAPMAN, S. D. 'The transition to the factory system in the Midlands cotton-spinning industry', *Economic History Review*, 1965, **18**, no. 3.

CLAPHAM, SIR J. H. 'The transference of the worsted industry from Norfolk to West Riding', *Economic Journal*, 1910, **20**, no. 78.

CRUMP, W. B. (ed.) *The Leeds Woollen Industry, 1780–1820*, Leeds, 1931 (Publications of the Thoresby Society, 32).

DANIELS, G. W. 'The cotton trade during the Revolutionary and Napoleonic Wars', *Transactions of the Manchester Statistical Society*, 1916.

DANIELS, G. W. *The Early English Cotton Industry*, Manchester–London, 1920 (Publications of the University of Manchester, Historical Series, no. 36).

DEANE, P. 'The output of the British woollen industry in the 18th century', *Journal of Economic History*, 1957, **17**, no. 2.

EDWARDS, M. M. *The Growth of the British Cotton Trade, 1782–1815*, Manchester, 1967.

FITTON, R. S. & WADSWORTH, A. P. *The Strutts and the Arkwrights*, Manchester, 1964.

HEATON, H. *The Yorkshire Woollen and Worsted Industries*, Oxford, 1920 (Oxford Historical and Literary Studies, vol. 10).

PONTING, K. G. *A History of the West of England Cloth Industry*, London, 1957.

SIGSWORTH, E. M. *Black Dyke Mills: a history with introductory chapters on the development of the worsted industry in the 19th century*, Liverpool, 1958.

SMELSER, N. J. *Social Change in the Industrial Revolution: an application of theory to the British cotton industry*, Chicago, 1959.

UNWIN, G. *Samuel Oldknow and the Arkwrights: the industrial revo-*

lution at Stockport and Marple, with chapters by A. Hulme and
G. Taylor, Manchester, 1924 (Publications of the University of
Manchester: Economic History Series, vol. 1).

WADSWORTH, A. P. & MANN, J. DE L. *The Cotton Trade and Industrial Lancashire, 1600-1780*, Manchester, 1965.

(v) *Other industries*

BARKER, T. C. *Pilkington Brothers and the Glass Industry*, London,
1960.

CLOW, A. & N. L. *The Chemical Revolution: a contribution to social
technology*, London, 1952.

COLEMAN, D. C. *The British Paper Industry, 1495-1860; a study in
industrial growth*, Oxford, 1958.

LORD, J. *Capital and Steam Power, 1750-1800*, 2nd ed., London,
1966.

MATHIAS, P. *The Brewing Industry in England, 1700-1830*, Cambridge, 1959.

ROLL, E. *An Early Experiment in Industrial Organization, being a
history of the firm of Boulton & Watt, 1775-1805*, London, 1930.

(vi) *Area studies*

BARKER, T. C. & HARRIS, J. R. *A Merseyside Town in the Industrial
Revolution: St Helens, 1750-1900*, London, 1959.

CHAMBERS, J. D. *The Vale of Trent, 1670-1800: a regional study of
economic change*, London-New York, 1957.

DODD, A. H. *The Industrial Revolution in North Wales*, 2nd ed.,
Cardiff, 1951.

GREEN, E. R. R. *The Lagan valley, 1800-1850: a local history of the
industrial revolution*, London, 1949 (Studies in Irish History,
vol. 3).

HAMILTON, H. *The Industrial Revolution in Scotland*, London, 1966.

HAMILTON, H. *An Economic History of Scotland in the Eighteenth
Century*, Oxford, 1963.

JOHN, A. H. *The Economic Development of South Wales, 1750-1850:
an essay*, Cardiff, 1950.

MARSHALL, J. D. *Furness and the Industrial Revolution: an economic
history of Furness (1711-1900) and the town of Barrow (1757-
1897)*, Barrow-in-Furness, 1958.

ROWE, J. *Cornwall in the Age of the Industrial Revolution*, with an
introduction by A. L. Rowse, Liverpool, 1953.

(vii) *Innovation and technical change*

GILFILLAN, S. C. *The Sociology of Invention: an essay in the social causes of technical invention and some of its social results, especially as demonstrated in the history of the ship*, Chicago, 1935.

HALL, A. R. The historical relations of science and technology (inaugural lecture, London, 1963).

HARTWELL, R. M. *The Industrial Revolution in England*, London, 1966.

MUSSON, A. E. & ROBINSON, E. 'The early growth of steam power', *Economic History Review*, 2nd series, 1959, **11**, no. 3.

MUSSON, A. E. & ROBINSON, E. 'The origins of engineering in Lancashire', *Journal of Economic History*, 1960, **20**, no. 2.

MUSSON, A. E. & ROBINSON, E. 'Science and industry in the late 18th century', *Economic History Review*, 2nd series, 1960, **13**, no. 2.

SCHMOOKLER, J. *Invention and Economic Growth*, Cambridge (Mass.), 1966.

SINGER, C., HOLMYARD, E. J., HALL, A. R. & WILLIAMS, T. I. (eds.) *A History of Technology*, vol. IV: *The industrial revolution, circa 1750 to circa 1850*, Oxford, 1958 [for reference].

USHER, A. P. *History of Mechanical Invention*, rev. ed., Cambridge (Mass.), 1954.

WRIGLEY, E. A. 'The supply of raw materials in the industrial revolution', *Economic History Review*, 2nd series, 1962, **15**, no. 2; reprinted in Hartwell, *Causes of the Industrial Revolution* (1967).

CAPITAL ACCUMULATION
[*see also Banking*]

ASHTON, T. S. *Economic Fluctuations in England, 1700–1800*, Oxford, 1959, ch. 3.

CAIRNCROSS, A. K. *Factors in Economic Development*, London, 1964, Pt. II, particularly ch. 7.

CAMERON, R. E. *et al. Banking in the Early Stages of Industrialization: a study in comparative economic history*, New York, 1967, chs. 1, 2, 3.

CROUZET, F. 'La formation du capital en Grande Bretagne pendant la révolution industrielle', *2nd International Conference of Economic History*, 1962.

DEANE, P. 'Capital formation in Britain before the railway age', *Economic Development and Cultural Change*, 1961, **9**, no. 3.

HEATON, H. 'Financing the industrial revolution', *Bulletin of the Business History Society*, 1937, **11**, no. 1.

POLLARD, S. 'Capital accounting in the industrial revolution', *Yorkshire Bulletin of Economic and Social Research*, 1963, **15**, no. 2.

POLLARD, S. 'Fixed capital in the industrial revolution in Britain', *Journal of Economic History*, 1964, **24**, no. 3.

POSTAN, M. M. 'Recent trends in the accumulation of capital', *Economic History Review*, 1935, **6**, no. 1.

PRESSNELL, L. S. *Country Banking in the Industrial Revolution*, Oxford, 1956.

PRESSNELL, L. S. 'The rate of interest in the 18th century', in Pressnell, L. S. (ed.), *Studies in the Industrial Revolution*, London, 1960.

See also an industrial case history, e.g.:

COLEMAN, D. C. *The British Paper Industry, 1495–1860; a study in industrial growth*, Oxford, 1958, ch. 9.

EDWARDS, M. M. *The Growth of the British Cotton Trade, 1780–1815*, Manchester, 1967, chs. 9, 10.

MATHIAS, P. *The Brewing Industry in England, 1700–1830*, Cambridge, 1959, chs. 8, 9.

THE ENTREPRENEURS

BENDIX, R. *Work and Authority in Industry: ideologies of management in the course of industrialization*, New York–London, 1956, pt. 1.

COONEY, E. W. 'The origins of the Victorian master builders', *Economic History Review*, 2nd series, 1955, **8**, no. 2.

GRUBB, I. *Quakerism and Industry before 1800*, London, 1930.

HABAKKUK, H. J. 'The economic functions of English landowners', reprinted in H. G. J. Aitken, *Explorations in Enterprise*, Cambridge (Mass.), 1965.

HUGHES, E. 'The 18-century estate agent', in H. A. Cronne, T. W. Moody & D. B. Quinn (eds.), *Essays in British and Irish History*, London, 1949.

MANTOUX, G. *The Industrial Revolution in the 18th Century*, rev. ed. tr. by M. Vernon; reprinted London, 1964.

MATHIAS, P. 'The entrepreneur in brewing, 1700–1830', *The Entrepreneur*, special issue of *Explorations in Entrepreneurial History*, 1957 and in H. G. J. Aitken (ed.), *Explorations in Enterprise*, Cambridge (Mass.), 1965.

MCKENDRICK, N. 'An 18th-century entrepreneur in salesmanship and marketing techniques', *Economic History Review*, 2nd series, 1960, **12**, no. 3.

MCKENDRICK, N. 'Josiah Wedgwood and factory discipline', *Historical Journal*, 1961, **4**, no. 1.

MCKENDRICK, N. 'Wedgwood and Thomas Bentley: an inventor-entrepreneur partnership in the industrial revolution', *Transactions of the Royal Historical Society*, 5th series, 1964, **14**.

MINCHINTON, W. E. 'The merchants in England in the 18th century', *The Entrepreneur*, special issue of *Explorations in Entrepreneurial History*, 1957.

POLLARD, S. 'Factory discipline in the industrial revolution', *Economic History Review*, 2nd series, 1963, **16**, no. 2.

POLLARD, S. *The Genesis of Modern Management: a study of the industrial revolution in Great Britain*, London, 1965.

ROBINSON, E. 'Eighteenth-century commerce and fashion: Matthew Boulton's marketing techniques', *Economic History Review*, 2nd series, 1963, **16**, no. 1.

SMILES, S. *Industrial Biography: iron workers and tool makers* [1863], ed. L. T. C. Rolt, Newton Abbot, 1967.

SMILES, S. *Lives of the Engineers . . .*, 5 vols, London, 1904.

WESTERFIELD, R. B. *Middlemen in English Business, particularly between 1660 and 1760*, New Haven, 1915 (Transactions of the Connecticut Academy of Arts and Sciences, 19).

WILSON, C. H. 'The entrepreneur in the industrial revolution', *History*, 1957, **62**, no. 145.

BANKING AND INVESTMENT

(i) *Banking*

ASHTON, T. S. & SAYERS, R. S. (eds.) *Papers in English Monetary History*, Oxford, 1953.

CAMERON, R. E. *et al. Banking in the Early Stages of Industrialisation: a study in comparative economic history*, New York, 1967.

CLAPHAM, SIR J. H. *The Bank of England: a history*, 2 vols, Cambridge, 1944.

COPE, S. R. 'The Goldsmids and the development of the London money market during the Napoleonic Wars', *Economica*, new series, 1942, **9**, no. 34.

FEAVERYEAR, A. E. *The Pound Sterling: a history of English money*, Oxford, 1931.

JOSLIN, D. M. 'The London private bankers, 1720–1785', *Economic History Review*, 2nd series, 1954, **7**, no. 2.

KING, W. T. C. *History of the London Discount Market*, London, 1936.

LOVELL, M. C. 'The role of the Bank of England as lender of last resort in the crises of the 18th century', *Explorations in Entrepreneurial History*, 1957.

MORGAN, E. V. *Theory and Practice of Central Banking, 1797–1913*, Cambridge, 1943.

PRESSNELL, L. S. *Country Banking in the Industrial Revolution*, Oxford, 1956.

THORNTON, H. *An Enquiry into the Nature and Effects of the Paper Credit of Great Britain*, edited with an introduction by F. A. von Hayek, London, 1939.

(ii) *Monetary policy*

CANNAN, E. *The Paper Pound of 1797–1821*, n.p., 1920.

HAWTREY, SIR R. G. *Currency and Credit*, 4th ed., London, 1950.

HORSEFIELD, J. K. 'The cash ratio in English banks before 1800', *Journal of Political Economy*, 1949, **57**, no. 1.

SCHUMPETER, E. B. 'English prices and government finance, 1660–1822', *Review of Economic Statistics*, 1938, **20**.

SILBERLING, N. J. 'British financial experience, 1790–1830', *Review of Economic Statistics*, 1919, **1**.

SILBERLING, N. J. 'Financial and monetary policy of Great Britain during the Napoleonic Wars', *Quarterly Journal of Economics*, 1924, **38**, Feb. and May.

VINER, J. *Studies in the Theory of International Trade*, London, 1937.

6 The human dimension

POPULATION

Research into British population history has just gone through the destructive phase of historiography, where previous generalizations that have held the stage for a generation and more have been completely undermined by new evidence. The facts about what happened to total numbers in the country are not in serious dispute. Every indication is that Gregory King's calculations from 1688, which showed total numbers in England and Wales to be about $5\frac{1}{2}$ million, were reasonable. At the first – and defective – census of 1801, numbers were 9 million for England and Wales; $1\frac{1}{2}$ million for Scotland. By 1851 numbers had risen to 18 million in England and Wales; 3 million in Scotland (21 million); by 1901, to $32\frac{1}{2}$ million in England and Wales; $4\frac{1}{2}$ million in Scotland (37 million). The rise in numbers in Ireland had been equally formidable in the century after 1750 – that is until the famine of 1846. From $2\frac{1}{2}$ million in the mid-eighteenth century Irish population reached 5 million by 1800 and over 8 million in 1841. Then came disaster. By 1851 numbers in Ireland had fallen to $6\frac{1}{2}$ million; in 1901 they were $4\frac{1}{2}$ million.

The rates of growth represented by these changes are also, of course, broadly agreed. Growth in England and Wales was negligible as a whole for a century before 1741. From 1741 to 1781 numbers rose from 4 to 7 per cent per decade. Then right through from 1781 to 1911 population in Great Britain increased by over 10 per cent per decade. Rates of growth then fell equally dramatically to under 5 per cent per decade. At its peak between 1811 and 1821, the rate of growth in Great Britain was 17 per cent per decade. This is high, but much less dramatic than in some developing countries in the twentieth century, and a very long way from the biological maximum.

The important and controversial thing, however, is to find out how numbers rose; to examine the mechanism of growth; to find out why numbers rose; that is, to discover how this demographic revolution was associated with economic growth. In what ways was it a cause of growth; in what ways a consequence of industrialization? Of course, the analysis of the causes and mechanisms of population growth will have a very strong bearing upon the analysis of the relationship between population change and economic growth. It is still a great cause for argument and poses the fundamental question mark at the present time for a country like India, in a very different context.

One factor can be settled at the start. The increase in the case of Great Britain was mainly caused by natural rates of growth, not by immigration. There was considerable internal migration but the inflow from Ireland, the greatest source of immigration to Great Britain, was broadly balanced by a net outflow.

The previously accepted explanation for the onset of sustained population growth was a rapidly falling death rate, occasioned primarily by the progress of medicine, with a roughly constant birth rate. We can look over our shoulders in our own day to see the death rates tumble in countries such as Ceylon, when the teams move in to eliminate malaria and many other killer epidemic deseases by insecticides, mass inoculation and antibiotics. More regular nutrition (if standards of consumption are very low) and high-quality personal doctoring and hospital medicine will also have major demographic results. This is the working of an 'exogenous' factor, unconnected with any deepseated economic or social changes in the country. But for eighteenth-century England this explanation has been discredited as an adequate explanation for population growth.

In the first place, the statistics cannot support the argument that the death rate did fall heavily after 1780. This theory rests upon the assumption that registrations of births and burials remained as efficient, or improved in efficiency after 1780. Mr Krause has proved that, in fact, the parish registration system collapsed in efficiency and the gap between recorded baptisms and burials, and actual births and deaths, grew much wider. There were many reasons for this. The Anglican church became less efficient, with increasing pluralism and benefices; its parochial organization not covering the rising industrial and mining areas very effectively. There was also the growth of dissent. In addition, religious indifference was increasing in some rapidly growing areas (which has been demonstrated for Sheffield). Private burial grounds also grew in number, as well as dissenters' burial grounds. By 1810 there were more than 2,000 such burial grounds not included in the parish returns. Parish burial statistics were particularly deficient for recording death rates because only baptized persons could enjoy an Anglican burial service.

The effect of all these developments was such that burials probably underestimated deaths by as much as 25 per cent in 1800–20. Cornish parish registers, for example, recorded an infant death rate of 60 per 1,000 in 1800. The infant mortality rate for England and Wales in 1900 was 140 per 1,000 – so probably more than half the infant deaths in Cornwall were not being registered in the early nineteenth century – and possibly one-third of the adult deaths. This fall in efficiency of the Anglican registrations as a means of finding out about national birth and death rates completely eliminates the falling death rate. Equally, the steady improvement in registrations after 1820, leading up to the start of civil registrations in 1836, can wipe out the assumed increase in the death rates in the period 1820–50.

Quite independently of these criticisms of the registration system, historians of medicine have demolished the argument that medical and sanitary improvements could have improved the death rates much between 1780 and 1820. Most hospitals were erected in the more important towns; and they affected the health or survival of a very small proportion of the population. Some of the main advances in medicine were expensive, so again they did not affect the doctoring of the mass of the nation, or the standards of midwifery most mothers experienced. Inoculation, vaccination, country dispensaries and some outpatient departments of urban hospitals, were probably the only improvements to penetrate far down the social scale in village and urban England. It may well prove that smallpox, in particular, was brought under control by improved medical practice, and this was a widespread scourge. However, it has been said that the virulence of smallpox, as a killer disease, was on the decline before the great spread of inoculation and vaccination; and it remains doubtful if the incidence of smallpox as a cause of death was sufficiently high to account for the general rise in population when that incidence declined. A proportion of those saved by inoculation from death by smallpox would have died in the same age group from other things.

There is also no evidence at all that eighteenth-century hospitals did improve their patients' chances of survival. They were hot-beds of infection so that the danger of mortality rose when a patient entered one. Hospitals may have had a good effect in removing infection from the community at large, but in any case, London and the older, larger towns probably only maintained their numbers by the flow of migrants from the countryside, so improvements here would only cut down a wastage rather than explain an increase in numbers in the nation as a whole.[1] The sanitation revolution in the towns also came after 1840 in the main, after the great enquiry into the health of towns in 1841–2; after Edwin Chadwick, just as the revolution in hospital care came after Florence Nightingale. Urban death rates, particularly in fast-growing industrial towns, were shown to be very much higher than the national average in 1851. Other things – like iron beds, cotton clothing, better social habits of cleanliness, probably began to affect a significant proportion of the population only well after the sustained rise in numbers had begun.

The conclusions from the medical evidence and the social evidence suggest that the explanations must be sought mainly in the environment of the medically unimproved rural areas – village England – where two-thirds of the population were living in the 1750's. They may well lie in changes which induced a higher birth rate and a decline in infant mortality – which, it now seems, were two major variables in explaining the great rise in some numbers after 1750. Some things operated *both* to induce higher birth rates and lower death rates. Influences upon

[1] The work of Dr E. M. Sigsworth may lead to a revaluation of these generalizations about eighteenth-century hospitals.

the birth rate are very much more directly responsive to economic and social conditions than death-rate changes influenced by medical improvements: the rate of marriage (the numbers per 1,000 who get married), the age of marriage and the fertility of marriage. Moreover, the economic effects of a cut in infant mortality are demographically similar to a rise in the birth rate: more children survive into the working age groups, and into reproductive age groups than before, thus leading to an increase in the number of marriages and hence a cumulative effect upon demographic growth. Detailed research into local history – parish records, town and diocesan surveys – will provide the answers about age-specific death and birth rates in time, but it is only just beginning with these new questions to ask of the records.[1]

Different regions, it seems, were experiencing different rates of population increase. Even in the first half of the eighteenth century such counties as Lancashire, the West Riding of Yorkshire, Warwickshire, Staffordshire, were growing noticeably, while the agricultural south was stagnant or in decline. This was probably not explained much by migration before the 1750's. If anything, migration might have been away from these counties, as from other counties, to London. The movement of differential growth rates in different regions intensified when total numbers began to move up and was then stimulated by internal migration. There was no large-scale inter-regional migration, just creeping local movements from agricultural hinterlands to mining areas, ports, industrial towns. Hence changes in the distribution of population which set in during the eighteenth century and continued through the nineteenth century – the north and west growing fastest, and more densely than the south which was previously the most densely populated area – are not to be explained by large-scale movement between the two areas. It is becoming clear that the industrial regions were helping to produce their own labour supplies by a much higher than average natural increase in numbers. Mechanisms which

---

[1] The Cambridge Group for the History of Population and Social Structure have launched large-scale research on parish records using 'family reconstruction' techniques. See E. A. Wrigley, *An Introduction to English Historical Demography*.

explain these different rates of growth between areas may well include birth-rate differentials, which relate very intimately to changing economic conditions and the offer of employment.

First came higher marriage rates in the industrial regions. Lancashire and the West Riding showed the maximum increases in rates of marriage over the century; southern England came below this; while central and north Wales counties were the lowest of all.[1] The same phenomenon seems to have existed between the rural parts and the industrial areas within a single county. In the age group 17–30, 40 per cent were married in 1800 in industrial Lancashire; 19 per cent in rural Lancashire. These differences would be influenced strongly by migration. The sort of people attracted to rising industrial areas were young working people, so the age structure there was likely to be favourable to high marriage rates. But this is far from a complete explanation. The great expansion of employment opportunities had something to do with it, without benefit of migration.

All this evidence may be confirmed by data about the age of marriage, for which the Anglican parish records give more accurate evidence than for much else. The age of marriage in some rapidly expanding areas seems to have been lower than that in purely agricultural areas by about three years. Professor Chambers has found this in Nottinghamshire; there are hints from Gloucestershire marriage registers, and for Lancashire and Yorkshire. In the early eighteenth century, the average age of marriage appears to have been about 27. In the textile and mining areas in 1800 it was about 20 and about 23–4 in other areas. A general fall, therefore, took place, but with the industrial areas leading. This again can relate directly to expanding employment opportunities, which removed a restraint on early marriage. In the new trades there were seldom long apprenticeships which postponed marriage. The practice of labourers on farms, and elsewhere, 'living in' – which meant staying unmarried – declined. A farm labourer in a cottage needed a wife.

[1] Controversy exists about ages of marriage and rates of marriage, for which no national evidence – or that of representative samples of parishes – is yet available. I have taken conclusions from the work of Professor Krause and Professor Chambers.

Higher wages could be earned earlier in life; children were not so much of a burden in the textile areas, both under the domestic system and in the spinning mills, where they could become earners at an early age. Restraints against marriage and children were therefore lessened. When visiting the Halifax textile area of small-holdings Defoe wrote in the 1720's: 'Neither indeed could one-fifth part of the inhabitants be supported without them [manufactures] for the land could not maintain them.'

For a combination of these reasons the number of marriages in areas of expanding employment increased. One of the characteristics of rural society, where trade and manufactures were not prevalent, remained a high proportion of unmarried adults and marriage at a late age. It has been argued (but not proved) that the increased local mobility of people, encouraged by economic change, stimulated marriage rates by removing local surpluses of men or women as the area widened from within which marriage partners were chosen. Others have pointed to a specific genetical improvement this might also have produced – although it has yet to be documented that local mobility in pre-industrial England was insufficient to avoid these hazards.[1]

Supporting the increase in marriage rates came enhanced fertility rates (the number of children per marriage) in the expanding regions. In particular a lower age of marriage (more particularly the age of first marriage of women) extended the child-bearing years of marriage back into the healthier, more fertile, age zone and made more children per marriage possible. These trends may have enabled birth rates to expand enough to account for the rise in numbers: increases in births become cumulative, as does the decline in infant deaths, when the new crops of babies grow up to marriageable age themselves, even though high infant death rates would take their toll of the extra babies. Equivalent extensions of life in the older age groups would not have had this cumulative effect. Developments that encouraged a rise in the birth rate must not be seen simply as alternatives to others that brought a fall in the death

---

[1] Mobility within a generation or more has been amply demonstrated. This may not prove mobility on a short-term basis affecting such variables as the choice of marriage partners.

rate. Some could be interdependent, such as a fall in the death rate of infants and children or women during their child-bearing period.

The first fruits of 'parish-register demography' concerned with pre-industrial England seem to add more weight to these suggestions. Compared with some non-European patterns of population growth, where rapid advances in numbers led into the cataclysms of major famines, growth rates were very modest, particularly in the seventeenth and early eighteenth centuries. In Malthusian language 'preventive' checks held back population growth a great deal. A high percentage of people did not get married; the age of marriage was high; some family limitation was practised within marriage, it seems. In response to bad times marriages were postponed. Such responses in the formation of new households had much to do with the availability of employment, it appears, and with the opportunities of settling on a holding. Given the strength of these various restraints, rising demands for labour will tend to lead to a relaxation of them, which can act as an important mechanism in encouraging population growth.

Greater survival rates, particularly amongst babies, do not only depend upon improvement in medical skills. The rising manufacturing and trading regions offered higher and more regular money wages than other, more purely agricultural, areas, even though subject to greater short-run trade-cycle depressions in occasional years. This created the opportunity of buying food and fuel more regularly, if not in greater quantities and of improved quality. Food prices were low in the period 1730-50. Quite a lot of evidence suggests that beer sales per head were rising towards the end of the century; that the working masses were demanding wheaten bread and meat more insistently in the 1780's than when the century opened. More potatoes and vegetables were being eaten as supplementary foodstuffs. Such an improvement in diet, responding to higher money incomes, could take place despite deteriorating environmental conditions in industrial towns in the early nineteenth century.

Improvements in nutrition, more particularly in protein intake, on the part of mothers, can effect a dramatic increase in the survival rate of babies. The rate of miscarriage may fall; more babies will be born stronger; mothers become able to feed their babies more adequately. And such a decline in the rate of wastage between conception and the early months of life will appear demographically as a rise in the birth rate. Economic historians have not yet begun to think seriously about the health of the mother and her nutrition in the eighteenth century. Yet this is one of the first things for which biologists would seek evidence. But this comes back again to the conditions of employment.

These conclusions being reached by modern research do constitute in part a return to the ideas common at the time. Most observers then thought that the state of population related to the offer of employment, and Malthus proposed that the remedy for over-population should be postponing the age of marriage.

Several complications have been thrown into this argument. It seems that in Sweden after the 1720's there was a decline in the virulence of epidemic diseases. Plague was absent; smallpox was becoming less of a killer, even before inoculations began to influence quite large numbers of people. The reasons for this are obscure, but the great jagged peaks which cropped up on the death-rate chart in occasional years, coming from epidemic disease, do die away after the mid-eighteenth century. This may be an 'exogenous' factor, a decline in the potency of diseases from various causes, particularly a change in climatic conditions. It may also be linked with better human resistance to disease coming from better nourishment. Pestilence and diseases strike with greater mortality at a population weakened by famine, as we know from Indian experience. In the 'positive checks' of Malthus famine is the parent of disease. The demographer is concerned more with the mortality than the incidence of disease – a variable much influenced by nutrition.

The work of Dr Hollingsworth on the dukes and the peers, a very well-documented group, has revealed that their families tended to increase, and more children survive, from the 1740's in common with national trends. But this particular group was obviously not responsive demographically to better employment

or more food, fuel and shelter. Nor were they representative, of
course, and this may just be coincidence – or inoculations.

Ireland shows certain parallels and certain differences. The
mechanism of growth seems similar – medical improvements
(with the possible exception of inoculation) had negligible
effects, the age of marriage fell, the rate of marriage rose, there
were more children per marriage as birth rates rose. But there
the similarities stop. The social and economic mechanisms encouraging this to happen in Ireland were not expanding employment from economic growth and industrialization as in
England. Family increases came with the extension of potato
cultivation. Population growth was most marked exactly in the
rural areas most strongly influenced by the potato. This was
nutritionally almost as good as any cereal as a staple food, if
supplemented by a little skimmed milk.[1] And it was a much
more intensive crop, in spade cultivation. Families could thus
be supported on smaller patches of ground and the size of holdings
fell as numbers multiplied in virtual monoculture with potatoes.
No check came from landlords in the west of Ireland against this
movement: there was still universal access to land.

In seeking to trace the links between the onset of self-sustained
economic growth in Britain and the beginnings of an equally
sustained growth in numbers, one must recognize a mutual dependence, that population growth, in its turn, served to influence
the course of economic change.

In England the economic impact of rising numbers was
moulded by their redevelopment in the economy. The productive capacity of the nation rose while its structure changed towards the sectors where there were increasing returns, advancing
productivity – in manufacturing industry, mining, trade, transport. With a labour force developing in these sectors, higher

[1] Adam Smith commented: 'The chairmen, porters, and coalheavers in
London, and those unfortunate women who live by prostitution, the strongest
men and the most beautiful women perhaps in the British dominions,
are said to be, the greater part of them, from the lowest rank of people in
Ireland, who are generally fed with this root. No food can afford a more
decisive proof of its nourishing quality, or of its being peculiarly suitable
to the health of the human constitution.' (*Wealth of Nations*, Book I, Ch. XI.)

output per head and increasing returns were more likely than for extra labour in agriculture, with lower output per head and probably diminishing returns after a certain point. Migration towards sectors in the economy with increasing returns became the crucial aspect of the demographic revolution in Britain, which contrasts it to experience in Ireland at the time: the rate of change in the structure of the economy became geared into the rate of change of population. Rising numbers probably allowed it to happen more quickly by providing a rapidly growing labour force.

Increasing numbers, too, being in employment as paid labour (and at higher money incomes usually than in agriculture) and not insulated from the market economy in largely self-sufficient peasant households, provided the purchasing power of a widening internal market. This stimulated economic expansion on the demand side, as well as the labour supply side. The internal market could expand as fast with rising incomes *per capita* within a constant population as by a rising population without marked changes in income *per capita*. This would give rise to different structural developments in demand, however, as people used their rising incomes to purchase better quality articles, rather than to purchase more of basic staple items, which was a consequence of extending the same pattern of demand – or the same broad level of purchasing power *per capita* – over larger numbers.

Population growth had other important economic effects. By making greater demands on food supplies, it placed a greater strain on agricultural output and required greater investment in agriculture. Rising numbers also made greater demands on investment generally. Even if no expansion in the amount of capital per head of the labour force took place (which happened with the deepening of investment coming with industrialization), more capital would be needed to employ the extra numbers at static levels of technique. This is expansionary in making demands for extra investment. But if shortage of capital was a constraint to economic growth – which we have argued was not the case in eighteenth-century England – the extra need for investment to cope with a population increase could pose an extra problem as much as providing an extra incentive. With urbanization developing at the same time as population growth much greater requirements of social investment greatly increased the demand for total investment. A mobile population was also *qualitatively* advantageous. Migrant labour flowed naturally to the 'pressure points' of the economy, where demand for labour was greatest and the supply in particular categories of jobs most lacking. Where population density increased, innovations in transport and other improvements, such as in the distributive trades and retailing, became more worth while and could pay their way better. Social hardships, on the other hand, coming with population increases, migration and urbanization, are likely to be increased in a context of rising numbers, and the social costs of industrialization heightened.

In Ireland numbers multiplied largely as poverty-stricken peasants. Diminishing returns set in in agriculture, with output per head and income per head falling as population rose. Within the boundaries of Great Britain the Malthusian threat of overpopulation proved a false one. Malthus' theory that numbers expanded in geometrical ratio always faster than food supplies implied that numbers would always press against the margin of subsistence. When the first *Essay on Population* was published in 1798, the theory received wide publicity, boosted in 1801 by the shock of the first census which proved how rapidly numbers were rising. But the economic expansion was such that income for the purchase of raw materials and food beyond the indigenous resources of the country in return for exports gave the opportunity for a general rise of material comforts to the numbers increasing so unprecedentedly.

This was a new phenomenon in the world's history and it occurred only with industrialization. It is not surprising that Malthus writing towards the beginning of this process did not fully understand its significance from the predominantly rural parts of England he himself knew, and drawing evidence from other contemporary societies like Sweden and Norway, which were mainly agrarian, or from history – that is from other mainly agrarian societies. He missed, in the *Population* essay, the most important long-term trend in the century 1750–1850, but he had every excuse for anticipating eventually diminishing returns in the major sector of the old economy – agriculture – as did Ricardo – even though agriculture in England was resilient, expanding and improving its techniques. This was exactly the fate that was being worked out in Ireland and the North-West Highlands of Scotland at the time. National income per head fell; the people got closer to the margin of subsistence; the extra offer of labour bred only more unemployment. The respect which some contemporaries paid to the industrialist, to the businessman, in England cannot be understood unless one relates it to this issue – it was a respect, they thought, properly owed to the persons who, by offering employment, were the instruments saving society from the fate predicted for it by Malthus and being worked out for all to see across the Irish Sea.

The industrial counties grew much faster than the national average (mainly by higher natural rates of increase) and agricultural areas much slower than the average. Local migration became intense by the early nineteenth century. In 1801–11 Monmouth county population grew by 36 per cent; Lancashire by 23 per cent. This was still the creeping movement from rural areas in the immediate hinterlands of industrial settlements, and from immediately adjacent counties. The impact of migration was even more marked with individual towns. In 1851 less than half of the inhabitants of Manchester, Glasgow and Liverpool had been born in the towns. Liverpool grew by 46 per cent in the decade 1821–31, and Manchester by 40 per cent. There were 115,000 people in Liverpool in 1811; 453,000 in 1851 – an increase of 338,000 of whom 222,000 were migrants. The same story occurred in most rapidly growing urban centres. Of the 6·6 million people living in London and the 71 largest English and Scottish towns in 1851, 3 million were migrants to them. These rapidly growing towns were helped by such migration to have higher than average natural rates of increase also, because the high proportion of young adults among the migrants gave the resulting age structure to the towns a higher than average proportion of people in child-bearing and marrying age groups.

Internal migration was not exclusively a traffic linked to times of agricultural depression. It pulsated with demands for employment from the expanding areas as well as with the state of agriculture. The flow, for example, ceased temporarily in the acute depression in 1841-2, but continued through prosperous times for agriculture in 1850-70, and in fact increased then. Probably the railways gave this extra stimulus to the restructuring of the economy which stepped up migration flows.

Irish migration – perhaps any migration that involves a sea voyage – did seem to follow the 'push' of bad conditions in the country of exodus rather than a pull from the receiving country, as far as timing is concerned. Irish emigration quickened in the small famines of 1817-18 and 1822, which provided portents of the future. The flow increased before 1846, but became a torrent in the decade following the disaster: 200,000 persons left in the year of the famine and a million and half within a decade. Those who came to Britain went mainly to London and to the industrial centres in Lancashire and Glasgow, also to south Wales. In 1851, one-tenth of Manchester's inhabitants and one-sixth of Liverpool's were Irish. There were over 100,000 Irish in London, 250,000 in Scotland, 500,000 in England and Wales.

They became hand-loom weavers, textile operatives, labourers, domestic servants, navvies. As early as 1824, one of the leading cotton spinners of Glasgow could remark, 'our manufactories are principally supplied from Ireland', and in 1835 a writer said of the flax-mills of Leeds that they would be at a standstill but for the influx of Irish. The character of this permanent migration was very different from the traditional, mainly temporary, migrant work of the Irish in England in the eighteenth century – doing all the very heavy work, as Adam Smith suggested, that the English poor neither would nor could do. The Irish swamped occupations of easy entry (such as builders' labouring, hand-loom weaving, domestic service). They could underlive the native English just as they traditionally outworked them. And, with the Irish, came the most frightening standards of squalor known in early Victorian England, which was what

Engels principally described in Manchester in 1844. This was the result of the translation of the standards and habits of rural peasant Ireland, where poverty was worse than that known in industrial England, into urban Lancashire. Even the laws against keeping pigs in towns were aimed at Paddy's ingrained rural habits.

CONDITIONS OF WORK AND SOCIAL ATTITUDES

Changing conditions of employment have to be related to their context before they can be evaluated historically. The first point is to remember the very poor standards existing before industrializing began. Comparisons must begin from here, not from later standards. Gregory King's views about mass poverty were accepted as commonplace by all his contemporaries, considering half the nation as paupers, needing charity if not poor relief to make ends meet. The conditions of much employment available were sporadic, much subject to natural interruptions, with much underemployment on the land. John Law in 1705 assumed that the poor in agriculture, where there was no out-work in textiles available, were 'idle one half their time'. Defoe called such areas 'unemployed counties'. A very similar phenomenon of concealed unemployment or underemployment exists today in under-developed agricultural economies with fairly primitive techniques. Miserably low real incomes remain inevitable in these circumstances because national income remains very low with techniques of such low productivity.

The age structure of the population, with high birth rates and high death rates, added to the problem because probably about 40 per cent of the people were under 15. Gregory King thought this was so in 1696; it was true in the early nineteenth century. The proportion now is almost half this. Because of high death rates the fraction of the population in the working age groups, aged 15–60, was about half in the late seventeenth and eighteenth centuries probably – whereas it is two-thirds today. The conclusion is that a very high proportion of dependents existed at the same time as production and productivity was low. A large family could only stave off want by child labour or poor relief.

Women's and children's labour was virtually inescapable and universal in these economic circumstances, where the opportunity for it existed. Defoe, Hanway and a long tradition of philanthropists – the most humane of men in their generation – could only see the advantage in extending the opportunities for women's and children's labour – as one of the most important benefits that could come in the eternal struggle against poverty. Possibly the more surprising thing is how limited was the role of women's labour in agriculture in England, compared with eastern European, African or Asian experience.

The general legal emphasis was for keeping wages down. Justices of the Peace officially had power under the Statute of Artificers to fix maximum wages. The use of this provision to exert pressure on wage levels was also closely related to economic circumstances. Before the rise of high-productivity technology, labour was the dominant factor in production. With fairly stable technology, wage costs, with raw material costs, were the main determinant of prices. At the same time the textile industries were already much committed to export markets, with the consequent fear of low-wage competition from other nations. Defoe, John Carey, Dudley North and one or two other commentators were unusual in advocating a high-wage economy. Changes in attitudes became more common in the mid-eighteenth century with the awareness that mechanization, by extending capital in production and raising output per head of the labour force dramatically, could equate high wages with great increases in production at lower prices for the first time. They stressed the improvement in the quality of labour that high wage rates could bring, as well as a better market for industry.

Many other conditions of work common during the first half century and more of industrialization were inherited from the pre-industrial context. Child and women's labour are an example of this. The 12-hour shifts common in the textile mills in 1800 existed in the original Lombe silk factory of 1718. Equally, the worst examples of long hours, evil conditions, harshness of treatment, and miserliness of reward in the factories can be matched by those in the industries that remained organized on the putting-out system until the late nineteenth century. Long after the Factory Acts imposed minimum standards on all factory employers, the conditions in the sweat shops of the London garment industry survived to shock Charles Booth and Beatrice Webb in the 1880's. These piece-rates were not subject to legislation until 1909.

Conditions of work

One main organizing theme to labour history in this period is family employment. Family labour became a bridge between the conditions of employment in the old world of the putting-out system and the new factory world. A natural adoption took place, therefore, of women's and children's labour, which still operated as family units very often, within the mill or the mine. Children worked for their father or their mother as they had done at home, collecting wastes, tying threads and 'piecing'. The adult migrant tended to enter the mills with his family – and the fact that discipline was imposed on the children largely by their own parents made the harshness of the new disciplines socially tolerable. In Robert Peel's mill at Bury, 95 out of the 136 employees belonged to 26 families in 1801-2: relatively few of this labour force were adult males. The same was true in the mines, where colliery owners contracted with a pitman for family labour, the children as 'trappers' working ventilation flaps and stacking, the women hauling, the men hewing. Often, the isolation of pit villages, causing a lack of alternative employment and low incomes, conspired to reinforce this family tradition of employment. The worst conditions of employment under industrialization existed in these circumstances – where the colliery owner or the mill owner did not accept direct responsibility for conditions of labour, hours of work or employment of children at a specific age, but had sub-contracted these functions to an intermediary. In the mines 'butty masters' negotiated with groups of miners and their families; small charter masters did the same in other industries; mill owners struck bargains with the heads of families in textile mills, for the labour of the whole unit. It resembled leasing a concession, sometimes, more than direct employment of individuals. There is evidence for this in the fact that employers sometimes had to take children too

young to be economic assets in order to oblige parents maintaining a family economy in the mill. Jedediah Strutt took children
at 7 in the 1770's; but reluctantly, wanting them at a minimum
of 10! These children were necessarily involved in the same
hours of work as the adults for whom they worked.

Factory Acts did not at once break down this association. Up
to the 1820's the main pressure for limiting hours of work and
imposing a minimum age for work in the mills did not come
from the workers themselves but from external sources –
humanitarians, doctors, enlightened employers occasionally,
Tory radicals. Peel's Factory Act of 1802 applied only to pauper
apprentices in the factories, outside the kinship system, upon
whom *family* discipline could not be imposed. Most trade
societies in the mills tried to maintain the rule that only the
children or relatives of the adult spinners could be trained in the
mill as skilled spinners – seeking to maintain recruitment, discipline and earnings largely within this kinship system. The
attack on child labour from the workers coincided with the
break-up of these kinship links under technological advance, as
much as from factory legislation. When the automatic mules of
Richard Roberts came into the textile mills after 1824 an adult
spinner needed as many as nine young assistants in the place of
the one or two under the older mules. Similarly, power-loom
weaving broke the tradition of family employment on this side of
the industry. When standards of discipline and work were imposed by foremen and managers, rather than by the family
groups, they became intolerable and a wave of protest came from
the workers against harsh conditions, immorality and long hours.
The facts of the case had not changed so much but attitudes
swung radically.

The 1833 Factory Act limited the hours of work of children
between 9 and 13 to 8 hours per day, of those between 14 and
18 to 12 hours per day (with no night work). It also outlawed
the work of children under 9, and tried to force mill owners to
provide elementary schooling. By snapping the link between
the children's shifts and the adults, this legislation broke the
kinship system to pieces. Labour reactions were initially to
demand *either* bringing down adult working hours to those of

the adolescents, *or* a 12-hour day for the children. Then the movement swung behind the campaign for the 10-hour day. This was gained in 1847, and the traditional forebodings of employers about the loss of export markets were not realized. An act of 1844 had already limited the hours of work of children between 8 and 13 years old to 6½ hours daily. After the break with the old pattern in 1833, made effective by the corps of salaried factory inspectors, the legislation of the 1840's and subsequently, ensured improving standards within the new system by making more time for mothers and children outside their place of work. But down to 1853 the Factory Acts were confined to textile factories, and no limitations were imposed on adult men in the mills, even though the Ten Hours Act usually meant that they had to stop work with the women and children. Only in 1878 was the system extended to cover all factory and workshop trades.

The horrors of the old system in the mines were exposed by a parliamentary investigation of 1840 (this was the first Blue Book to have pictures of the worst evils), after which the Mines Act of 1842 promptly killed it by prohibiting the employment of women and boys under 10 underground. An Agricultural Act of 1867, which outlawed the employment of children under 8, or women and children with men in a field-gang, broke up family employment in that field (even though it still went on with migrant labour in harvesting and 'hopping'). An Act of 1864 did the same for the infamous practice of children's employment in chimney sweeping. A long list of equivalent controls over the working conditions of women and children followed. National, eventually compulsory, education statutes followed in 1870 and the 1880's to complement this industrial legislation.

One or two other points need to be remembered when considering the standards of industrial employment of women and children, which were horrific compared with the standards we instinctively relate them to today. Contemporary treatment of children in general was very harsh. Wesley's instructions for a child's upbringing read horrifically; so also was the savagery meted out to the cadets of the ruling families at public schools. Life was generally brutalized, judging by later standards of gentility and civility, as evidenced in such things as popular sports and entertainments, gaols, the army and navy.

Some of the evidence of bad conditions of work and life should also properly be seen as evidence of the determination and the campaign to get things changed. This is true, above all, of the Blue Books, that vast series of Parliamentary Papers beginning in 1797. In part these were deliberate attempts by forward-looking groups in Parliament, and outside it, to shock public opinion and the public conscience by using the rules of evidence and the selection of witnesses as ruthlessly as they could. This was still the unreformed House of Commons. In an age of rising standards of humanitarianism the few were determined to impose higher standards on the many; and were able to exploit developing means of mass-communication to do it. The mere exposure of traditional practices in a factory setting, advertising their presence in large mills in the middle of densely populated towns, could lead to a demand for action unthinkable when the conditions were those of private homes, isolated mines, or the agency of disciplined parental authority.

In this sense the new industrial system, looked at from the point of view of standards of employment, the context of work, quickly broke up traditional patterns which had existed for centuries, as much as it created new problems. Living in industrial towns, the context of life rather than work, did create new and terrifying problems. But having stated that, it remains true that industrialization vastly increased the power of a few men over the lives of a multitude of families, but no more than that of a great landowner. In the logic of the circumstances this increased first the possibilities of abuse and then the inevitability of the imposition of social controls by public authority. Older patterns of employment appropriate to the conventions and conditions of a pre-industrial economy got carried into the new context where different conditions brutalized and degraded the older practices and made the same practices appear more brutal and degrading, as standards of expectation rose. Some of the apostles of *laissez-faire*, who resisted every limitation imposed upon employers by statute in the name of individual liberty and the bogy of impending commercial disaster, deserved to end up on the lowest ledges of Dante's inferno. It is a false assumption that industrialization had no tragedies or iniquities to hide.

The main, and most publicized, tragedy of the industrial revolution was that of the hand-loom weavers in the cotton industry, themselves a creation of the great leap in yarn output with factory spinning. Wage rates in hand-loom weaving dropped from a peak of 23s. per week in 1805 (when mechanized spinning had created a tremendous demand for weaving capacity) down to 8s. 3d. per week in 1818 and to 6s. by 1831. Yet the numbers of hand-loom weavers in the cotton industry increased, as social tragedy intensified, until after the collapse of the 1825 boom. Over 250,000 heads of families were involved. One cannot explain this simply on economic grounds: rather the motivations which made the tragedy such an extended one defied the operation of simple economic incentives. At the end of the Napoleonic Wars the writing was on the wall for everyone to see. There could only be one solution – get out of hand-loom weaving. Why, therefore, did numbers increase for the next generation?

The rate of expansion of production in the textile industry was so great that manufacturers could install power looms and still have work for hand-loom weavers in good times. Part of the tragedy was that they were always the first to be laid off in bad times, because a manufacturer could not afford to allow expensive factory weaving plant to lie idle, whereas it cost him nothing to stop handing out work to cottage weavers. A large proportion of the weavers were part-time workers and women. In addition, because of technical difficulties in adapting the new looms to different styles and qualities of yarns and fabrics there was a very slow rate of diffusion of power-weaving over the face of the industry – it proved to be a long drawn-out process of attrition not a brutal, but short, shock such as happened to the hand combers in the few years after the main combing machine was patented in 1851.

To cling on in the face of wages which involved hours of work, squalor and ill-health worse than any factory conditions required the stamina of social as well as economic inertia: the large-scale invasion of poverty-stricken Irish labour, seeking employment on almost any terms, did much to drag down the levels of reward in hand-loom weaving. But, apart from this, the cohesion of family employment and the social bonds of a way of life resisted economic incentives. The husband and father remained at the centre of family earning power and status; there was the independence of setting one's own self-imposed pattern of working and discipline. These are exactly the same motivations, involving the values of a whole way of life, that keeps a poor peasant slaving away on a marginal plot of land for monetary returns far less than those of an agricultural labourer – but preserves status with a way of life and a nominal title to land.

The scale of the new factory and large-plant employment, relative to employment in other fields, needs to be borne in mind throughout this discussion. Very few large units of industrial employment existed in the early stages, up to 1850, apart from the textile industry, the iron and non-ferrous metal industries, and one or two other trades like glass-making, bleach-making, railway workshops, dockyards, and a handful of breweries, paper-making, some mining areas.[1] The work-shop, putting-out trades and farming were no longer the most strategic areas of the economy – nor the fastest growing – but the progress of the new technology, the new social relationships in industry over the economy at large was slower than textbooks often suggest.

Conditions of life

The new urban environment, affecting a steadily rising proportion of the nation, brought problems of discipline in living, of social controls, just as much as factory employment brought the problem of discipline and regularity in work. Industrialists solved their problems – often harshly – more efficiently than local government, police and public administration solved theirs. Money wages were higher and more regular, on the whole, in urban manufacturing industry than in agriculture, but the pattern was broken by short periods of intense cyclical unemployment. At the same time, in this context, negligible public provision was made for loss of earnings at such times, or for the cessation of earnings for any cause of dependence – accident,

[1] See below, pp. 261–72.

sickness or old age. Spending habits appropriate to the old style of rural life, as well as other inherited social habits and conventions, increased social problems when translated into the new environment. The weekly wage packet was now the family's only protection against distress: in the rising industrial towns there were seldom gardens, small holdings or payments in kind. Everything needed to be purchased in shops, and rent paid, from wages. In the older style of life money – actual cash – often did not possess this unique importance. It could be squandered (and was, particularly on drink) without such drastic social harm resulting. When higher, more regular, wages were fed into these traditional spending habits in industrial communities much greater social problems resulted.

Some other attributes of rural life also proved lethal when translated into high-density urban housing in the absence of strict local government regulations – sanitation being a clear example. The context of urban life proved socially more lethal than the context of work. Environmental decline was, and remains, the most intense social problem resulting from industrialization. Not until the second quarter of the nineteenth century was the general administrative basis for effective social controls in towns successfully evolved. With lagging public provision and public initiative, encouraged by the anti-interventionist philosophy prevailing at Westminster – even the absence of a national educational system – great scope remained for the spontaneous evolution of appropriate social values by social elites. A set of social norms, embodied in emergent social institutions, did develop in response to these new needs, however imperfectly they were practised. The virtues of hard work – the gospel of work preached by Samuel Smiles – saving, thrift, sobriety became the new social imperatives dinned into the heads of the working classes by their social betters by every known means of communication. They were enshrined in Nonconformist and evangelical doctrine. In Sunday schools, pulpits, the mechanics' institutes after 1824 and all forms of literature in the hands of middle-class publicists, were preached the golden rules as they attempted to diffuse the bourgeois virtues down the social scale. Many of these values were also championed by working-class publicists as a logical response to the new environment of life and work, being supported by Chartist orators and newspapers, trade unions, clubs and friendly societies.

Undoubtedly hard work and thrift proved the twin, universal virtues of the industrializing society. On the part of the businessman they gave the chance of ploughing back profits in investment for expansion; for the working family they brought the chance of security for bad times. The lack of either quality could ruin a family as easily as a business. Both attitudes were significant of a period when the state did very little to help either industrial progress or its social casualties. Social mechanisms and institutions growing spontaneously from social needs were the prime movers before 1850.

Friendly societies became the main institution embodying these values and motivations. They grew out of trade societies and clubs – incipient trade unions – which were almost universal in urban and artisan employment in the eighteenth century. The printers' chapels, for example, spanned from Tudor guild regulations right through to trade union organization. One finds a system of fines the characteristic way in which self-discipline was imposed in the friendly and early trade societies (as well as in the factories). All the printers' chapels whose rules have survived, show traditional 'solaces' for swearing and fighting or 'suggesting sending out for drink'. One function was clearly to impose work-discipline. But there were others, some mutually antagonistic. The fines went towards a fund which was used to help printers in social need, aiding with burial expenses, sickness, accident and unemployment. In the early nineteenth century printers' 'chapels' provided small sums to unemployed printers belonging to other 'chapels', tramping through local towns looking for work. This 'tramping artisan' system, which existed in several trades, showed that these societies were nation-wide. But contributions and the fine-money also went towards the 'Chappell Drink' on Saturday nights. Conflict clearly existed in these undifferentiated trade and friendly societies between their social solidarity purpose and their social welfare purpose – even if they were usually called the 'Sons of

Prudence' or 'Daughters of Oeconomy'. Most of them met at public houses, and used the publican or his brewer as their banker. Progressive employers tried to institutionalize the good purposes (as they saw them) at their works and surprisingly often one finds a small levy being made on wages to provide a doctor, sometimes a schoolmaster and accident benefits. William Marshall set up such a club in 1790 at his new flax mills in Leeds to be run by employees primarily from their contributions. The Strutts did the same at Belper, with their own schools outside the factory and a co-operative store in 1821. Wedgwood also did the same sort of thing. These instances are characteristic – and it was enlightened self-interest that made it worth while for industrialists to encourage the social virtues amongst their own employees, to seek to raise the quality of their labour force by changing their motivations.

The law was also invoked to encourage the socially useful friendly societies by statute. In 1793, provided their rules and treasurers were approved by the local J.P.s, friendly societies received legal protection. In 1829 a register of friendly societies was set up in London and funds could be deposited with the Commissioners of the National Debt, earning – in non-inflationary times – a safe income. No less than 700 friendly societies registered in 1801; by 1850 supposedly two-thirds of the employed population in Lancashire were on the books of such organizations. A second such institution was the savings bank, another example of consolidation and specialization taking place with a more generalized social utility. These were protected in a similar way by statute in 1817. When the savings bank legislation was consolidated in 1828, 408 banks were operating, possessing £14 million in deposits.[1]

Encouraging these institutions by statute was mainly important for allowing them legal protection to recover funds and sue for debt. The real purpose of registering friendly societies and letting J.P.s inspect their rules was, of course, to prevent

---

[1] In 1807 proposals were made that the state should establish a national network of savings banks, guaranteeing deposits and a fixed rate of interest, using the post-office organization, but that was not done until 1861, by Gladstone.

incipient trade unions from enjoying the privileges accorded to socially 'useful' institutions. But many associations with the purpose of influencing the bargain struck between worker and employer did cloak this aspect of their life under the statutory favours being shown to self-help and thrift, particularly after the Combination Laws were passed in 1799 to clamp down on trade societies.[1]

Just as the problem of intemperance was a widespread feature in the new society so temperance campaigns became a characteristic response. Given the spending habits of the poor in the eighteenth century some social device to divert earnings into more responsible channels was vital. Hence temperance became a theme of Chartism, the trade union movement and the co-operators. Establishing a temperance hotel was one of the original purposes of the Rochdale pioneers in 1844. It was equally favoured by upper-class philanthropic opinion. The Queen eventually became patron of the Church of England Temperance Society with the entire bench of bishops drafted as Vice-Presidents. Not accidentally Lancashire became the centre of the movement, which was particularly marked in the industrial areas and taken up by Nonconformist circles. The movement sprang from the 1830's as a spontaneous self-help phenomenon, with rapid foundation of societies to implement it – even though, as with the other virtues, they had been preached by the upper classes to the poor for a very long time.

These self-help movements reveal very clearly a certain diagnosis of the cause of social problems. At their most naïve and pretentious they implied that poverty and dependence of the able-bodied sprang from an individual moral failing, a personal responsibility, which might be cured by a moral campaign for the social redemption of the individual by his conversion to the true social values. In effect they became secularized forms of simple evangelism, casting out the devils of drink or sloth, conducted in terms of missions with banners and hymns, conversions and signing pledges. Such an intellectual analysis sought to remove, or at least minimize, the responsibility for poverty and dependence by society. The solution was self-help. It did

[1] See below, pp. 366–7.

not require any fundamental redistribution of income for large public expenditure on social institutions. It did not need any great enlargement of the role of the state in society, or increased taxation. Charity and self-help were the two main private responses sufficient to overcome the social problems thrown up in a changing society according to this analysis.

Not surprisingly the radicals, such as Robert Owen or Thomas Spence, refused to accept such an analysis of the causes of poverty, or the diagnosis for its cure. Owen, for example, with regard to temperance saw the problem as a symptom and immediate cause for social tragedy. Anyone would know of individuals ruined by drink but one could still maintain that poverty was primarily a result of the economic and social system and could only be redressed by institutional changes. Drunkenness, in this analysis, was the cheapest Utopia for those whose lives were being brutalized; a gin-shop stupor had become the quickest road out of Manchester.

Both views were partially correct. In any case it took time before new social values could respond to the new environment. But, clearly, in the long run the institutional problems of poverty, education, health, sanitation and the conditions of employment were such that the role of the state was transformed by the social implications of industrialization and urbanization. It was irrelevant to suggest that moral regeneration, a change of individual values, could cure unemployment resulting from the trade cycle or the investment cycle. The new Poor Law of 1834 did make this assumption – that unemployment was voluntary for able-bodied poor, that work was available for the willing. Hence the justification for the principle of 'less eligibility' or deterrence in the workhouses. The idea was that, if conditions inside were worse than those prevailing outside, then the able-bodied poor would take the rational decision to stay out of the workhouse and work. Not surprisingly this principle, although maintained through the nineteenth century as official dogma, soon broke down in practice. All this is not to say, however, that philanthropy and social self-help were not major forces in the moulding of nineteenth-century society.

In the much publicized endeavour to engender new social

norms responsive to the needs of the new environment, one must always distinguish between intentions and results, between hope and reality. Early Victorian society did not, in fact, operate in the way propagandists for social discipline said it ought to. Beer and spirits consumption *per capita* rose, on trend, to 1899. The continuance of the campaigns and legislation show the truth of the matter. The revelations of Mayhew about London society in 1851, and of Charles Booth and Seebohm Rowntree about the extent of poverty in London and York in the last quarter of the nineteenth century, showed the gap between the ideal and the actual. This is true also of middle-class Victorian attitudes to sex. Charges of hypocrisy levied at the Victorian age were symptomatic of the attempt to impose higher standards, higher expectations upon a brutalized society.

The self-help movements all made one assumption that the new employment, save in years of depression, did offer a money wage greater than that needed for immediate consumption – itself, of course, a subjective standard. If this were not so, none of these movements could have prospered. In point of fact, the poorest paid section of society without such a margin above subsistence needs – the agricultural labourers – had the poorest record of membership of friendly societies, and the highest record of receipts from poor relief funds. In the 1840's even Engels was complaining to Marx that he had doubts about the social solidarity of the proletariat in the class sense; because of their widespread adoption of bourgeois values. This partial *embourgeoisement* of working-class attitudes, in so far as it happened, was the justification for so much of this self-help and charitable activity in the first half of the nineteenth century.

STANDARDS OF LIVING

There are two sorts of calculations by which to approach the question of the standard of living on a systematic basis. The first is from 'national income' calculations to work out the annual total value of goods and services produced over time, divided by population numbers. One can also look at wages and prices and try to find out how much a man or a family could buy

with his wage packet at different times. These types of calculation can then be supported in principle, by direct estimates of
consumption of different commodities. All are inadequate in the
circumstances of the eighteenth and early nineteenth centuries
because of the absence of systematic data.

National income calculations are 'guestimates', like Gregory
King's of the seventeenth century, but the broad conclusions of
a trend rise are not in doubt. Price inflation during the Napoleonic Wars gave a monetary increase to the aggregate values in
current prices; but when allowance is made for this by looking
at the values in 'constant' prices, there is still no doubt about
the conclusions. Of course, this has to be seen in relation to
rising population, and when this is done, the trend of national
income per head still indicates a rise, although this is no longer
the case during the Napoleonic Wars.

These figures do not prove that the standard of living was
going up. That depended in large part on how the national income was being distributed. We know that rates of investment
were rising, with industrialization, but only gradually, probably
from below 5 per cent of the national income in the 1750's to
somewhere near 10 per cent by the 1840's. This would leave a
lesser proportion of the rising total for consumption, even though
little remains of the argument that a very steep increase in the
rate of investment at the beginning of industrialization gives a
strong *a priori* reason for anticipating a decline in consumption levels. Secondly, no firm data exist about how the proportion which was going to consumption was divided between rents,
profits, salaries and wages. Certainly it seems logical to assume
that distribution was becoming more unequal and that the
Napoleonic Wars, in particular, saw farmers, holders of government stock and receivers of profits getting a much greater share
during inflation at the expense of the wage-earners. Transfers of
income from taxation to holders of the national debt remained
important long after 1815, absorbing about £30 million per
annum.

The gradually increased share of investment and, more

importantly, the changes in the distribution of income for consumption, could easily have been sufficient to nullify this increase
in the national income *per capita* figure as far as the labouring
masses of the nation were concerned, right through to the mid-
nineteenth century. There can be no certain conclusions drawn
from these figures about what *was* happening to the standard of
living. But that is not entirely negative. The national income
was rising steeply enough to make a rise in living standards a
feasible hypothesis: it is not ruled out of court by these calculations, as similar calculations would rule it out of court for
Ireland.

Figures and graphs showing wage rates, prices and national
income figures for this period are exceedingly deceptive and
need much explanation. To start with, the phrase 'standard of
living' is an economist's concept and subject to the limitation
that the only facts caught in this net are those which may be
expressed in money terms. Much escapes. In a boom town, for
example, money wages might be very high, attracting migrants
rapidly, so that population density rapidly outstripped the provision of special capital. Housing conditions and sanitation can
deteriorate despite the upward movement of real wages – but a
smoky atmosphere, the smell of drains and a high disease rate
cannot be seen on the graphs. Economic growth is also likely to
involve the corrosion of certain cultural values; even though
one can hope that other cultural forms will emerge from the new
environment. The crofting life of the Highlands was the vehicle
for a culture. Perhaps a ballad literature, for example, can
spring only from the stony soil of a harsh material environment.
Matthew Arnold, the Lake poets, Marx, Cobbett and a host of
other, equally diverse, critics then and since, have condemned
the poverty of life in industrial Britain in cultural terms.

Most figures and graphs are inevitably national abstractions –
they conceal important differences within the national pattern,
which defy averages. Most prices, which form one half of a 'real
wages' index, are taken from the wholesale prices paid by institutions like Eton College or Chelsea Hospital, usually in the

south of England, whose records have survived. These are not
necessarily the same as weekly retail prices in south Wales or
Lancashire. The same is true of money wages, the other side of
a calculation of real wages. These varied very much in different
parts of the country and in different trades and in different years
with economic fluctuations. The figures which tend to have
survived are also weekly wage rates. These are not the same as
actual earnings or income. The real guide would be actual family
earnings over the year – the unit of domestic economy being the
household, which shares certain overheads like rent and fuel,
and can economize to some extent on clothes. But there is usually
no allowance made in the graphs, nor can there be, for unemployment and overtime (two great unknowns), or the income of
wives and children, or receipts in kind while at work (which
were very common with farm labourers). One must relate evidence to its precise context in time and place and not draw
national hypotheses from sectional evidence. This is particularly
important during a time of rapid economic expansion and structural change. More than in the centuries before the mid-
eighteenth (when less structural change was in progress), more
than after 1900 (when much greater national co-ordination
existed in trends in wages and employment) one should expect
diversity – contrasting experience between groups in different
industries, different regions, different social groups in the
period 1750–1850. Another problem of interpreting evidence
relates to its dating. Many of the most socially damaging effects
of the new industrial society came from short-term fluctuations
in economic activity. Evidence about unemployment therefore
has to be related exactly to its chronology with the trade-cycle,
investment cycle – or still the harvest cycle. It was also a time
of very little public provision mitigating the effects of these
changes.

Technical problems also exist about drawing up an index for
the cost of living. One takes a particular 'basket of goods' chosen
to represent the actual pattern of purchasing, and then sees how
this has changed its money value over the years. But patterns of
spending change and the basket of goods gets more and more
unrepresentative as an index of prices. New commodities appear;

others decline in importance. Yet if the 'weighting' of the basket
is changed, comparability is lost. Further problems relate to
spending habits. Among certain groups in society – miners,
dockers, agricultural workers, often when at a very low standard
of living with casual employment – there develop traditional,
largely inherited, patterns of expenditure for the minimal necessities of housing, clothes and food – at least in the short run.
The surplus income above that mortgaged to this traditional
'basket of goods' was often poured away in increased leisure and
liquor. This attitude, fairly common today in certain groups in
some parts of the world, could mean that a rise in prices, or a
fall in wage rates, could result in more work being done (where
more work was available) to maintain these traditional standards;
while a rise in wages could lead, in some measure, to less work
offered, extra leisure or more drunkenness. A cost of living index
and a real wage index cease to have much meaning in such circumstances. The 'basket of goods' on which the most famous
index, of Professor N. J. Silberling, is based suggests that the
'Silberling man' did not live in a house (at least he paid no rent);
he did not drink, he did not gamble and he did not smoke. He
was scarcely representative, therefore, of the English working
man.

Having issued these warnings, which become more necessary
as one goes back in time before 1800, the evidence must now
be examined to see what was happening to wages and prices.
During the eighteenth century wage rates of unskilled labourers
in agriculture in the south and west of England remained fairly
stable. The figure for Oxfordshire, for example, remained on
trend at 1s. 2d. per day from 1700 to 1770 and then rose to
another plateau of 1s. 4d. per day for the rest of the century. In
Lancashire daily wage rates began the century well below this,
between 8d. and 1s. But the important difference was that they
rose to pass the Oxfordshire figure in the course of the century.
Between 1760 and 1765 Lancashire rates rose to 1s. 6d. and rose
again to 1s. 10d. and above between 1780 and 1790. London
wage rates were higher, but more stable on average, standing
between 1s. 10d. and 2s. throughout the century. Thus the main

trend in the regional variations in wage rates was the rise of Lancashire rates, mirrored by those in other industrial centres from below the rates current in the rural south to equal the London rates between 1760 and 1790.

This is a much steeper rise than occurred in food prices. These declined on trend in the first half of the century: being a little above half in the 1740's to what they had been in the 1690's – years of war and poor harvests.

Between the 1750's and the 1790's grain prices rose again, but not to the same levels, before the outbreak of war in 1793. With this went increasing standards of consumption, clearly recorded by literary evidence. The move towards wheaten bread, away from bread of mixed grains, barley and rye, meant a move towards the most expensive grain. Costs of diet in workhouses at the end of the century, and calculations for supplementing wages by poor relief, were both calculated on the price of the wheaten loaf. The consumption of tea and sugar increased several times over during the century – sugar from 4 lb per head to 13 lb per head, despite the expansion of beer output and spirits output per head over the century as a whole, and despite the rise in price of these food articles. Most movements are most clearly marked between 1760 and 1790: virtually all excised commodities, like beer, tallow, spirits, tea, printed fabrics, soap, increased in output at a rate more than double that of the rise in numbers. Doubtless some substitution was taking place from commodities of which no production figures survive, but the conclusion of a rise in the standards of consumption seems clear.

The picture changes during the war years, between 1793 and 1815, because the gentle rise in prices, particularly food prices, then became much faster. Partly this sprang from the inflation of unconvertible paper currency but there was a steeper rise in food prices, which were the main factor in the cost of living for the labouring masses. Wheat prices, which were 47s. a quarter on average for the decade before 1793, averaged 77s. from 1793 to 1801. Between 1803 and 1813 they averaged 92s., being no less than 126s. per quarter in 1812. Although money wages rose, real wages did not fully keep up with rising prices, real wages of London artisans falling by about a quarter. Money

wages of agricultural labourers almost doubled and this particular index did keep in step with prices. All this, supported by
literary evidence, suggests deterioration: bleaker diets (but with
the poor still demanding wheat), a decline in non-food purchasing, with standards probably lower than at any other time since
the wars at the beginning of the eighteenth century.

After the coming of peace in 1815, the evidence of real wages
up to 1850 is still subject to the weakness that no allowance can
be made for unemployment, figures still being based entirely
on wage rates, not 'take-home' wages. The falseness of this
picture as an indication of the true state of affairs can be seen
from the fact that wage rates of London artisans remained
virtually static and conventional, with the tiniest upward bump
visible at the peak of the boom in 1824–5, and a scarcely visible
gradual decline in the 1830's. The index of wage rates in the
textile industry was not quite as unresponsive to events. There
was a decline at the end of the war years, a gentle decline after the
boom of the 1820's ended in 1825, but recovery in the 1830's.
Money wage rates rose save in the bad years of trade, 1841–3,
1846–7. One qualification should be made to this conclusion
for cotton operative wages. They relate to individual grades of
skill, and during this period there was an extension in the
employment of women and adolescents, whose wages were much
less, relative to those of adult men. The curve of money wage
rates in agriculture was the only series to fluctuate markedly,
showing a steep plunge in the post-war years and then violent
dips in every depression year. The reaction to the bad years
1841–3 was particularly marked.

These agricultural wages of adult men ranged between 8s. and
10s. per week in most counties, compared with wages of 18s. and
more per week in industrial unskilled employment, excluding
particular depressed groups such as the hand-loom weavers.
London skilled artisans were earning about 25s. to 40s. per week,
according to their trades, in the early nineteenth century. A
printer (or a top paper maker) was at the upper end of this
scale, a cobbler or a carpenter at the lower end. Cotton industry
wages ranged from 20s. to 25s. per week for skilled men.

The sharp declines in agricultural wage rates in bad times

underline the conclusion that agriculture was the great reservoir of marginal producers, having much less resistance to adverse movements in the labour market than wages in the expanding industrial areas. The new money-wage standards were being set here, as they were in the eighteenth century. Equally, in the industrial counties agricultural wages were being boosted by industrial competition in the labour market. In 1837, for example, agricultural wages in Cheshire and most of the northern counties were 12s. per week; but in counties like Devon, Dorset or Wiltshire 8s. and below. The sharp dip in the 1840's showed that even the rewards of those who stayed on the land were protected by the departure of migrants thence to industry (both by their removal from the agricultural labour market and in their continuing demand for food). The severe crisis of 1841–3 in industry stopped this migration movement. Immediately the reaction on agricultural wages was sharp. That is to say, the dynamics of the labour market were being set by industry. It is on the land, too, that stark hunger riots spread in 1812, 1816, 1830–1, and where the greatest intensity of poverty existed – apart from groups of operatives clinging to handicraft skills doomed by advancing technology. This certainly gives the lie to critics who expressed their hostility to the rising industrial world by painting an idealized romantic vision of rural life.

One can follow lower wage rates with the migrants from agriculture into occupations of easy entry in the urban, industrial world; builders' labourers, sawyers, domestic service, dock labour, hand-loom weaving – where there were no barriers of skills to be overcome, or very low ones. In contrast to this the adult male spinners in Lancashire or the iron-foundry, copper and tin-plate workers in south Wales were protected by their skill and experience from the immediate impact of migrant labour from agriculture and thus had higher and more stable wage rates.

The conclusion to be drawn from wage rate movements is that earning power, within each grade and sector of the economy, was more dependent on variations in the volume of employment available, and on variations in prices, than on changes in wage rates. No exact, quantifiable indication of unemployment is available, and the figures do not exist yet to be able to make an index of the volume of employment. But the crucial variations seem to lie in the cost of living over time, even if the 'basket' of goods whose prices are being analysed for change over time is a little unreal. The big swings in prices are apparent. The index of London prices, the cost of living index of the Silberling man, the price of a 4-lb loaf in London, all tell broadly the same tale because food prices were the most important single constituents in the cost of living.

A great post-war fall in prices occurred, greater even than the extent of the fall in the money wages of agricultural labourers. A lesser rise and fall took place in the 1820's; similarly in the 1830's. From 1835 followed a fairly sharp rise to 1840, with rising grain prices, then a fall again in the early forties. When this steeply moving price level is translated against fairly constant wage rates, ignoring fluctuations in employment, real wages come to depend almost completely on changes in prices. The real wage index of London artisans thus becomes virtually a mirror image, the inverted curve, of the cost of living index. The conclusion is interesting, however. As far as the London artisans are concerned, it suggests the title of the 'Hungry Thirties' rather than the 'Hungry Forties', because this was the decade when living standards were sapped most by rising prices, after a similar episode during the Napoleonic Wars. The point was essentially one of food supplies. The very high prices in agriculture during the wars had induced such a great expansion in capacity that there was relative over-production, in conjunction with imports, for a generation. By 1836–7 the expansion in population had once more caught up with the supply of food and prices moved up once more. Even wage rates in agriculture responded a little to this. Possibly, too, very heavy fixed investment in railways, mines and factories caused some little inflation in these years.

In some years all these conclusions were nullified by heavy unemployment: 1816, 1819, 1826–7, 1830–1, 1842–3. As industrialization gathered weight so a regular cyclical pattern of boom and slump strengthened. There was said to be 60 per cent unemployment in Bolton in 1842, an astonishing figure; but also astonishing was how quickly intense depression came and departed in the cotton industry. Where periods of cheap food coincided with good employment – as in 1821–6, 1832–6, 1842–6, 1848–50 – almost all groups in society advanced, in those things that could be measured.

Can one hope to draw conclusions about the changes in the standard of living between 1790 and 1850? There is no agreement now; there has been no agreement by contemporaries arguing ever since those days. Both sides agree that after 1850 the national income was expanding so fast that, even with wider gaps between rich and poor probably developing, the poor were benefiting from the expanding economy and industrialization – again in those things that could be measured.

The lack of a consensus means that one cannot yet speak with confidence of a single entity, 'the national economy', as far as the standard of living is concerned. The question is whether the hand-loom weaver was more representative than the adult in the factories who maintained wages in the face of falling prices. Is the bad year 1842 more typical than the good year of 1845? A lot of evidence, favourable and unfavourable, depends on these two questions: which sector of the economy does it apply to, and to which particular year?

The worst evils, short-term unemployment and technological unemployment, were acute problems, almost the economic antithesis of the chronic disease of underemployment on the land. But this was still an unsatisfied society as violent social protests repeatedly made clear, whether of Luddites smashing machines in industry in 1812; agrarian violence in 1816 and 1830; Peterloo in 1819; the Rebecca Riots of 1838–9 and Chartism – even if these protests were involved with very much more than movements in the long-term standard of living.

But continuing debate today means that probably no marked general change took place, certainly no *general* movement towards deterioration, such as occurred between 1795 and 1815 from war inflation and high food prices and a shift in distribution of income away from wage-earners. This absence of drama in turn may be considered very dramatic given the increase in the population that had to be supported – from under 9 million to over 14 million in these 60 years after 1790; given the tragedy being played out in the non-industrial Ireland, and given the fact that the economic system, consolidated in this period, was going to pay off in increasing material benefits for all after 1850.

Reading list

POPULATION

(i) *Malthus*

COONTZ, S. H. *Population Theories and the Economic Interpretation*, London, 1957.

EVERSLEY, D. E. C. *Social Theories of Fertility and the Malthusian Debate*, Oxford, 1959, ch. 9.

GLASS, D. V. (ed.) *An Introduction to Malthus*, London, 1953 [esp. chapter by H. L. Beales].

MALTHUS, T. R. *First Essay on Population* [1798], reprinted London, 1926.

MCCLEARY, G. F. *The Malthusian Population Theory*, London, 1953.

SMITH, K. *The Malthusian Controversy*, London, 1951.

SPENGLER, J. J. 'Malthus's total population theory: a restatement and reappraisal', *Canadian Journal of Economics and Political Science*, 1945, **11,** nos. 1, 2.

(ii) *Population and economic growth*

CHAMBERS, J. D. 'Population change in a provincial town: Nottingham, 1700–1800', in L. S. Pressnell (ed.), *Studies in the Industrial Revolution*, London, 1960.

CHAMBERS, J. D. *The Vale of Trent, 1670–1800: a regional study of economic change*, London–New York, 1957.

CIPOLLA, C. M. *The Economic History of World Population*, Harmondsworth, 1962.

CONNELL, K. H. 'Some unsettled problems in English and Irish population history, 1750–1840', *Irish Historical Studies*, 1951, **7,** no. 28.

CONNELL, K. H. *The Population of Ireland, 1750–1845*, Oxford, 1950.

GLASS, D. V. & EVERSLEY, D. E. C. *Population in History: essays in historical demography*, London, 1965, chs. 2, 4, 7, 9, 10, 15, 17.

HABAKKUK, H. J. 'Population problems and European economic development in the late 18th and 19th centuries', *American Economic Review*, 1963, **53**, no. 1.

HOLLINGSWORTH, T. H. 'A demographic study of the British ducal families', *Population Studies*, 1957, **11**, no. 1.

HOLLINGSWORTH, T. H. 'The demography of the British peerage', *Population Studies*, 1964, **18**, no. 2, supplement.

JONES, E. L. & MINGAY, G. E. (eds.) *Land, Labour and Population in the Industrial Revolution*, London, 1967; New York, 1968 [articles by J. T. Krause and P. E. Razzell].

KRAUSE, J. T. 'Changes in English fertility and mortality, 1781–1850', *Economic History Review*, 2nd series, 1958, **11**, no. 1.

KRAUSE, J. T. 'Some implications of recent work in historical demography', *Comparative Studies in History and Society*, 1959, **1**, Jan.

KRAUSE, J. T. 'Some neglected factors in the English industrial revolution', *Journal of Economic History*, 1959, **19**, no. 4.

MCKEOWN, T. & BROWN, R. G. 'Reasons for the decline in mortality . . . in the 19th century', *Population Studies*, 1962, **16**, pt. 2.

RAZZELL, P. E. 'Population change in 18th-century England: a reinterpretation', *Economic History Review*, 2nd series, 1965, **18**, no. 2.

REDFORD, A. *Labour Migration in England, 1800–1850*, 2nd ed. revised by W. H. Chaloner, Manchester, 1964.

TUCKER, G. S. L. 'English pre-industrial revolution population trends', *Economic History Review*, 2nd series, 1963, **16**, no. 2.

WRIGLEY, E. A. 'Family limitation in pre-industrial England', *Economic History Review*, 2nd series, 1966, **19**, no. 1.

WRIGLEY, E. A. (ed.) *An Introduction to English Historical Demography from the 16th to the 19th Century*, London, 1966.

CONDITIONS OF WORK AND SOCIAL ATTITUDES

BENDIX, R. *Work and Authority in Industry: ideologies of management in the course of industrialization*, New York–London, 1956, pt. I.

BLAUG, M. 'The myth of the old poor law and the making of the new', *Journal of Economic History*, 1963, **23**, no. 2.

BLAUG, M. 'The Poor Law Report re-examined', *Journal of Economic History*, 1964, XXIV.

COATS, A. W. 'Changing attitudes to labour in the mid-18th century', *Economic History Review*, 2nd series, 1958, **11**, no. 1.

COATS, A. W. 'Economic thought and poor law policy in the eighteenth century', *Economic History Review*, 1960, XIII.

COATS, A. W. 'The classical economists and the labourer', in E. L. Jones & G. E. Mingay (eds.), *Land, Labour and Population in the Industrial Revolution*, London, 1967; New York, 1968.

COLEMAN, D. C. 'Labour in the English economy of the 17th century', *Economic History Review*, 2nd series, 1956, **8**, no. 3; reprinted in E. M. Carus-Wilson (ed.), *Essays in Economic History*, vol. 2, London, 1962.

EDEN, F. M. *State of the Poor* [London], 1797, ed. A. G. L. Rogers, London, 1928.

HAYEK, F. A. (ed.) *Capitalism and the Historians: essays* by T. S. Ashton, L. M. Hacker, W. H. Hutt, B. de Jouvenel, London, 1954.

HECHT, J. J. *The Domestic Servant Class in 18th-century England*, London, 1956.

MARSHALL, J. D. *The Old Poor Law, 1795–1834*, London, 1968.

MARSHALL, D. *The English Poor in the 18th Century: a study in social and administrative history*, London, 1926.

MARSHALL, D. 'The old poor law', *Economic History Review*, 1937, VIII.

PINCHBECK, I. *Women Workers in the Industrial Revolution, 1750–1850*, London, 1930.

SMELSER, N. *Social Change in the Industrial Revolution: an application of theory to the British cotton industry*, Chicago, 1959.

STANDARDS OF LIVING

ASHTON, T. S. 'Changes in the standard of comfort in 18th-century England', *Proceedings of the British Academy*, 1955, **41**.

ASHTON, T. S. 'The standard of life of the workers in England, 1790–1830', *Journal of Economic History*, 1949, supplement; reprinted in F. A. von Hayek (ed.), *Capitalism and the Historians*, London, 1954.

COLLIER, F. *The Family Economy of the Working Classes in the Cotton Industry, 1784–1833*, ed. R. S. Fitton, thesis, Manchester [1964].

DRUMMOND, SIR J. C. & WILBRAHAM, A. *The Englishman's Food: a history of five centuries of English diet*, London, 1939.

HAMMOND, J. L. 'The industrial revolution and discontent', *Economic History Review*, 1930, **2**, no. 2.

HARTWELL, R. M. 'The rising standard of living in England, 1800–1850', *Economic History Review*, 2nd series, 1961, **13**, no. 3.

HOBSBAWM, E. J. 'The British standard of living, 1790–1850', *Economic History Review*, 2nd series, 1957, **10**, no. 1.

HOBSBAWM, E. J. & HARTWELL, R. M. 'The standard of living during the industrial revolution: a discussion', *Economic History Review*, 2nd series, 1963, **16**, no. 1.

NEALE, R. S. 'The standard of living, 1780–1844: a regional and class study', *Economic History Review*, 2nd series, 1966, **19**, no. 3.

POLLARD, S. 'Investment, consumption and the industrial revolution', *Economic History Review*, 2nd series, 1958, **11**, no. 2.

TAYLOR, A. J. 'Progress and poverty in Britain, 1780–1850', *History*, 1960, **45**, no. 153; reprinted in E. M. Carus-Wilson (ed.), *Essays in Economic History*, **3**, London, 1962.

TAYLOR, P. A. M. (ed.) *The Industrial Revolution: triumph or disaster?*, Boston [1958].

WILLIAMS, J. E. 'The British standard of living, 1750–1850', *Economic History Review*, 2nd series, 1966, **19**, no. 3.

7 Economic fluctuations

The process of economic change in Britain, as elsewhere, has not been steady but subject to unbalance and fluctuation. Analysing the nature of these economic fluctuations is important in itself; but also gives insights into the process of growth, the changing structure of the economy and the social hardships brought by industrialization and economic change.

Fluctuations and cycles can be of two kinds for the economy. Some result from forces inherent in the economic process itself, which operate in a cyclical way. Some of these are internal to the national economy, some impinge upon it from the international context – and both internal and external pressures interact. But economic history is not a self-contained system which operates under the stimuli of just economic pressures. It is also concerned with the economic and social consequences of the historical process as a whole. Some of the pressures which create fluctuations are 'autonomous', being imposed on the economy from causes which are not inherent within the economic process.

The greatest of these was probably war.[1] In foreign trade war could kill or create a market. Capturing a French sugar island could make prices tumble and set off a series of pulsations in markets. Napoleon's Continental System sealed the north European market, so that a surge of activity resulted in 1814–15 when the bulging warehouses could at last discharge their contents. When the navy had swept French merchant shipping from the seas, other distant markets might prosper as merchants sought new outlets, as with the South American boom of 1807–8, when the famous ice-skates were sent to Rio. Internally, government boosted the demand for iron, so that peace brought over-capacity and a painful time of re-adjustment when the building of new

---

[1] See above, pp. 43–7.

plant temporarily stopped. Equally, peace might bring back prosperity to some consumer goods industries like brewing and milling, where mass consumption had been sapped by high wartime taxation. Construction industries also received a boost when the government moved out of the loan market after a war, and the rate of interest fell, which encouraged borrowing in industries heavily dependent upon credit for mortgages. Very close links existed in the eighteenth century between government loans for war, a high rate of interest and depression in building. Bad news from the front or a naval defeat could also induce a wave of panic in banking and the money markets, as in 1745, or 1793, or 1797.

From 1815 to 1914, however, war became an infrequent and minor factor in setting up these pulsations, so that the rhythms inherent in the economic processes themselves were dominant. During the Crimean War government spending in the years 1854–6 did outrun income from taxes by over £30 million so a considerable boost was given to the economy in that year, particularly to demand for shipping and the heavy industries. Rearmament, especially naval ship-building, had a similar effect after 1900, but was more sustained.

More important than war, however, as a creator of fluctuations were the harvests. In the eighteenth century and in the first half of the nineteenth century the most potentially powerful agents of fluctuations were the elements themselves. Professor Ashton has remarked: 'What was happening at Westminster or in the City was of small account compared with what was happening in the heavens.'[1] And again, as with war, no regularity existed in the cyclical rhythm stemming from harvest fluctuations. One would expect the variation in food prices and farmers' incomes to be one of the most important sources of economic fluctuations at a time when agriculture was the greatest single component, either more or less directly, in the national income, the largest industry by its capital and its labour force, and when two-thirds or three-quarters of the purchasing power of the masses of the nation was mortgaged to buying food and drink.

How did harvests affect the economic flow? First came their

[1] T. S. Ashton, *Economic Fluctuations in England, 1700–1800*, p. 2.

internal effects on purchasing power. The demand for food-stuffs, particularly grain, was very inelastic: demand did not fall off very much even when prices rose sharply. People still had to eat, so that food was the last thing they could economize on. Equally in a year of glut demand did not increase much for grain, even though prices were very low, because there is a limit to the amount of bread people will and can eat. Demand was much more variable for the more expensive sorts of food like meat, butter or fruit. A relatively small movement in the amount of grain coming on the market, in these conditions of demand, thus had an exaggerated effect on the movement of grain prices: price swings remained much more dramatic than the fluctuations in the yield of crops in the fields. The farmers looked forward unashamedly to a short harvest; Cobbett spoke of 'the dreadful evils of abundance' and the toast on his travels in 1821 was always, 'Here's to another war or a bad harvest.'

When food cost more, less was left over in the family budget to spend on other things, particularly clothes, which probably took up the next largest fraction of purchasing power devoted to commodities. Hence it was very usual for a crisis in internal demand to face the textile market after a bad harvest, and for home sales to turn up in a year of glut. A standard proverb in Bradford in the nineteenth century was, 'When the poor live cheaply, they clothe well.' Alexander Somervell was brought up in a desperately poor Scottish family at the beginning of the nineteenth century and wrote about this as follows: '. . . the chief reason for my not being sent sooner to school, I believe, was the want of clothes . . . something else than rags, and these were not to be had until 1818 when markets fell and food being cheaper it became possible to get clothes.'[1] In this way a bad harvest brought a considerable redistribution of purchasing power towards agriculture – or towards the farmers explicitly in the short run, not to landlords or labourers. Some of this flow was sterilized by being saved, or hoarded underneath the traditional mattress; some was diverted into other channels of expenditure by the farmers about their farms, or elsewhere (there were always complaints that farmers' daughters were

[1] *Autobiography of a Working Man*, p. 13.

being brought up like debutantes at these times). What found its way back into the economic system via deposits in country banks or direct spending did so only after an interval, and in different channels. The distortions away from the normal flows of purchasing power still occurred.

Bad harvests also had parallel effects in the international economy through the need to import corn in a bad year after the 1760's. Until the mid-nineteenth century this corn-trade was irregular, mainly from the Baltic, and because of its sporadic nature a sudden wave of grain imports tended to be paid for largely in bullion. £10 million in gold supposedly flowed out of the country in 1838 to pay for grain – and grain caused a greater fluctuation in the balance of trade position than any other commodity. A sudden leap in import values meant that some purchasing power which would have been devoted to home products was spent on imports, causing a deflationary effect at once on home demand. This was, of course, the same sort of income effect as the internal redistribution of income, but the farmers receiving the purchasing power were in another country. However, when the payments were in gold another monetary effect was added to the 'drain' abroad. An outflow of gold from circulation and from the reserves of the banking system put pressure on the entire financial structure of the country. Note issues were cut back as the bullion base of the circulating media contracted; bankers pulled in loans to cover their shrinking reserves; the Bank of England put up its discount rate – bank rate – to protect its own reserves. The other side of the wave, when prices fell again, could bring distorting effects as well. Many corn merchants would be caught with stocks they had bought at the high price. As they went bankrupt the banks that were crediting them got squeezed. If any of the banks declared bankruptcy this could set off a loss of confidence generally in the banking system, and a collapse of credit in the economy as a whole. This sequence was played out in the last of the great harvest crises in 1847; one set of problems being created by the great potato famine and grain-shortage year of 1845-6; followed by a Liverpool corn merchant and banking panic in 1847 when corn prices fell. The uneven rhythm of harvest crises can be traced throughout the eighteenth century: 1710, 1725, 1767, 1773, 1783, 1792–3, 1795–6, 1799–1800.

In one other sense it is possible to see longer swings originating in agricultural prices, through which distortions in the pattern of investment in the economy occurred. The period 1793–1813, for example, was one of high grain prices on trend, with restricted imports and poor harvests. Poor real wage levels were associated with a tremendous switch of resources to agricultural investment. Over-capacity then resulted which, with a better run of harvests on average and easier corn-imports, took until 1835–6 to work off, the period 1814–35 being one of low grain prices on trend, depression and little investment in agriculture. This was brought to an end by the continuing rise in population finally outrunning capacity in agriculture once more. But such a longer phasing of fluctuations in farming is more properly an investment cycle, inherent within the process of expansion in this sector of the economy, rather than a short-term harvest cycle round a stable trend, imposed upon farming by the weather.

From the mid-nineteenth century onwards, the influence of the harvest diminished relatively as a main cause of economic fluctuations and social hardships. Its power died as the stake that agriculture had in the economy shrank and as the power of cyclical influences stemming from trade and industry became relatively more powerful. The international effect of food imports also changed when they became established on a more regular basis, from several non-European countries.[1] Then the mounting values were not settled by an export of bullion, but became part of a regular trading system. Purchases of foodstuffs from non-European countries intensified under free-trade conditions after 1840. These regular food imports then became a spur to the general expansion of the economy, as much of these sterling credits earned by foreign countries by their sales of food to Britain became, in turn, available for purchasing British exports. Before the 1840's this was just a sporadic trade, depending on the hazard of whether the harvest was good or bad in Britain – and the imports were largely paid for in gold. Much

[1] See Table 22, p. 473.

of this was hoarded, or at least returned very slowly into the international economy so that the net effects of corn imports to Britain, coupled with high internal food prices, were very deflationary. Corn caused greater short-term fluctuations in the balance of payments than any other commodity in British foreign trade in the period 1770–1850.

Trade

The second main source of fluctuations was the process of foreign trade itself, quite apart from the impact of war or political disturbance on it. And as the stake that foreign trade had in the national income expanded with the change in structure of the economy, so the British economy became more exposed to the inherent periodicity involved. This 'trade cycle', or inventory cycle, had a duration of between 4 and 7 years. It existed also in internal trade, but historically this was much more difficult to measure.

When conditions in trade were good manufacturers and merchants were tempted to enlarge their production and their consignments. Much might be sent as speculative consignments, rather than for orders on firm contracts. In the conditions of the time, without telegraph or cable communication before the 1860's, markets could change radically in the long-distance trades between the time when orders were placed and when the ships arrived. All the hazards of crop failure, war, revolution and famine could affect the foreign customer. And when income conditions changed in Britain, from several causes, this affected demand for imports quickly and dramatically, and, through this fluctuation, the purchasing power available abroad for buying British goods was affected. Once warehouses were glutted for any of these reasons, it took time for stocks to be cleared. Meanwhile prices slackened, orders for more deliveries dried up, would-be buyers held off from the markets hoping that prices might fall even lower, and this fall in trading activity was quickly reflected back to produce a fall in production in those industries working for export markets. With profits reduced and sales dragging, industrialists had neither the incentive nor the means to expand their plant in these years; they did not take investment decisions. This itself had important consequences. If production had to be cut down or wages lowered the effects spread out into the national economy by a decline in purchasing power and spending from the families affected by the shortage of employment.

When stocks had run down the reverse sequence would ensue. Demand and prices picked up, confidence and optimism returned. Buyers became more active, thinking that prices were on the way up if they held off. When the ripples of the trading revival reached manufacturers they expanded production. The volume of employment increased, perhaps wage rates rose if labour became short, both effects expanding internal purchasing power. With prices moving up and production expanding, profits increased. This gave industrialists the resources to think about increasing capacity by installing more plant and building more factories, while prevailing trade gave them the confidence to want to do it. If this revival was sufficiently strong and sustained it would outrun their existing capacity; they would order more machines; put up more buildings; need more transport. This would bring another rhythm into play: the investment cycle.

Just as an increase in imports could produce, in the short-run, a deflationary effect in the economy, equally an export boom could inject extra purchasing power into the economy. Making the exports created wages, but the goods produced by this labour did not absorb purchasing power on the home market but went abroad. This is a stimulating process for demand. It might also result in an inflow of bullion which could have a stimulating effect on enlarging the circulating media and bank credit.

W. W. Rostow believes that an export boom pulled the British economy out of almost every depression in the nineteenth century by boosting home demand in this way. This certainly was important when considering British trading relations with the United States. Here was a sophisticated trading economy subject to its own cyclical pressures, and the extent of the 1836 boom in foreign trade and the 1841 slump were magnified just because British responses fed into these American fluctuations and deepened their rhythm. But many other economies were primarily linked just to Britain in their external relations. Their purchases of British goods could be very dependent on the quantities and prices of their sales to Britain. When fluctuations in purchasing power within Britain affected these sales, then British exports to them would react in consequence. Hence in these markets a boom in British exports to them might be the echo of an import boom in their sales to Britain. The importance of the cyclical nature of expansion in foreign trade for the British economy is revealed by the proportion of production destined for export in some major industries – probably more than half of all textiles, except for silk, linen and jute; possibly more than half of output of the Sheffield and Birmingham trades. The latter two groups of industries were particularly dependent on the United States market in the first half of the nineteenth century. And this was subject to very wide swings in values. Exports to the United States totalled £12½ million in value in 1836, at the peak of the boom of the 1830's, and under £5 million in 1837. This degree of fluctuation brought intense distress to particular areas of the country. So localized were some of the textile and hardware trades in particular that one village might specialize in the production of a particular kind of blanket or watch-spring and sprocket, or a particular kind of knife blade destined for one particular foreign market. National averages of unemployment rates, national aggregates in the values of total foreign trade could therefore mask dramatic local variations.

Investment

The third main source of fluctuations, also deepening as the process of industrialization intensified, was that of investment. Capital goods industries, such as coal, iron, ship-building, construction, machine-building, the engineering industries of all kinds, stood at the back of the consumer-goods industries, such as food processing and textiles. They were dependent for a large part of their prosperity on orders flowing from manufacturers in the consumer-goods industries and from general demands for investment in housing and transport and public utilities of different kinds. Durable consumers' goods demand (for housing, or pots and pans) falling on the capital goods industries, was postponable in bad times.

Manufacturers' demands, to take one side of this, tended to cluster at the peak of their trade cycle, when returns were good, profits buoyant and confidence high. A trade boom could therefore lead into an investment boom. Projecting many investment schemes, such as domestic housing, canals and railways, or public utilities, meant heavy reliance upon pre-mobilized capital; from mortgages in the case of house-building or from publicly-sold shares in the case of transport and mining (which was also a joint-stock affair to a large extent). This at once linked their timing to the cost and availability of credit – to the state of the money market and the Stock Exchange. Here another pressure added to the violence of the swings: speculation. In the peak of a boom optimism led to a general lowering of critical standards by people offering credit and seeking outlets for capital. Bankers accepted bills of exchange of doubtful probity, some of them 'accommodation bills' not representing real transactions at all. Merchants discounted bills, and then discounted the lading lists for the same cargoes. On the Stock Exchange the sharks moved in with bogus companies, patents for perpetual motion and other fraudulent schemes. Persons came into the market to play for capital gains, ready to jump out again as soon as prices showed any hesitation. When the smash came investors were scared out of the market for some years. Initially, in the rush for liquidity, interest rates leapt, credit vanished, share prices slumped. No canal or railway projectors could then get a scheme launched.

Confidence, cheap credit, good profits, high demand meant that the trade cycle and the investment cycle (as far as the *projecting* of investment was concerned) were locked together, although every trade boom did not trigger off an investment boom. Fluctuations affecting trade and purchasing power got reflected with a multiplier effect upon the capital goods industries, and as the investment cycle was longer in its rhythm than the trade cycle so it was more intense in its effects on these industries. In turn, because many of the goods they turned out did not enter immediately into consumption, they did not mop up purchasing power. The purchasing power created by wages

in the investment industries therefore had a multiplied effect
on boosting demand in the other consumer goods industries;
and a reverse depression effect on demand when the investment
goods industries were slack and not generating a high volume of
wages.

This was the pattern in abstract. As the weight of the basic
industries developed in the economy, their markets being primarily internal ones, so the fluctuations inherent in their process
of growth got more powerful. They were of small account in
the early eighteenth century, by 1841–2 they were rivalling
trade in intensity; by the end of the nineteenth century, and in
the inter-war period, investment fluctuations had become the
crux of the problem of unemployment to which Keynes turned.
Thus 'major' cycles were marked by boom in investment projects, and their slumps by unemployment and slack in the basic
industries.

Investment booms can be traced back to the eighteenth
century: 1791–3 for canals; in 1809 a 'boomlet'; 1825, 1836,
1845, 1854, 1866, 1872. Depressions in the basic industries
centred on 1816, 1826–7, 1842–3, 1848–9. Iron prices and the
phasing of expansion in the iron industry marched step by step
with these waves of investment decisions, particularly in railways during 1830–50. The intensity of the 1842–3 depression,
possibly the worst two years in the whole century after the
famine that opened it, was explained by the fact that internal
demand had collapsed through the investment cycle at the same
time as depression had come in foreign trade. The investment
cycle was at its low point as a result of the maturing of the main
investment projects carried through the 1836 boom. No railways were being projected or built in 1842–3. For the first time
textile manufacturers found that sales did not respond at all to
cuts in prices. Britain climbed out of this deep depression
through a revival in foreign markets and a series of good harvests, which triggered off another investment boom, as full
employment once more inflated internal demand. Investment
booms at this time tended to be killed off by mania in the Stock
Exchange, a crisis of confidence and a shortage of ready cash to
pay the first instalments on shares purchased. Most sound pro-

jects which did get through seemed to face relatively little further trouble over shortage of capital to complete the projects, or shortage of any of the materials or labour needed to carry them out. The ceiling of a boom in investment in the twentieth century is often thought to be some physical bottleneck in capacity of investment industries or labour supply at the height of it. These do not appear to have set the limits before the mid-nineteenth century.

The construction industries moved contra-cyclically with textiles in the late 1830's and 1840's, apart from 1841-3. If, from the working of economic forces, the depression phase had coincided in both foreign trade and investment cycles in 1848; if 300,000 families had been sustained by railway employment, (with the iron, coal and construction industries also slack), the political consequences might have been more dramatic than they were. Despite very high local unemployment rates, in the years of depression, recovery from the trade cycle in industries which were expanding on trend proved rapid so that personal savings might go some way towards tiding families over the fairly short gap. Economic fluctuations had a pronounced influence on labour organization. In the early part of the century the upswing of the cycle brought wide organization, attempts to found national unions and the assembling of strike funds. As effective instruments these almost all collapsed at the first touch of depression. Only the most favourable conditions in the labour market allowed them brief continuity. Depression years saw a swing towards the political expression of dissatisfaction in the first part of the nineteenth century and to what Dr Hobsbawm has called 'collective bargaining by riot'. In the latter part of the nineteenth century the deepening rhythm of investment depressions meant that miners and iron and steel workers might be slack for months or years at a time. When the boom came, of course, expansion could be feverish and the miners drank champagne, as in 1872. But intervening years of attrition helped to make the miners' trade unions the most radical in their demands for protection against natural economic forces. It is not coincidental that the main demands for limitation of production, work quotas, minimum wages, after 1870, should come from organized labour facing the problems of the investment cycle. The bitterest strikes, and the highest incidence of violence over labour troubles, also occurred in these investment industries.

Of course, all these swings in activity were on a rising long-term trend. Over-capacity was worked off by rising population, rising demand coming from a rising national income. When new bursts of trade and investment occurred they took production to much higher levels. But possibly the fact that expansion was an unstable, jerky affair increased the pace of the process, both as far as foreign markets were concerned in the trade cycle, and as far as the expansion of capacity was concerned in the investment cycle. If so, this is yet another example of the general truth that economic gains were so often made, in the short run, at the expense of social gains in the nineteenth century. At every point the problems of short run economic fluctuations rested upon the fundamental forces operating for long-run economic expansion.

Reading list

ASHTON, T. S. *Economic fluctuations in England, 1700–1800*, Oxford, 1959.

BEVERIDGE, SIR WILLIAM. 'The trade cycle in Britain before 1850', *Oxford Economic Papers*, 1940, no. 3.

COONEY, E. W. 'Long waves in building in the British economy in the 19th century', *Economic History Review*, 2nd series, 1960, **13**, no. 2.

GAYER, A. D., ROSTOW, W. W. & SCHWARTZ, A. J., with the assistance of FRANK, I. *The Growth and Fluctuation of the British Economy, 1790–1850: an historical, statistical and theoretical study of Britain's economic development*, 2 vols, Oxford, 1953.

HABAKKUK, H. J. 'Fluctuations in house-building in Britain and the USA in the 19th century', *Journal of Economic History*, 1962, **22**, no. 2.

HALL, A. R. 'Long waves in building in the British economy of the 19th century: a comment', *Economic History Review*, 2nd series, 1961, **14**, no. 2.

HOBSBAWM, E. J. 'Economic fluctuations and some social movements since 1800', *Economic History Review*, 2nd series, 1952, **5,** no. 1.

HUGHES, J. R. T. *Fluctuations in Trade, Industry and Finance: a study of British economic development, 1850–1860*, Oxford, 1960.

MATTHEWS, R. C. O. *A Study in Trade-cycle History: economic fluctuations in Great Britain, 1833–1842*, Cambridge, 1954.

MATTHEWS, R. C. O. *The Trade Cycle*, Cambridge, 1959 (Cambridge Economic Handbooks).

MATTHEWS, R. C. O. 'The trade cycle in Great Britain, 1790–1850', *Oxford Economic Papers*, new series, 1954, **6,** no. 1.

ROSTOW, W. W. *British Economy of the 19th Century: essays*, Oxford, 1938, chs I, II, V, VI.

SAUL, S. B. 'House building in England, 1890–1914', *Economic History Review*, 2nd series, 1962, **15,** no. 1.

THOMAS, B. *Migration and Economic Growth: a study of Great Britain and the Atlantic economy*, Cambridge, 1954 [for 19th century] (National Institute of Economic and Social Research: *Economic and Social Studies*, no. 12).

TOOKE, T. & NEWMARCH, W. *History of Prices and of the State of Circulation from 1793 (to the present time)*, 6 vols, London, 1838–1857.

WARD-PERKINS, C. N. 'The commercial crisis of 1847', *Oxford Economic Papers*, new series, 1950, **2,** no. 1.

PART II

The evolving industrial economy: to 1914

8 The century ahead—changing structure of the British economy

The broad perspectives of change in the economy are most usefully summarized by statistics and charts – although these shorthand ways of stating what happened cannot directly answer the questions how they happened or why they happened.

Table IV(a) shows, broadly, movements in national income. The figures for 1900–9, 1945–54 are the annual averages for

TABLE IV: *The changing economic structure of Great Britain*

(*a*) *National income of United Kingdom* (constant prices 1865–85)

1801	£190 m.	£12 per head U.K.
1851	£560 m.	£20 ,, ,, ,,
1900–9	£2,081 m.	£49 ,, ,, ,,
1945–54	£3,750 m.	£75 ,, ,, ,,
(1945–54 current prices)	£10,750 m.	(£215) ,, ,, ,,

(This table does not indicate changes in the standard of living because no indication is given about distribution of the national income between consumption and investment; between wages, salaries, profits and rents etc.)

(*b*) *Structure of national product of Great Britain* (as percentages of national income). Share of government, defence, domestic service etc. not separately shown.

	Agriculture, forestry, fishing	Manufactures, mining, building	Trade, transport
1801	34	28	16
1851	21	40	19
1907	6	37	28
1935	4	35	28
1955	5	50	25

TABLE IV—*continued*
(*c*) *Distribution of the population of England and Wales by occupation*

	1831	*1951*
Agriculture and fishing	34%	5%
Trade, manufactures, handicrafts	46·5%	60%
Others, not in these 2 categories	19·5%	35%

(*d*) *Dependence of Great Britain on imports*

	Population m.	*Ratio of value of retained imports to National Income*
1688	7·4	$5\frac{1}{2}\%$
1820	20·9	12%
1850	27·4	18%
1900	41·5	26%
1951	50·2	32%

(*e*) *Composition of Great Britain's exports as a percentage of total exports*

	Manufactured exports	*Textiles*	*Metals and engineering*	*Coal*
1830	91	67	11	1
1850	93	63	18	2
1870	91	56	21	3
1913	79	34	27	10
1937	78	24	35	7
1951	88	19	49	1

(*f*) *Composition of Great Britain's imports as a percentage of total imports*

	Food and livestock Total	(*grain*)	*Raw materials* Total	(*for textiles*)	*Finished manufactured goods*
1820	31	(4)	60	(24)	9
1850	34	(10)	59	(32)	7
1870	35	(9)	50	(28)	15
1900	42	(9)	39	(16)	19
1913	37	(9)	43	(17)	20
1933	46	(8)	41	(13)	13

After E. A. G. Robinson, 'Changing Structure of the British Economy', *Economic Journal*, 1954.

these decades, expressed in constant prices to give valid comparisons avoiding monetary differences. The latter figure is given at current prices also, which shows the degree of monetary inflation since 1914 – almost entirely a phenomenon of the two world wars and the post-1945 period. The national product was growing most rapidly in the second half of the nineteenth century; and it also in this period that the standard of living was advancing most definitely – a conclusion that must be remembered through all the discussions of the slowing down in the rate of growth of industrial output, the problems of advancing competitors abroad and the dangers of a maturing economy at home that became more and more insistent after the 1870's.

Some more positive content is given to this by Table IV(b), which shows that many of the trends emerging in the late eighteenth century and early nineteenth century carry on into the twentieth. The most marked of these has been the sustained decline in the relative proportion of the national income going to primary production in agriculture, fishing and forestry. Proportionately the most rapid redistribution here came in the second part of the nineteenth century, with a decline from 21 per cent to 6 per cent between 1851 and the first census of production in 1907.

In looking at the increase of other sectors it may well be that the 40 per cent in manufacturing shown in 1851 is an overstatement. But perhaps not. One of the remarkable things about the redeployment of the national income and the employed population in the later stages of industrialization is that the 'tertiary' sector – trade and services – often grows more rapidly than the 'secondary' industries – manufacturing. The 'services' in question are partly services directly supporting industry: transport, trade, banking, insurance, finance, commercial services concerning the City. Apart from servicing British trade, and quite a lot of the trade of the rest of the world, a great deal of activity here flowed in the wake of the export of capital. Capital was flowing abroad at a greater rate than it was being invested at home in some years after 1850, and the more rapid rise in national income from trade, transport, and 'tertiary' industry than manufacturing industry is partly a consequence of this. Other 'services' increasing rapidly in the last hundred years were not so closely linked with the productive side of the economy: government employees nationally and locally, social services like health and education, the entertainment industries.

The share of trade and transport, which increased at a faster rate than secondary industry, reflected the enormous outlays going into the railway system, and the enormous expansion of world trade after the 1840's, a very high proportion of which was being carried in British ships. Equating the balance of payments with the growth of trade reveals exactly how important shipping was in the economy in the later nineteenth century. Some reflection of the growth of service-trades in the later stages of industrialization can be seen in Table IV(c), where the third group of occupations grows at a faster rate than the occupied population in trade, manufactures and handicrafts: white collar 'black-coated' office workers in their legions, teachers, nurses, government employees at national and local level, cleaners, servants and the like.

One of the main social developments accompanying these redistributions of the national product and the occupied populations was of course urbanization. The 1851 census report commented that, 'it is evident . . . the great cities will not be like camps or the fields in which the people of other places exercise their energies and industry but the birthplace of a large part of the British race'. At that time the population was roughly evenly divided between country dwellers and town dwellers (in communities above 5,000). But the astonishing rise of the ports servicing industrial hinterlands and the industrial towns had taken place mainly by internal migration in the previous fifty years.[1] This same flow continued after 1851 and was supplemented by an outflow of emigrants also in the second half of the century, when the inward flow of Irish tailed off. Although the rural areas were not depopulated to any extent at all in England and Wales, 4 million of their increments in numbers were decanted away from them between 1841 and 1901. English towns attracted over 3 million and the colliery districts over half a million. The North-West Highlands of Scotland, which suffered

[1] See Appendix, Table 3, p. 451.

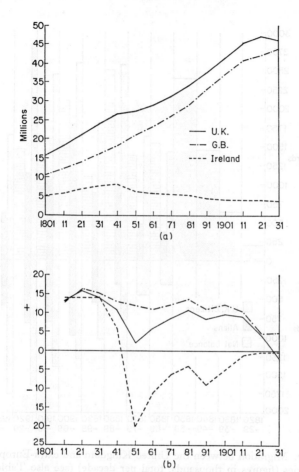

Fig. 6. Population growth in Great Britain and the United Kingdom, 1801–1931. (a) Total number of persons. (b) Rate of growth of population (percentage change per decade). (See also Table 1, p. 449.) After Mitchell and Deane, 1962, pp. 8–10.

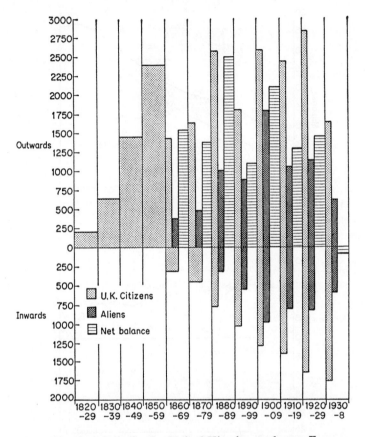

Fig. 7. Migration between the United Kingdom and extra-European countries (figures in thousands, total per decade) (see also Table 4, p. 452). After Mitchell and Deane, 1962, pp. 47–9.

a potato famine on a comparable scale with Ireland in the 1840's, became the only rural area to experience demographic devastation similar to Ireland in its aftermath. But the nineteenth century saw 'the representative Englishman turn town-dweller' and by 1900 three-quarters of the nation lived in towns.

Table IV(d) shows the increasing stake that foreign trade had in the economy as industrialization and population growth proceeded. The growth of international trade was profoundly important, both before and during the beginning of the process of industrialization in Britain. No other industrial power (including Japan) has had foreign markets at such a strategic place in development. After 1850 most increments in food grains came from imports, as the continuing expansion of numbers did finally outrun the expansion in domestic agriculture. Equally British dependence on the international economy grew on the raw-material import side, for the continuing expansion of productive capacity increasingly outstripped home supplies. All the cotton, of course, in the most strategic expanding industry came in through the ports; but by the end of the 1850's half the wool used was being imported; and by 1913 over four-fifths. As the technological base of manufacturing industry advanced so the resource position deteriorated: all the oil, most of the cellulose were imported; the mines of Cornwall and Derbyshire became exhausted or uneconomic and almost all non-ferrous metals then came from abroad by 1914.[1] So did much non-phosphoric iron ore for steel-making – because most British deposits were of low-grade impure ores. By 1913 the position had been reached whereby about seven-eighths of raw material supplies – apart from coal – and over half of food supplies were imported. An industrial structure weighted in this way and a population grown sixfold from 1750 thus had its existence, let alone its relatively high standard of living, made more and more dependent on providing the world with capital, goods and services in return. In 1913 the nakedness of this position was concealed to a large extent by the income from foreign investments: £200 million was flowing in each year from a capital of £4,000 million invested abroad, mainly since 1850. This protected the trading

[1] Appendix, Tables 15, p. 466 and 33, p. 485. See aso Fig. 12, p. 309.

accounts with the world from some of the consequences of failing to compete. Total exports were under £500 million per annum at this time, so an investment income of £200 million went a long way towards covering an import bill of over £600 million and providing yet more of a surplus for re-investment. This *rentier* position in the world economy was abruptly threatened by the sale of many overseas assets in the 1914–18 war.

Table IV(*e*) reveals how the export pattern changed in accordance with this changing international position. At once the meaning of the phrase that textiles were the strategic sector of the British economy in the first stages of industrialization becomes apparent – at least as far as foreign trade is concerned. Fully two-thirds of exports were composed of textiles, with virtually one-half of exports in the single staple of cotton cloth and yarn, in 1830 and 1850. The other conclusion which is apparent from these figures is the extraordinary extent to which international specialization had developed in the world economy. By the mid-nineteenth century 93 per cent of British exports were composed of manufactured goods and the same proportion of imports primary, unprocessed, produce. Only 7 per cent of imports were finished manufactured goods. This was at a point when Britain dominated the world economy, with over 40 per cent of the entire world output of traded manufactured goods produced within the country and about a quarter of the world's international trade passing through British ports. It was confidently considered by all save a few engineers, who had studied some light industries in the United States, that increasing world trade would continue to lead to increasing specialization in the international economy in Britain's favour. The United States was confidently presumed to be – correctly – the great reservoir of grain and meat as soon as railways could unlock the middle west, just as she had proved the great reservoir of raw cotton in the previous half century.

The official policy of free trade, to which Britain had become committed in the 1840's, the export of capital, currencies linked to gold, and the growth of the world economy without the distortions produced by political restraints were collectively assumed to be leading towards a more complete complementarity between Britain's position as the workshop of the world and other tributary economies as primary produce suppliers – whether they were part of the formal British Empire, as India or Australia, part of the 'informal British Empire' such as Argentina, or such politically independent countries as Portugal, Sweden, Denmark. Thus the Great Exhibition of 1851 was celebrated as a symbol of such an interlocked world economy: it was an international exhibition, with Britain taking most of the prizes for industrial products and other nations for food-stuffs, handicrafts and raw materials (save that 'Yankee ingenuity' was also demonstrated to the world). A free-trade policy, by urging Britain faster in the same direction as she was being driven by the developing economic logic of her position was even championed by Cobden and others in the hope that it would make wars impossible, despite the machinations of the politicians, by making nation so dependent upon nation. 1851 was thus a secular shrine to the peace which freely developing commerce would bring in its wake. This uncritical ideology had neatly reversed all the seventeenth-century assumptions about economic philosophy, that trade meant war.

These were the results of a unique set of circumstances in world history: never before and never since has one country so dominated the world economy. This, then, is the unique ex-perience to be explained – not that other nations eventually caught up and surpassed. Being the first to break out of almost medieval levels of industrial productivity, to take the first giant strides in costs and prices coming from massive production and new skills, British export industries were enabled to undercut the rest of the world's handicraft industries in cheap cloth and basic iron products, even where the standards of living and wage levels of competitors were much lower than in Britain. In a con-text where empty continents were awaiting immigrants, capital and equipment, at the same time as this new enormous source of industrial momentum arose in Britain, powerful pressures were set up for the international economy to develop along complementary lines with the rest of the developing world being drawn into trading relations with Britain as primary producers. In a pre-railway age, given the very slow means of diffusing technology at this period, the first nation to make the jump enjoyed a lead of two or three generations.

As Britain assumed this dominant role in the international economy, exploiting the unique advantages of a unique position, so the prime dynamic in the economy became the industrial sector, and within that, directly and indirectly, the export industries. A very 'distorted' industrial structure thus developed with the few giant industries – textiles, coal, ship-building, engineering – responding with alacrity to the opportunities of this very special habitat, with the economy becoming dependent – to what would now be considered an alarming extent – on its ability to sell cheap cloth, cheap iron, machinery and coal, and to provide the ships to carry the cargoes, to the rest of the world. In a fundamental change of habitat in the world economy these few successful giants of the nineteenth century were all too likely to find themselves the gasping dinosaurs of the twentieth. This mid-nineteenth century position itself bristled with ironies. Trading links were being extended by war in China; by the use of aggressive diplomacy in the Middle East and parts of Africa; by establishing protectorates; by the shadow of British naval power which lay over every ocean in the world. British capital in American railways was allowing a giant economy with a resource position favourable to its development as an industrial competitor, as well as a trading partner in raw produce, to flex its muscles.

A rival logic was also developing within the British economy, intimations of which may be seen from the two final columns in Table IV(e). As the share of textiles in British foreign trade shrank (although the total quantities and values of cotton goods increased up to 1913) so the share of metal and engineering products mounted. With this went coal – which provided 10 per cent of total exports in 1913 – paradoxically the first mass export of a raw material that the British economy had known since the decline in the exports of raw wool in the fourteenth century – and appearing in a maturing industrial economy. The two were closely linked. The engineering industry had developed initially in the textile areas in response to the needs of the mill owners for machine builders and repairers. Many of the most famous firms had been completely sponsored in their early years in this way. But once specialized out as an industry in its own right its leaders claimed the right to export markets of their own. Engineer after engineer argued thus before the Parliamentary Committees on the Export of Machinery in 1824 and 1843. They claimed that the French would soon be supplying the needs of would-be industrialists in other countries if Britain did not; and the net result would be the same for the British textile magnates, who were opposing the export of textile machines, while the country would also have lost a rising export market in machinery. The export of capital goods, in fact, might more than outweigh the loss of consumer-goods exports, when other nations were competing successfully at this stage. The export of capital and railway building provided extra impetus for the same trend: over 40 per cent of the £4,000 million invested abroad went into railway building. The export of coal provided some of the fuel and power to run the capital equipment being exported. The conclusion of this process was that developments within the British economy – the differentiation process which brought an independent engineering industry into existence and the build-up of forces which encouraged the flow of capital abroad – actively encouraged the progress of industrialization in some other countries abroad. The claim for export markets by the engineering industry, speaking for all the manufacturers of capital goods, meant sowing dragons' teeth abroad – even if a lot of their products, like motor cars today, did not exactly fall under this definition. But many of the looms of Japan and New England and the Calcutta jute mills, did feature in this rising proportion of exports in metal products and engineering.

In some ways Table IV(f) reflects the changes shown in earlier tables. The first column, indicating a fairly steady trend increase in the proportion of food and livestock imports, is a consequence of the continuing rise in population. The British market was importing 55 per cent of its grain by 1913 (70 per cent in the mid-1930's) and about 40 per cent of its meat (60 per cent in the mid-1930's). Over half total food supplies, in those products which could be produced in Britain, came from abroad in 1913 (two-thirds between the wars). While dependence on imported raw materials strongly increased, they fell as a percentage of total imports, that fall being almost completely explained by the shrinking share of textile raw materials. But the preponderance of textiles in the export pattern of the mid-nineteenth century had brought the consequence that one-third of total imports, no less, was to feed the textile mills.

The other main trend was that of the increase in imports of manufactured goods, shown in the last column of Table IV(f). Two main reasons lay behind this movement. The first was increasing wealth which brought demands for an increasing diversity of goods and services: the market expands, becomes more discriminating, more sophisticated as it becomes more diversified. Extending the range of demand would naturally lead towards such a conclusion as this series shows – a natural, beneficial conclusion, in terms of economic satisfaction, to the whole process of expanding national wealth and living standards. But another reason was enlarging the dimensions of the trend, more dangerous as a portent in the later nineteenth century. It was that new industries were not growing as rapidly in Britain as in some other countries, so that for whole ranges of articles dependence upon imports was increasing. Germany had picked up the main European export trade in chemicals, Germany and the United States in electrical engineering products, and in coal derivatives such as dyes. The Dutch had developed a mass export trade to Britain in margarine; the Americans (and to a lesser extent the French) in motor cars. This was not a case of everyone taking in everyone else's washing – as in the motor car trading pattern after 1945 – but that Britain had few advantages to offer other nations in certain fields. The reasons for these lags will be explored later: the conclusion was that this change in the structure of both the export and the import trade was overshadowed by the rise of Germany and America, and after 1900 to a lesser extent Japan, as industrial states.

This was a perfectly inevitable process once they set about the job, given railways and the advancing technology in large part pioneered in the British Isles before 1850 and actively being disseminated abroad by British enterprise and British capital. And given the size, population and resource endowment of these large nations, the vigour and skills of their people, the effectiveness of their governments, it was inevitable that they should become powerful industrial states. By 1913 Great Britain was producing 8 million tons of steel, Germany 13·5 million and the United States 31 million. When half a continent starts to develop then it can produce more than a small island. This is not surprising. To repeat: the unique phenomenon was the combination of factors which allowed Britain such world dominance in manufactures and trade in the mid-nineteenth century, not the fact that others began to catch up. Nor is the process of living as an industrial state in an industrializing world an impossible or unfavourable one in principle. Nations have been doing it for many generations – even Britain – with a good record of prosperity and growth. Indeed, industrialization creates great national wealth, a diversification and expansion in demand for imports, so that new markets should be developing of benefit to everyone. The United States is Britain's best single customer today; Britain was Germany's best single customer in the generation before 1914; and Germany was Britain's second best customer. In short, industrialization is not a zero-sum game. Since 1945, moreover, the group of rich, highly industrial nations have tended to trade between themselves more than with other less-developed nations, to invest spontaneously amongst themselves more than with other less-developed nations, and to grow faster and richer than the less-developed nations.

Of course, it is impossible to keep ahead in all fields all the time while this process of the spread of industrialization in the world economy is going on. Always, in certain lines, competitors will have an advantage in cheap raw materials, or cheap power, or developing skills, or cheap labour, which will enforce new specializations in the world economy. This means there are always problems of transition for an industrial economy in an industrializing world. But provided new sectors, new skills, new products are coming forward to replace the older staple industries and skills under challenge the problem will not be mortal. Essentially after 1870 Britain was facing the problems that traditional markets were growing more reluctant to accept traditional textiles and cheap iron; that the mechanization of textile industries and basic metals was usually amongst the first of the new industrial skills to take root elsewhere. The decline in traditional markets in textiles, iron and hardware in the United States and northern Europe, at the same time as British demands for imports from there grew more insistent, led to a developing balance of trade problem – and also with continental Europe, South Africa, New Zealand, Canada – and even Argentina by 1910. The advantages of being first in the field – accumulated capital, expertise, a trained labour force, modernized institutions, established commercial dominance – were being increasingly counteracted by new liabilities. Certain of these lay in the changing logic of the international context, external to the British economy. Trends there were bound to be more prejudicial to British exports, based on an older dominance, than to those of other countries. The British economy, given its highly specialized industrial structure based on the export possibilities of a unique historical context, was more exposed to attrition than others. The fact of tariffs abroad, springing up in all the rising industrial nations from the late 1860's, had to be accepted.

But several characteristics about the internal developments in the economy after the 1870's did bode ill for a country such as Britain living in an increasingly competitive world. New sectors, such as the chemical industry, electrical engineering, the motor car industry, were not coming forward fast enough to replace older industries – or at least to replace them as earners of sterling credits in exports. Secondly, the older industries themselves were not accepting innovations, or investing capital for re-equipment on a large enough scale. Productivity was falling in coal mining faster in Britain than elsewhere. Thirdly, the whole tempo of industrial advance was slowing down. Rates of growth of industrial production had been above 3 per cent per annum since 1820; after 1880 they fell to below 2 per cent; the rate of growth of productivity and the rate of capital accumulation at home all showed a similar rate of fall. Even when trade values surged after the period of depression 1880–95, and prices and profits picked up, these key ratios of productivity, the rate of capital accumulation, and the rate of growth of industrial production did not respond significantly. More cotton factories were built in Lancashire after 1896 (it was a period of great expansion of capacity and exports) but without any general re-equipment of the industry with the latest cost-reducing technology. This last great boom for Lancashire was floated with exports to the last unexploited mass markets in the world for unsophisticated cheap cloth. It seemed as though the industrial machine, at the centre of British economic fortunes in the new competitive world, was slowing down. With capital pouring abroad at the rate of almost £200 million per annum before 1914 and investment income pouring in, Britain's position was becoming to some degree that of a *rentier* in the international economy, and attitudes in part *rentier* attitudes. After a successful and active industrial youth, it seemed that the country's economy was settling down to a less strenuous, less competitive but still comfortable middle-age. All these assumptions were then shattered by the experience of total war in the next four years, and the economics of depression in the next generation.

Reading list

GENERAL READING AND TEXTBOOKS FOR PART II

ASHWORTH, W. *An Economic History of England, 1870–1939*, London–New York, 1960.

CHAMBERS, J. D. *The Workshop of the World: British economic history from 1820 to 1880*, London, 1961.

CHECKLAND, S. G. *The Rise of Industrial Society in England, 1815–1885*, London, 1964.

CLAPHAM, SIR J. H. *An Economic History of Modern Britain*, 2nd ed., 3 vols, Cambridge, 1950-2 [for reference].

COURT, W. H. B. *A Concise Economic History of Britain from 1750 to Recent Times*, Cambridge, 1954.

COURT, W. H. B. *British Economic History, 1870–1914: commentary and documents*, Cambridge, 1965.

DEANE, P. & COLE, W. A. *British Economic Growth, 1688–1959: trends and structure*, 2nd ed., Cambridge, 1967.

GAYER, A. D., ROSTOW, W. W. & SCHWARTZ, A. J., with the assistance of I. FRANK. *The Growth and Fluctuations of the*

British Economy, 1790–1850: an historical, statistical and theoretical study of Britain's economic development, 2 vols, Oxford, 1953 [for reference].

KINDLBERGER, C. P. *Economic Growth in France and Britain, 1851–1950*, Cambridge (Mass.), 1964.

LEWIS, W. A. *An Economic Survey, 1919–1939*, London, 1949; reissue London, 1963.

MADDISON, A. *Economic Growth in the West: comparative experience in Europe and North America*, New York–London, 1964.

MITCHELL, B. R. *Abstract of British Historical Statistics*, Cambridge, 1962 [for reference].

POLLARD, S. *The Development of the British Economy, 1914–1950*, London, 1962.

ROSTOW, W. W. *British Economy of the 19th Century: essays*, Oxford, 1948.

SAVILLE, J. (ed.) *Studies in the British Economy, 1870–1914* (Special edition of the *Yorkshire Bulletin of Economic and Social Research*, 1965).

SAYERS, R. S. *A History of Economic Change in England, 1880–1939*, London, 1967.

SVENNILSON, I. *Growth and Stagnation in the European Economy*, Geneva, 1954.

YOUNGSON, A. J. *The British Economy, 1922–1966*, London, 1967.

9 Occupational structure and industrial organization in the mid-nineteenth century

The occupational structure of Britain in the mid-nineteenth century, taking the cross-section at the 1851 census, shows how far the progress of industrialization had affected the employed population after almost a century. The main conclusion that emerges from the table is the high proportion of people whose context of employment was still outside the factory and the mine, or outside large plant 'industry', as generally defined, altogether. This is not to say that the lives and jobs of such people were unaffected by industrialization, of course, but the figures are still remarkable. First comes agriculture. By numbers alone agriculture was still for Britain, in Clapham's words, 'by very far the greatest of her industries'. Over 1·75 million persons were engaged in it – over 1·5 million men and a little under ·25 million women. Over a quarter of all men over the age of 20 were directly concerned in agriculture, over 1·25 million as agricultural labourers, about 280,000 as farmers and graziers. Most of the women employed in agriculture were 'indoor farm servants' (domestic servants but also helping in the dairy, cheese making, etc.).[1] This was much the largest occupational group, and total numbers in agriculture had been rising right through the first half of the nineteenth century, even though at a much smaller rate than numbers employed in other sectors of the economy. Some of the corollaries of this fact are worth making in the social history of rural England. No English county experienced rural depopulation in the first half of the nineteenth century. Numbers in all counties went up, despite the generally current fear

[1] 28,000 were listed as farmers in their own right, one suspects mainly the widows of farmers.

259

TABLE V: *Principal occupation groups in Britain in 1851 in order of size*

	Male	Female
Total population	10,224,000	10,736,000
Population of ten years old and upwards	7,616,000	8,155,000
Agriculture: farmer, grazier, labourer, servant	1,563,000	227,000
Domestic service (excluding farm service)	134,000	905,000
Cotton worker, every kind, with printer, dyer	255,000	272,000
Building craftsman: carpenter, bricklayer, mason, plasterer, plumber, etc.	442,000	1,000
Labourer (unspecified)	367,000	9,000
Milliner, dress-maker, seamstress (seamster)	494	340,000
Wool worker, every kind, with carpet-weaver	171,000	113,000
Shoe-maker	243,000	31,000
Coal-miner	216,000	3,000
Tailor	135,000	18,000
Washerwoman		145,000
Seaman (Merchant), pilot	144,000	
Silk worker	53,000	80,000
Blacksmith	112,000	592
Linen, flax worker	47,000	56,000
Carter, carman, coachman, postboy, cabman, busman, etc.	83,000	1,000
Iron worker, founder, moulder (excluding iron-mining, nails, hardware, cutlery, files, tools, machines)	79,000	590
Railway driver, etc., porter, etc., labourer, platelayer	65,000	54
Hosiery worker	35,000	30,000
Lace worker	10,000	54,000
Machine, boiler maker	63,000	647
Baker	56,000	7,000
Copper, tin, lead-miner	53,000	7,000
Charwoman		55,000
Commercial clerk	44,000	19
Fisherman	37,000	1,000
Miller	37,000	562
Earthenware worker	25,000	11,000
Sawyer	35,000	23
Shipwright, boat-builder, block and mast maker	32,000	28
Straw-plait worker	4,000	28,000
Wheelwright	30,000	106
Glover	4,500	25,000
Nailer	19,000	10,000
Iron-miner	27,000	910
Tanner, currier, fellmonger	25,000	276
Printer	22,000	222

Employers making returns and employed in certain trades in England and Wales, 1851

I	II	III	IV	V	VI	VII	VIII	IX
Trade	*Masters making returns*	*No men or number not stated*	*1 or 2 men*	*3–9 men*	*10–19 men*	*20–49 men*	*50–99 men*	*100 and upwards*
Tailor	10,991	4,239	3,852	2,456	343	80	10	1
Shoe-maker	17,665	7,311	6,016	3,644	444	181	38	31
Engine and machine maker	837	160	152	295	90	72	40	34
Builder	3,614	292	417	1,541	701	498	113	52
Wheelwright	2,057	670	982	373	20	11	1	–
Tanner	349	31	41	147	68	39	8	5
Woollen cloth manufacture	1,107	131	199	329	156	179	41	82
Worsted manufacture	154	27	14	24	20	26	12	31
Silk manufacture	272	36	30	72	22	37	29	46
Miller	2,394	403	1,147	722	84	23	13	2
Brewer	776	120	228	319	67	34	3	5
Lace manufacture	317	58	54	123	28	26	9	19
Cotton manufacture	1,670	482	81	174	124	216	172	411
Earthenware manufacture	378	68	68	112	31	56	7	36
Blacksmith	7,331	2,282	4,035	967	31	15	1	–

Census of 1851, Ages and Occupations. After J. H. Clapham, *An Economic History of Modern Britain* (1932), vol. II, p. 24.

of redundant labour in the agricultural counties. Rural pauper-ism proved to be the greatest single scourge of the 1820's and 1830's. Poor rates rose to a peak of £7 million per annum in the early 1830's. When the incidence of poor relief costs is plotted by counties, it is at once apparent that they were highest exactly in the regions where agricultural employment dominated local employment patterns. The 1834 Poor Law Act was particularly designed to combat the evils of rural destitution by encouraging, if necessary in a brutal way, migration away from areas where employment did not offer a living minimal wage for a family. The practice of supplementing wages with poor relief payments, started in 1795 by the Berkshire magistrates meeting at Speenhamland by Newbury, had proved a serious social and economic liability as a long-run solution of this problem. As an emergency method of coping with the crisis of high food prices in the Napoleonic Wars, it might also have served as an acceptable short-term device for relieving the cyclical unemployment in manufacturing areas during occasional depression years. In fact the practice spread mainly in rural areas in the south in response to the chronic problem of subsistence-living standards in agriculture. In this context it demoralized the labourers who received help, induced a lowering of ordinary wages by farmers in anticipation of poor relief supplements to make up the difference when bread prices were high or work scanty and acted as a brake against migration – which was the best long-term economic and social solution to the problem of rural underemployment and destitution. In this sense the Speenhamland system took over where the Settlement Laws left off as a device which discouraged the free mobility of labour.

The Benthamite poor law of 1834, written by Edwin Chadwick, Secretary of the Commission, by aiming to stop the provision of out-door relief to able-bodied paupers, became one factor in the migration of increments of population in the rural areas away from agriculture. It also assumed a quite false diagnosis of the ills of industrial society, for unemployment in cyclical depressions or from technological change was involuntary rather than a deliberately chosen option. Of course the new Poor Law was only one pressure, helping to create a 'push' from the agricultural counties. Other 'pull' effects operated from the reception areas for agricultural migrants: expanding industries, the railways after 1830, better wages and faster expanding employment in industry than in agriculture. Migration continued even after the worst years of agricultural distress had ended in 1836–7, and in decades after rural pauperism had declined during the high farming boom of mid-Victorian times until the 1870's. This suggests that migration was a function of the 'pulls' towards industrial employment as much as it was a 'push' away from agricultural regions. The position after 1851 changed slightly. But only 1 or 2 per cent at most of rural depopulation developed between 1851 and 1881 (depending on how 'rural' is defined) in the group of 15 counties which were most agricultural. The worst hit of all, Huntingdonshire, lost 12 per cent of its population, which was quite exceptional. In fact, the 1921 census still recorded 1·3 million adult men employed in agriculture, which was still much the largest single occupational group. Of course, *proportionately* a steady decline continued away from

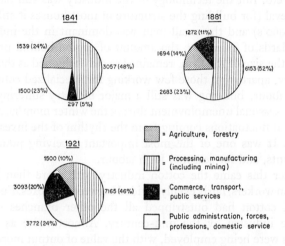

Fig. 8. Labour force in the United Kingdom (figures in thousands). After Mitchell and Deane, 1962, pp. 60–1.

agriculture, the most consistent general trend in the occupational structure in the nineteenth century. Over 33 per cent of families were in agriculture in 1831; 15 per cent of the working population of England and Wales in agriculture in 1871 but only 7·6 per cent in 1911.

After agriculture, domestic service – employing over 1 million persons (905,000 of them women) – in 1851 stands out as the second largest occupational group, again a surprising conclusion for the most advanced industrial economy in the world. Some link is discernible here between this very large occupational group (mainly unmarried) and the fact that more women than men migrated within Britain at this period.

Building was probably the next largest industry: 442,000 craftsmen alone are enumerated and a good proportion of the 367,000 unspecified labourers were probably labourers in building. At one end of this industry were the very few large-scale contractors, such as Cubitts, and the great railway contractors like Peto. But the technology of the industry was still basically medieval (for building the structure of most houses it still is in the 1960's) and the small man was dominant in the industry. Standards of efficiency, the amount of capital behind production, the size of the firm, remained as old-fashioned as the technology, apart from those few working for specialized contracts. For labour, building was still a major industry suffering very heavy seasonal unemployment during the winter months, as well as great fluctuations coming from the rhythm of the investment cycle. It was one of the most important receiving points for migrants, and for seasonal Irish labour.

After this came the cotton industry with more than half a million workers, fairly evenly divided between the sexes. Furthermore, cotton had outstripped all the other branches of the textile industry by the mid-century. Almost twice as many hands were being employed, with the value of output more than twice as much as in the woollen industry, including all the different branches of manufacture using wool as a raw material. In turn the woollen industry was more than twice the size of the silk industry, with flax and hosiery and lace smaller still. Altogether there were just over 1 million in all sides of the textile industry; and in almost every branch more women than men were employed – although only to a fairly small degree. This was by far the largest industry properly speaking (excluding agriculture and domestic service).

How far had the factory system taken over production for this million of workers in textiles and how far was the context of employment still the 'out-worker' system in small workshops or cottage weaving lofts? On the spinning side, of all the branches of textiles, factory production had already triumphed completely and the average size of plant was very high. This was already true by 1820 for cotton, flax yarns for linen, silk and wool. Even the coarsest fibre of all, jute, had been adapted to the spinning machines in Dundee by 1838. Great technical battles had been waged to adapt machines pioneered on the most tractable fibre of all, cotton, to stiffer materials. This was accomplished and established factory production of wool and linen yarn in full stream by the 1820's. Jute had defied all efforts made by the linen-spinners of Dundee to adapt it to the powered machines until it was found that whale oil softened its fibres sufficiently. And these experiments were made profitable in the 1830's by the glut of oil on the market after the erection of the local gas-works had put the town lighting onto gas.

On the weaving side of textiles the picture was still far from complete in 1851. Cotton was the most advanced in the progress to factory weaving by power loom and the tragedy of the hand-loom weaver was virtually over. Only for very expensive, highly complex, specialized weaves was the worker still operating a hand-loom. Perhaps up to 50,000 hand-looms were still at work in highly specialized grades of cloth. When Edward Baines wrote his *History of the Cotton Manufacture* in 1835 he could comment:

> It is by iron fingers, teeth and wheels moving with exhaustless energy and devouring speed that the cotton is opened, cleaned, spread, carded, drawn, roved, spun, wound, warped, dressed and woven [a sequence of eleven processes with distinct machines] . . . The various machines are proportioned to each other in regard to their capability of work . . . All are moving at once – the operations chasing each other – and all derive their motion from the mighty engine.

He remarked that these machines had all been invented in the last 70 years, adding, 'it must be acknowledged that the cotton mill presents the most striking example of the dominion obtained by human science over the powers of nature of which modern times can boast'.

Power-weaving had been introduced mainly by the leading cotton spinners (the men of capital and initiative in the industry). As localization developed on the towns of the Lancashire plain so the combined spinning and weaving firms rose to dominance. These integrated firms had the largest amount of horsepower and the largest labour forces even though they numbered only just over 500 out of a total of 1,580. The average number of workers per factory for this group was over 300; and each combined firm averaged over 300 looms and almost 20,000 spindles. But cotton manufacture was the *only* branch of the textile industry where the large plant was dominant. At this point it seemed likely that vertical integration was going to be the dominant feature of the cotton industry, with unified control within a single firm over the span of processes from raw materials to final product markets. But after 1850 different commercial and technical pressures quite reversed this trend so that by 1900, the cotton industry was dominated by separate firms in spinning, weaving and often finishing. The integrated firm, like Horrocks of Preston (originally in spinning), that controlled everything down to the position where it could 'brand' its fabrics was an exception.

In the worsted industry, centred on Bradford, the great patent battle to get an effective combing machine had only just been won in 1851, by Lister and Holden and Donnisthorpe. Only the 1850's and 1860's saw the preparatory operations and weaving follow spinning into an integrated sequence of factory processes. Jute weaving, being a very coarse low quality trade, was already mechanized. Crossleys of Halifax had just taken out steam-loom patents for the coarsest kind of weaving of all – carpets. Linen weaving was mainly in the factory by 1851 but much of hosiery and lace making still depended on outwork organized from Nottingham through the 'bagman' – but the basic innovations which brought factory production in their wake were already changing the structure of these industries. Most of the Spitalfields silk weavers still worked in houses and small workshops. In the clothing trades were another half a million persons, the tailors and seamstresses – as many as the complete labour force in cotton – quite divorced from the context of factory production. Clapham concluded that outwork was still, on the whole, the characteristic form of occupation in manufacturing industry.

Textiles were almost the only branch of industrial employment at this time where women were represented in comparable numbers with men, except for the quasi-textile outworking trades of gloving and straw plaiting, both of which were still organized mainly by handicraft methods on a putting-out system. In the 1850's the Blake stitcher came into shoe making; sewing machines (at first only treadle-powered), steam-powered stocking frames, and powered cutting machines for mass-tailoring, all came into use. But these secondary branches of textiles and clothing trades were still much concerned with outwork in 1900. The triumph of steam power and the semi-automatic machines here were delayed into the era of gas engines and electric power. The great evils of working conditions and low piece-work rates in these sweat-shops and attics long survived the era of the Factory Acts.

Coal mining was already high on the scale of industries with 219,000 employees, almost exclusively a male labour force by 1851 following the Mines Act of 1842. The characteristic mine in the north-east coalfield and the midlands was, by 1851, a large unit, deeply sunk with vertical shafts, employing a large labour force and very heavily capitalized. The steeply rising curve of coal production implied a steady trend to deeper, larger, more costly pits. Many shafts had been sunk to over 1,000 ft in the 1830's, taking 3 years to win. A few 1,000-ft pits had been sunk on other coalfields but they were exceptional. Capitals were equally impressive. Some of the biggest coal owners, landed magnates like Lords Ravensworth and Londonderry or the Earl of Durham, had more than £·5 million each sunk in pits. A capital of £·25 million put a man into the second rank. These men were in no sense mere 'corn-law lords'; their stewards acted as the department managers of vast mining concerns. Total production of coal was about 13 million tons in 1815, 30 million in 1830 and 65 million in 1856. About a third of the whole was raised in the single great field of Northumberland and Durham, where coal had been the breeding ground for most of the experiments in steam-powered traction. In the 1850's, however, the most rapidly rising new market for coal was already driving the Rhondda pits in south Wales: steam coals for

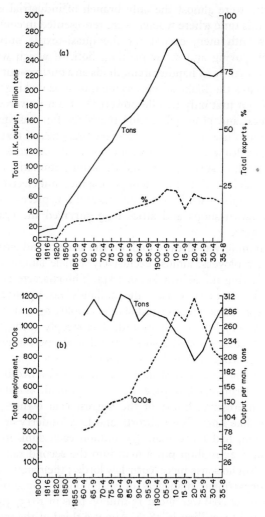

Fig. 9. Coal. (a) United Kingdom output, and total exports as percentage of output. (b) Total employment and output per man. (See also Table 29, p. 481.) After Mitchell and Deane, 1962, pp. 115–21.

steam-shipping and for export to the world's coaling stations. Exports had reached 2 million tons per year by 1851.

As the uses of iron in production and construction industries advanced, this meant a more than quadrupling of the increase in the demand for coal by these industries; each ton of refined iron using over 4 tons of coal in its production and other metals much more. Probably about one-third of all the coal raised was used in iron works and for refining metals at this time. Even though coal and iron are not particularly prominent in these occupational groupings, as strategic industries they clearly were giving Britain the material basis for successful industrialization throughout this period. A later Victorian economist, Stanley Jevons, remarked: 'Coal stands not beside but above all other commodities' in importance.

The iron industry, with cotton and coal, was the other industrial field where the large unit had triumphed and the full consequences of massive technology on the size of plant and the extent of the labour force at the single plant had been revealed. Over 6,000 workers were on strength at Sir John Guest's works at Dowlais, near Merthyr Tydfil, in the 1840's, producing 20,000 tons of pig-iron a year. Over £1 million capital was engaged in the business. This was exceptional but it was not uncommon for a large south Wales, Staffordshire or Scottish works in the 1840's to have over 1,000 men on the payroll. South Wales had the largest plants, profiting mainly in the market for cheap rolled iron and cheap castings, particularly for railways. Higher-cost Staffordshire and Shropshire works were attempting to develop higher quality markets in constructional goods; art-castings, bridges, steam-engine parts, high-quality iron for nailers and the Birmingham trades. Then, after Neilson, the manager of a Glasgow gas works, had invented the 'hot blast' in 1828, the new Clyde valley iron works became the pace-makers in expansion and in pricing. They also prospered on the cheap mass market for rolled iron and castings; whereas the older eighteenth-century Scottish works, such as the Carron Company, were trying to develop the quality trade, like Coal-brookdale, in domestic appliances like stoves and garden furniture. The catalogue of the 1851 Exhibition is highly instructive in revealing the great expansion in the iron markets as more and more objects were being contrived from metal. Total iron production for Great Britain had risen from a little over 100,000 tons per annum in 1802 to over 2 million tons by 1850. Scotland was then producing over one-quarter of the whole; whereas under 5 per cent came from Scotland in the 1820's. The two great new markets were constructional uses of all kinds and the railways.

In the iron towns, like Merthyr Tydfil, technology had brought the iron masters into the position of being lords of their communities, as the cotton lords of Lancashire mill towns, with an absolute divide separating the owners of capital in the industry and their workers. When at least £50,000 was needed to set up as a master, the gap between master and worker had become impossible to span. Class consciousness and class bitterness in bad times ran high in these places. But such an extreme local industrial class structure was as unusual as was the massive technology in the national economy of 1851. The secondary metal trades, centred on the Birmingham district, Sheffield and many Lancashire villages, were very different in their structure of production and collateral social relationships. The average size of workshop still had less than 10 employees. There were some firms, like Boulton and Watt, whose toy business and small metal-ware workshops (separate from the engine business) employed over 200 persons. But a man could set up as a small master fairly easily, if he saved £60–100, renting 'rooms and power' for his workshop. Social relations here were always held up as the example for the rest of the kingdom (particularly for south Wales and Lancashire). A feeling of solidarity existed in the region and hostility was expressed more against the distant monopoly-seeking copper and iron magnates forcing up raw material prices by collusion, as the Birmingham men believed, rather than against the owners of property in the industry within Birmingham. The great crises came from fluctuations in export markets for which no local people could be held responsible.

The same was true of the Sheffield edge-tool and cutlery industries, all using the highly-priced raw material, steel, that could only be produced from small furnaces before Bessemer's invention of the 1850's. In the 1830's over 500 tiny furnaces were producing cast and shear steel and the entire range of Sheffield industries used only 12,000 tons of high-quality, mainly Swedish, bar-iron as its annual intake of raw materials. The trend in both places was towards a gradual increase in the size of plant, which had been the case long before 1851. But not until the 1860's did steel become a mass-production material, and not until the 1880's did automatic stamping and cutting machines begin to revolutionize the traditional craft-skills and the small workshop employment of these secondary metal industries, and also nailing in the Birmingham area. Joseph Chamberlain spoke of these innovations 'depriving [Birmingham] of its special characteristic, viz. the number of its small manufacturers' in 1865–6. But as older trades and some processes were absorbed into massive production, small businesses expanded in other new lines. At the end of the century, and even in the mid-twentieth century, the small firm prospered among the giants more easily in the Sheffield and Birmingham trades than almost anywhere else.

Other large-plant industries had an even smaller place in the pattern of total employment in 1851 so that glass, non-ferrous metal mining and smelting, iron mining and paper were not at all representative as employment types. Railways were 'large plant' employers themselves and indirectly through the engineering workshops associated with railways and supplying railway needs. Cornish mines, still in full production at the mid-century, had over 150 men employed per mine on average; as highly capitalized as coal mining in the north-east. In ship-building the naval dockyards and one or two Thames yards in the 1850's were still among the largest units of employment anywhere (over 5,000 men worked at the largest naval yard in wartime). Most other shipyards were very small. Five breweries employed over 100 men, but they were all in London and unrepresentative of the industry as a whole. The general size of plant was very much smaller. The same sort of pattern is true of potting, milling and building. One or two large firms existed, but the characteristic unit of production was still tiny.

The first conclusion to be drawn from this analysis of the employment pattern in 1851 is that the general pattern of employment, the immediate context within which most people earned their living, was still very different in 1851 from the picture one might anticipate from studying the expanding parts of the economy. The change from this position was also fairly slow, if steady. But, secondly, the numerical importance of certain categories of employment does not give the true picture of their strategic or dynamic importance, as instruments of industrial and commercial growth. Even if a large proportion of people did not come immediately within the orbit of industrialization as far as their jobs were concerned, all were affected by it at just one stage less directly. The fortunes of the labour force in agriculture, meagre as they were, were dependent on the absence of those who were migrating to industrial employment; the demands for domestic servants and tailors were expanding under the impact of rising industrial and commercial wealth. The contribution of industries to gross national product or to total capital investment remained, of course, very different from their importance in the scale of employment generated because of the great differences in productivity and in capital engaged per head of the labour force in different industries.

Over time, the move towards manufacturing industry in this occupational pattern may not appear very significant as a category. The relative decline in agriculture was more to trade, distribution, services, finance, transport than to manufacturing. From 1870 to 1914 little change came to the percentage of the labour force engaged in manufacturing, mining and industry, which was between 43 and 46 per cent. The percentage had been as high as 41 per cent in 1831. Within the industrial sector in the second half of the century a certain change of emphasis took place. Heavy industries, capital goods industries (particularly coal) grew faster than consumer goods industries. Coal (employing over 1 million men by 1913) and construction, iron and steel, engineering and ship-building had become of much greater relative importance by 1900; whereas textiles were much more dominant in the employment pattern in 1851.

Industrialization not uncommonly involves a higher rate of increase in non-industrial employment than in manufacturing. The total population of Lancashire, for example, may be rising at a faster rate than the number of operatives in the cotton industry: the proportional significance of cotton in employment may appear actually to decline. But such statistical revelations can mislead. In Lancashire the shipping, the Liverpool dock activity, the growth of towns, the banks, the local transport, the shopkeepers, the domestic servants, were all, either more or less directly, much dependent for their growth in numbers and prosperity upon the cotton industry – the greatest flywheel of expansion in Lancashire at this time and the great initiator of growth in these other sectors. Manchester was quite rightly christened 'Cottonopolis'. One cannot set out to increase the national income or expand the economy by increasing the number of clerks and lawyers and dock workers, even though as a result of industrial expansion these groups may rise and profit more than manufacturing groups. The initiative which determined economic expansion and the redeployment of the labour force was firmly centred in the manufacturing and the transport sectors and derived from the vast increases in productivity made possible by steam power.

Reading list

(i) *Poverty and poor law*
    [*see also pp. 224–5*]

BEALES, H. L. 'The new poor law', *History*, 1931, **15**, no. 60; reprinted in E. M. Carus-Wilson (ed.), *Essays in Economic History*, vol. 3, London, 1962.

BLAUG, M. 'The myth of the old poor law and the making of the new', *Journal of Economic History*, 1963, **23**, no. 2.

BLAUG, M. 'The poor law re-examined', *Journal of Economic History*, **24**, no. 2.

MARSHALL, D. 'The old poor law', *Economic History Review*, 1937, **8**, no. 1.

ROSE, M. E. 'The allowance system under the new poor law', *Economic History Review*, 2nd series, 1966, **19**, no. 3.

SAVILLE, J. *Rural Depopulation in England and Wales, 1851–1951*, London, 1957.

(ii) *Industry*
   [*see also pp. 178–83*]

BLAUG, M. 'The productivity of capital in the Lancashire cotton industry during the 19th century', *Economic History Review*, 2nd series, 1961, **13**, no. 3.

CHAPMAN, SIR S. J. *The Lancashire Cotton Industry: a study in economic development*, Manchester, 1904 (Publications of the University of Manchester, Economic Series, no. 1).

CLAPHAM, J. H. *An Economic History of Modern Britain*, 3 vols, Cambridge, 1950–2, vol. II, 1952, ch. 2: 'Free trade and steel'.

ELLISON, T. *The Cotton Trade of Great Britain, including a history of the Liverpool cotton market*, Liverpool, 1886.

ERICKSON, C. *British Industrialists: steel and hosiery, 1850–1950*, Cambridge, 1959 (National Institute of Economic and Social Research, Economic and Social Studies, no. 18).

HABER, L. F. *The Chemical Industry in the 19th Century: a study of the economic aspect of applied chemistry in Europe and North America*, Oxford, 1958.

MORRIS, J. H. & WILLIAMS, L. J. *The South Wales Coal Industry, 1841–1875*, Cardiff, 1958.

PAYNE, P. L. *Rubber and Railways in the 19th Century: a study of the Spencer Papers*, Liverpool, 1961.

PORTER, G. R. *The Progress of the Nation in its Various Social and Economic Relations from the Beginning of the 19th Century* [1851], rev. ed. by F. W. Hirst, London, 1912 [chapters on industries].

TAYLOR, A. J. 'Concentration and specialization in the Lancashire cotton industry, 1825–1850', *Economic History Review*, 2nd series, 1949, **1**, no. 2.

WOODRUFF, W. *The Rise of the British Rubber Industry During the 19th Century*, Liverpool, 1958.

10 Railways

The ways in which improved transport methods augmented economic activity apply to the railways in relation to canal transport, as they applied to canals. Railways performed the same economic functions as the canals, of shifting bulk staples of low value density at low costs – with all that implies – but added to this all the other, complementary functions that the best late eighteenth-century post-roads gave: rapid communication for people and specialized freights, such as mail, samples of goods and gold. In both functions railways were superior, so that they had knocked out all the long-distance coaches by 1850 and had made most of the canals unprofitable (but not until the era of the lorry in the twentieth century did the canals become derelict). Steam brought improvements over water when applied to transport as it did when applied to power.[1] Canals, like the water wheels, were subject to all the limitations of drought and flood and freeze. The routeing of canals and their efficiency in operation in speed and costs was much limited by the nature of the country. Locking up the two miles to Devizes on the Kennet and Avon canal could take half a day. Cotton took 36 hours to get from Liverpool to Manchester at the best of times by canal and river. Huskisson fought to get the Liverpool and Manchester Railway Bill through Parliament with the plea that the canal monopoly was holding merchants and manufacturers wanting to distribute raw materials and foodstuffs inland from Liverpool up to ransom, and that cotton was taking longer to reach the mills from Liverpool than it was on the voyage from New Orleans. Tolls were cut from 15s. per ton to 10s. per ton as soon as the railway opened in 1830. Equal freight rates thus

[1] No sophisticated 'cost-benefit' analysis to measure the extent of the economic advantage of railways over canals as a transport medium for the economy has as yet been attempted for the U.K.

made it much more attractive to send goods by rail than by canal. Indeed, the canals lost traffic even though their average level of freight rates was lower than that of the railways. With higher speed and greater regularity, a further enormous advantage of a railway over a canal was in the higher intensity of traffic able to work a line (and hence cut overhead costs by expanding the volume of traffic sharing them). Roads in the twentieth century, with effective lorry transport, have allowed even greater intensity of use. Many of the costs of transport are incurred in breaking bulk and trans-shipment: the longer the hauls in railway logistics, the greater the economies between shipment points – at least in Britain. Here the railways had another advantage over the canals. It was technically very much easier for industrial and mining plants to be directly connected to the rail-net, by spur lines and sidings, than to a canal net. Of course, lorry haulage had an even greater advantage in eliminating breaking bulk and trans-shipment than railways. Local deliveries from stations increased enormously during the nineteenth century. Thus, although the coach proprietors were right in thinking that railways would kill the long-distance, high-speed runs, which were the pride of the turnpikes, in fact the vast increase in the traffic deployed on the railways meant an increase in the demand for horses. The numbers of dray and cab-horses increased much more than the numbers of coaching horses declined.

In short, when viewed from the angle of efficiency in time or costs, or ability to move the expanding volume of goods in transit, the railways were the only form of transport able to respond to the rising momentum of mechanized industry and the urban revolution with which it was associated. Although the canals carried rising traffic, and the preponderant part of the freight that moved, for many years after 1830, the main increments in the demand for transport were sustained by the railways, without which the whole momentum of industrialization and urbanization would have been slowed. When an innovation characterizes an age as much as the railways did that of early Victorian England, one should anticipate that they would enter the nation's folklore. For the United States even more than Britain, the railroad took the place that the forest holds in

Scandinavian and German myth. One superb expression of this, on a tombstone in the South porch at Ely Cathedral, commemorates the death of the engine driver and stoker of the Norwich to London train which crashed on Christmas Eve 1845, and is a sort of steam-powered Pilgrim's Progress, entitled: 'The Spiritual Railway'.[1]

The Up-Line

The line to Heaven by Christ was made
With Heavenly Truth the Rails are laid . . .
God's Word is the first Engineer
It points the way to Heaven so dear . . .
God's Love the Fire, his Truth the Steam . . .
That drives the engine and the train
In First and Second and Third Class
Repentance, Faith and Holiness . . .
Come then poor Sinners, now's the time
At any station on the Line
If you'll repent and turn from Sin
The Train will stop and take you in.

The idea and practice of railways was well known before 1800. The demands of any heavy traffic in bulk goods along a regular run tends to induce a 'rail' concept. This had been implemented since the seventeenth century and was widely practised in the eighteenth: for quarries at Bath, ore-mines (as in Cornwall) or for coal transport. Tramways from the coal and iron mines at Coalbrookdale were using cast-iron rails from 1767. By 1800 about 200 miles of tramways serviced coalmining 'staithes' along the rivers of the north-east coast coalfield, mainly the Tyne. Twenty-three public railway acts had been passed by Parliament before the Stockton and Darlington line was projected in 1823, most of them short horse tramways with a range of up to 15 miles. Almost all of them were projected to shift coal. In the decade after 1800 about half a dozen persons, for the most part colliery engineers, were struggling to adapt the steam engine for traction: Trevithick at Merthyr Tydfil; Blenkinsop at Middleton; Blackett at Wylam and George Stephenson at Killingsworth.

---

[1] For complete text see J. Warburg (ed.), *The Industrial Muse* (1958), pp. 28–9.

Stephenson had already proved that the friction of an iron wheel on an iron rail was quite sufficient to provide enough grip for heavy haulage (a point about which great scepticism existed at the time). He had transferred the flange from the rail, which had previously been L-shaped in section, to the wheel; and he and Timothy Hackforth in 1810 simultaneously lighted on the crucial technical trick which made steam locomotion effective – the steam-blast. By throwing the exhaust steam up the boiler-fire chimney the power of the fire and steam-raising capacity were much increased. This did for the locomotive what Watt's separate condenser had done for the steam engine in the 1770's.

However, the victory of the locomotive over the horse and the fixed engine using cables was long in coming. The Stockton and Darlington line, opened in 1825, at first used locomotives for only a relatively short level section of the route. Primary motive power came from stationary engines. The real proving ground for the locomotive was in 1829 at the famous Rainhill trial, where the proprietors of the Liverpool and Manchester Railway Co. held a public competition to determine their choice of engine, laying down very strict specifications for size, weight, power and reliability. There were many entries, with many more being kept out of the competition by the strict limits imposed on weights. Stephenson's victory and the triumphant success of the line when it was opened in 1830 established the monopoly of the locomotive, which was the sole motive power there from the start – an unprecedented thing. This also set up George Stephenson and his son Robert as the leading railway engineers, riveting their gauge of 4 ft $8\frac{1}{2}$ in. over most of the lines in the country built by them and their pupils.

Several conclusions should be drawn about the development of railways up to this point. Innovation in transport was one of the clearest examples of being induced by economic necessity as the need intensified. Successful innovation came after a ferment of experimenting in many different parts of the country. Almost all the early projections had freight as their prospective earning power, not passengers. The Stockton and Darlington line, for example, was projected by the Quaker businessmen Pease, Richardson and Backhouse, to break the monopoly established in coal production by the noble coal owners of the Tyne hinterland by developing new collieries to the south and opening the way to water carriage on the Tees at Stockton. Liverpool merchants distributing inland were behind the Liverpool and Manchester line. In the case of the north-east the 'mineral lines' did prosper mainly on coal freights, but the surprise of the 1830's was that of the enormous potential passenger traffic revealed. Receipts from passengers, even on the Liverpool and Manchester line, were more than double freight receipts until 1845. Freight receipts first exceeded receipts from passengers only after 1851. This is not surprising in retrospect. Fares second class (in covered, upholstered carriages) were about half the coach fares, and passengers saved much expense in tips, meals and beds on the longer coach runs – quite apart from the convenience of faster, safer, steadier travelling. This tapped a new market of travellers quite unsuspected in 1830: 400,000 persons travelled in the first year of its opening; ·5 million travelled in the first year of the London and Birmingham line in 1839; and 1 million were using this line annually by 1845. Perhaps the most difficult result of the railway system to evaluate is the effect of this increase in human mobility, the speed of being able to do business and the increased assurance in business that rapid communication allowed.

Up to the mid-1830's the lines faced outwards towards the coast in the main, reaching towards rivers or canals, feeding existing waterways, extending water carriage. They were thus of local significance or tributary to water carriage rather than providing inter-regional transfers by creating interior lines of communication across the country as the canals were doing. The building of the main trunk lines came in the 1830's and 1840's. Up to 1830 the development of the railway system had not owed very much to the rhythm of the trade cycle. Acts had tended to concentrate in years of prosperity but this was as much due to the fact that, at such times, existing transport facilities were strained to their limit as it was to Stock Exchange booms at the peak year of the trade cycle. The rich Quakers did not need to follow the ebb and flow of Stock Exchange funds and confidence: most of their capital was raised through their

TABLE VI : *Railway mileage*

Date	Mileage sanctioned	Mileage opened	Total sanctioned (Cumulative)	Total opened (Cumulative)
1832	39	26	419	166
1833	218	42	638	208
1834	131	90	769	298
1835	201	40	970	338
1836	955	65	1,925	403
1837	544	137	2,469	540
1838	49	202	2,518	742
1839	54	227	2,573	970
1840	—19	528	2,553	1,479
1841	14	277	2,568	1,775
1842	55	164	2,623	1,939
1843	90	105	2,717	2,044
1844	810	192	3,524	2,236
1845	2,816	294	6,340	2,530
1846	4,540	606	10,881	3,136
1847	1,295	740	12,176	3,876
1848	373	1,253	12,549	5,129
1849	16	811	12,565	5,939
1850	7	618	12,572	6,559
1851	126	243	12,698	6,803

SOURCE: H. G. Lewin, *Early British Railways*, 1928, and, *The Railway Mania and its Aftermath*, 1936. Fractions of a mile omitted.

kinship groups and from persons hoping to profit commercially by using the line. In any case the Stockton and Darlington Bill was held up for four years by purely parliamentary obstruction. The initial impetus for the Liverpool and Manchester line came from the failure of the canal to cope with increments of traffic with the expansion of trade in 1821. Parliamentary and technical delays put the bill back from 1824 to 1826; but the sources of capital were mainly from Lancashire, and this largely disconnects the timing of the project from the mania of 1825 on the London Stock Exchange. The projectors did, in fact, suffer from the tightness of credit in 1827 in the aftermath of that crisis and they got a loan of £100,000 out of £510,000 total capital as a temporary help from public funds. From the opening of the Liverpool and Manchester line in 1830, when railways were fully launched on the national consciousness and the public realized exactly how profitable they could be, further projections during the next 20 years did fall in the pattern of the investment cycle, clustering in the two periods 1834–7, 1844–7. The state of confidence in the money market, the availability and cheapness of credit, conditioned this rush of capital.

The importance of the coming of the railways as a service for the economy as a whole lies in the fact that they enabled economic activity in all other sectors of the economy to expand. But the railways were also important as an industry in their own right, creating employment, using capital and demanding economic resources. In this sense they became one of the most important industries in the country by the 1840's. A town like Middlesbrough was the creation of the railway system as a service to the economy – it was the site of a new 'Quaker' port opened up by the new transport. Crewe, Swindon and Wolverton were creations of the railways as an industry – being the sites for the workshops and engine and carriage building plants of main-line companies. The largest contracting firms and the largest engineering works in the country in 1850 were those working for railway business.

The timing of the projection of railway companies is different from that of the commitment of resources and labour in actually constructing the lines. The boom of the 1830's centring on 1836 had a 3–4 year gestation period before the investment came to fruition in 1840. Nine hundred and fifty-five miles were projected in 1836; mileage constructed reached 227 in 1839; 528 in 1840; 277 in 1841. The dimension of the boom of the 1840's was two or three times that of the 'thirties and the gestation period of railway investment then was slightly less – 2 years – the peak in the sanctioned mileage being in 1846 and the peak construction year 1848. In 1846, 4,540 miles were sanctioned; in 1848, 1,253 miles were constructed. By 1851, 6,800 miles were open. The difference was partly accounted for by the fact that the 1836 boom was characterized by the construction of long trunk lines – London to Birmingham, Birmingham to Lancashire, Yorkshire to Derby, Bristol to London. The rise of the great contractors, and the improvement of their organizations, meant that the lines of the 1840's were built more speedily. Morton Peto was employing 14,000 in specialized construction gangs and Thomas Brassey 8,000 in the 1840's. Housebuilding, shipping and other capital goods industries had a gestation period for investment of about a year (that is, between the placing of the orders and the completion of the project). The fact that railways dominated the construction activity of the 1830's and 1840's and had a much longer interval between projection and completion is of the highest significance. These industries often moved contracyclically with the trade cycle because of this time-lag, as in 1839–40 and 1847–8.[1] The labour force in construction touched 100,000 in 1840 and 300,000 in 1847; quite apart from the 60,000 persons employed in running the system in 1850.

British railways were very expensive: their cost averaged £40,000 per mile, which was three or four times larger than for American and continental railways. About £250 million had been raised in nominal capital by 1850. It is very difficult to discover exactly how much capital went into actual income raising flows which stimulated economic activity. Certainly, it was not the same figure as the nominal capital raised by the companies. Not all of this had been used to pay wages or buy materials. Possibly 10–20 per cent went to purchase land (very often being 'paid for' in shares). The London and Birmingham line paid out £·75 million to landowners as the easiest way to soften potential parliamentary opposition. A great deal of parliamentary corruption helped to wash the waves of railway bills through both Houses: 178 M.P.s were directors of Railway Companies by 1847. Over £·5 million was spent in lobbying by both sides when George Hudson was trying to block the projection of the direct Great Northern line from London to York in 1845–6. These expenses were usually 'transfer payments' in paper, subsequently proving a drain on the profits of the companies, but not generating income flows through the process of railway construction. Other reasons for the very high cost of British railway construction were the nature of the country, particularly in the

[1] See above, pp. 236–7.

north and in Wales, and also the very high costs foisted on the companies by their chief engineers. The railways became an engineer's paradise – sometimes a megalomania – with elaborate stone-built bridges, stations, engine sheds, expensively bedded tracks and the like.[1]

As far as can be calculated, the boom of the 1830's produced about £50 million (1833–43) in such income raising flows; and the boom of the 1840's £125 million (the peak flows being £9 million per annum in 1839 and £30 million in 1848). In 1846–8 railway investment was absorbing 5–7 per cent of the national income (about half total investment and very much the largest single slice). This was equivalent to two-thirds the value of all domestic exports, and entailed a £16 million wage bill for a 250,000 labour force. The point of all this, remembering the labour figures too, is that swings in railway investment created at their peak almost as much employment as the entire cotton industry, while the income raising flows were greater than all the fluctuations in foreign trade in these years. At the times of the railway booms domestic investment was the prime mover in the economy. As expected, the prices of iron and coal and bricks moved in parallel with the timing of railways contracts, their most important single market at these times being rolled iron for rails, castings for 'chairs' on sleepers, and constructional iron. In 1850 locomotives were using 1 million tons of coal per year for steam raising.

The economic impact of the railways as a stimulus to the economy cannot be measured by their direct effects only in creating demands for coal, iron and constructional materials, and in generating flows of wages. Coal used in current consumption by railways for steam raising, for example, was less than 2 per cent of national production. Higher demands were made indirectly, through the use of coal in metal production and brick production destined for railway contracts. Less directly still, the railways were instrumental in encouraging urban growth, and industrial expansion not having direct links with inputs to

---

[1] Stamford's local station is a fine example, all in dressed stone with elaborate ornamentation (including the engine shed) – a worthy scenic neighbour to Burleigh House.

railway construction, through their effects as a service to the economy generally. They were also one of the main breeding grounds for the complex of new – and scarce – engineering skills which modernization of the economy required on an ever-increasing scale. The capital market was also helped.

One can see what a wasteful process railway investment was in this country up to 1851 by the fact that less than half the mileage projected was, in fact, constructed. But, however wasteful, the boom of the 1830's at least laid the foundations of the trunk-line system and saw 1,500 miles of track in operation at its close. With the exception of the matrix of local lines on the north-east coalfield, the same regional demands induced the same priorities in the development of the railway system as with the canals. The list of canals in order of the relative profitability of the different navigations in 1825 has broadly the same distribution of traffic as the 1850 railways. Lancashire was the site of the opening of the railway age, apart from mineral lines, in 1830, as she had priority in the canal age. The first trunk routes were from the north-west to the midlands; and from the midlands to London; then followed the north-east to the midlands to London, then the midlands to Bristol, London to Bristol. East Anglia lagged behind in both canal development and railways.[1] The Eastern Counties railway remained an unprofitable line; and it was losses on the Eastern Counties that exposed the weaknesses of George Hudson's finances in 1849 and ruined him.

After 1840 several indications show that the railways were at last beginning to weld the economy together along interior lines of communication, translating the new scale of costs and efficiencies onto inter-regional transfers. On trunk routes between London and Liverpool, York, Bristol and the south coast by 1850, speeds were averaging between 30 and 40 m.p.h. In 1839 Bradshaw, a Manchester Quaker, first published his *Railway Guide* for the convenience of his Quaker friends – the first national timetable. Also in the 1840's a trend developed towards the amalgamation and consolidation of regional systems under the control of the company controlling the main through-routes, which became the spines of the regional systems. The

[1] A similar priority is now developing in motorways.

controllers of these main routes adopted a quasi-military strategy designed to tap through-traffic and block through-traffic flows to their rivals, further evidence for the changing nature of the railways' role.

George Hudson controlled 1,000 miles of track opening out from York in 1840. He amalgamated the Midland Counties with the Birmingham and Derby to collect all the London and North Eastern traffic. Then he bought his way into the Birmingham and Gloucester to protect the south-west flank and feed that traffic into his system. In 1847 he drove the east-coast route to Scotland, to control in all 1,500 miles of track and £30 million in capital. But he had been concealing losses and paying dividends out of capital. Only a great increase in traffic could have saved him in 1847-8, so he was caught out by the trade depression and forced into bankruptcy. George Carr Glyn[1] the London banker had developed a similar regional control based on the London and Birmingham, and thence to Lancashire.

I. K. Brunel had consolidated the Great Western and its tributary companies and feeder lines between London and the south-west, based on the Bristol to London trunk route. All this regional system was on the 7-ft gauge in contrast to Stephenson's 4 ft 8½ in. The problem of the gauges, which arose in 1847 when the Great Western (on 7 ft) met the Midland (on 4 ft 8½ in.) at Gloucester and Cheltenham, was yet another sign that inter-regional trunk traffic was becoming important. Parliament took the decision, in principle, to support Stephenson and his pupils but the problem only ended in 1892 when the Great Western reluctantly converted to the narrow gauge.

Two other points also show how the national economy was being geared up to the trunk railway system. In 1842 Glyn founded the Railway Clearing House, an association of the main-line companies to settle inter-company accounts between themselves. Then as the system became consolidated after 1850 with over 6,000 miles of track in operation, two routes to Scotland opened with the links to Holyhead and the Channel ports all

---

[1] He became Lord Wolverton, taking his title from the small village which the workshops of the London and Birmingham line, of which he was chairman, had made into a bustling, grimy, little town.

operating, receipts from freight climbed level to passenger earnings and passed them in 1852. More than half the tonnage was coal. Only bulk goods where time was no object went by canal, and very few canals paid dividends after 1850.

A financial as well as an operational consolidation was proceeding from the 1840's. Most new capital was raised initially by *pro rata* issues to existing shareholders after 1847, much of it *subsequently* jobbed on the Stock Exchange by re-sales. Capital at first came predominantly from the counties where lines were being built (judging from the lists of addresses of shareholders for Lancashire and Yorkshire railways) and from London. From the boom of the 1840's the net became nationwide – anonymous, *rentier* capital 'seeking its 5 per cent', but Lancashire capital also contributed prominently to many trunk lines in the 1830's and 1840's, as the 'Liverpool Party' of shareholders in such railways as the Great Western, the London to Southampton, London to Birmingham, and the Eastern Counties showed. Long-term capital was pouring out of Lancashire as well as being sucked in. The existing main-line companies extended their financial controls by subsequently buying feeder lines. The epoch of the take-over bid was well established in the railway world by 1850. The 200 companies of 1843 had been brought into 22 regional groups by that year, and the skeletons of the present regions of British Railways were already there.

Financial consolidation pyramided capital into the main companies in a very wasteful way. Competitive lines still went on being built – stupid, petty railways. The profitability of the main lines kept tempting further construction in advance of traffic, such railways being built 'on faith'. Capital was cheap, while the railway preference share had become the safe middle-class alternative to gilt-edged – which again tempted excessive construction. Yet another main line was built to London in 1899, the Great Central from Sheffield to Marylebone, giving London its thirteenth main-line terminus. Of course, an essential service which suppliers of risk capital perform in a market economy as investors is to lose their money occasionally. Many local railways and canals never paid a dividend but were able to cover their current costs of operation and thus kept operating – a financial failure but an economic asset. By 1880, 18,000 miles of track were in operation, with a great proliferation of sidings and buildings. The total network of the United Kingdom in 1900 was 22,000 miles and in 1914, 23,000. British Railways now rue the day that capital was so plentiful and optimism so great: £1,300 million was in the system in 1914 – the most expensive heritage of Victorian success. But there were no more manias after 1846 and railway building no longer dominated the investment cycle in quite the same way as it had done between 1830 and 1850.

The battle of the gauges and competitive trunk and local lines give evidence for the absence of national planning in the British system, the price of such unrestricted private initiative in transport, in contrast to the Belgian or Prussian system. An official enquiry in 1917 called the system a 'riot of individuality'.[1] All sorts of inefficiencies resulted from this lack of co-ordination, increasing the obstacles for long-distance transfers which had also made the canal system much less useful for trunk traffic, without trans-shipment, than it might have been. The carters profited, but everyone else lost by the obstacles of getting freight between termini on the opposite sides of large towns. A link existed on the map between Liverpool and Hull via Manchester in 1840, but through traffic across Manchester was not established until 1844 without trans-shipment.

Apart from great wastage and corruption in the projection of the lines; heavy overcapitalization in individual lines and in competitive lines; costs were high in operating the system, and in engineering, very often high technical standards came at the expense of competitive standards in costs, with too many types of engine and rolling stock. Very little technical standardization occurred between railway companies.

At one point, in 1844, it appeared that state intervention, under the unlikely patronage of Mr Gladstone at the Board of Trade, was going to establish a certain national uniformity by statute. The Railway Act of that year laid down some important conditions. An inspectorate was set up to enforce minimum standards of safety, signalling and braking and telegraph

[1] One company had 41 different types of handbrakes in use on its wagons.

systems. Companies were compelled to run one covered-carriage train a day, stopping at all stations, offering a fixed fare third class which could not be raised without parliamentary permission – the so-called Parliamentary Train. More remarkably the Act contained provisions to allow the state to buy out all the companies when their charters expired in the 1860's. But vested interests in the companies, and a general hostility to such dramatic state control over functions which were much more than protecting women and children at work, meant that the Board of Trade did not father the British national railways of the 1860's. Bankruptcy in the 1930's and the war ensued before the nationalization of the 1940's.

Reading list

BAXTER, R. D. 'Railway extension and its results', *Journal of the Statistical Society*, 1867, reprinted in E. M. Carus-Wilson (ed.), *Essays in Economic History*, vol. 3, London, 1962.

BROADBRIDGE, S. A. 'The early capital market: the Lancashire and Yorkshire Railway', *Economic History Review*, 2nd series, 1955, **8,** no. 2.

KENWOOD, A. G. 'Railway investment in Britain, 1825–1875', *Economica*, 1965, **32,** no. 127.

LAMBERT, R. S. *The Railway King, 1800–1871: a study of George Hudson and the business morals of his time*, reissue, London, 1964.

MITCHELL, B. R. 'The coming of the railways and UK economic growth', *Journal of Economic History*, 2nd series, 1964, **24,** no. 3.

POLLINS, H. 'The finances of the Liverpool and Manchester Railway', *Economic History Review*, 2nd series, 1952, **5,** no. 1.

POLLINS, H. 'The marketing of railway shares in the first half of the 19th century', *Economic History Review*, 2nd series, 1954, **7,** no. 2.

POLLINS, H. 'Railway contractors and the finance of railway development in Britain', *Journal of Transport History*, 1957, **8,** nos. 1, 2.

ROLT, L. T. C. *Isambard Kingdom Brunel: a biography*, London, 1961.

ROLT, L. T. C. *G. and R. Stephenson: the railway revolution*, London, 1960; cf. SMILES, S. *The Life of George Stephenson and his Son Robert Stephenson*, rev. ed., London, 1868.

SAVAGE, C. *An Economic History of Transport*, rev. ed., 3rd imp., London, 1966.

SIMMONS, J. *The Railways of Britain: an historical introduction*, London, 1961.

286 RAILWAYS

SAVAGE, C., An Economic History of Transport, rev. ed., 3rd imp., London, 1966.

SIMMONS, J., The Railways of Britain: an historical introduction, London, 1961.

11 The free trade system and capital exports

THE COMING OF FREE TRADE: IDEAS AND POLICY

The opposition to the protective system surrounding British foreign trade came from four quarters: writers, independent commentators and economists; ministerial circles in government and officials in some government departments; the business community; and – finally – the legislature, without the concurrence of which the old statutes and duties and restrictions could not be abandoned. The arguments for free trade, or a less restricted trade, were both theoretical, derived from a general system of analysis in the case of certain writers and thinkers, and practical, *ad hoc*, sectional, from the belief that freer trade in certain particulars would bring direct commercial gain to the interest group advocating the change.

The theoretical challenge developed in the mid-eighteenth century, long before the momentum of industrialization had gained any strength.[1] It took almost another century before the weight of commercial interests was added to these criticisms on a scale large enough to impress Parliament. Just as revenue demands for war finance had been the most important influences in raising the tariff walls round Britain at the end of the seventeenth century, rather than any ostensible intention to protect home industry, the claims of the revenue, desperately short of acceptable alternative sources of income from taxation, were the most important single influence in postponing the dismantlement of the protective system in the early nineteenth century. There is thus a certain paradox to the fact that the process of industrialization in Britain was nurtured for a century under protection. Fiscal necessity, reinforced by the accretion of

[1] See above, p. 89.

vested interests, explained this situation more than ideological conviction.

The theoretical economic arguments were elaborated by Adam Smith in 1776, formalized by Ricardo, Bentham, James and John Stuart Mill, and spread by a host of popularizers such as J. R. McCulloch. Many cross-currents created this stream: one can trace predecessors to Hume and Adam Smith (hunting the pedigree is always a favourite game) but the *Wealth of Nations* made the great impact in this theoretical battle and had gone into 8 editions in English and several other languages within 20 years. The essence of the argument was that a system of freely-operating market prices, under naturally competitive conditions, would ensure the lowest effective prices to the consumer and produce the most efficient allocation of resources between the different branches of economic activity. The ultimate test of efficiency and welfare thus became a freely moving price level not distorted by legislative interference. Parallel arguments applied the same sort of analysis to the operation of competition within a national economy as to its operation between nations in the international economy. Smith's analysis of the mercantile system concluded that it was a plot against the interests of consumers, who faced higher prices as a result of all the interference by political action with the free flow of the market economy. Such a generalization covered the tariffs prejudicing the import of corn, or French wine, or non-Empire sugar and timber, and the bounties boosting the export of British goods, and the monopoly of trade in specific areas given to the Levant Company or the East India Company. 'Consumption,' concluded Smith, '. . . is the sole end and purpose of all production . . . But in the mercantile system the interest of the consumer is almost constantly sacrificed to that of the producer and it seems to consider production and not consumption as the ultimate end and object of all industry and commerce.' This is exactly the argument echoed by the Report of the Committee on Import Duties in 1840, which heralded Peel's free trade budgets: 'The real question at issue is, do we propose to serve the nation or particular individuals' – that is everyone as consumers, or a few persons as producers. The fiscal slogan adopted to support this thesis was: 'Taxation for revenue purposes only'. The budget, that is to say, was not to be used to divert natural economic flows for political objectives. This argument made very large assumptions – about employment, strategic weaknesses, the development of industrial competition, anti-social activities of different sorts and so forth. Many writers and economists made certain qualifications to its general thesis. Adam Smith thought the strategic purposes of the Navigation Acts, supporting naval strength, had a certain justification. Ricardo thought that landowners deserved a small fixed duty on corn to compensate them for the burden of the land-tax.

Smith and other writers added more practical arguments. The fact that the *Wealth of Nations* appeared in the same year as the Declaration of Independence was appropriate. Dean Tucker of Gloucester, an earlier writer on economic affairs, emphasized these political consequences of colonial restrictions in the 1740's and 1750's. He regarded the Americans as an ungovernable mob who would always trade in the best markets and heed British commercial laws only as long as they were frightened of the French. The revolt of the colonists proved to most people that in colonies where legislative restrictions seriously challenged their natural course of development the political problems created would be more trouble to live with for Britain than their economic advantages were worth. And then came the self-contradictory conclusion (also held by Dean Tucker) that, in any case, Britain was the best customer for the Americans; that the American continent would naturally develop, by the force of economic logic alone, as a great raw material and food supplier to Britain and a great market for British goods, Navigation Acts or no Navigation Acts. This, in fact, seemed proved by experience after 1782, when exports to the United States were growing more rapidly than those in any other market. By 1836 almost a quarter of British exports (£12·5 million out of £53 million) went to the United States, and four-fifths of Lancashire's cotton came from there. With this great example of the successful development of complementary economies without political subservience, the argument for free trade and against the colonial system was generalized.

Radicals like Tom Paine, Cobbett, Cartwright and John Bright (who knew America well) were against colonies anyway, because they thought imperial power was usurpation of freedom. But free trade had an anti-imperial aspect to it for such as Cobden and Lord Brougham also. Even the young Disraeli spoke about colonies dropping away like ripe fruit in the 1850's. The strategic argument in favour of 'colonies, shipping and the navy' as the common toast went, also dissolved before free trade logic. Cobden was a free trader because he thought the interlocking of the world economy by free trade, as international specialization developed, would prevent war – despite the politicians doing their worst. Free trade meant international peace – in 1851 the first great International Exhibition became the symbol of this. Thus mercantilist logic had been reversed. The existence of British naval hegemony was not part of this particular argument and debates on naval estimates were on an altogether different day in the House of Commons. One of the reasons that persuaded other nations of English hypocrisy at the time was such a discovery that political restraint in trade was wrong, coming conveniently at a point when it was assumed not to ensure any economic advantages. Another was that the anti-imperialist trend was flourishing in British politics in Westminster in the mid-nineteenth century, while quite a lot of the map in India and Africa was being painted red.[1]

Up to 1820 these arguments had not received very powerful support from business interests looking for direct commercial advantages from a change in laws. The business communities had been bitterly divided over their attitude to Pitt's proposals for freeing trade to some degree with France and Ireland in 1785-6. No great commercial battle was waged from the provinces to get the monopoly of the East India Company (a London group of merchants) abolished in 1813. Indeed, the struggle against Napoleon put back the evolution of free trade policy as much as it did the course of parliamentary reform. The commitment of the business world to the struggle for free trade is usually said to date from 1820 when the London merchants

---

[1] J. Gallaher and R. E. Robinson, 'The Imperialism of Free Trade', *Economic History Review* (1953).

petitioned Parliament for free trade policies, their document containing 'all the great principles of commercial policy', as Huskisson acknowledged. But this really antedated the commitment of business leaders. The real promoters of the petition were the members of the Political Economy Club, founded by Ricardo and his friends to promote the new truth in economics, a club composed mainly of writers, publicists and officials, several of whom had failed in business before taking to the desk or the pen. Another irony was that some of the most aggressive free traders, such as James Mill, John Deacon Hume, John McGregor, were officials in the East India Company headquarters, the Customs and Excise and the Board of Trade – exactly the bodies controlling monopolies and administering the tariffs and the Navigation Acts. The Board of Trade, in particular, was rife with free trade officials, busily trying to educate their political chiefs. Thomas Tooke, a member of the Political Economy Club, wrote the petition for the London merchants in 1820 and then hawked it round the business leaders he knew to get it signed. Eventually he found support, led by Samuel Thornton, a disgruntled Russia merchant prejudiced by the duties favouring Canadian timber. But it was a struggle. He had found more sympathy from Lord Liverpool and rising young statesmen like Huskisson and Canning, and wrote wryly: 'the truth is that the government were at that time far more sincere and resolute free traders than the merchants of London'.

The next 20 years did see the support of commercial opinion mount, until the real attack on the old system came with Peel in 1841. Undoubtedly the main centre of opposition became Manchester and Liverpool, led by the Manchester Chamber of Commerce, which had been founded explicitly to press for the removal of restraints upon Lancashire trade. Its members were not necessarily persuaded that this was a new absolute truth, with an abstract vision of ultimate efficiency and justice, but they protested where the shoe pinched and were quite happy to use any arguments to support a case based on expediency. Their first complaint was of exclusion from lucrative monopolies established by statute. The abolition of the East India Company's monopoly over the Indian trade in 1813, which allowed ships from the outports to trade direct east of the Cape for the first time, had resulted in a tremendous rise in the exports of Lancashire cotton goods. From under 1 million yards exported by the Company in 1814, consignments reached 56 million yards by 1832. This success redoubled the pressure from Lancashire to abolish the 'China monopoly' of the trade between British India and China – still reserved for the East India Company until 1834 – and the Levant Company monopoly of near-eastern trade, abolished in 1825.

The next problem was one of raw materials, which invoked the whole structure of the colonial system. The tremendous expansion of production in textiles had made the search for low-cost raw materials increasingly important, and was developing the commercial and political influence of the leaders of the industry. By 1820 it was clear that only the United States could increase cotton supplies fast enough to cope with rising Lancashire demand. Egypt, India, the African Coast, the West Indies had all been swamped as sources for cotton by the plantations of the Carolinas and Georgia, and by the new boom area of the Mississippi valley. Lancashire men were determined that they should not be prejudiced by duties designed to protect Empire cotton. The raw material duties were very low compared with those on timber, or coffee and sugar, but the cotton interest was much better equipped to make an issue of cotton import duties. The principle was not fully admitted, however, until 1845.

An even more pressing problem was the opposite constraint of export markets. Industrialization was exerting equal pressure on developing new export markets to clear the mounting flood of cotton goods from the mills. Empire areas could never be the natural or sufficient outlets for this. Lancashire and Scottish merchants were attempting to break into or develop a whole series of new, unsophisticated, non-Empire countries – south-east Asia, Brazil and Argentina, the west coast of Africa, Australia and the west coast of Central and South America. These countries had relatively little connection with the world market, in many cases, save through these British and Scottish merchants attempting to open them up with mainly bi-lateral links in world commerce, with Great Britain. In such areas

great difficulty arose in developing a trade to balance their purchases of British goods; and in the nature of the case the only
feasible exports which could be developed in these countries
were those of primary produce: cash-crops like timber, coffee,
cocoa, hides, grain, wool. But many of these raw products,
which such economies might develop quickly as exports to pay
for British goods, were excluded by the heavy tariffs protecting
Empire produce like sugar, coffee, timber, or native British
agricultural produce. Merchants in some of Lancashire's export
markets slowly became convinced that exports to them were a
dependent variable to Britain's accepting imports from them.
Foreign countries needed to acquire sterling credits before they
could purchase British goods.

A particular shipping problem also existed in these markets,
which reinforced the other arguments. Shippers complained of
a lack of return freights once ships had reached a country like
Brazil with British goods. Coffee, or other primary produce, was
said to be the sole means of providing direct return cargoes, but
these were prejudiced by high import duties. Shipping would
be made very uncompetitive with other nations if return
voyages had to be made in ballast. Stories were being told that
non-Empire coffee was being taken across the Atlantic to touch
at a British possession in Africa in order to get under the tariff
wall, and that timber had been sent from the Baltic to Canada
and then brought back again to Britain to escape the 65s. per
load duty on non-Empire timber.

In sophisticated markets, where effective independent governments were able to enforce policy – such as the United States
and northern Europe – exporters became increasingly worried
that, if Britain maintained discrimination against their exports,
British exporters would face rising tariff barriers in retaliation.
One of the first main compromises of the tariff system came from
Canning's and Huskisson's acknowledgement of the force of this
argument in 1822. Between 1823 and 1830 they established a
series of 'reciprocity treaties' with most European states to
remove this threat.

The intensity of the pressure for free trade legislation from
Lancashire mounted in every depression in foreign trade in the

second quarter of the century. It had become apparent by the end of the 1830's that the vastly increasing flow of textiles abroad was not paying off in equivalent increases in the value of exports. British exporters (and the balance of trade) were being cheated of the rewards of the increases in volume by falling export prices. The analysis ran that this was occasioned by the lack of opportunities for some of these countries to sell primary produce to Britain. The terms of trade between primary produce imports and manufactured goods exports were deteriorating during the 25 years after 1815.

All these arguments were gathered up into one general creed and focused by two events in the late 1830's – the failure of foreign markets to pick up again in steady expansion after the collapse of the trade boom in 1837 and the foundation of the Anti-Corn Law League as the depression began to deepen in 1839. By 1841–2, in the trough of the worst trade depression of the century, the most vocal business interests had become convinced that the only remedy for their problems lay in a stiff dose of free trade legislation. Indeed, by 1841 they were ready to face the unpleasant fiscal medicine of a new income tax, the precondition that made it financially possible for the government to give away revenue from customs.

The Anti-Corn Law League brought specific arguments for cheap food into the battle. Their strongest argument was a variation on the problem of the effect that high food prices had in depressing home demand. If food could be cheaper then purchasing power at home would be released to expand the demand for manufactured goods in the home market. Possibly, too, more food imports from some areas would do something to help British exports and shippers if the food import trades could be regularized and the sterling credits, created by food imports to Britain, be devoted to buying British goods in return rather than causing an outflow of bullion. These arguments were accompanied by conflicting assumptions about the usefulness of lower food prices for lowering wage costs. Some manufacturers hoped that their competitiveness in export markets would be enhanced if cheap food brought lower wages (on the assumption that the 'floor' of wage rates was determined by the price of bread). This was not an argument to be used very forcibly in public debate if mill owners wanted their windows to remain unsmashed but it was possibly the one heeded by the urban proletariat in Lancashire, who did not give much support to the Anti-Corn Law League.

Members of the Manchester Chamber of Commerce were still not completely uncritical in the support they gave to the free traders. They painted an alarming picture of the disasters that would befall Britain if the export of machinery, particularly textile machinery, was allowed. They battled against the engineers who pleaded before a Parliamentary Committee in 1824 for the right to export markets, and they kept up a running fight against the Board of Trade officials licensing machinery export until it was authorized by statute in 1843. Some manufacturers protested equally hard when Parliament allowed the emigration of skilled artisans in 1825. Others, the weaving firms and finishers, wanted a heavy tax on the export of textile yarns, but interests were obviously divided here. Liverpool timber merchants and some Liverpool shippers put pressure on Huskisson to maintain the high differential duties against non-Empire timber, to protect their Canadian interests. Liverpool was reluctant to face the competition of American shippers (who had taken over from the Dutch as the main rivals in shipping) and hence opposed the repeal of the Navigation Acts. Equally, business communities were not slow to demand government protection of trade in politically insecure countries, wanting British consuls to be appointed in South American states. They sought pressure from Whitehall to force reluctant governments to allow British merchants to distribute goods under reasonable conditions, and even military and naval expeditions or the occupation of particular areas when a hostile power, such as China, refused to allow British merchants access to the interior of the country. The abolition of the East India Company monopoly was proved not sufficient to make China a second India for Lancashire. It needed two wars in 1839-42 and 1856 before the truths of free trade became acceptable to the Chinese. Sometimes the logic of free trade needed a little political and naval emphasis, or even some colonizing.

The economic logic of Britain's developing industrial economy thus in the long run lay at the back of these increasingly powerful commercial arguments for free trade. The logic of an expanding population also in the long run would demand the lowering of tariffs on food imports. But legislation was a long time in coming. Economic change, particularly changes in economic policy, remains very dependent on institutional processes, and political sequences, which have a rhythm and a logic of their own to some degree.

In 1830 Henry Parnell, the leading financial expert of the day, commented that if free trade was the right policy the work of introducing it still remained to be done. Apart from the partial dismemberment of the East India Company monopoly and a few reciprocity treaties very little had been changed by that date. Huskisson had relaxed the Navigation Laws a little to allow the colonies some direct trade with Europe. A chaotic jungle of customs regulations (over 500 Acts which only James Deacon Hume was said to understand) had been reduced to a simple code and in the process duties had been slightly lightened. In 1828 an important change had been secured in the Corn Laws. Between 1815 and 1828 no wheat could be imported when the price was below 80s. per quarter; but no duty was imposed when the price was above this figure. Then Huskisson introduced a sliding scale of duties which steadied the corn trade and lowered the general incidence of the duty.

But the government throughout the 1830's did not feel strong enough to introduce more direct taxation and hence did not have the financial resources to dismantle the protective duties, which yielded over £24 million per annum – almost enough to pay the interest on the national debt. Despite presidents of the Board of Trade being pressured by their officials to be free traders, coupled with mounting business pressure after 1825, very little was done until an influential parliamentary enquiry into the customs system took place in 1840 – the Committee on Import Duties. This was virtually rigged by the Board of Trade officials who supplied most of the evidence and were interrogated by dedicated free-trade members of Parliament who had got themselves appointed to the Committee. The report publicized the fact that only a handful of commodities produced large revenues: tea and sugar and tobacco between £3 million and £4 million per annum each; spirits, wine and timber between £1·5 million and £2·5 million each per year; coffee almost £1 million. In 1840 the corn duties yielded over £1 million. Under 20 articles produced 95 per cent of the customs revenues: the remaining 1,000 petty impositions were, in the Committee's words, 'merely vexatious'. Yet the government was still acting with curious indecision.[1]

The Committee reported flatly against the protective system, and the depression of 1841–2 at last fully roused the Lancashire interest. When Peel was returned in 1841 his government was secure enough in Parliament to be able to implement free trade policies at last, and collect an extra £5 million a year by the income tax to replace lost duties. The 1842 budget brought the first strong blow. The sliding scale for corn duties was lowered and Empire wheat let in at a nominal rate, turning the flank of the landed interests. Other duties were brought down and the vigour of the trade revival was such that Cobden, the government and the country were persuaded that free trade had been responsible for this improvement. In 1845 the second major budget continued the work. Whereas the 1842 budget had lowered all duties, maintaining imperial preference, in 1845 preference was itself attacked. Duties on the import of raw cotton and wool (already low) were abolished. Those on non-Empire timber were slashed from 55s. per load to 10s.; the coffee duties reduced from 1s. 3d. per lb to 2d.; sugar from 63s. per cwt to 34s. (with the anti-slavery movement in Parliament powerful enough to keep the old rate of duty imposed on slave-grown sugar; slave-grown cotton was another matter). More important for the landed interests, the duties on cattle, meat, fish, butter, fat and cheese were abolished or reduced.

So by 1846 the Corn Laws were the last isolated citadel under

[1] The debates are strongly reminiscent of ministerial statements in the late 1950's about the government's attitude to Europe; full of allusions about their responsibility to home agriculture and to the Empire/Commonwealth.

attack, and a mine had been sprung under them by allowing Empire wheat in without duty. The 1842 budget, with another sliding scale, had also greatly reduced their effects. 1846 is not the turning point in free trade policies, but the last symbolic political surrender. The timing of the battle was immediately related to the potato famine in Ireland and Scotland, but another short harvest or a business depression would doubtless have set off a similar sequence within a short time if the logic of events of Peel's ministry was any guide. By 1846 the Anti-Corn Law League was the most powerful national pressure group England had known, and upon their techniques of mass meetings, travelling orators, hymns and catechisms a good deal of later Victorian revivalist and temperance – and even trade union – oratory was based.

Despite the parliamentary crisis that the repeal of the Corn Laws brought on there was no question of reversing the swing of policy towards free trade. The Navigation Acts were abolished without any parliamentary squall in 1849, and Russell in the 1850's and Gladstone in the budget of 1860 completed the work, killing off the remnants of the duties on such things as cheese, sugar and timber. Undoubtedly the final acknowledgement of the new system was Cobden's free trade treaty with France in 1860. This did involve the sacrifice of the Coventry ribbon trade to French imports and brought social disaster to the town for some years – a price which had to be paid where high-cost industries were being sheltered from competition.

The only duties remaining on imports were on one or two deliberately chosen articles such as tea, simple to administer, which became the remaining contribution of the working classes to indirect taxation by foreign trade. Free trade's final justification was fiscal: so great was the increase in the volume of trade after 1850 that the vastly reduced rates of tariff brought in almost as high a net total of cash as all the duties in the first half of the century. Customs receipts were about £22 million per annum on average between 1840 and 1870 and dropped only to £20 million at their lowest in 1890. As a proportion of public revenue, however, customs revenue fell from 46 per cent of the total in 1840 to 25 per cent in 1880; from above 30 per cent of import values in 1840 to below 10 per cent after 1865.[1]

If the Anti-Corn Law League had become the most per-
suasive force in the anti-tariff campaign, the arguments deduced
in favour of cheap food underlined the paradoxes of the affair.
The leading advocates of the League were Lancashire employers;
and its most vociferous opponents landowners – which could
have been anticipated. Beyond this, allegiances were less obvious.
The League failed to gain the enthusiastic support of the urban
industrial proletariat (whom cheap bread would presumably
benefit) but did pick up strange allies in farm labourers and
farmers (on the specious argument that only the landlord's rents
were likely to suffer (in the long run?) from cheap corn, not the
farmer's profits or the labourers' employment). Just as the Corn
Laws had not prevented low prices and depression in agriculture
for 20 years after 1815, so, after 1846, their abolition did not
bring lower food prices until the 1870's. Hence the further
paradox that the effective argument *ex ante* in political terms,
that free trade would bring its greatest benefits through the
mechanism of lower food prices, proved quite without foundation, *ex post facto*, for a generation. The free-trade battle over
corn, in this sense at least, was a political mountain that brought
forth an economic mouse. Wheat prices remained between 50s.
and 60s. per quarter from 1815 to 1875 – taking the average of
10-year periods – only falling on trend after 1870, to reach
below 30s. per quarter by 1890–1900. Before this could be
brought about many other changes were necessary apart from
tariff legislation.[2]

Doubtless prices would have been pushed up if the Corn
Laws had been maintained after the 1840's. But meat, butter
and cheese prices did rise steadily – particularly meat prices.
The great gains of free trade came from stabilizing wheat prices
and developing steadier, rising food-import trades which did
create purchasing power abroad for British exports and fed a
great increase in international trade in a generation when
Britain was the pivot of the international economy. The main
immediate gain from free trade thus became the increase in

[1] See Appendix, Table 12, p. 462.
[2] See below, pp. 337–49.

export markets as imports to Britain expanded, not a fall in food prices.

FOREIGN TRADE, SHIPPING AND THE BALANCE OF PAYMENTS

Some of the main generalizations about the movements of British foreign trade, the effects of industrialization on the structure of trade and the export of capital in the nineteenth century have been altered by the work of modern scholars recasting the statistical evidence upon which older conclusions and assumptions were founded. The root of the trouble lay in the inadequacy of the information recorded by contemporaries. Before 1854, no record existed of the actual costs of imports based on current prices. Details of current cost of exports were only collected by the customs men after 1798. This meant that the only comparable series of imports and exports available until the second half of the nineteenth century were the old 'official value' figures based on fixed prices. The complicated reconstruction of the actual current values in foreign trade has produced considerable revision of views. During the eighteenth century the pattern of prices between imports and exports did not change greatly, it seems, except for re-export commodities like sugar and coffee. But in the first half of the nineteenth century the 'official value' figures completely misrepresent the balance of trade position, while at the same time completely concealing the most important trends in the values of foreign trade.

The official values (and the older textbooks) tell the following success story: once the factory system had become established in textiles the resultant flood of cotton goods created a steadily mounting surplus in the balance of trade. Exports of British produce (excluding re-exports) were counted at under £40 million per annum in 1816–20; they were £90 million per annum in 1836–40 and almost £150 million per annum in 1846–1850. This satisfyingly simple and apparently logical deduction derived from the vast increases in quantities of textiles and other goods produced and exported. Meanwhile the 'official value' figures for imports crept up at a much slower pace, falling more

and more behind exports, making, with re-exports, a comfortably rising surplus on the balance of trade: £17 million per
annum in 1816–20, over £70 million in 1846–50 and over
£230 million in 1870. Here, obviously, was the source of the
capital lent abroad in the nineteenth century – the natural
result of the surplus of exports produced by industrialization.

The trouble about the explanation is that it ignored the steep
fall in the price of exports in this half century compared with
the prices of imports; the terms of trade growing less favourable in these years. In such circumstances more had to be sold
abroad to earn the same amount of imports. In fact the net barter terms of trade index (of import/export prices) deteriorated
by over 100 per cent between 1800 and 1860, which meant that
Britain had to sell twice as much by quantity to earn the same
amount of imports in 1860 as in 1800. This adverse movement
of the terms of trade did not necessarily mean that the economy
was getting worse off in any real sense. The index continued to
sink in good times, such as 1850–60, as well as in bad times (such
as 1837–43). Indeed its movement in this period was mainly
determined by the falling prices of cotton goods – the major
export – and here falling prices were occasioned mainly by a
steep fall in costs through mechanization, and a steep fall in the
price of raw cotton (not reflected as prominently in the import
price index). Cotton remained an expanding and profitable
industry on trend throughout the period so that the terms of
trade index by itself does not tell very much about the determinants of growth and profitability in the cotton industry, or in the
economy as a whole. Table VII shows the actual sequences.

However, the conclusions are still remarkable enough when
price changes are taken into account in the new current value
figures of trade. The balance of trade shows that industrialization did not produce an accumulating surplus, but a mounting
deficit on trend right up to the 1914–18 war.[1] The surplus
flowing abroad in foreign lending did not therefore come from

[1] The deficit on visible trade, and income from 'invisibles', is maximized
by the accounting conventions of costing all imports c.i.f. (i.e. price on the
dockside in Britain, including carriage, insurance and freight costs) and all
imports f.o.b. (free on board – net of these costs).

TABLE VII: *Balance of payments and export of capital in the United Kingdom, 1796–1913*

Year (annual average for 5-year period)	Net imports (a)	Exports of British products (b)	Balance of commodity trade (c) = (a)+(b)	Income from services (d)	Income from interest and dividends (e)	Balance on current account (f) = (c)+(d)+(e)	Accumulating balance of credit abroad (f)
1796–1800	36·6	32·9	−3·7				
1801–1805	47·9	39·9	−8·0				
1806–1810	54·0	42·2	−11·8				
1811–1815	50·3	42·9	−7·4				
1816–1820	49·3	40·3	−9·0	14·5	1·7	7·2	46
1821–1825	45·4	37·3	−8·1	14·2	4·2	10·3	98
1826–1830	48·7	35·9	−12·8	10·6	4·6	2·6	111
1831–1835	53·6	40·5	−13·1	14·1	5·4	6·4	143
1836–1840	73·8	49·8	−24·0	18·6	8·0	2·6	156
1841–1845	71·0	54·0	−17·0	15·4	7·5	5·9	185
1846–1850	87·7	60·9	−26·8	22·0	9·5	4·7	209
1851–1855	116·4	88·9	−27·5	23·7	11·7	8·0	249
1856–1860	158·0	124·2	−33·8	43·5	16·5	26·2	380
1861–1865	201·2	144·4	−56·8	57·1	21·8	22·0	490
1866–1870	246·0	187·8	−58·2	67·9	30·8	40·5	692
1871–1875	301·8	239·5	−62·2	86·8	50·0	74·6	1,065
1876–1880	325·9	201·4	−124·5	93·0	56·3	24·9	1,189
1881–1885	336·5	232·3	−104·2	101·0	64·8	61·6	1,497
1886–1890	327·4	236·3	−91·1	94·6	84·2	87·6	1,935
1891–1895	357·1	226·8	−130·3	88·4	94·0	52·0	2,195
1896–1900	413·3	252·7	−160·6	100·7	100·2	40·3	2,397
1901–1905	471·5	297·0	−174·5	116·6	112·9	49·0	2,642
1906–1910	539·6	397·5	−142·1	136·5	151·4	145·8	3,371
1911–1913	623·2	488·8	−134·4	152·6	187·9	206·1	3,990

1. All columns save final are annual averages. Final column (f) represents total in final year, in each quinquennium.
2. All figures in £m. and in current prices.
3. Income from services includes shipping credits, insurance, banking, emigrant funds, tourist spending, profits from foreign trade, etc. Columns (d) and (e) represent net figures.
4. Bullion transfers and ship sales not included.
5. SOURCE: A. H. Imlah, *Economic Elements in the Pax Britannica.*

commodity trade *directly* at all, even though intimately associated with these commercial flows. The deficits there were made up, and the surplus on the balance of payments entirely created, by the earnings of 'invisible' exports – services of various kinds rather than goods. Free trade legislation in the 1840's also came, not after a period of soaring values in exports, but after almost half a century of virtual stagnation in export values, as manufacturers were robbed of the rewards of increasing quantities sold in foreign markets by ebbing prices. In the quinquennium 1801–5 exports were just on £40 million per annum, and they hung about this total until after 1835. Import values were always higher than exports and the gap increased during this period.

The next conclusion to be drawn is the immense leap in values in foreign trade under the stimulus of free trade. The great boom goes on until 1875, by which time annual exports were running at £240 million and the import bill was £300 million. The deficit also increased (it was £62 million per annum in 1871–5) but it did not keep pace with this vast increase in values. But then came a new phase in the movements of foreign trade. Exports ran into difficulty, and values did not continue to rise. In fact there was stagnation in export values for 20 years, until 1895. Then the march upwards continued again at a quickened pace between 1896 and 1913, doubling from the level exports had averaged between 1875 and 1895. This was the Indian summer of the free trade system, when after a generation beset by doubts and questionings, expanding volumes, rising prices and profits gratified the mercantile community again. On the import side also a slower rate of growth occurred after 1875 than before, but no real stagnation, apart from the years 1886–90. But import values moved ahead even more rapidly than exports after 1895. The result of all this was that the deficit on the balance of trade doubled after 1875, to reach the very formidable figure of £175 million after 1900. One must distinguish in this post-1875 period the variation in the price and the variation in the volume of exports and imports. Quantities continued to rise between 1875 and 1895, but at a slower pace than before. The

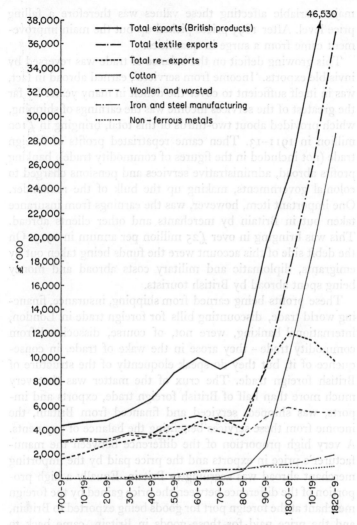

Fig. 10. Principal exports, 1700–1829 (official values, see note to Table 14. See also Table 15, p. 466). Annual average per decade. After Mitchell and Deane, 1962, pp. 279–81, 293–5.

major variable affecting these values was therefore a falling price level. After 1895 prices picked up but the main improvement came from a surge in quantities.

This growing deficit on the balance of trade was reversed by invisible exports. 'Income from services', earned abroad in fact, was in itself sufficient to cover the deficit in many years. By far the greatest of the services income was the earnings of shipping, which provided about two-thirds of this total, bringing in £100 million in 1911–13. Then came repatriated profits of foreign trade (not included in the figures of commodity trade), banking profits abroad, administrative services and pensions charged to colonial governments, making up the bulk of the remainder. One important item, however, was the earnings from insurance taken out in Britain by merchants and other clients abroad. This was bringing in over £25 million per annum in 1913. On the debit side of this account were the funds being taken out by emigrants, diplomatic and military costs abroad and money being spent abroad by British tourists.

These profits being earned from shipping, insurance, financing world trade, discounting bills for foreign trade in London, international banking, were not, of course, dissociated from commodity trade – they arose in the wake of trade, in consequence of it, but they do speak eloquently of the structure of British foreign trade. The crux of the matter was that very much more than half of British foreign trade, exports and imports, was shipped, serviced and financed from Britain, the income from these services benefiting the balance of payments. A very high proportion of the difference between the manufacturer's price in exports and the price paid by the importing merchant abroad was accruing to Britain. Equally a high proportion of the difference between the price gained by the foreign merchant at the foreign port for goods being exported to Britain, and the price paid for those goods in Britain, came back to Britain. If British trade had been mainly carried in the ships of trading partners, and the trade organized and financed by them rather than by British businessmen in sterling, then little income from services would have been generated to solve the problem of the deficit on the balance of trade.

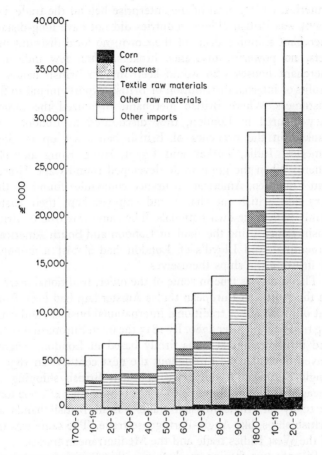

Fig. 11. Principal imports, 1700–1830 (official values, see Table 14, p. 465). Annual average per decade. After Mitchell and Deane, 1962, pp. 279–81, 285–9.

But in the new foreign markets being created by British merchants, India, South-east Asia, Australia, Africa, South America, China, most of the enterprise behind the trade, both ways, was British. These countries did not have long-distance merchant shipping fleets of their own, no local discount markets, no powerful insurance brokers, often few indigenous merchant houses who would keep in non-British hands the profits of internal distribution of British exports inland to final customers. Where British merchants organized the cargoes, they insured in London, they discounted in London, they banked in the branches of British banks set up in South America, India, Turkey and Egypt, Hong Kong and elsewhere. When the grain trade developed round Cape Horn to San Francisco, American insurance companies found to their fury that British merchants and shippers kept their custom firmly with their own nationals. The same was true of British businessmen using the Bank of London and South America in Argentina. And Lloyd's of London had almost a monopoly of insuring the ships themselves.

The same was true in some of the older, traditional markets. In the Northern European trades Amsterdam had been frozen out of much of her traditional international business and carrying trade by war after 1780. By 1815 the main European discount and insurance market was firmly based in London, where it stayed unchallenged throughout the next century. In 1830, in Anglo-European trade, twice as much British shipping was engaged as foreign shipping (950,000 tons against 463,000 tons). Virtually all Anglo-Russian trade was in British hands and British ships, like Anglo-Portuguese trade. The same was true of the West Indies trade and the Mediterranean trades.

In only two foreign markets was this British hegemony in shipping broken, and even there the financial servicing and the insuring of the trade was on sterling account. The minor example was the Scandinavian timber trade, where Norwegians and Swedes built, manned and provisioned their ships more cheaply than the British, so that foreign tonnage was twice that of the British. One of the main arguments of the Liverpool and Canadian timber interests against a reduction of the duties on

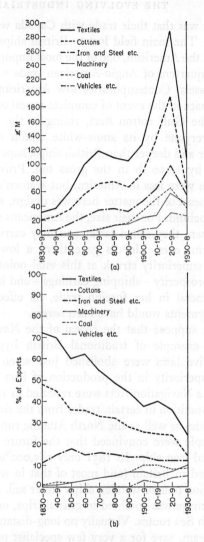

Fig. 12. Exports from the United Kingdom at current prices, 1830–1938. (a) Exports. (b) Percentage of total exports. (See also Table 17, p. 468.) After Mitchell and Deane, 1962, pp. 303–6.

Baltic timber was that their trade with Canada was entirely in British ships. The main field lost to British ships up to 1860, however, was the American, one of the most important markets, where three-quarters of Anglo-American trade was carried in American vessels. Contemporaries saw American shippers as the main menace in the event of complete repeal of the Navigation Acts. The Gulf cotton fleet, riding in the Mersey, was known to everyone by its snow-white cotton sails – superb vessels, longer and deeper than British ships, superior in carrying capacity by 1,000 lb in the gross ton. Provisioning and building costs were less in America, but seamen's wages were higher. The heart of the matter here was design, where Britain was 20 years behind. For their size, the Americans were manned with fewer men, they sailed faster and they carried more. To British chagrin, even Lloyd's gave them a lower insurance rating. Such superiority struck at this vital point in Britain's commercial prosperity – shipping earnings – and had this position been general in her foreign trade, its effects upon the balance of payments would have been severe.

One might suppose that the repeal of the Navigation Acts was another example of traditional British hypocrisy – that these restrictive laws were abolished just when Britain was assured of superiority in the production of iron steam ships. But in fact the Navigation Acts were repealed in 1849 at a time of severe competition in certain trades from the Americans – in the China trades as well as the North Atlantic runs. And at the time few people were convinced that the future lay with the steam-powered iron ship. In 1851 only 185,000 tons of steam tonnage existed in Britain (and most of that in wooden ships) and 3·66 million tons of wooden ships under sail. Almost all of the steam tonnage was confined to coastal trips, or in the Irish and the North Sea routes. Virtually no long-distance commerce was under steam, save for a very few specialist passenger and mail lines, and it long remained under sail. The dominance of the iron steam ship was a long time in coming. For a time sail benefited as much from the iron- or steel-hulled ship as did steam.[1]

[1] See Table 37, p. 489, and opposite.

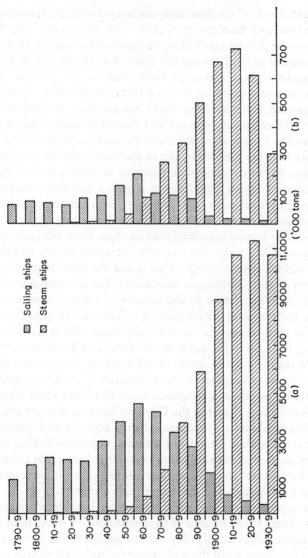

Fig. 13. Shipping, 1790–1938 (see also Table 37, p. 489). After Mitchell and Deane, 1962, pp. 217–22.
(a) Shipping tonnage registered in the United Kingdom. (b) Ships built and first registered in Britain.

Britain shook off the American challenge during the transition to the iron and then the steel ship. The Americans, already ceasing to be the serious challengers they had been in the 1840's, fell seriously behind during the Civil War in the 1860's and subsequently never recovered their place in the general expansion of world shipping. By 1890 Britain had more registered tonnage than the rest of the world put together. In 1910 over 40 per cent of tonnage entered and cleared in world trade was still British. British ships were also the carriers of the world – not only with her own trade, but in the tramp markets carrying the trade of third parties not touching at British ports. The west coast of South America was largely a Scottish preserve, for example. This was one of the only sectors in the economy where Britain kept the world dominance after 1870 that she had enjoyed over a wide industrial field in 1850. Even the basic innovations in shipping – the multiple expansion engine and the steam turbine – were British. This is not the place to continue the story of ship-building as an industry, but shipping must be stressed here in relation to the balance of payments position. Where trade was in British ships it usually meant that all the financial and commercial services associated with it flowed to Britain. In a very real sense the evolution of London as the world's main centre of international banking, finance and insurancing was a function of the dominance of British shipping in world trade. It is not accidental today that Leadenhall Street and Gracechurch Street in the City (the location of many shipping line headquarters) are immediately adjacent to Lombard Street and Cornhill. One of the essential objectives behind the Navigation Acts of the seventeenth century, of reserving British trade for British ships, was thus continued with increasing success into the hey-day of the free trade economy.

The export of capital, which is further considered below, relates closely to the balance of payments position in the light of these figures. A relatively slow rate of accumulation of capital abroad continued until the mid-century – under £8 million per annum save for 1821–5. Only just over £200 million had piled up by 1850 and the annual interest on this, at £11·7 million, was not very significant in comparison with the values current in trade or the income earned from services. But the annual income from abroad in interest and dividends was usually more than the new foreign lending. The net result for the foreign balance was that all the yields on past investment were just not being repatriated. From 1856 to 1875 a new pattern developed. This was a phase of very much higher capital exports, reaching £75 million per annum in the years between 1870 and 1875. The total accumulated leapt to over £1,000 million in this 20 years, with the dividends from this piling up at £50 million per annum at the end of it. But in this period more capital was flowing abroad than could be provided from the interest accruing. Income from services made up this balance. A further change came after 1875. From then until 1910 the yield of the already invested capital more than covered new lending, even when the annual totals rose so dramatically in the decade before 1914. As before 1856, this was a period of 'secondary export' of capital, created without finding new net resources from domestic saving, with foreign lending pulling itself up by its own bootstraps. Just before 1914, however, the flow once again became larger than the interest, at unprecedented levels. Clearly, once a large pile already existed overseas the further accumulation process could take place without much strain on the rest of the economy, sometimes almost automatically. This is doubtless what multi-millionaires mean when they say that the only real problem is making the first million. The export of capital, just as the 'invisible earnings', was also, of course, intimately associated with exports of the capital goods themselves. Dividends were created by the earnings of capital equipment largely supplied by British industry particularly up to the 1870's.

The conclusion to be drawn from Britain's accounts with the rest of the world in 1913 is to see to what a great extent the economy was being protected, or cushioned from the failure of exports to pay for imports, by the £4,000 million of capital invested abroad. The balance of payments deficit was completely concealed by this; income from investments had now become a more important source of revenue than the income from 'invisible exports', so there was the comforting feeling that 'coupon-clipping' would both cover the gap and provide for a flow of yet more capital abroad. Even quite a marked degree of failure in the competitive standards of some British export industries might be tolerated without much strain, as long as the £200 million came in as interest each year.

But how had these problems of balance of trade payments intensified under cover of the foreign lending? To what degree was it a failure within the British economy; to what extent was it merely a consequence of what was happening in other countries, and thus beyond British control, and responsibility? The first major external disrupting influence was the industrialization of the United States and Germany and their development into creditor nations in the world economy, running surpluses on their balance of trade. As a consequence of this came tariff barriers to protect their industries. At the same time as American metal and textile industries conquered their own national markets, excluding some traditional British exports of hardware, metal products, tin-plate and textiles, British dependence on the United States for cotton, and foodstuffs like wheat, cheese, fats, ham and bacon, mounted until 1900. Imports of oil and non-ferrous metals grew. American steel production surpassed Britain's in 1886. But the hangover of a debtor attitude from the first half of the century meant that the traditional American attitude was that 'every import is an insult'. The first main tariff against imported manufacturers came in 1861. Its average level was 47 per cent at the end of the 1860's. In 1890 the McKinley tariff had raised this to 50 per cent; by 1897 the Dingley Tariff was up to 57 per cent.[1] A rash of similar tariff barriers against British goods (as the main rivals) appeared in Europe in the late 1870's: Russia in 1877; in Germany for coal, iron and textiles in 1879; and in agriculture in 1885; in France after 1878. Defensive reactions were taking place all round as industrialists became a sufficiently powerful political interest to claim the aid of governments hitherto dominated by the desires of agricultural interests and consumers for cheap imports of industrial goods.

---

[1] The degree of effectiveness of a tariff in diverting trade cannot, of course, be measured just by its effect upon prices. The elasticity of demand for the products, and other indirect effects, have also to be considered.

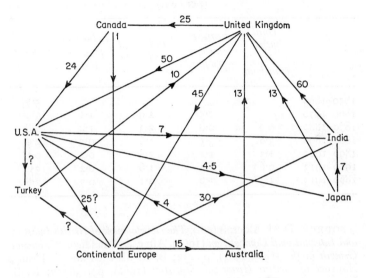

	Debit						Credit				
U.S.A.	.	.	.	.	50	India	.	.	.	.	60
Continental Europe		.	.	45	Australia.	.	.	.	13
Canada	.	.	.	.	25	Japan	.	.	.	.	13
Straits Settlements .		.	.	11	China (incl. Hong Kong)	.	13
South Africa	.	.	.	8	Turkey .	.	.	.	10
New Zealand	.	.	.	4	Uruguay.	.	.	.	6
Argentina .	.	.	.	2	British West Africa	.	.	3
Total	.	.	.	145	Total	.	.	.	118

Fig. 14. Pattern of world settlements and British trade balances, 1910. Figures in £m. per annum, representing balances of trade. Arrows point towards countries in surplus. Source: Saul, 1960, p. 58.

TABLE VIII: *Rates of growth*

(a) *Average annual rates of growth of selected economic indices* (UK)
(per cent)

	Total output per man-hour	Real income per head	Industrial production	Industrial productivity	Exports
1850–1860					5·7
1860–1870		2·5	2·9	1·1	3·2
1870–1880	0·9	0·8	2·3	1·2	2·8
1880–1890	3·8	3·5	1·6	0·5	2·9
1890–1900	1·3	1·2	2·8	0·2	0·4
1900–1913	0·6	0·4	1·6	0·2	5·4
1860–1913	1·5*	1·6	2·1	0·7	2·8

* 1870–1913.

SOURCE: D. H. Aldcroft (ed.), *The Development of British Industry and International Competition* (1968). After, A. Maddison, *Economic Growth in the West* (1964), p. 232; B. R. Mitchell and P. Deane, *Abstract of British Historical Statistics* (1962), pp. 367–8; K. S. Lomax, 'Growth and Productivity in the United Kingdom', *Productivity Measurement Review*, August 1964, p. 6; E. H. Phelps Brown and S. J. Handfield-Jones, 'The Climacteric of the 1890s: A Study in the Expanding Economy', *Oxford Economic Papers*, October 1952, pp. 294–5; A. H. Imlah, *Economic Elements in the Pax Britannica* (1958), pp. 96–8.

(b) *Long-term rates of growth, 1870/71–1913* (per cent per annum)

	Total output	Output per man-hour	Industrial production	Industrial productivity	Exports (1880–1913)
UK	2·2	1·5	2·1	0·6	2·2
US	4·3	2·3	4·7	1·5	3·2
Germany	2·9	2·1	4·1	2·6†	4·3
France	1·6	1·8	3·1*	n.a.	2·6

* 1880–1913.   † Rough estimate only.

SOURCE: Aldcroft, 1968. After, output and export data based on A. Maddison, *Economic Growth in the West* (1964), pp. 201, 232, and

'Growth and Fluctuation in the World Economy, 1870–1960', *Banca Nazionale del Lavoro*, June 1962, p. 185. Industrial production and productivity data calculated from: (for UK) K. S. Lomax, 'Growth and Productivity in the United Kingdom', *Productivity Measurement Review*, August 1964, p. 6, and E. H. Phelps Brown and S. J. Handfield-Jones, 'The Climacteric of the 1890s: A Study in the Expanding Economy', *Oxford Economic Papers*, October 1952, pp. 294–5; (for US) J. W. Kendrick, *Productivity Trends in the United States* (1961), p. 465; (for Germany) P. Jostock, 'The Long-term Growth of National Income in Germany', *Income and Wealth*, ed. S. Kuznets, V (1955), p. 103, and D. J. Coppock, 'The Climacteric of the 1890s: A Critical Note', *The Manchester School*, January 1956, p. 24; (for France) S. J. Patel, 'Rates of Industrial Growth in the Last Century, 1860–1958', *Economic Development and Cultural Change*, April 1961, p. 319. (These rates may be subject to revision in the light of much research now in progress.)

While this put an additional curb on the rise in British exports, Britain's own 'open' ports policy put no restraint at all on the rise in her import bill. She became the dumping ground for cheap food and subsidized sugar from all over the world – to the immense gain of all consumers and serious loss to wheat farming. By 1910 the balance of payments with the United States was running at a deficit of £50 million per annum and with continental Europe at £45 million per annum. In other countries such as Canada, South Africa, New Zealand, Argentina and South Africa, where Britain had very heavy import bills, the balance was also negative. In the Canadian and the Argentine case it was already being worsened by American exports to these countries taking the place of British. Quite certainly the hard core of the deficit problem lay with the United States in 1900. How were these accounts settled? The United States was in deficit herself from many tropical areas like India, Ceylon, Brazil, Japan, West Africa, Malaya, for raw materials and foodstuffs which could not be grown in the United States. It was Britain's surplus on balance of trade to these areas, particularly India, that enabled the other deficits to be cleared by the operation of multi-lateral settlements. India had become the most important trading area, as far as the surplus of trade was concerned, bringing in £60 million per annum in 1910, followed by China, Japan and Australia.

Britain had become increasingly dependent upon markets taking a traditional style of product in textiles, as well as a mounting proportion of capital goods like railway rolling stock and machinery. But these were increasingly the less sophisticated markets of the world, while she was being relatively squeezed out of the wealthier markets, demanding new ranges of imports, as they began to be able to make cheap cloth and cheap iron and steel. That is to say the problem of the declining balance of trade with the United States and Europe was not just a question of tariff barriers, but involved the internal problem of the structure of the economy, innovations and the failure to develop new export lines. This brings part of the problem back to what was happening in industry in Britain after the 1870's.[1]

It seems clear from this picture of world trade that the export of capital, which was providing the means to stave off the problem of the balance of payments, was partly responsible for creating these problems of balance of trade. Much of the capital exported was to provide railways in countries such as Canada, Argentina, the United States. Those railways enabled such a flood of raw materials and foodstuffs to pour out of these countries to Britain that it swamped her ability to supply them with exports in return. One can see from this how vitally British fortunes depended on the functioning of a system of multi-lateral payments before 1914. If she had not been able to square her deficits with the United States and Europe through a surplus with India and the Far East she would have run into exactly the sort of dollar problem before 1914 that was faced in 1945. Here, in the deficits with the advanced economies before 1914, lay the root of the balance of payments problems which threatened between the two world wars, and would have brought disaster immediately after 1944 without American aid.

THE EXPORT OF CAPITAL[2]

The main financial inducement behind the export of capital for investors not hoping to profit commercially from their offer of

---

[1] See below, pp. 404–26.
[2] See tables on pp. 305, 469–70 and Fig. 15 on p. 327.

capital – the *rentier* interest alone – remained the higher rates of return possible to investors abroad than in British government stock and, after 1875, in railway stock. Returns on foreign lending were not necessarily higher than on investments in industry or in property in Britain. Higher risks, of course, brought fancy margins, but even the absolutely secure foreign bonds, such as Indian railways where dividends could be paid out of taxes levied and administered by British civil servants, had higher returns. This first became apparent in the early 1820's when government borrowing could at last be curtailed in the peacetime economy and wartime loans funded and consolidated at lower rates of interest. Three per cent Consols climbed from 73·5 in 1823 through to 96 in November 1824, thus bringing 'gilt-edged' rates of interest almost down to the 3 per cent 'par' price. Refunding operations also brought the 5 per cent stock down to 3·5 per cent between 1822 and 1824. At this time loans being broked to secure European governments by the Rothschilds and Barings brought in 8 per cent. More dubious South American governments had to pay even more. Another analysis of interest rates between 1900 and 1910 shows that British government stock was then yielding well under 4 per cent (3·2 per cent in 1900–4; 3·6 per cent in 1905–10), while 'blue-chip' foreign bonds were at or above 5 per cent. Here lay the continuing motive for such an outflow of capital, even without enquiring if the organizers of the investment, as well as some of those who provided the capital, hoped to benefit from its results in other ways.

The apprenticeship for organized lending overseas, and the breeding ground for confidence, came when the Rothschilds and the Barings became loan mongers for the legitimist regimes of Europe after 1815, using the Congress of Europe meetings as their auction rooms. Barings broked the £10 million loan which solved the problems of the French war indemnity in 1817–19, being old customers of the French since 1809 when they handled the 'Louisiana purchase' sale for Napoleon during the wars. They organized a further £2 million loan for the Czar of Russia. Meanwhile the Rothschilds had broked £5 million for Prussia and another £1 million for Austria. These successes, plus the regularly ensuing payments of interest, led directly into the speculative mania of the two years 1824–5, encouraged by the fall in the rate of interest at home. Irresponsible governments in Greece, Mexico and South America, feckless mine-owners and the promotion sharks reaped the benefit of this growing investors' confidence. The faith spread that only capital was needed (at 8–10 per cent, of course) for the permanent benefits of productive enterprise to be realized in these lands. About £24 million was actually paid to these governments, most of it for mining schemes. Foreign lending was at the root of the Stock Exchange mania in 1825. Investors were able to buy stock with an initial 'call' – or down payment – of 5 or 10 per cent of the holding taken up. A rise in price, with a quick sale, could thus net a handsome gain for a small initial payment of capital. In December 1824 the £400 shares of the Real del Monte mine (on which investors had paid an initial call of £50 to acquire the title) stood at a premium of £550. Once prices stopped rising, of course, all those playing for capital gains on fraudulent or extravagant schemes sold out and the bubble burst with it, in December 1825, bringing the British banking system momentarily to its knees. Frightened City men thought the country was within 24 hours of barter.

Almost all these investments proved a dead loss. In the Greek case £3 million had been raised in London in the rosy glow cast by Lord Byron and a classical education. The only things that reached Greece as a result were about £·5 million in cash and supplies and two small frigates in 1828. In South America some even greater farces were played out. The governments defaulted on their debts, as in Greece (in some cases until the 1870's), while constructive results from productive investment in the long run were virtually nil. Almost all the mines collapsed, producing no bullion, and subsequent investments in South American railways and public utilities in the cities were associated mainly with the development of the economy for the export of primary produce such as hides, wool, grain and meat – not bullion or metals. In the short run trade to South America was boosted a little, for some government loans were taken up in military equipment, hardware and cloth. Some British mining equipment and miners also went out to the mines. The loss was not of capital alone. Robert Stephenson himself went out to Bogota as engineer for a 'bubble' mining company. Edward Pease called him back from this futile waste in 1827. On his way home, at Cartagena, Stephenson met the great Trevithick, penniless and alone, a loss to Britain and to engineering ever since he went out to invest in a Peru silver mine in 1816.

The effect of the disaster in 1825 was to dry up the flow of funds abroad for some years, and then to switch its direction north of the Rio Grande. The 1830's were characterized by a similar boom and crash in American investment, the United States being the main target for foreign investment in this decade. By 1830 there was probably not much more than £6 million (25 million dollars) of British capital in the United States. Seven million dollars of New York State bonds, for financing the Erie Canal, had been sold in London. Most American stocks were not launched publicly on the Stock Exchange at this time, but distributed through the banks and through private channels by Barings. Then in 1828 and 1831, Barings broked 8·5 million dollars in loans for Louisiana banks, the contracts containing important provisions that interest was payable, and stock redeemable, at fixed exchange rates in sterling. Thus inflation in the United States or any manipulation of paper currency could not defraud British investors of their due. Often these loans were also underwritten by state governments – they agreed to use tax receipts to pay dividends if the loan did not result in productive investment able to pay its own way. These were the essential provisions that underlay most of the capital pouring away from Britain in the second half of the century. Unprofitability of enterprise and bankruptcy were, of course, still a risk with private lending; while a political risk still remained in the case of stock underwritten by a public authority.

In the 1830's, the main openings for loans in America were state bonds covering transport investment and banks. This was particularly important in servicing the expansion of cotton growing in Louisiana. But these capital transfers were also underpinning the whole structure of Anglo-American trade at the time. America had a chronic deficit on current account in her balance of payments with Britain which was being covered by British funds flowing into the United States on capital account. The boom in trade in 1836 was mirrored by the boom in loans. British holdings rose from 66 million dollars in 1834 to 175 million in 1837 – and there were reports of Nicholas Biddle's agent crossing the Atlantic with 20 million dollars' worth of scrip in his brief-case. The crash came in 1839 (after a temporary falter when the trade boom collapsed in 1837). Nicholas Biddle, the head of the Second Bank of the United States, attempted to use British loans to rig the cotton market (against Lancashire!) and knock out his banking competitors in America at the same time. He was finally ruined by the decline in cotton prices. Falling trade values in 1839 then set off a general financial panic in the United States. By 1841, nine states were defaulting on loans and it was embarrassing to be an American in London. The flow of capital from London to the States did not revive much until after 1850; nor did trade with America.

With the American loan market dead in 1840, a second switch took place in the direction of the flow. This time it was towards railway building on the continent. Stephenson had drawn up plans for some Belgian trunk lines in 1834 and eventually built some of them with British navvies. The same was true of one of the major French lines in the 1840's – the Paris–Rouen – constructed in 1843 by Edward Blount and British labourers, with the help of £600,000 raised in London. It was a similar story with the Paris–Boulogne route in 1845; and there were strong British interests in the lines across France to Geneva and the Mediterranean. At the peak of the boom in 1845 £80 million was on call (if not finally paid up) in London for French railways.

After the 1848–9 political troubles, railway building in Europe picked up rapidly. Barings handled a £5·5 million loan for the St Petersburg–Moscow line in London in 1851, and £3·5 million went to Cavour for Italian railways. Later in the 1850's the first large Indian railway loans began, with guaranteed interest of 5 per cent. After the mutiny in 1857, railway construction became a matter of urgent policy in India, while the lines themselves by aiding troop movements helped to create the security

that investors required. The greatly increased flow of capital
abroad was then dominated by railway building – it became the
era of the great international contractors like Thomas Brassey,
who built over 30 lines and had contracts running in as many as
12 countries. Undoubtedly the most rapidly extending railway
market of all was in the United States, with 25,000 miles of
track in 1872 and 100,000 miles in 1880. Even the Civil War
debt in the 1860's is said to have been held by Europeans to the
extent of 1 billion dollars.

Meanwhile a new, stable government in Argentina in 1865
welcomed foreign investment and the flow started again, even
though the shareholders of almost £3 million from 1824 were
still waiting for their first dividend. £23 million of British
capital had been invested in Argentina by 1875; £45 million by
1885 and £175 million by 1890. Most of this had gone into
government loans, railways, banks and urban utilities such as
gas works, but British managers acquired a powerful stake in
sheep and cattle farming in some of the richest regions of the
republic. Argentinian loans stopped abruptly in 1890 and the
confidence of all investors in foreign lending was shaken for a
decade by the Baring crisis of that year. Over-confidence had
led to a typical over-extension of lending on unsound projects
in the preceding years, which Barings had backed without much
investigation. The extent of their commitment was enough to
shake the London money market to its foundations, to the
extent that the government secretly agreed with the Bank of
England to stand half the loss involved in propping up the firm.
Had they let Barings go the Chancellor of the Exchequer forecast a crash which would have made the collapse of Overend
and Gurney in 1866 appear 'but a trifle'.

The reduced scale of lending in the 1890's was particularly
involved with mining booms in South Africa and the Rhodesias
– with diamonds, gold and copper. The world search for gold
and non-ferrous metals had brought feverish loans and capital
imports to such places as California and Australia since 1850.
When the flow really revived to massive proportions after 1900
the white dominions, Canada, Australia, South Africa, were the
favourite markets. By 1914 not quite half the total investment

(of £4,000 million) was reposing in the Empire, but three-quarters of this imperial lending had gone to the white dominions, which were fiscally autonomous, and not directly administered by British civil servants, like the Indian railways. Europe had less than one-twelfth of the total. British investment was slight in Russia (mainly in railways, a little in textile industry plant and metals) compared with French capital, where it directly supported diplomatic strategy against Germany in a way alien to the motivation and direction of British investment.

No less than 41 per cent of the total British foreign lending had been in railways, a figure which excludes the stock lent to governments which may have been used eventually for railway building. Of this American railways had the largest single share (16·4 per cent) at about £650 million; dominion and colonial railways had about half this total (8·2 per cent or £325 million); Indian railways 3·7 per cent or £150 million; other foreign railways in Europe, South America and China 12·4 per cent or £500 million. Very little publicly-raised capital flowed directly into industrial or commercial investment abroad, most of which was created through the establishment of subsidiary enterprise by British firms overseas. This is very difficult to quantify.

Effects on British trade

A clear link developed between the export of capital and the rising proportion of metal goods and engineering products in British export trades, particularly in the early decades. In many parts of the world raising capital in London for railway building presumed ordering the complete railway in Britain: the engineer, the iron, the rolling stock, sometimes even the foremen and a key group of navvies. Up to 1880 much iron was exported for American railroads financed in Britain, but from very early on the Americans supplied their own locomotives and organized their own labour. But in countries like India, China and South America it was usually a complete 'packaged deal'. Over a third of Indian railway loans were spent in Britain. South Wales and Scottish iron masters benefited enormously from orders for rails. When at Maintz on the Grand Tour in 1843 Lady

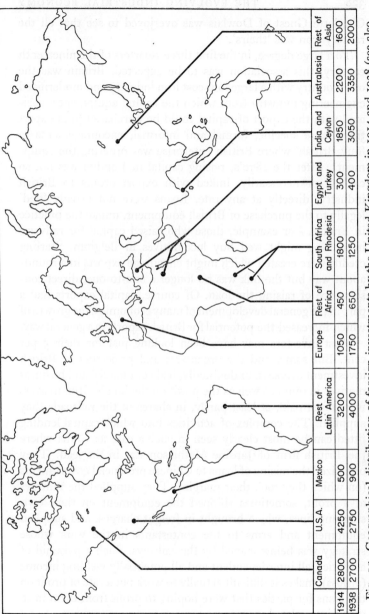

	Canada	U.S.A.	Mexico	Rest of Latin America	Europe	Rest of Africa	South Africa and Rhodesia	Egypt and Turkey	India and Ceylon	Australasia	Rest of Asia
1914	2800	4250	500	3200	1050	450	1800	300	1850	2200	1600
1938	2700	2750	900	4000	1750	650	1250	400	3050	3350	2000

Fig. 15. Geographical distribution of foreign investments by the United Kingdom in 1914 and 1938 (see also Table 19, pp. 469–70). Figures in $m. After W. Woodruff, *Impact of Western Man*, 1967, pp. 154 and 156.

Charlotte Guest of Dowlais was overjoyed to see that all the railway iron was 'theirs'.

To a large degree, in the first three-quarters of the nineteenth century, this association was to be expected. Britain was the only country with a large low-cost iron industry and modernized engineering industry from which the capital equipment associated with the export of capital could be purchased (quite apart from more specific, formal and informal, encouragements to 'buy British' where British enterprise was ordering the equipment). After the 1870's, raising capital in London was not so closely, or necessarily, linked with export orders to British industry, directly at any rate. Loans were not usually 'tied' legally to the purchase of British equipment, unlike the practice in France. For example, those who raised capital for railways in sterling might well buy locomotives in Belgium. Sterling credits were created which might encourage exports in a roundabout way but the link was no longer a one-to-one, direct consequence of raising the loan. Of course, capital exports had a part in the general development of many economies, the growth of which increased the potential for British exports in a general way.

Most investors may have been looking just for their 5 per cent. But some, and the organizers and projectors of British investment overseas, undoubtedly, had commercial and business motives in mind as well as the profit on the bonds. Iron masters were often paid, at least partly, in shares of the railroads they supplied. The complex of activities into which capital lending fitted can be most clearly seen in such a case as China where the British firm of Jardine Mathieson was in the lead. They organized the raising of loans to Chinese provincial governments (on which they took their margin). They supplied the railways at a profit, sometimes shipped the equipment on their own shipping lines, which brought in freight charges, and supplied equipment and arms to the contestants in the wars whose strategy was being shaped by the railways. Such a pyramid of activities, all interdependent and all potentially yielding income (or loss), makes it difficult actually to work out a rate of profit on the loans for parties that were hoping to profit from them in so many interrelated ways.

On the import side, the effects of foreign lending on the pattern of trade were even clearer. Railway building in countries such as the United States, Australia, Canada, South Africa and Argentina was instrumental in opening up these vast land masses and developing export sectors in primary produce – foodstuffs, hides, wool, metals – for Britain. In enabling a flood of raw materials and foodstuffs to pour out of these countries to Britain this capital investment tended to add to the balance of trade problem by swamping Britain's ability to supply these markets with enough exports in return.

Plotting the way in which transport investment and investment in other enterprises in the United States – banks, mortgage companies, cattle and sheep ranching, mining – were linked to the export trade to Britain, it becomes clear that this was not just 'blind capital' but the 'blind capital' of *rentiers* organized by financiers and businessmen very much with a view to the trade that would be flowing when the enterprise was under way. A few examples can make this clear. The clustering of British investment in Louisiana in the 1820's and 1830's was orientated to the development of cotton exports. The main 'British' railroads in the United States were from the mid-west to the eastern seaboard and in the south – exactly the lines tapping the wheat belt and the middle western hog and cattle rearing areas in the Chicago hinterland. Thomas Lipton invested in some of these lines and then set up one of the biggest meat packing plants in Chicago in the 1880's, originally to serve his shops. He did the same with tea plantations in Ceylon. British investors showed very little interest in transcontinental lines linking the mid-west with the west coast. Scottish enterprise and capital in Texas and the cattle ranches of the west was a story of its own. Some ranches of 2 million acres and vast firms like the Texas Land and Mortgage Company were organized from Scotland in the 1870's and 1880's. The object here was in part the leather, tallow and then meat export trade to Britain, although the American market was larger and also booming. Clearly, some of the shrewdest businessmen and financiers in Scotland – mainly from the Aberdeen and Dundee hinterlands it seems (the cattle regions of Scotland) – had decided that if the prosperity of the Scottish cattle trade was going to be threatened by imports from the New World they were going to have a share in the new trade. And if Scottish graziers, who knew what a well-bred Aberdeen Angus looked like, could be shown a Texas longhorn, they saw also that there was money to be made by getting improved British stock into the new world. Railways and this sort of investment in the United States, Australia and Argentina gave the immense benefits of cheapening raw material prices and food in Britain after 1875.

Apart from these specific connections with British foreign trade, perhaps the main utility of the export of capital lay in its effect in releasing a brake curbing the rate of expansion in world trade. The expansion of many markets, for both exports and imports of Britain, depended on very heavy capital investment in strategic technology, which, in the nature of the case, in the nineteenth century could only come from Europe. Without foreign lending there could also have been a chronic 'sterling shortage', a chronic curb on the ability of some other countries to absorb British products unless their deficits on current account were being covered by capital transfers (as with the United States in the 1830's). In this way, the investment of capital abroad was one of three basic conditions governing the rate of expansion of world trade after the 1840's, accompanying 'open' ports in Britain without tariff restrictions on imports, and the system of multi-lateral payments, which in turn depended upon the operation of the 'gold standard'. Even if Britain had a balance of trade deficit her overall balance of payments was heavily in surplus.

The first possible debit entry in the ledger of capital exports is wastage. Obviously much that was invested in the 1820's proved to be a write-off for investors and the economy alike, yielding neither productive result from the investment nor any dividends. Perhaps the two should be synonymous but, where interest payment was guaranteed by governments out of tax revenue if necessary, the bondholders could be satisfied even without productive results. This sort of situation came about sometimes where the investment was not put to productive use, and in these cases one cannot see capital exports helping the expansion of the international economy. Then the question becomes relevant whether what was good for the British bond-holders was also good for the country receiving the loans. On the whole, as far as the British economy was concerned, the record of outright wastage, pouring money into useless mines and the like, was reasonable, according to the standards of the time. The positive results of this lending were to be seen in the world economy, and in the £200 million annual income from dividends in 1913. This has to be judged, for most of the nineteenth century, against the astonishingly high rate of risk, fraud and waste in domestic floatations on the Stock Exchange. Relatively few sound concerns survived from the waves of bubble companies projected at home in 1809 or 1825, and an analysis of the joint-stock companies launched under the incorporation and limited liability statutes of 1856 and 1862 also revealed a very high rate of mortality.

The next charge is that investment in industry in Britain, showing a low rate of capital formation, would have given a more worthwhile return on this capital. Was some of the British failure to adopt new innovations and to re-equip traditional industries after 1870 linked to the flow of capital abroad? Was there a haemorrhage of capital, remembering that in 1913 the rate of flow abroad was about 7·5 per cent of the national income annually – almost double the rate of capital formation at home, of about 4·5 per cent?[1] It can be argued that foreign lending kept up interest rates to some degree. But the problem was of *low* interest rates in home industry tempting capital abroad. *Potential* yields from home industrial investment could have been comparable with those in business enterprise abroad. Little sign is visible at home of a shortage of capital for those who actively went out to get it; and certainly not in equivalent

[1] The very special circumstances in the British economy and the international economy which made this spontaneous flow of such a magnitude possible are underlined when one considers the difficulties found by the rich, industrial nations of the world in the 1960's in investing 1 per cent of G.N.P. in the developing countries during the United Nations 'development decade'.

forms of capital stock like railways or gas works. More particularly, the problems of innovation and lack of investment in certain British industries were very much more deep-seated and institutional than a mere 1 or 2 per cent gap in the cost of capital.

One extension of this argument is that if this money had been invested in home industry it would have expanded British exports and made them more competitive. Britain might have developed a great export trade in chemicals or electrical engineering products or motor cars which would have earned the economy more by trade than was gained by the dividends on investment abroad. The German economy, for example, developed very little foreign investment but massive expansion and re-equipment of home industry provided a consequent expansion in exports. This may have some importance as a theoretical argument but in nineteenth-century conditions it is an unhistorical alternative, ignoring much about the process of investment and innovation in home industry and taking much for granted about the ease of creating markets abroad for exports without the flow of capital into the international economy.

Another argument maintains that there would have been greater social advantage in Great Britain if some of this capital had been diverted for social investment at home. Undoubtedly domestic housing, schools, hospitals, city improvement could have mopped up a great deal of this money to immense advantage. But such social benefits would have been bought at some social costs. In the short run foreign investment might help to push up prices at home, because it took a long time to mature (while yielding profits to the stockholders), but in the longer run it paid dividends to everyone in lower prices, particularly lower food prices. Cheap food is on one side of the social balance; poorer housing on the other.

A further, less tangible, point remains. For good or ill the root of success for the new industrial state was the efficiency of its productive machine. If that failed disastrously, in an industrializing world, then national disaster would undoubtedly follow. Did the cushion of income from foreign investment, which was masking certain industrial problems and hiding the absence of new export sectors by increasing *rentier*-status in the world, encourage the breeding of *rentier* attitudes? Was Britain becoming another Holland of the eighteenth century, moving from industry and trade towards finance? The point was that the springs of wealth from financial income were less secure, less resilient, more subject to disturbance under the stress of political insecurity abroad or the shock of war than the solid indigenous strength of an efficient system of production and trade. It needed two world wars, the sale of the investments, and Marshall Aid to shake Britain out of this *rentier* attitude and to arouse the national consciousness to the job of putting the national workshop and sales system in order, to start earning a way in the world without much investment income. Perhaps the £200 million annual income from investments in 1913 had something to answer for.

One question remains to be considered, strictly outside the terms of reference of this book but needing a mention: the effect of importing capital on the country that borrowed it. The issue is part of the much wider area of debate concerning political controls or influences that sometimes (formally or informally) followed the loans in the empire, in the Middle East, or in South America. In other cases they did not – as in the European states or in the United States. The main potential economic evil, which might well offer grounds for political influence, lay in the loans not being used productively, which was made clear by the fate of Egypt. French and British financiers organized a flood of alien capital, at fancy margins for themselves, to feed the feudal extravagances of a profligate ruler. The context into which this capital poured was only partly that of a modern economic world of railways, irrigation and the Suez Canal. Too much of it fed an older world of values in which productive investment had no meaning – lavish palaces, enlarged harems, greater personal extravagance. Even with the financing of the Canal the financial burden, enlarged by the rapacity of international bankers, was too crippling for its economic benefits. The Egyptian state became bankrupt and could not pay the interest on the loans. The unusual thing about this (compared with the South American, Greek and Turkish defaults) was that it coincided with broader strategic and imperial interests, and ended by British and French political intervention and the finances of Egypt being run by honest European administrators in the interests of European bondholders, to create their dividends at the expense of the wretched *fellaheen* paying most of the taxes levied. The more general charge, applicable particularly to tropical colonies and India, was that the import of capital under the auspices of alien enterprise developed the primary product export sectors of these economies, to the detriment or neglect of their general development.

In other countries, notably the United States and the dominions (which received the greater proportion of capital exported from Britain), foreign capital did not have such economic or political consequences. Indeed the general rule was that government interference and the encouragement of particular governments abroad was, in the main, only in the interests of British trade, enterprise and merchants, not British bondholders. Foreign investment bore its own risks, as did gambling in domestic stocks and shares. The British government refused to touch intervention in Mexico in the 1860's or in South America. A concept of 'informal Empire' flourished in South America, as in other parts of the world, but it was not primarily concerned with securing dividends.

Reading list

THE COMING OF FREE TRADE: IDEAS AND POLICY

BARNES, D. G. *A History of the English Corn Laws, 1660–1846*, London, 1930.

BROWN, L. *The Board of Trade and the Free-Trade Movement, 1830–1842*, Oxford, 1958.

CUNNINGHAM, W. *Rise and Decline of the Free Trade Movement*, 2nd ed., Cambridge, 1905.

FAIRLIE, S. 'The 19th-century corn law reconsidered', *Economic History Review*, 1965, **18**, no. 3.

GRAMPP, W. D. *The Manchester School of Economics*, Stanford–London, 1960.

IMLAH, A. H. *Economic Elements in the 'Pax Britannica': studies in British foreign trade in the 19th century*, Cambridge (Mass.), 1958.

MCCORD, N. *The Anti-Corn Law League, 1838–1846*, London, 1958.

REDFORD, A. *Manchester Merchants and Foreign Trade, 1794–1858*, 2 vols, vol. I, Manchester, 1934.

SCHUYLER, R. *The Fall of the Old Colonial System: a study in British free trade, 1770–1870*, New York, 1945.

FOREIGN TRADE, SHIPPING AND THE BALANCE OF PAYMENTS

ASHWORTH, W. *An Economic History of England, 1870–1939*, London–New York, 1960.

BROWN, A. J. 'Britain and the world economy, 1870–1914', *Yorkshire Bulletin of Economic and Social Research*, 1965, **16**, no. 1.

IMLAH, A. H. *Economic Elements in the 'Pax Britannica': studies in British foreign trade in the 19th century*, Cambridge (Mass.), 1958.

KINDLEBERGER, C. P. 'Foreign trade and economic growth: lessons from Britain and France, 1850–1913', *Economic History Review*, 2nd series, 1961, **14**, no. 2.

PARES, R. 'Economic factors in the history of empire', *Economic History Review*, 1937, **7**, no. 2; reprinted in E. M. Carus-Wilson (ed.), *Essays in Economic History*, vol. 1, London, 1954.

SAUL, S. B. 'The export economy', *Yorkshire Bulletin of Economic and Social Research*, 1965, **16**, no. 1.

SAUL, S. B. *Studies in British Overseas Trade, 1870–1914*, Liverpool, 1960.

SCHLOTE, W. *British Overseas Trade from 1700 to the 1930s*, translated by W. O. Henderson & W. H. Chaloner, Oxford, 1952.

THE EXPORT OF CAPITAL

CAIRNCROSS, A. K. *Home and Foreign Investment, 1870–1913: studies in capital accumulation*, Cambridge, 1953.

COONEY, E. W. 'Capital exports and investment in building in Britain and the USA, 1856–1914', *Economica*, new series, 1949, **16**, no. 64.

FEIS, H. *Europe, the World's Banker, 1870–1914: an account of European foreign investment and the connection of world finance with diplomacy before the war*, New Haven, 1930.

FORD, A. G. 'Overseas lending and industrial fluctuations', *Yorkshire Bulletin of Economic and Social Research*, 1965, **17**, no. 1.

HALL, A. R. (ed.) *The Export of Capital from Britain, 1870–1914*, London, 1968.

HALL, A. R. 'The English capital market before 1914: a reply', *Economica*, 1958, **25**, no. 100.

HALL, A. R. (ed.) *The London Capital Market and Australia, 1870–1914*, Canberra, 1963 (ANU Social Science Monographs, no. 21).

HALL, A. R. 'A note on the English capital market as a source of funds for home investment before 1914', *Economica*, 1957, **24**, no. 93.

HOBSON, C. K. *The Export of Capital* (thesis), London, 1896.

JENKS, L. H. 'British experience with foreign investments', *Journal of Economic History*, 1944, Supplement.

JENKS, L. H. *Migration of British Capital to 1875*, London–New York, 1927; reissued London, 1963.

LANDES, D. *Bankers and Pashas*, London, 1958.

12 Agriculture, 1815–1914

From 1815 to 1835 peace brought distress to the farming community, despite the Corn Laws and despite the stimulus to demand from a continuing increase in population, of which the proportion growing their own food steadily declined. Furthermore, relative demand for wheat probably increased as London standards of white bread spread (as most social habits spread) from the south and east to the north and west, even in the times of poverty. In 1852 it was said that only parts of Wales, Westmorland and Cumberland survived as 'barley bread areas', although the wheaten loaf still had much ground to conquer in Scotland from oats. Over-capacity in wheat production laid down in the Napoleonic Wars was still not absorbed by rising population until the mid-1830's. Until this happened, in the average to good harvest year, the Corn Laws could do little to hold up prices, which were being set by domestic gluts. What was wanted was stability to enable adjustment to peacetime schedules. This had happened by 1830. Rents were down by a third or a half (depending on the region) from their wartime heights, wages had been pulled down from 18s. to 10s. a week on average – both necessary prerequisites for profitable peacetime farming. When wheat prices fell to 64s. in 1815, witnesses to a parliamentary enquiry claimed that capital values had dropped by half in arable areas. By 1822 wheat prices reached 43s., the lowest since 1792. The prices of stock and meat did not fall so severely, or the prices of butter and cheese. Hence in the midland counties, such as Leicestershire, the pattern of land use moved back to traditional pasturing and dairying which had existed before the tillage boom of the war period. The same is true of other areas like the high chalk downs of the south and much upland pasture. By the time of another parliamentary enquiry in 1833 only the wheat farmers on heavy soils were complaining.

337

This set the traditional pattern of distress in British agriculture, repeated in the years after 1873, and after 1921. On the heavy clay lands wheat was the only feasible straw crop and pasture was not good. When this land was low lying also flexibility in use became further restricted. Wet, stiff clays, such as parts of Cambridgeshire (but not the black silt fen soils) and Huntingdonshire, suffered the worst falls in farming profits and rents at these times. They were suitable primarily for arable farming, yet they had later seed-times, shorter growing seasons, fewer days working on the land, a higher ratio of bad seasons, and heavier labour costs and horse costs. Yields were more chancy and the more profitable rotations using the Norfolk system of barley, turnips and sheep could not be adapted very successfully, because sheep and barley do not like wet, stiff lands. Stock were mainly important in these clay regions to keep land fertile for straw crops.

When wheat prices revived to above 60s. a quarter for a few years after 1838, an increasing flow of capital began into even the heavy wet lands. Poor relief burdens, mainly in agricultural regions, had fallen by almost half since the 1834 Poor Law; the Tithe Commutation Act of 1836 had also helped. Then rising prices kicked off the revival of investment, which had been flowing on the light barley and stock farming lands since 1831-2. On these light lands Norfolk rotations were extended and barley demand increased markedly when the beer duties were removed in 1830. Malt consumption rose by one-third in two years. Light iron implements, which could be drawn by one or two horses, lowered costs in these regions, whereas they were still unsuitable for many clay soils. This was a period of great expansion in Ransome's of Ipswich, selling light iron ploughs with interchangeable parts to the progressive farmers of East Anglia. The sandy soils of western parts of Nottinghamshire were becoming another Norfolk at this time, with the Dukes of Portland playing the role of the Cokes of Holkham.

On the heavy lands the most important technical improvements in this period involved improved drainage. In the Fens, from 1830 onwards, steam drainage was taking over from windmill-drainage wheels, enabling the land to dry out much more and hence take crops of wheat and potatoes in place of oats. This was cheap and efficient drainage. Drainage rents were levied at an annual rate of only 2s. 6d. per acre; while one engine could keep 6,000–7,000 acres under control.[1] Such engines cleared fen soils, the rich black silts, not clay lands in the main. For the latter, expensive under-drainage was the only answer, and this depended on landlord capital. New techniques for effecting such drainage were coming into operation in the 1830's, such as mole-ploughs which burrowed out a trench. Tile-making machinery then produced the possibility of very cheap efficient conduits, invented in Essex, also under the stimulus of the same incentive, in 1843. When an Act of Parliament enabled public loans to be made to farmers for drainage in 1846, tile drainage developed into an East Anglian boom on the heavy lands. This did for the clays what the Norfolk rotations were doing for light soils. Sir James Caird claimed that this Agricultural Drainage Act was more beneficial than the Corn Laws for farmers: £15 million went into drainage loans, both public and private, in the 30 years after 1848. The steam engine was hitched to this job also in the 1850's, when teams of contractors with stationary engines and tackle made a business of mole-plough drainage and pipe-laying.

In these ways both the cultivated area and productivity per acre were extended, although the process of enclosure was almost complete by 1820. After 1850, only the historical curiosities of open fields remained – as at Laxton. Contemporaries anxious to improve the efficiency of farming at this time were concerned to consolidate holdings into larger, more efficient units which could profit by expensive machinery and improved rotations. 'Deduct from agriculture all the practices that have made it flourishing in this island,' was the resurrected text from Arthur Young, 'and you have precisely the management of small farms.' Some consolidation undoubtedly did occur, as small family farmers had their capital drained away in the 20 years of low prices after 1815. Many of those who had bought their farms as sitting tenants in Leicestershire, when

---

[1] There survives at Stretham, near Ely, one of the most famous of these fen pumping engines, installed in 1832.

profits were very high during the wars, now sold out again. Even so, in 1831, 95,000 out of 235,000 occupiers of land in England employed no labourers – the family-worked farm was very far from dead. And in 1851 the average size of farm in England and Wales was only just over 100 acres, while by numbers over two-thirds were under the 100-acre limit. No significant change came to these figures, in fact, in the second half of the century. Including Scotland, two-thirds of the farms remained under 50 acres. This, of course, was a national average and averages often conceal the truth. Within farming regions quite a significant movement developed. In arable and pasture farming areas the average size of farm did rise, while in areas round the cities and in counties like Kent, Worcestershire and Herefordshire the more intensive cultivation of land under hops and fruit and garden crops increased greatly – which was mainly a smallholding – or, at least, a small acreage – operation. Obviously this changing structure of land use helped to keep the national averages fairly steady while important changes away from the norm were taking place in opposite directions in different regions of the country.

From 1850 to 1873 farming, like most other industries in the country, enjoyed a generation of high prosperity and expansion, with resilient prices and profits. After the awful warnings sounded by the farmers and landowners in the campaign for the repeal of the Corn Laws, this 25 years reconciled them to the advantages, or at least to the innocuousness, of the free trade system. Why was it that free trade in corn did not, at once, lead to that reduction in prices so widely canvassed by the Anti-Corn Law League before 1846? On the demand side, of course, numbers continued to grow, while better employment and money wages increased consumption per head. Supplies coming to market increased, but not fast enough to overwhelm this expansion in demand and break prices. Imports certainly increased enormously at this time, as did the production of British farms. Even though repeal of the Corn Laws did not reduce the price of bread greatly (as free trade legislation did not reduce the price of cheese or sugar either very much in the short run because of the increase in demand) – undoubtedly, without repeal, bread prices would have gone up. Average annual imports of wheat to the UK were 14 million cwt in the 5-year period 1851-5 and 32 million cwt in the period 1866-70. Imports of barley, oats and butter trebled also in this period. The main curbs on imports were the small available European corn surplus and the time needed to develop transport facilities and open up new wheat lands outside Europe. In 1850 four-fifths of British corn imports came from European countries (France, Russia and the Baltic countries) plus the Black Sea provinces of Russia. The United States supplied most of the remaining fifth. But the European population was also growing rapidly and most lands there were already settled and cultivated, so the rate of expansion of the export surplus in grain from European countries was fairly circumscribed. Yet developing more distant sources meant heavy long-term investment in iron ships on the ocean routes, railways into the interiors of new countries, and the whole process of settlement and breaking in of new lands there. Such settlement, and investment, and new technology, and transport took a generation after 1850 to be realized. Most of the increments in British imports did come from beyond Europe: in 1870 about 60 per cent of British grain imports were coming from new countries (about half the total from North America) and by 1900 87 per cent of the whole came from beyond Europe. In the long run, therefore, the British farmer was right to see prairie wheat as his main rival.

Wheat prices during the prosperous years of Victorian high farming lay usually between 45s. and 55s. a quarter, a little lower in fact than the average of prices between 1820 and 1840. But progress in the efficiency of farming at home was enabling the farmer to tolerate these price levels with equanimity. Improvements continued to spread in the previous fields: animal and plant breeding, better rotations, the use of seed-drills and iron ploughs and other implements, drainage. But two other important innovations began to come in which characterized 'high farming'. Caird's best-known pamphlet was called *High-farming . . . the best substitute for Protection* (1848) and it preached the virtues of increasing output per acre by the very heavy importation of fertilizer onto the farm. Guano was coming into the country at the rate of over 100,000 tons a year in the 1850's, superphosphates were produced from coprolite deposits in Cambridgeshire and from bones treated with sulphuric acid. Nitrates and potassium fertilizers were all developed in this same period. The great increase in the import of feed for stock also allowed more stock to be carried per acre, and more fertility per acre to be derived from stock for arable production. This broke through traditional limitations on output where farms were mainly dependent on their own resources, without additional inputs, for maintaining fertility. Increasing output per acre in this way brought greatly improved outputs per head in consequence. The other great advance came with the beginnings of mechanized harvesting. Thrashing by steam (often done, like drainage, by peripatetic contractors) had been well known in the 1820's and 1830's, but the mechanized reapers and binders had little effect until after 1850. They too had been patented in the 1820's by Englishmen and Scots. They were not made commercially, however, until McCormick's American machines received wide publicity in 1851 at the Great Exhibition, and spread relatively slowly. The conclusion of all this was that output of meat and grain rose rapidly while the labour force declined by 300,000 between 1851 and 1871. Productivity increased much faster under this new sequence of innovations than under those that characterized the classic 'agricultural revolution' of the seventeenth and eighteenth centuries.

Even during this time of prosperity for arable and mixed farming warnings were being delivered by some of the shrewdest and most experienced commentators. They pointed to the growing importance of livestock farming and dairying in the pattern of national farming, forecast cheap wheat in the near future and claimed that movements in demand at home would give progressively greater stimulus to meat, butter and milk than to cereals. While cereal prices had tended to move only marginally in these mid-decades of prosperity, prices of mutton and beef had almost doubled. The trends in production followed these changing factor prices.

Partly this was a question of import difficulties over importing meat and cattle (apart from preserved pig meat) in the days before refrigerated ships; partly it was a question of time before cattle-ranching investment and settlement and transport could be built up in Argentina, Australasia and the United States. But it was also a question of changing demand conditions in Britain. Demand itself continued to rise after 1871, of course, when wheat prices started their trend decline. Ten million extra mouths appeared between 1871 and 1901, in the time of distress, whereas 5 million was the increase in the 20 years of prosperity between 1851 and 1871. And in the earlier period real wages rose by less than 1 per cent per annum; in the second period by about 2 per cent per annum. In these conditions the aggregate demand facing the food producer would seem to be highly favourable. But rising wealth usually leads to a rising demand for proteins, for milk and meat, at the expense of demand for the cheaper starches. One of the signs of prosperity in the twentieth century has been, in fact, a falling bread consumption. One commentator summed it up in 1899 by saying: 'the sort of man who had bread and cheese for his dinner forty years ago now demands a chop'. Even though imports of meat and butter went up at faster rates than wheat after 1871 (beginning from much lower absolute quantities), they did not have nearly so dramatic an effect on prices at home. The wheat farmers suffered both from the rise in imports and from the changing pattern of demand.

In textbooks a tale of woe has blanketed British agriculture after the harvest of 1872. Wheat prices were below 50s. per quarter in 1875; below 40s. per quarter after 1883 and below 30s. per quarter after 1893. Slight recovery took place after then, but not consistently. Prosperity to wheat farmers came again only with war in 1914. On average, it is said, farm incomes fell by 40 per cent. Rather than let farms fall vacant, landowners lowered their rents on average by a third. Such was the tale of woe given in the evidence before two full-scale parliamentary enquiries. Can one doubt its truth as a national generalization when the wheat and barley acreage fell by 2 million between 1866 and 1911 (1·5 million of the loss being in wheat acreage)?

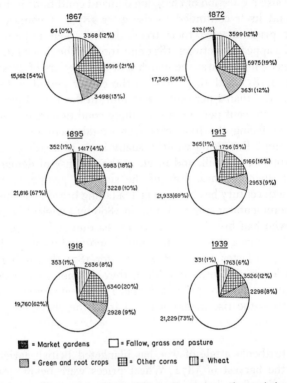

Fig. 16. Crop acreage in Great Britain (in thousand acres) (see also Table 24, p. 476). After Mitchell and Deane, 1962, pp. 78–9.

One ought to. The best-known textbooks were written by people closely connected with farming, in the south of England. The parliamentary committees were dominated by large landowners from arable farming areas asking questions of substantial farmers coming mainly from wheat growing areas. This was the post-Napoleonic War pattern of distress over again: the heavy wheat lands, which were high-cost farming areas with less flexibility in switching crops, were the ones which mainly suffered when wheat prices fell. There is no doubt of this. The point is to what extent income from wheat was characteristic of income from farming as a whole. Wheat was pre-eminent in 1870 – composing about half the total arable output. It earned farmers as much as the value of beef and mutton together, and was probably responsible for over a fifth of the value of gross output. But, by 1895, wheat was only a sixth of the arable output. The value of the output of dairy produce, and beef and mutton and pig meat and even poultry was each greater than the value of wheat output. The fall in gross output of British farming at current prices was entirely accounted for by the decline in wheat: livestock output in all its forms rose. Evidence from the midlands, the west country, Lancashire and Cheshire was much scarcer than the tale of disaster from the arable lands.

By and large in the pasture country, where cattle raising and dairying were the mainstays of profits, things were not too bad. Even though prices of meat, butter and cheese fell under the competition of mass imports in the 1880's (later than the tumble in wheat prices), so did one of the main constituents of farming costs in these areas: the price of feed. These farmers were interested in the price of cereals as buyers more than producers. Home-bred meat was still of better quality than the imported, so that a wide spread of prices emerged in these markets, and British cattle farmers did not get their returns set by a fixed world price. In fact they remained better off than the cost-of-living index of meat prices, based on cheaper import prices, might suggest. Wheat, on the other hand, was a homogeneous commodity with a fairly uniform world price – and the British farmer was at the further disadvantage that his crops could not make as 'strong' a flour as the harder prairie wheats. As usual, farmers on the lighter soils were better off, even in arable areas. They could raise more mutton than on the heavy lands, their costs were lighter, and British malting barley remained supreme in quality. Price and acreage in barley did fall, but neither as heavily as with wheat. Beer consumption rose throughout this period (reaching a peak in 1899) and long-term malting barley contracts remained a sheet anchor of prosperity for many East Anglian farmers on light lands.

As far as changes in land use are concerned, when fairly near an urban market and on suitable soil, a general move occurred towards more intensive crops at higher values per acre and per worker in vegetables and fruit farming. This was the time of the development of a mass production cheap jam industry and the beginnings of widespread commercial canning. Many factories sprang up at Bermondsey on the perimeter of London facing the north Kent soft fruit regions. In the Vale of Evesham and in scattered favoured places from Dundee to the Lea valley such conversion continued. This acreage more than doubled after 1873–1907 with reports of this being 'successful and progressive' – and coming 'most opportunely to the assistance of the farmer'. Corn and cattle farmers would certainly not bring market gardening and fruit within their definition of 'proper' agriculture, and only farmers favoured by soil, situation and marketing facilities, and owning a little capital too, could take these opportunities to cash in on green crops and fruit that a rising standard of living was making progressively more popular. On the rich soils of the fens in East Anglia, potatoes, beet, carrots and the like brought salvation. The main response, however, was to turn to grass for milk and meat and poultry. In the market where no imports were possible (and still are not) – liquid milk – prices were maintained and even advanced a little in this 30 years. Milk production meant more capital to some extent for buying cows, but thereafter lower running costs on the farm with fewer men per acre and much reduced prices of feed. Six million acres were added to permanent pasture lands between 1866 and 1911, when only 2 million were lost to arable.[1]

[1] For statistics of these changes see Appendix, Tables 24 and 25, pp. 476 and 477, and Fig. 16, p. 344.

By 1911 16 million acres were under grasses, 5·5 million acres under corn, and 2·25 million acres under green crops (roots, potatoes, etc.). The population of cattle almost doubled (from 3·8 to 5·9 million) and numbers of sheep and pigs also rose.

It was a great epoch of expansion for the dairy companies in the west of England. Thomas Kirby, a London milk dealer, founded the first in 1871 and had six collecting depots by 1889. The Anglo-Swiss Condensed Milk Company (later Nestlé's) put up the first large-scale milk factory at Chippenham in 1873 and the Wilts United Dairies brought seven companies into amalgamation in 1896 – prospering on the liquid milk trade to London, creameries, butter factories and condensed milk. Conversion of land from mixed farming to dairying in west of England counties like Wiltshire and Somerset did cause sharp social consequences, from the fall in employment for agricultural labourers and a high rate of migration from villages in these regions to London, the dominions, and the United States. Numbers of agricultural labourers fell by 340,000 (from 962,000 in 1871 to 621,000 in 1901) in 30 years of rapid transition. With a rise in the value of total output of almost 10 per cent in the same period, according to one index, this represented a rise in productivity of no mean order in a generation afflicted by depression.

The proudest of the corn counties in the old days was Essex – the granary of London and the finest, most prolific wheat growing area in the island. Conventions there were set firmest in the arable traditions and farmers thought it beneath their dignity and certainly outside the realms of possibility (or even know-how, perhaps) to run cattle. They therefore hung on longest to their staple wheat growing and their fate became the hardest of all. When their capital had leached away they had no chance to buy stock in any case. Farms were vacated, arable tumbled down into rough pasture and land was sold at knock-down prices by equally disillusioned landlords to Scottish cattle farmers. This Scottish invasion of Essex was not a conversion to high-grade pedigree cattle-farming to take the cream of Smithfield prices – but the old extensive pasturing of ranging scrub-cattle. In the view of traditional farmers it was a humiliating decline in technique, but this was at least land use that could prosper in the changing structure of agricultural costs and prices.

In summary one can say that new standards of commercial efficiency were forced upon British farmers, sometimes at the expense of higher technical standards. But the response varied according to site and soil and opportunity: higher quality products, changing products, more intensive cropping, lower cost farming. The most recent attempts to make an index for total agricultural output (including vegetables, poultry and eggs) suggest that the decline in arable farming was more than offset over the nation as a whole, but not in wheat farming areas on heavy soils, by the increase in animal products and market gardening. One output index goes up by 8 per cent between 1870 and 1900 and a further 5 per cent between 1900 and 1913 (which is not, of course, a record of profits). Putting land down to grass, by far the most widespread response to the fall in wheat prices, was also an insurance policy for the future – maintaining fertility in the soil which would build up a valuable capital stock to draw on when wartime emergencies demanded the maximum production of cereals once more. All these trends repeated themselves when the world price of wheat slumped again in 1921 and wartime emergencies brought out the plough to its full usage again in 1939.

The impact of these changes, and a certain contraction in the rate of growth of farm output in the last quarter of the nineteenth century, did not have as severe effects upon the rest of the economy as in some other European countries. The agricultural depression itself was not as severe as it might have been, because of the flexibility available in switching to non-cereal production – agricultural production was comparatively differentiated in its sales pattern. Agriculture was also a smaller sector in the total economy than in most European countries so that the multiplier effects of a slowing down of growth rates were less. Real wages of the agricultural labour force were maintained (even if numbers fell), while cheaper food stimulated consumer demand in the economy generally. Nor was farming very important, it seems, as a source of investment demand for the products of British industry. The redeployment of such a large section of the labour force contributed to the efficiency of the economy, particularly as the process was accompanied with rising productivity in agriculture.

Reading list

FLETCHER, T. W. 'The great depression of English agriculture, 1873–1896', *Economic History Review*, 2nd series, 1961, **13**, no. 3.

FUSSELL, G. E. & COMPTON, M. 'Agricultural adjustments after the Napoleonic Wars', *Economic History*, 1939, **4**, no. 14.

JONES, E. L. 'The changing basis of English agricultural prosperity, 1853–1873', *Agricultural History Review*, 1962, **10**, pt. 2.

JONES, E. L. *The Development of English Agriculture, 1815–1873*, London, 1968.

MOORE, D. C. 'The corn laws and high farming', *Economic History Review*, 2nd series, 1965, **18**, no. 3.

ORWIN, C. S. & WHETHAM, E. H. *History of British Agriculture, 1856–1914*, London, 1964.

SPRING, D. *The English Landed Estate in the 19th Century: its administration*, Baltimore, 1963.

THOMPSON, F. M. L. *English Landed Society in the 19th Century*, London–Toronto, 1963.

THOMPSON, F. M. L. 'The second agricultural revolution, 1815–1880', *Economic History Review*, 2nd series, 1968, **21**, no. 1.

TRACY, M. *Agriculture in Western Europe: crisis and adaptation since 1880*, London, 1964 [sections on Britain].

TROW SMITH, R. *English Husbandry: from the earliest times to the present day*, London, 1951.

Victoria County History. Leicestershire, 5 vols, London, 1907–64.

Victoria County History. Wiltshire, 8 vols, London, 1957–65.

WHETHAM, E. H. 'The London milk trade, 1860–1900', *Economic History Review*, 2nd series, 1964, **17**, no. 2.

13 The evolution of banking and the money market, 1825–1914

The main new arrival on the British financial scene in the 1820's was the joint-stock bank, its coming timed to some extent by the great banking crisis of 1825. Scotland had long enjoyed the advantages of joint-stock banks – in the eighteenth century she had several chartered banks and many multi-partnered banks that functioned as joint-stock companies. The late arrival of commercial and industrial advance on a large scale in Scotland, shortage of local capital and the need to raise large amounts quickly and spread risks widely prompted the joint-stock principle of deposit banking there. It was a response to a less mature business environment as much as to a more tolerant legal code. The Scottish business community profited much from the greater willingness of joint-stock banks to lend on overdraft at 5 per cent, and from the greater stability that large capitals in a common fund made possible. English businessmen had noticed that the Scottish banking system had been far less troubled by the 1825 panic than the English. Thomas Joplin, a Newcastle merchant and banker, thereupon successfully challenged the Bank of England's claim to monopoly. In 1826 joint-stock banks were legalized outside a 65-mile radius from London, and in 1833 joint-stock banks, but without rights of issuing notes, were legalized within the Bank of England monopoly area and London.

The boom in joint-stock banking that followed added considerably to the banking capacity of the country. Within 10 years over 100 joint-stock banks had been established, 59 in the boom year of 1836 alone, where bank promotion was part of the investment boom of that time. From this legislation of 1826 and 1833 the era of private banks drew to a close, although the number of branches of joint-stock banks in the provinces did not begin to exceed the numbers of private partnership banks until 1838. In London, the London and Westminster bank was launched in 1834, as a joint-stock venture, against the united hostility of all the established bankers in the capital. There were 5 joint-stock banks in London by 1844, but until that year the Bank of England tried to freeze them out of the bill market by refusing to extend credit, or rediscount bills, underwritten by the London and Westminster. In other words the Bank virtually refused them an account, or aid in getting cash in a crisis. Until 1854 they were not allowed the convenience of being members of the London Bankers Clearing House, established to settle accounts daily between themselves without the need for complicated cash transfers. But the trumps were on the side of the larger concerns and in time the older members of the banking community had to come to terms.

The invasion of the joint-stock banks did more than just extend the capacity of the banking system. They made it more competitive, more aggressive in the search for business. In fact, the argument that the joint-stock banks would be more stable cut both ways. They were, indeed, safer. With many more partners, or directors, than the smaller country banks they could grow more rapidly to a greater size and assemble greater capitals. But this greater size and security in normal conditions of trade allowed them to take greater risks and survive on smaller margins. In addition, they were *arrivistes* on the banking scene. They had to bid for custom from established interests. Joint-stock banks therefore tended to offer slightly higher interest rates on deposits; interest was even paid on some current accounts. Bills of exchange were accepted for discount of more doubtful quality than the standards demanded by the more cautious of private bankers. In particular the joint-stock banks rediscounted in London a great deal of the bills of exchange they accepted for discount. That is to say they underwrote such commercial paper (accepting its risks) and then sent it off to London for conversion into cash, profiting from the margins available between the higher rates of interest they charged in the provinces for accepting bills on unknown traders and the lower ones current in London for bills backed by first-class risks in the provinces (the joint-stock banks). They were able to do these things and were hated for them, because they turned over as much business as possible on very low profit margins. They had to keep lower cash reserves and employ all their deposits as actively as possible to survive on these margins. New and expansionist practices were thus introduced in the wake of the joint-stock banks and in turn forced upon rivals who wished to keep their trade. The new bankers, in a way, brought to their business the same aggressive instincts and a similar technique of expanding turnover and cutting margins as the new industrialists.

The expansion of joint-stock banking was halted temporarily by stricter controls imposed on them in the 1844 banking legislation – they had fed the speculative troubles and bank-ruptcies of the years 1836-9. But when limited liability was given to joint-stock banks (but not to their note issues) in special Acts of 1858 and 1862 another leap forward came. Bar-clays converted to joint stock in 1862, Lloyds in 1865. By the 1880's the number of private banks in the provinces was down to 172, while the joint-stock banks – also shrinking in numbers (but not in branches) by amalgamation had more than half of total bank deposits. From this period the five main joint-stock banks – Barclays, Lloyds, Midland, District, Martins – drove on to establish national networks of branches, sweeping up the private bankers into their organizations. 164 different banks contributed to the structure of Lloyds in 1923. These five deposit banks were some of the greatest alligators of all in the amalgamation movement in British business after 1870. The last country bank, Gunner and Co. of Bishop's Waltham in Hampshire, was taken over by Barclays in 1953, but country banks of any sort were becoming historical curiosities after 1900.

This consolidation brought a consolidation of conservative lending policy with it. Many local country bankers in the eighteenth century were much more unstable, much more risky in their lending policy. But the growth of national joint-stock banks eventually spread more conservative banking principles. Branch managers' freedom of action became limited by the London head office. The banking system became a very stable, very efficient instrument for short-term accommodation without being an important instrument for financing investment, unlike in Germany where the banks initially sponsored the growth of great new industries. In Britain, the City to a large extent had its back turned to industry. This theme makes another strand to the story of the industrial problems of the late nineteenth century which are discussed below.

The Bank of England and banking legislation

We must now turn to the changes that took place in the Bank of England at the head of the financial system, as joint-stock banking was developing. To do so means discussing general legislation affecting the powers of the Bank of England and banking generally. Even though its directors still refused to acknowledge their formal public responsibilities here, claiming they were just another private bank in law, the logic of their position was to place them above the money market, not in a directly competitive position within it, and in practice they had acted as such.[1] The depression years were intensified between 1819 and 1821 as the Bank deflated its note issues and accumulated gold ready for convertibility again in 1821. Subsequently the Bank had to bear some responsibility for intensifying the mania and panic of 1825. It had not attempted to curb activity, as the speculative fever mounted, by pushing up its discount rate or cutting back the volume of its notes in circulation. Then, in the panic which followed, the directors retracted too late, too suddenly and too hard by refusing to discount, rationing accommodation loans by quota and not by price (by charging a high rate of interest) alone. If other bankers and merchants know they can get cash, but will have to pay dearly for it, panic is not spread. When bankers found that they were not assured of unlimited rediscount facilities at the Bank of England, this at once set off the rush for liquidity – for cash. Only on 1 December 1825 did the directors acknowledge that their responsibilities in such an internal crisis of confidence were to lend as boldly as possible. They then lent to the limit of the famous lost box of notes that a clerk discovered in the cellars.

[1] See above, pp. 172–3.

But the corner was only turned on 19 December when £·5 million in gold arrived from the Bank of France through the Rothschilds, and then £2 million in silver destined for Ireland.

The 1826 banking legislation showed the general diagnosis of this panic. The blame was not put on the Bank of England but on the country banks, with the paper currency of the country banks accused of being the main agent of over-expansion of credit. Joint-stock banking was therefore encouraged in the provinces, as we have seen. All bank-notes under £5 in value were prohibited, and the Bank of England was authorized to set up branches in the provinces, to push gold and its own notes into circulation and help keep local bank-notes down, or at least under control. In retrospect it seems hard to believe that small-denomination provincial bank-notes had much responsibility for the crisis. Being used for wages and fairly small retail transactions they were just not the medium involved in the speculative mania which had really conditioned the 1825 crisis. But some alteration of the banking system had to come after that crisis, when 60 banks went bankrupt, for it dominated the minds of merchants, industrialists and bankers for months. Pressure against private note issues was increased in 1833, when rights of issue were denied to joint-stock banks opening in the London area.

From 1826 the Bank of England, and its branches, did not attempt to bid very actively for discount business. Bank rate was kept at 4 per cent when the commercial rate charged by the commercial banks in Lombard Street was well below this. Normally, therefore, bill brokers and bankers handled the bulk of this trade without interference from the Bank of England in normal times. The bill brokers, led by Samuel Gurney, from the crisis of 1825 had received the immediate cash reserves from the deposit banks in London 'at call'. With this float of short-term capital (from country bankers also) they themselves began to act as principals in discounting bills, and not merely as intermediaries channelling bills through to accredited banker customers for discount. Whenever Lombard Street was short of funds, therefore, the immediate demand for cash now fell on the bill brokers – the discount houses as they had come to be called – who held the first reserves of cash in the system. If they could not absorb the demand, their line of retreat lay to the Bank of England, to whom they would present bills they had accepted for rediscount, in order to get into cash themselves. Thus in any move for liquidity after 1825 the bill brokers were placed between the bankers and the Bank of England.

At such times the Bank still occasionally rationed accommodation by quantity rather than by price. In 1836, 1839 and 1847 it did this temporarily. The bill brokers at once ceased to discount bills until they were sure of their own line of retreat, which meant that credit was at once frozen in Lombard Street. In a sense this was the continuation of a tradition formed in the time of the Usury Laws (before 1832) when 5 per cent was the maximum permitted rate of interest. In 1836 another smaller crisis developed, caused by the collapse of the Stock Exchange mania of that year. And then, three years later, another crisis came out of a blue sky, with no great increase in country currency, no Stock Exchange mania, no previous collapse of confidence at home. This time it was an external drain of gold from the Bank of England, flowing out of the country to pay for corn imports, aided by a continental panic that caused short-term loans to London to be repatriated. A temporary threat faced Lombard Street when Gurney was momentarily refused rediscount facilities. But still the gold reserves were flowing away and the bank rate had to be jacked up strongly to stop the haemorrhage. £2 million in gold from France again saved the day.

From these two differing crises, 1836 and 1839, was born the most important banking legislation of the century, Peel's 1844 Act. The diagnosis this time was that continuing financial instability was caused by over-issues of Bank of England notes (even though formally limited, like country bankers' note issues, by the rights of holders of Bank of England notes to present them over its counters for gold). Provincial paper, went the argument, could not be tamed until all freedom of action over Bank of England issues had been removed from the power of the Court of Directors. The currency school, the old Bullionists of 1810, who diagnosed uncontrolled paper currency as the root of all the trouble, had finally triumphed. Active steps were taken in 1844 to prevent any bank which was not a note issuer from becoming one. Other banks of issue were persuaded to suspend their issues by being offered privileges of accommodation with Bank of England branches. If they declined there were ways in which they might be frightened at times when they needed help. Once a bank had suspended its note issues it could not start again. Provincial paper currency was thus to be allowed to die a natural death. The last country bank issuing notes was Fox Fowler and Co. of Wellington, Somerset, who did so up to the time of their absorption into Lloyds in 1921. In fact, even in the 1840's at the time of the Act over three-quarters of the notes circulating in the country were Bank of England notes and their proportion had been growing before 1844. By the end of the century most country paper had disappeared (under £250,000 remained in 1910).

The Bank of England itself in 1844 was allowed a fiduciary note issue, uncovered by gold, of £14 million above which all its notes had to be covered pound for pound in bullion. The issue department was made quite independent of the banking department, and gold reserves covering the note issues were not allowed to be used to help the banking department when that was under strain. After 1839 the Directors of the Bank had themselves proposed to limit their fiduciary issue in this way in response to criticism, but they had not thought of preventing one set of reserves from being utilized in an emergency. They realized, as did some other observers, that their notes would not lose the confidence of the public and be presented for gold (being actively sought as cash at these times). It was clear that the real shock of a crisis fell on the banking department, lending cash on discounts and as loans to the business and banking world. This was exactly what happened in the 1847 crisis. The Directors paid out almost all their reserves in the banking department while the vaults were stacked with useless gold covering their notes. Only a Treasury letter releasing this gold saved them, although it was not then used. The provisions of Peel's Act had to be broken again in a crisis of 1857 (set off by an American financial panic) when the Bank printed more notes without gold cover to them. The Overend and Gurney crisis of 1866 almost required permission again. The 1890 Baring crisis almost certainly would have done if the government had not agreed privately to support Barings. Only the foresight of the Directors in keeping such a high reserve in their banking department enabled them to survive so often.

Immediately, the 1844 Act had an ironic effect. The Directors of the Bank had allowed themselves to be persuaded that variations in the supply of bank-notes had been responsible for financial instability. This had now been cured by the 1844 Act, releasing them from discretionary power and all responsibility for causing speculation. They therefore plunged into the discount market, dropped the bank rate for discounting bills to 2·5 per cent in September 1844 and went out to collect discount business from Lombard Street. This brought all discount rates down as the discount market tried to keep its trade and led the country once more along the cheap-money road to expansion and speculation. Even at the end of 1846 bank rate was still below the market rate of 3 per cent. Although no recriminations were made against the Bank in legislation for this policy, in fact, from this date (as between 1825 and 1844) the Bank stayed out of the bill market, by keeping bank rate above the market rate of interest, allowing the market to come to them only when liquid funds in Lombard Street were too short to meet the demand for accommodation. Conflict between the public responsibilities of the Bank in acting above the money markets as a regulator and a final resort for cash, and the opportunities for pursuing private gain by seeking business in the money markets as a banker, had finally been resolved. Although a private institution until the Nationalization Act of 1944, the Bank acted with the motivations and policy of a central bank after 1847. And it was certainly a private institution with a very special relationship to the public authorities.

The main problems of the Bank of England in relation to the successive crises of the later nineteenth century were not because the Directors did the wrong thing in emergencies. Indeed, their clever anticipating action, bold use of bank rate and a full awareness of their responsibility to maintain the liquidity of the London money market and, through that, the world money markets, all contributed to make the international gold standard work fairly smoothly, at least as far as Britain was concerned. Drastic American banking crises in 1900 and 1907 were cushioned by effective action in the Bank of England. The trouble was that the size of the Bank's resources in the banking department had not grown commensurately with the expansion of the money markets as a whole, and hence the Bank could not be as effective in throwing its weight into the market at times of crisis as it might have been. But with the steady growth of joint-stock banking on a national scale and the steady extension of conservative banking principles in these more stable banking institutions, the days of internal panic in banking had waned – and only the Stock Exchange or foreign banking business provided the headlines for sensational speculative manias. The 'gold standard' worked efficiently, on the whole, for Britain. When money was short a rise in the rate of interest would attract gold from all over the world to London, as the order went out to British managers of local banks, and merchants and bankers looked to gain from higher interest rates. But stability at the centre was often bought at the price of very great instability at the periphery. The currency base and the level of bank lending in far-flung countries fell, and economic activities contracted, as the gold flowed out to London.

An institutional change also came to the operations of the bill brokers and discount houses in the second half of the nineteenth century. At first the development of joint-stock banks had increased the flow of bills from the provinces through London for discount and the bill brokers, as we have seen, were at the centre of the money market in the 1840's. Inland bills were still the most important media for transferring funds in the country. In the 1840's, when the discount houses were employing all the available balances loaned to them 'at call' by the banks they were doing more discount business in their own right than all the London banks together. The greatest of them was still Overend and Gurney (as Richardson and Gurney had become) with £6 million on deposit at any one time in this decade. They were three times larger than the second-rank firms in the discount market, Alexanders and Sandersons. Over 30 other smaller discount houses flourished at this time. The collapse of Overend and Gurney in 1866 brought on the worst panic in the City since 1825. They failed with liabilities of £18 million and Friday 11 May 1866 became known as Black Friday. The Bank of England paid out nearly £4 million on that day to support liquidity. Overend and Gurney had been shaky for some years (rumours were circulating in the City about this) having underwritten much doubtful commercial paper. The unsound business they were carrying was exposed by the general crisis of that year.

By the 1860's the volume of inland bills of exchange was declining as a proportion of business done. Increasingly, deposit banking was spreading through the commercial community, and more and more of the capital and savings of the nation were coming to rest in bank vaults. This made for enhanced economic efficiency, for these savings were then put actively to work by the banks to earn income. Bank deposits grew to be several times the value of circulating media and currency as the banking habit spread over the nation.[1] But a consequence was that inland transfers of credit were increasingly done by cheques and drafts drawn directly on other bank deposits. This was true of industrialists and merchants settling accounts in their normal way of trade, quite apart from private persons conducting their household expenditures. These transfers passed within the banking system, needing no financial intermediaries outside it like the bill brokers. The extension of multi-branched joint-stock banking with national networks encouraged this further. As the inland bill declined in importance so the business of the London discount market moved steadily towards financing international trade, still mainly afloat on sterling bills. One of the most important functions of the merchant bankers of London was then underwriting bills of exchange drawn upon foreign merchants whom they guaranteed. The signatures of famous houses like Barings, Rothschilds and

[1] See Appendix, Table 39, pp. 492–3.

Hambros, made an enormous volume of foreign bills negotiable in London. This created a further problem for the Bank of England, trying to regulate the London money market in times of instability. The dimensions of this market were now not confined to British commerce alone, but covered the whole sterling area. It would be more accurate to call the international commercial system one of the 'sterling standard' than the gold standard. The resources of the Bank of England were relatively less powerful when they had to be deployed against the momentum of forces in this huge international sterling market.

And then a complementary movement took place in credit. Not only did London become the main centre of a world-wide flow of bills of exchange seeking discounts, but a main target for unemployed short-term capital the world over seeking profitable short-term investment in discounting. The discount houses developed a call market for international funds in the second half of the century as they had developed a call market for British banking surpluses in the first half of the century. 'Foreign short-term money discounted foreign-drawn bills.' This was the hey-day of the London discount market – the most remarkable example of international finance operating under purely private institutions, responsive only to the price mechanism and the laws of the international gold standard. As we now have reason to realize, it was the product of very special historical circumstances and a very special economic context. It has to be very closely related to the structure of world trade and world shipping. London's financial hegemony was the reflection in a golden mirror of commercial and maritime strength. How much success and strength in this international finance depended on the stability of the pound, and exchange rates, large gold reserves, and a strong balance of payments position, we know only too well. Between the wars and now London still attracts much short-term capital on call from Zurich and Frankfurt and New York. But no capital could be more restless. It migrates mysteriously and swiftly at the hint of a balance of payments crisis, a rise in the bank rate in New York, the suspicion of a rumour about devaluation that the Chancellor of the Exchequer has taken seriously enough to deny. And in these circumstances such short-term capital can be as much of a liability as an asset, nationally, when an economy is operating close to the wind on its bullion reserves and the balance of payments. This international delicacy of confidence is reminiscent of the state of affairs common to banking within the country in the early nineteenth century. In the words of the *Morning Chronicle* lamenting the 1825 crisis, 'Credit, like the honour of a female, is of too delicate a nature to be treated with laxity – the slightest hint may inflict an injury which no subsequent effort can repair.'

Reading list

ASHTON, T. S. & SAYERS, R. S. (eds.) *Papers in English Monetary History*, Oxford, 1953.

BAGEHOT, W. *Lombard Street: a description of the money market*, with a new introduction by F. C. Genovese, Homewood (Ill.), 1962.

BLOOMFIELD, A. *Monetary Policy under the International Gold Standard, 1880–1914*, New York, 1959.

CLAPHAM, J. H. *The Bank of England: a history*, 2 vols, Cambridge, 1944.

CRICK, W. F. & WADSWORTH, J. E. *100 Years of Joint-stock Banking*, London, 1936.

FORD, A. G. *The Gold Standard, 1880–1914: Britain and Argentina*, Oxford, 1962.

GREGORY, T. E. *The Westminster Bank through a Century*, Oxford, 1936.

HAWTREY, R. G. *A Century of Bank Rate*, London, 1938.

HIGONNET, R. D. 'Bank deposits in the United Kingdom, 1870–1914', *Quarterly Journal of Economics*, 1957, **71,** no. 3.

KING, W. T. C. *History of the London Discount Market*, London, 1936.

MORGAN, E. V. & THOMAS, W. A. *The Stock Exchange: its history and functions*, London [1962].

PALGRAVE, R. H. I. *Bank Rate and the Money Market in England, France, Germany, Holland and Belgium, 1844–1900*, London, 1903.

SAYERS, R. S. *Bank of England Operations, 1890–1914*, London, 1936.

SAYERS, R. S. *Central Banking after Bagehot*, Oxford, 1957.

SAYERS, R. S. *Lloyds Bank in the History of English Banking*, Oxford, 1957.

SAYERS, R. S. *Gilletts: In the London Money Market, 1867–1967*, Oxford, 1968.

SCAMMELL, W. M. 'The working of the gold standard', *Yorkshire Bulletin of Economic and Social Research*, 1965, **17,** no. 1.

TAYLOR, A. M. *Gilletts: Banking in Banbury and Oxford*, Oxford, 1964.

THOMAS, S. E. *The Rise and Growth of Joint-stock Banking*, London, 1934.

14 The organization of labour and standards of living

LABOUR ORGANIZATION

Looking back on the labour movements which developed in an industrializing society it is clear, with hindsight, that the future lay with those that sought to accept the fundamentals of the emergent industrial society and mould its influences in favour of the working man – the friendly society, the co-operative store, above all the trade union – rather than with attempts to organize the rejection or destruction of the new society. But until 1850, with the uncertainties and hardships of the first century of transition, much misguided energy and enthusiasm were poured into many different sorts of reaction.

One frequent response proved to be a quest to resurrect an imaginary, historical 'rural utopia', a recessive deathwish for a society without exploitation or extremes of wealth, without cotton mills or stock jobbers or paper money, where a new nineteenth-century yeomanry could prosper by digging allotments under spade husbandry. £112,000 in chartist pennies backed this dream in O'Connor's Land Plan of 1846. 'I would make a paradise of England in less than five years,' he claimed. How regressive these efforts were only the farm labourers and Irish peasants really knew. This was just fighting the logic of history: in an increasingly overcrowded land no return to the peasant society was possible. A variant on ruralism were the utopian industrial communities of Robert Owen and others, artificial parallelogram communities inspired and created by philosopher-industrialists – another impossibly exotic growth of blue-prints for brand new societies, often appealing to groups under great social and economic stress. A third characteristic reaction of the times to the new society was the attempt to destroy it, Luddism. These outbreaks of machine breaking, which came in the worst years of distress, 1800, 1812, 1816, 1826–7, 1830, were not a new theme but the survival of a reaction characteristic of the pre-industrial world – the peasants' revolt – a negative response nowhere more characteristic than in agriculture, where its symptom in Britain was rick burning.

These different negative reactions – and in some ways one might add Chartism to the list – came in conditions where it was impossible to organize a collective response to the new environment; that is by accepting the fundamental structure and then shaping its operations to favour labour. In many contexts conditions in the labour market in the early nineteenth century made effective bargaining through a trade union inconceivable: in agriculture, in occupations of low skill with easy entry or unskilled occupations, in enclaves of traditional skills facing the direct challenge of the new technology. With rapidly rising population, great labour mobility, immigration from Ireland, very low real incomes, great economic fluctuations – and a hostile law – effective general unionization was quite inconceivable.[1]

Effective trade societies were first confined to the skilled handicraft workers – the 'aristocracy of labour'. In most fields where workshop skills were traditional – papermakers, printers, wool combers, skilled cloth finishers, tailors and hatters, shoemakers, shipwrights and carpenters in the dockyards, millwrights – local collective action long predated the coming of the factory and the industrial state. Where such evidence for local societies existed, they were confined almost exclusively to skilled personnel. The new factory trades, in turn, quickly gave birth to societies corresponding to the old handicraft artisan societies. The Stockport and Manchester Spinning Society was in existence at latest by 1792, and by 1799 local combinations of spinners had come into existence in almost all the cotton towns. Public investigations into the woollen industry in 1806 similarly revealed universal and open organization, correspondence between the different woollen areas to organize concerted petitioning, a joint paid secretary, and concerted action against employers who refused to agree to minimum wage rates.

[1] Above, Chapters 6 and 7.

On the whole these skilled societies were responsible bodies from the start and stayed so throughout the troubled decades after 1790. They sought direct practical measures. They were not seduced very much by visionary hotheads. Their rules forbade violence and hostility to masters just as much as they sought to enforce a closed shop and prevent blacklegging between plants when there was a turn-out. Their skills, in fact, gave them incomes high enough to provide some savings for use in turn-outs, and a position to defend against incursions into their ranks from below, from unskilled workers, as well as a status from which to bargain with employers. Long before the industrial revolution the printers were trying to enforce 7-year apprenticeships, the exclusion of 'foreigners' from the trade, restrictions on the numbers of apprentices – exactly the traditional printers' demands of the early nineteenth century. The Lancashire skilled adult spinners' societies charged 10s. 6d. entrance fee for a non-local person, they sought to make apprenticeship the compulsory mode of becoming a spinner, and they then sought to limit apprenticeship to the children of members of the society, or children of friends nominated by members of the society – a self-perpetuating enclave. They refused entrance on principle to Irishmen.

The weaknesses of these societies were apparent. A rapidly expanding labour force, extensive migration and rapidly changing industrial location, as expansion and technical change progressed, weakened the strength and continuity of combinations. With rapidly expanding industries one of the main enemies was the small, newly-established master, undercutting in price, overworking labour, breaking apprenticeship agreements and living, in some cases, more precariously than the skilled journeymen in their societies. This context prevented effective unions altogether amongst unskilled grades.

Economic fluctuations also found out the weaknesses of the artisan societies, and wage levels did not allow the accumulation of substantial funds to sustain strike action for long. Spreading organization on the upswing of the trade cycle, successful bids for higher wages at the peak of the boom when demand for labour was at its highest, gave way to falling membership, dissipated funds and a collapse of unity in depression years. Funds were soon exhausted. A petty strike could ruin a society for years. A general Manchester spinners' strike in 1810, for example, used up £1,500 of strike money and prostrated the society until 1818. After a year of revived activity it was enfeebled again until 1823. The collapse of the 1825 boom had the same effect. All these societies, even if their formal continuity of organization was preserved, were but the temporary flowers of years of good trade as far as their economic effectiveness was concerned.

These societies also faced the hostility of the law, but this was a very much less formidable weapon against the consolidation and effectiveness of combination at this time than economic circumstances. On paper the law was a ferocious enemy. One minor issue was over wages. Until 1813 and 1814 statutes existed which formally regulated wages. They were repealed, appropriately enough, as soon as the organized cloth workers produced petitions and put pressure on J.P.s to implement these statutes in the interests of labour, by raising the minimum wage rates. Public control of the wage bargain, even for women and children, began to creep back only in the twentieth century, when the 1909 Trade Boards Act and the 1912 Mines Act attempted to underpin the economic position of two important economic groups – women in sweat-shops and the miners. Where they could, competing parties used the law regulating wages as a weapon over wage rates, but the main determinant of wage rates remained the fundamental economic and social facts of the context within which the bargaining took place. The same conclusion stands for the effectiveness of legal restraints against combination in restraint of trade – the second and much the more important impact of the law upon labour.

This had respectable ancestry in both statute and Common Law. The assumption of the individualistic principle in the eighteenth century was that freedom of contract meant only that of an individual workman with an individual employer. The Common Law stood firm to safeguard this concept of freedom in wage contracts and outlaw conspiracy in restraint of trade ostensibly on the part of masters as well as workmen, both before the passing of the Combination Laws in 1799 and after their repeal in 1824. Only the new trade union legislation of 1871 and 1875 gave unions protection of their funds, access to courts as ordinary associations, and legal protection to their members acting peaceably in trade disputes, strikes and picketing. Between 1824 and 1875 unions were not criminal conspiracies by the mere fact of their existence, as they had been under the Combination Laws, but they began to be so as soon as their members took any action to withhold labour from employers. They could be sued for breach of contract or action in restraint of trade and, if union funds were stolen, members or officers could not take action for recovery in the courts unless the union had registered as a friendly society and disguised its economic purpose successfully from the J.P.s.

The existence of such formal legal restraints, both in statute and Common Law, certainly did not prevent combinations, which were endemic in skilled trades, before 1824 and afterwards, as the examples quoted suggest. In this sense the law restricting combination and collective bargaining was as ineffective in general terms as the wage-regulation statutes, or the prohibitions on the emigration of artisans (also repealed, with the Combination Laws, in 1824). The general conclusion of the parliamentary enquiry which resulted in repeal was to expose the ineffectiveness of the law as a negligible instrument of oppression, while employers acknowledged that the presence of these laws on the statute book bedevilled labour relations. The state of the law also made possible outbreaks of arbitrary persecutions, when local J.P.s or the Home Office became frightened about sedition, such as with the prosecution of the printers of *The Times* in 1810, or the agricultural labourers of Tolpuddle in 1834. These occasional victimizations, on balance, probably increased the sense of social solidarity amongst workers and provided the movements with their martyrs as much as they cowed would-be trade unions to inactivity through terror. The economic context was a much more potent barrier.

The next phase of trade union development from the 1820's to 1850 was a series of false starts and frustrated hopes. Much energy and ambition went into attempts to create national associations from the local and regional societies existing in skilled trades. This fell mainly under the head of utopian system-building rather than effective working-class labour organization at this epoch. The great schemes were effective mainly on paper, in the enthusiasms of their authors and travelling orators or in the uncritical fears of employers and the Home Secretary. All proved ephemeral. They collapsed at the touch of a trade depression, or with the arrest of some leaders, with other leaders defaulting with the funds or even by a strike which made the funds run out. The 'Grand General Union of the United Kingdom' of 1829 for all spinning societies never got beyond a loose association of Lancashire groups. John Doherty's 'National Association for the Protection of Labour' of 1830 attempted to embrace other trades as well as textiles. On this was styled Robert Owen's more famous 'Grand National Consolidated Trade Union' of 1834, which failed even on the rising wave of the boom between 1834 and 1836, which was the strongest bargaining position labour could hope for. These extended visionary schemes are to be considered more as fore-runners of Chartism, which focused so much working-class ambition in the 1830's and 1840's, than of the Trades Union Congress. Permanent successful organization developed only under the 'new model' craft unions, led by the Amalgamated Society of Engineers of 1851. It grew out of the earlier, local tradition of the craft societies, working in a fairly restrained way for immediate local objects, and translated these methods and aims over a wider context. This is quite another theme to those abstract blue-prints of total social engineering being canvassed by Doherty and Owen.

A similar metamorphosis overcame the co-operative movement. The 1820's and 1830's saw romantic but ephemeral schemes for complete co-operative communities, co-operation being considered as a total social ethic, an all-embracing way of life. The highly successful organizations built up in the second half of the century stemmed from the efforts, and the tradition, of the Rochdale Pioneers of 1844. The root of their success lay in the practical business of efficient shopkeeping – even though shopkeeping with a wider social vision – and a 'divvy'.

Five craft unions, a nice mixture of old and new skills, led the national revival of trade unionism in the 1850's and 1860's – the engineers, carpenters and joiners, iron founders, bricklayers and the boot and shoe operatives. The five leaders of the 'Junta' headed respectable, responsible organizations of trade societies, emphasizing that their funds were for social benefits in adversity rather than a war chest for strikes. They led the campaign in the 1860's for the legal recognition of unions and secured the protection granted in the 1871 and 1875 statutes. By their prominence they have given a partially false picture of a universally peaceful trade union movement under highly conservative leadership in the third quarter of the century. Some image of them can be seen from existing Victorian photographs, showing respectable bearded patriarchs, dressed like their betters, every visible waistcoat with a golden watchchain, that great status symbol of the times, across its stomach. This proved a London image to a large degree. A harsher, more militant edge and tone came to labour organizations in the north and in Scotland, pertaining to mining in particular. On the whole, however, it seemed that labour was at last learning to play the free enterprise game according to the rules: accepting the need for some decline in wages when prices fell or depression came, not effectively rationing work or preventing advances in productivity, acting peacefully. On the employers' side, truck and long pay was rapidly declining under the stimulus of legislation and Factory Acts were beginning to generalize minimum conditions of safety, hours of work, ages of work and decency at work, of women and children, although not yet of adult men. The wage bargain was still essentially a private contract.

The main theme of trade union history after 1850, and more particularly after 1880, was that unions penetrated through the economy into most industries even though progressing at different rates in different industries, and at different rates at different times. At every point progress was conditioned by two facts: the state of employment at the time, and the nature of the industry.

In the early 1870's the boom had brought great organization to the skilled trades everywhere, and the growth of skilled unions came fastest where the units were large - railways, coal, shipyards, iron works, engineering shops. Unionism came most strongly in certain circumstances. First where immediate social problems afflicted labour, such as the places where truck payments survived; more particularly in the older basic industries where there were longer traditions of industrial employment. Where employers faced wide swings in prices during the trade cycle (as in the capital goods industries), they were led to put great pressure on wage rates at times of depressed trade, which provoked organized reaction. Where employers faced export markets as much as home markets, and were very conscious of low-cost competition abroad, they strove to keep prices at a minimum and maintain pressures against wage rates. In most industries at this time, combinations and price agreements amongst employers were ineffective, which made individual employers in their turn very conscious of price competition. Large-plant industries where a few employers dominated employment in a locality created a further stimulus for skilled labour to organize. Moreover, in general from 1850 until after the boom of the 1870's, employment conditions were good and labour in expanding demand, which gave unions of skilled men with direct local objects to achieve, good chances to improve their bargaining. The increase in money wages ahead of prices at the time reveals this.

The problems of the following decade 1879–89 challenged the tradition formed in the previous generation and set new union growth off along more radical lines. The intense slump year of 1879 severely jolted the movement – breaking up many miners' associations (particularly in south Wales) – and most of the gains in wage rates and hours of work secured in the previous decade were lost. The 1880's continued this pressure. Unemployment rates rose, putting labour at a disadvantage in bargaining. Narrower profit margins and contracting exports in some trades made employers more aggressive against wage levels. Falling productivity, as in the coal industry, increased the pressure of wage costs. Falling prices then gave the opportunity for an attack on wages where sliding scale agreements had been started under pressure from unions in times when this device was a protection for labour against rising prices. The conservative tradition of the leading craft unions, enshrined in the Trades Union Congress attitudes since its foundation in 1868, became outmoded.

Characteristic of the change was the revolt of the miners of Yorkshire and Lancashire to form the Miners' Federation of 1888, opposing the older conventions of miners' unions, centring on Northumberland and Durham, which had accepted a sliding scale for wages and sought to collaborate with the mine owners as much as they could over hours of work. The new federation of local unions demanded a minimum wage, no sliding scale, a cut in the length of the day (in order to ration work) and was broadly socialist in outlook. Moreover, new aims brought changed methods: the miners were prepared for violence in aggressive strike action. They took the decision, as did other unions of railwaymen (the General Railway Workers' Union and the National Union of Gas-Workers and General Labourers) at the time, that funds were for strikes alone. 'We have only one benefit attached, and that is strike pay.' They resolved that their unions should be 'fighting ones', as the expression went, not encumbered with any sick or accident fund.

The brief revival in trade from 1888 to 1890 saw the new unionism penetrate unskilled trades, particularly in the wave of enthusiasm which followed the first successful London dockers' strike of 1889. This reversed the normal sequence – a successful and fairly spontaneous battle to secure a wage of 6d. per hour amongst unorganized labourers, was immediately followed by the establishment of a union to consolidate and maintain the victory. The union came after the strike. Industrial and general unions now took the lead in labour action, with the miners in the van, over the older more restrained craft unions. But 1889 was not some new beginning in 'new unionism' as the Webbs suggested. Many trends in this direction were to be discerned before this.

In 1885 probably less than 10 per cent of the adult male manual labour force was in effective unions, or could have afforded to pay the high friendly-society type levies of these restricted craft unions. By 1892 the proportion of employed

men in unions had doubled, and the movement had about
1½ million members. Over 300,000 were miners, and a further
300,000 were in the metal trades. Membership waxed and
waned with the state of employment, shrinking after 1892 for
a few years; then surging to 2 million by 1900; slackening again
in the five years of poor trade after that. The Taff Vale Case of
1901 put unions under pressure at law again (by making unions
liable in actions for damages by employers for civil wrongs
payable by union funds). Ideal conditions of growth then followed: a resilient demand for labour with expanding employment, with rising prices putting pressure on standards of living
which raised the incentives for combination at the same time as
the state of the labour market allowed it to become effective.
From 2 million members in 1905 enrolments doubled to 4 million in 1914. And then came the most favourable conditions of
all for making the power of labour in combination effective –
total war. There were almost 8 million trade unionists by 1919.
Well over half were in the mining, metal, and engineering
trades, and in transport. Dockers and railwaymen, in fact, then
numbered about 1 million.

The spread of mass unions induced violence on a widening
front. Serious riots in London in 1886–7 brought a foretaste of
the radical traditions of the northern coalfields to the capital.
Strikes probably did not become more frequent, but were certainly more prolonged and more intense when they occurred.
A 15-week lock-out took place in the mines in 1893 with gang
warfare in Ebbw Vale. The Amalgamated Society of Engineers
led a 6-month strike in 1897–8, fighting for the 8-hour day. The
combined action of miners, dockers and railwaymen – the so-
called Triple Alliance – of 1913 led to scenes of industrial strife
on a scale undreamed of since the days of Chartism. The labour
struggles which made the headlines and provided some of the
political drama of these years were highly concentrated in these
relatively few major sectors of industry, now heavily and
militantly unionized. This tradition had been developing since
1870. It is quite certainly connected with the incidence of
economic fluctuations, as the weight of the heavy industries –
the capital goods industries – was growing in the economic

structure. These tended to be large-plant industries, where technology and the labour force at a plant was at its most massive. These industries also responded to the investment cycle as much as the trade cycle; and the swings of the investment cycle were larger, the depressions more intense, the booms more feverish, the recoveries slower and less resilient.

With increasing bitterness in the labour struggle came the move to the left politically. The strategy of trade unionism remained practical, as were its immediate objectives. In organization and planning it was in no sense utopian. But from the 1880's the movement ceased to accept some of the assumptions of the free market economy, although this did not now mean a rejection of industrialization. A new generation of intellectuals helped swing the allegiance of the movement to socialism. Henry George's book *Progress and Poverty* made an extraordinary impact on its arrival in 1880. George was fêted as a prophet on his visits from the United States. Marx was translated in 1886. There were Fabians, Christian Socialists and the Social Democratic Federation – all influencing small but quite important minorities. Also from this point came the break with the liberals and the demand for labour's own political representation, with the foundation of the Independent Labour Party by Keir Hardie in 1893. Many miners' unions formally affiliated to the Labour Party in the decade before 1914.

The economic implications of all these changes stemming from the 1880's and affecting the capital goods industries and railways, in particular, are impossible to quantify. How much costs and output suffered from bad industrial relations and strikes is problematical; to what degree the failings in productivity, the problems of innovation, were increased by the new institutionalized reactions of labour is unknown. In fact, where labour troubles were most intense, in mining, the rise in output was most sustained, but the decline in relative productivity most severe. One can say that labour reactions in Britain in the 1880's and 1890's encouraged a very different attitude to output and productivity compared with American unions. American unions, although not at all strong by comparison at this time, did not worry much about rising productivity per man provided that they could ensure that labour received its share of the benefits of technical innovation. They encouraged re-equipment. They aligned to no specific political party or to socialism. This difference in attitude was confirmed by the experiences of the inter-war years.

What were the actual economic effects of unionization upon wage levels? Unions were probably much more effective in improving conditions of work than influencing the average level of money wages for a significant time. Employers offering lower wages or poorer conditions than the average could be constrained by effective unions. The actual impact of unionization upon wage levels is much more difficult to quantify; and very few of the studies of trade unions have considered the question systematically. The fact that labour problems and trade union leadership were so concentrated in heavy industry and in transport has a further implication. Labour problems were not nearly so severe in the new industries prospering very much upon the rise in real wages and working-class prosperity after 1850. Unionization was not nearly so complete, even though some units of production were quite large in industries such as soap, food processing or tobacco. In many cases labour costs were not as high a proportion of total costs as in industries like mining and ship-building, hence giving employers more room to compromise. Often much of the labour was done by women, notoriously more difficult to organize. But employers in the new industries were often enlightened men wanting a contented labour force which would mean higher production and lower costs – *better* labour, in fact. Often these industrialists were to be found in the van of social movements in the second half of the nineteenth century. Cadbury set up a model community at Bournville; William Lever later at Port Sunlight (and he advocated a 6-hour day). Lipton supported the Saturday half-day. Rowntree investigated social problems in York. These men usually remained firm paternal autocrats as far as control of their businesses was concerned. While they might well tolerate unions bargaining for better wages with equanimity, they bitterly opposed any attempt to usurp management responsibilities and they hated the new political affiliations of the unions. But in their own industries little pressure came from labour against technical change, and wage rates tended to be above the average. Moreover, the prosperity of these new industries was not much involved in export markets as a rule, so that the minds of the employers were not as obsessed with the fear of competition from low-cost production abroad. Rather, they knew that their prosperity depended upon good wages and employment at home, upon rising social standards, possibly on increased leisure; certainly upon the shopping baskets of a million housewives. Lever and Cadbury had good cause to know that the purchasing power of the working classes made them rich, and could more easily see that the economic implications of the trade unions might be a healthy influence, implying a wider home market and better standards of labour. That is to say, the assumptions from which they were operating came from a different world of values from those of the coal owners.

STANDARDS OF LIFE, 1850-1914

After all the debate about movements in real wages from 1790 to 1850 substantial agreement exists that industrialization paid off generally in higher real wages for all groups in society in the second half of the nineteenth century. As far as very rough estimates can indicate, the national income (at constant prices) rose from about £550 million in 1851; doubling by the 1880's and reaching over £2,000 million in the decade before 1914.[1] Population was still rising by over 10 per cent per decade until 1911, which dragged down the average per head. But even so, the rise was still impressive: from about £20 to just under £50 per head in these 60 years.

Having said that, the same reservations apply as for the earlier period. Such calculations of national income divided by population tell nothing directly about the shares actually going to the wage earners. Variation in the proportion of the national income retained for investment and savings will affect the amount available for consumption, and that residue was shared between rents, profits, salaries and wages in variable proportions. But

[1] See Appendix, Table 9, p. 457.

when one tries to make allowance for all these traps it is fairly clear that the aggregate calculations tally with what was happening to wages in various industries and to prices. All these calculations refer only to things which can be measured in money terms, of course, they do not deal with quantities of satisfaction

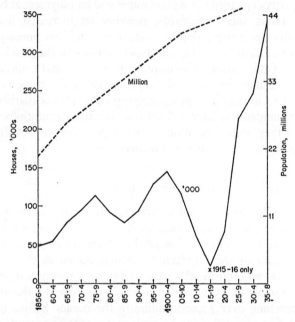

Fig. 17. Houses built in Great Britain and population growth, 1856–1938 (see also Fig. 6, p. 247, and Tables 1 and 38, pp. 449 and 490). After Mitchell and Deane, 1962, p. 239.

or happiness. They are also net of any 'transfer' payments; that is, they do not take into account the incidence of taxation or any 'free' receipts of public services like education or poor relief.

The qualification is worth making because some of the decades after 1870, when real wages were rising, happened to be times of increasing bitterness in class relations. Middle-class hopes that things were getting better were also shattered by the revelation of how widespread and deep-seated the problems of urban poverty still were. Charles Booth's massive survey of *Life and Labour* in London of 1889 uncovered the fact that 30 per cent of the inhabitants came below his poverty line. 8·5 per cent of all Londoners, he thought, were so poor – in 'primary' poverty – that they could not be fed or clothed or housed adequately by the income they earned – mainly casual, inter-mittent earnings. The greater shock was his conclusion that a further 22 per cent – in 'secondary' poverty – earned enough to make ends meet but only just at his minimum level, without the possibility of saving from income when at full work to provide for any help when work was not available for any cause – old age, sickness, accident or unemployment.[1] Seebohm Rowntree did a similar calculation for York in 1899 (adopting slightly higher standards in what was possibly a more prosperous town in a better year of employment) and found about 28 per cent of the total inhabitants in primary or secondary poverty – a com-parable figure to Booth's 30 per cent for London. 'We are faced', concluded Rowntree, 'with the startling probability that from 25 to 30 per cent of the town population of the United Kingdom are living in poverty.' This sort of contemporary statement needs stressing amongst the statistics of rising real wages at this time. There are, of course, a multitude of qualifica-tions which have to be made about the 'definition' of poverty – an essentially arbitrary thing. And if Charles Booth and Rown-tree had carried out their research in the 1840's or the 1870's no doubt their conclusions would have been even more alarming.

Changes in real income came through a combination of changing money wages, the volume of employment and price movements. Every index of money wages bears witness to the improvement in the cash bargain struck by labour after 1850 – that is in money wage rates (per week or per hour). Moreover, the general employment position improved too. There were only occasional bad years before the ending of the boom of the early 1870's – in 1857, 1866 – from which recovery was rapid.

[1] When Bowley did an exactly comparable calculation for the same districts in 1929 he found this 30 per cent in secondary and primary poverty reduced to just under 10 per cent.

Bad patches occurred in the 1870's and 1880's but money wage rates declined only in 1875-9, 1884-6, 1900-5. Money wages almost doubled between 1850 and 1910, rising by one-third between 1880 and 1914. They were astonishingly 'sticky' in bad times.

Prices moved even more dramatically in the opposite direction from 1874 to 1900, particularly food prices which took up more than 60 per cent of the cost-of-living indexes for this period. Prices rose on trend, with marked fluctuations, from 1850 to 1874, and then the fall began as the wheat and other staple products poured in from the New World. The prices that fell most were those of staple imports: tea, sugar, grain, lard, cheese, ham, bacon. As money wages slackened slightly in the late 1870's, prices tumbled by over 40 per cent, drawing real wages up (for those in employment) at a faster pace than had been experienced under the stimulus of rising money wages in the previous 25 years. Emphatically this was the harvest of exported capital, capital goods, mass emigration, improved technology in agriculture abroad and free trade at home. Home-produced products, such as milk, maintained their prices, while the release of new expenditure on meat, the food that mainly reflected increasing prosperity, was such that meat prices (which had doubled between 1840 and the 1870's) held fairly steady despite the rising flood of imports of frozen meat after 1880. The first refrigerated cargoes from Australia and New Zealand to Glasgow and London arrived in 1879 and 1881.

From 1895 retail prices began to move slowly up again, sharply curbing real wages in the years when money wages slackened. Standards of living gained since 1850 then came under pressure. In the main, however, employment after 1905 was good and trade flourished, but the tremendous shift of capital investment abroad (into projects which did not pay off quickly in increased imports and lower prices) made 1905-14 an inflationary decade. The harvest of yet lower import prices that might have come was lost in the general cataclysm of the world war. But in the crucial period from 1860 to 1900 the gain in real wages of the average urban worker was probably of the order of 60 per cent or more – even allowing for unemployment. A

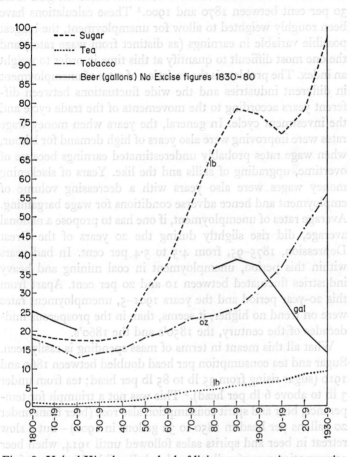

Fig. 18. United Kingdom standard of living: consumption *per capita*, 1800–1939 (see also Table 5, p. 453). Figures in annual averages per decade. After Mitchell and Deane, 1962, pp. 355–8.

calculation for Sheffield in more detail has made the gain there 30 per cent between 1870 and 1900.[1] These calculations have been roughly weighted to allow for unemployment, the biggest possible variable in earnings (as distinct from wage rates) and the one most difficult to quantify at this time in order to weight an index. The problem is the variation of rates of unemployment in different industries and the wide fluctuations between different years according to the movements of the trade cycle and the investment cycle. In general, the years when money wage rates were improving were also years of high demand for labour, when wage rates probably underestimated earnings because of overtime, upgrading of skills and the like. Years of slackening money wages were also years with a decreasing volume of employment and hence adverse conditions for wage bargaining. Average rates of unemployment, if one has to propose a national average, did rise slightly during the 20 years of the Great Depression, 1875–95, from 4·5 to 5·4 per cent. In bad years within this period, unemployment in coal mining and heavy industries fluctuated between 10 and 20 per cent. Apart from this 20-year period and the years 1901–5, unemployment rates were on trend no higher, it seems, than in the prosperous mid-decades of the century, the 1850's and the 1860's.

What all this meant in terms of mass spending is easily seen. Sugar and tea consumption per head doubled between 1860 and 1910 (sugar rising from 35 lb to 85 lb per head; tea from under 3 lb to above 6 lb per head).[2] This was not a triumph for temperance, beer and spirit consumption also rose (beer from under 20 gallons per head in 1850 to 32 gallons in 1900) – but a slow retreat in beer and spirits sales followed until 1914, when beer consumption was 26 gallons per head. Possibly this is one of the best pieces of evidence to suggest that money was tighter amongst the working classes. Ham and bacon imports rose from 4 lb per head to 18 lb per head between 1860 and 1910. The reason was not only that food prices at the ports became cheaper, but cheaper mass-production methods of food processing and food distribution aided the decline of prices in the shops. The

[1] S. Pollard, *A History of Labour in Sheffield*, Table 15B, pp. 339–40.
[2] See Appendix, Table 5, p. 453.

mass-production jam, chocolate and margarine industries all arose on cheap imports of sugar, cocoa and fats. Multiple retailing, spreading in the wake of mass food imports, took low profit margins on a mass turnover and added efficiencies of distribution to those of cheap imports. The greatest impact was made in the food trade (much the most important for family budgets), but other trades, such as chemists and newsagents, were involved. The co-operative societies were also expanding rapidly.

. Nor was this increase in real wages all absorbed in a wave of food buying. The age of Blackpool, as Lancashire's playground, had begun. Mass entertainment industries were growing, such as professional football, and that greatest mass entertainment industry of all – betting on dogs and horses. One of the great British innovations of the nineteenth century was the Bank Holiday. All this was symptomatic of rising working-class prosperity, as the petty luxuries long enjoyed by the rich became the necessities of the poor. This is what *social* democracy meant in England as the habits of diet, clothes, entertainments and holidays passed down the social scale in a society passionately concerned with equality, with many people in it equally passionately concerned with imitating the ranks next above them in the social pyramid.

Reading list

LABOUR ORGANIZATION

BRIGGS, A. (ed.) *Chartist Studies*, London, 1959; reissued London–New York, 1962–3.

BRIGGS, A. & SAVILLE, J. (eds.) *Essays in Labour History*, rev. ed., London–New York, 1967.

BROWN, E. H. PHELPS. *The Growth of British Industrial Relations: a study from the standpoint of 1906–1914*, London–New York, 1959.

CLEGG, H. A., FOX, A. & THOMPSON, A. F. *A History of British Trade Unions, since 1899*, Oxford, 1964, vol. 1.

COLE, G. D. H. 'Some notes on British trade unions in the third quarter of the 19th century', *International Review of Social History*, 1937, 2; reprinted in E. M. Carus-Wilson (ed.), *Essays in Economic History*, vol. 3, London, 1962.

COLE, G. D. H. *The Life of Robert Owen*, 3rd ed., London, 1965.

COLE, G. D. H. *A Short History of the British Working Class Movement, 1787–1947*, rev. ed., London, 1948.

COLEMAN, D. C. 'Combinations of capital and labour in the English paper industry, 1789–1825', *Economica*, new series, 1954, **21**, no. 81.

DUFFY, A. E. P. 'New unionism in Britain, 1889–1890: a reappraisal', *Economic History Review*, 2nd series, 1961, **14**, no. 2.

GEORGE, M. D. 'The combination acts reconsidered', *Economic History*, 1927, **1**, May.

HOBSBAWM, E. J. *Labouring Men: studies in the history of labour*, London [1964].

MATHER, F. C. *Public Order in the Age of the Chartists*, Manchester [1959].

PAGE ROBERTSON. *The Miners, a History of the Miners' Federation of Great Britain*, London, 2nd ed., 1953.

PELLING, H. *History of British Trade Unionism*, London–New York, 1963.

POLLARD, S. *A History of Labour in Sheffield*, Liverpool, 1959.

POLLARD, S. 'Trade unions and the labour market, 1870–1914', *Yorkshire Bulletin of Economic and Social Research*, 1965, **17**, no. 1.

SIRES, R. V. 'Labour unrest in England, 1910–1914', *Journal of Economic History*, 1955, **15**, no. 3.

THOMPSON, E. P. *The Making of the English Working Class*, London, 1963.

STANDARDS OF LIFE, 1850–1914

BOWLEY, A. L. *Wages and Income in the United Kingdom since 1860*, Cambridge, 1937.

CHECKLAND, S. G. *The Rise of Industrial Society in England, 1815–1885*, London, 1964.

POLLARD, S. *A History of Labour in Sheffield*, Liverpool, 1959.

POLLARD, S. 'Wages and earnings in the Sheffield trades, 1851–1914; real earnings in Sheffield', *Yorkshire Bulletin . . .*, 1954, 1957, **6, 9.**

WOOD, G. H. 'Real wages and the standard of comfort since 1850', *Journal of Royal Statistical Society*, 1909; reprinted in E. M. Carus-Wilson (ed.), *Essays in Economic History*, vol. 3, London, 1962.

15 Industrial maturity and deceleration

CHANGES IN THE FIRM

Incorporation and the Stock Exchange

How far had manufacturing business begun to draw on the general pool of national capital for long-term investment by 1914, instead of just local pools of capital coming in from the families and friends of the partners in business? We have seen that long-term capital was essentially a local, personal thing during the industrial revolution supplemented by some long-term lending by country banks and considerable mercantile credit. Supposedly the essence of capitalism in the nineteenth century was the presumption that here was a factor in production, perfectly mobile, with a single national market, all the savings of the nation being available for industrialists to tap by offering to pay the going rate of interest. To what extent was this concept of capital realized? Certainly, it became true for short-term credit, with the banking system and the bill brokers maintaining exactly such a single efficient national market. But the banking system did not make institutionalized savings in bank deposits available regularly to industrialists wanting long-term loans for capital investment in the later nineteenth century. Did the Stock Exchange do this, as the other main specialized intermediary for mobilizing the savings of the nation for investment?

Up to 1850 the answer was, scarcely at all for manufacturing business. Regular trading began in the Stock Exchange, specially built for the purpose, in 1773, after many years of jobbing in coffee-houses. But virtually all the stocks sold and traded at that time were government securities. A few mines and the great chartered trading enterprises of the century like the East India

Company were incorporated, but their shares were not usually bought and sold openly or even quoted on the Stock Exchange. Where they did change hands it usually happened through the company itself. By 1800, what was known as the 'docks and canals list' had appeared at the end of the weekly statement of prices quoted. Business was still completely dominated by dealings in government stock, but it had grown a small tail of public utilities, insurance companies, canal enterprise, and actually one brewery after 1809. No great changes came to this pattern as far as manufacturing business was concerned until after 1860. Railways brought a great new flood of business to the Stock Exchange in the 1830's and 1840's and after, when the middle-class investor was 'apprenticed in the school of Hudson' to look to the Stock Exchange for an alternative to gilt-edged. But industrialists did not do the same to any great degree, until well after the consolidating statutes of 1856 and 1862. These gave general permission for incorporation and limitation of liability to any firm wishing to take advantage of them. The idea that a great leap forward was being prevented in English business by a law hostile to incorporation until after 1844 is completely discredited by the failure to take place of a great surge of industrial borrowing on the Stock Exchange for another generation after the legal change. And even before general statutory permission arrived, the sophisticated legal devices evolved to allow firms to enjoy the benefits of incorporated enterprise suggest that the institutional legal forms developed fairly responsively when the need became great.

In each decade after 1862 there were Stock Exchange booms in domestic industry, their scale rising sharply. Most of the rapidly expanding industries with large plant technology, of the later part of the century, took advantage of incorporation, limitation of liability, and raising capital from the public: steel, shipbuilding, chemicals, brewing, food-processing, soap, etc. This was the only effective way of raising large quantities of capital very quickly, apart from large-scale links with banks. But, in 1913, home industry was still financed to only a fairly small extent by the Stock Exchange, in marked contrast still with 'public utility' investment, such as railways. In the investment boom just before the war about £45 million was going annually into home investment via the Stock Exchange (out of about £140 million invested in all), while the Stock Exchange was handling more than £200 million for new issues altogether – most being destined for foreign investment and government loans. Another estimate gave under £20 million per annum going into new issues on the Stock Exchange for home industry and trade in 1911–13. And some of the industries most committed to Stock Exchange capital were in the least strategic sectors of the economy in 1900. For example, the industry with most capital raised in this way was brewing, mainly to finance the race to 'tie' public houses – a separate Stock Exchange 'brewery list' existed in 1890. By 1900 over 200 brewing companies had quoted assets of £185 million. This means that the greater proportion of capital going into industrial investment – about three-quarters of it – was still coming from the older channels, particularly from 'plough-back'.[1]

Another important feature of the Stock Exchange floatations was that few new firms were launched in this way. The process was expensive – costs of legal fees, advertising, underwriting and attendant expenses seldom totalled less than £20,000 for an issue. The Stock Exchange itself was very reluctant to allow unknown newcomers to launch themselves in this way. Even though the basic denomination of the ordinary share was down to £1 and £5 units by 1890, the investors were mainly not small men in their thousands – or the traditional widows and orphans – but a small group of large investors and institutions. So the customers of the Stock Exchange were a relatively small group of mainly-established businesses, looking for capital for expansion, more than initial promotion; and the customers were also a relatively small group of mainly-established investors.

The volume of capital officially issued on the Stock Exchange to the public is also misleading. Many of the businessmen raising extra capital by the Stock Exchange had no intention of letting any outsider control their company. They usually sold largely fixed-interest preference shares or debentures to the public,

[1] Even now almost three-quarters of total industrial investment in Britain comes from retained earnings.

which did not carry voting rights, and issued most, if not all, of the ordinary shares to themselves, keeping control of their firms in their own hands or those of a few friends, ex-partners or their family. This was the case with Lever, who raised £1·5 million in 1886, with Lipton and a host of others. In such a case largely paper exchanges of power took place while the legal form of the business was revolutionized and extra capital acquired from the public, for the owners received the value of the business they legally 'sold' to the public back in the form of the ordinary shares which still carried control. The family dynastic control of these firms thus survived into the era of incorporation and shareholders' meetings. However much the shareholders might protest at a bad dividend, when all the proxy votes were counted they had no chance of challenging the board. This single annual – sometimes embarrassing – public appearance was the only concession these industrialists need make to the public providing much of their capital, at least until things got so bad that they failed to be able to pay any dividends on their preference share capital or debentures. Only then could investors seek ways of forcing the hand of the directors by appointing receivers or new directors and only then, in such dynastic concerns, was a revolution in techniques of raising capital likely to be followed by a managerial revolution. The managerial revolution in the board room long post-dated the legal and financial revolution of incorporation.

Conditions of competition

The idea of the perfectly competitive market was – and is – a fiction, in all save a few specialized cases, particularly commodity markets like the Chicago wheat exchange. In general firms were never in this perfectly competitive position. Between 1800 and 1850, as in the eighteenth century, many groups of industrialists attempted to fix prices, and in some cases to limit output in bad years in the iron, glass, silk, brewing, paper, salt, ship-building, coal mining and non-ferrous mining industries. The heavy industries, facing more severe fluctuations in prices and demand than the consumer goods industries, were more prominent in these efforts. But it is doubtful if these associations had significant economic effect. They were mainly regional affairs, operative in just depression years, and had no control over national outputs – indeed, very often their existence was really evidence of effective competition, lower prices and expanding output in other industrial regions. For example, the association of Staffordshire iron masters was the reaction of a high-cost region in the industry to the expansion of south Wales and Scottish iron masters, who were setting lower prices and dominating output. Despite these exceptions, evidence of intention rather than result, one can still regard the period from 1830 to 1875 as the hey-day of the competitive economy in Britain. Combination amongst employers was not a vital force. Labour was not organized in a way that had a marked influence upon the economy, through its organized effects at any rate. The government was also not acting in a way which consciously shaped the development of the economy. The theme song of these middle decades of the century was that of the music hall ballad of the times: 'Paddle your own canoe'.

From the late 1870's employers' associations took on a new power of growth. Falling prices, more severe competition, failing markets for some (but not for all), fears of the effectiveness of labour organization in some places, combined to make the period of the Great Depression, and afterwards, a fertile epoch for attempts to contract out of competition by individual firms. Trade unions symbolized the refusal on the part of their members to admit that labour was just another commodity, whose price was responsive to purely natural movements of supply and demand. Producers' agreements were also a refusal to admit the same criteria for industrial prices. Only in a post-Keynesian world did governments accept any economic responsibilities for maintaining levels of demand by public policy. Hence both labour and employers could only attempt to influence the prices of their commodities by restricting supply.

The first characteristic reaction to depression by industrialists was an extension of the older tradition of combination amongst producers: the trade association. Its essential object was almost invariably to agree on minimum prices. Very often additional objectives developed of limiting competition by establishing spheres of influence in marketing areas. The trade association was an informal pact – usually without institutional or financial or legal sanctions to it, the gentlemen's agreement – even though minutes were often kept at the meetings. The United Kingdom Soap Manufacturers' Association (of 1867) was a typical trade association, which had grown out of previous regional associations. Almost every trade possessed its groupings in the 1880's. As voluntary combinations without penalties they had very little economic effect, apart from encouraging co-ordinated responses to economic and commercial trends. If bad prices continued, in the words of one of the soap makers, 'some fool always cuts'. If the unit of production was fairly small new men were tempted to come into the trade, if prices did get held for any significant time. And on the upswing of the cycle, when prices hardened, the aggressive men broke out. W. D. Knight, the soap maker, concluded sadly in 1893: 'the history of our Association is a history of exploded agreements'. Indeed some of these associations had a further characteristic in common with their predecessors before 1850 in being mutual protection societies of smaller producers or distributors against the expanding William Lever, in soap-making, the Joseph Rank in the milling trade, Thomas Lipton in provisions, or Jesse Boot in drugs. The latter were all trades expanding very rapidly in the last quarter of the century on the new working-class prosperity.

National associations were very often at their most active just when the structure of an industry was changing most rapidly and small regional producers were facing a few individuals breaking through to capture the national market, and smashing the old marketing frontiers. So the mere existence of these price agreements and trade associations cannot be used *just* as evidence illustrating the brakes being placed on the operation of price competition: in some cases they are symptomatic of the *effectiveness* of competition. Once a movement towards collective action begins in a section of industry or commerce, strong forces are let loose to universalize such collective action amongst firms having dealings with the original group – as competitors, suppliers or customers. Such responses, to establish countervailing power, should also not simply be seen as evidence for the decline of competition in the economy. Competition usually continues but between, and within, different groupings. While on their way up the men like Lever and Lipton typically had nothing but scorn for those who suggested they might compromise on price or production policy. When the *arriviste* had arrived, however, he sometimes discovered the attractions of becoming friendly, or at least polite towards his neighbours in the national market. The great spread of employers' associations in the 1880's and later has also to be seen as complementary to the spread of trade unions, for the business of conducting wage negotiations and labour relations.

The second, more formal and institutional, method of limiting competition was the cartel. Sometimes even national trade associations, or large groups of firms in them, would consolidate into cartels, or trusts, when the forces creating incentives for curtailing competition proved stronger than the inherent centrifugal forces creating instability within informal price and output agreements. The cartel implied financial links between different independent companies, formed by exchanging some shares, or creating a common fund between them based on contributions from each member, calculated according to the proportion which their individual productions bore to the total output of the group. These more formal associations had consequently more ambitious aims. Regular price-fixing agreements got supplemented by production quotas and agreements over profits. Sometimes attempts were made to create legal sanctions against pirates in the group by signing written agreements authorizing agreed fines to be administered to blacklegs by private courts. But English cartels, as opposed to German or American, were very much more reticent about publicizing their existence. On the one hand industrialists seemed more embarrassed at being members, and on the other the state made no frontal attack on them, with 'trust-busting' legislation (as in the United States) which meant that their activities were often not brought to light. In Germany, too, there was no tradition of *laissez-faire*. The main economic philosophers there, Frederick List and Gustav Schmoller, had always regarded economic affairs as being in the service of a strong state, to be guided by government where necessary. Producers' agreements, cartels, were more accepted as constructive – natural and inevitable – in Germany, not as a somewhat guilty deviation from a competitive norm, as in England or in the United States. None the less widespread cartelization developed in many branches of British industry in the 1890's and afterwards, particularly in cotton which had been severely affected by 20 years of low prices and sagging exports. These were mainly 'horizontal' groupings of firms in the same line of business as competitors. The Bleachers' Association, for example, formed in 1900, brought 53 firms into a cartel, many of which had previously been in ineffective price agreements. The Bradford Dyers and the Calico Printers Association of 1899 were other typical examples.

The most effective and the most widespread attempt at cartelization was probably in shipping. The first, and classic, example of the shipping cartel was the Hangkow Tea 'conference' started in 1879. A group of shippers in this particular trade offered a 5–10 per cent rebate on freights if customers agreed to ship exclusively with them. The object, of course, was to limit the tonnage competing for trade and to enable all owners in the pool to secure full freights for their vessels. By 1900–5 most of the long-distance regular routes had been organized into such conferences. They proved more effective than similar attempts in other industries because of the vast capitals necessary before outsiders could break into the trade.

The third and most formal method of limiting competition, which was progressing rapidly after 1880, was the outright amalgamation of separate companies into combines. This could be accomplished simply by one company purchasing another, or offering its shareholders cash or the conversion of their shares in the company being absorbed into the shares of the host, or the alligator. The other way of consolidating a cartel was for the two or more firms coming into amalgamation to form a holding company to hold the ordinary share capital of each of the constituent companies, and hence control them. This again meant a share conversion offer being made to the ordinary shareholders of each company for shares of the new holding company, the directors of which would probably be chosen from the previous heads of the main original companies in the new group. The point about the combine was that it had ceased to be a voluntary association of separate firms operating revocable agreements, but had become a new legal entity which could not be unscrambled easily.

Absorption or amalgamation into combines was a feature of the creation of the Salt Union of 1888 – of 64 firms, including *all* those in Chesl ire – and the United Alkali Company of 1891, which brought 48 firms in the bleaching side of the chemical industry into union. The English Sewing Cotton Company of 1897 was engineered by J. and P. Coats to bring 14 competing firms into alliance, giving them virtual monopoly over the British market in sewing cotton, as the Salt Union had achieved in salt. In tobacco, the movement was even more dramatic. In 1901 the American Tobacco Company invaded the English market by purchasing the business of Ogdens Ltd and announcing that they had £6 million ready for investing in the European tobacco business. This frightened thirteen of the leading British firms into a combine, the Imperial Tobacco Company, with £12 million assets and this, in turn, brought 20,000 retail tobacconists into a dealers' alliance, the UK Tobacco Dealers' Alliance, to protect their interests. In salt and oil distribution and in sewing thread American invasions took place at the turn of the century, symptomatic of the changing centre of gravity of industrial power between the two economies. Some of these amalgamations were badly organized failures, such as the Salt Union and United Alkali Company. Others were successful and have survived in their own names until our own day.

Most of the combines which came together under pressure of adverse prices, adverse profits and severe competition in the late nineteenth century were of firms in competitive relations with one another in the same line of business. This 'horizontal integration' operated on the simple principle 'if you can't beat them, join them'. The advantages here, in principle, were several. The leaders of the various firms hoped to cut out competitive advertising between themselves, the costs of which in trades like soap, drug-selling, and the food trades, were already becoming important in the 1880's. Often they hoped to centralize research facilities for the group (where such costs were being incurred at all) and make results available to all the production companies. Other centralized services provided by the holding company might be a specialized law department for negotiating patents and property. There might be centralized printing facilities provided or transport after the days of lorry delivery had begun. Central negotiations on behalf of all production companies in a group might also secure favourable rates from suppliers or railway companies. Some of the greatest costs for manufacturers facing retailers, like the soap or food manufacturing groups, lay in the costs of travellers. The object of the 'soap trust' formed by Lever in 1906 of 11 regional soap businesses was partly that each company could act as the agent for all the others in its regional sales organization, while there would be exchange of technical expertise between all of them. However, each production company inside the new firm 'Lever Brothers' was to go on manufacturing its own lines as before, subject to a guiding hand from the central board, and each business was to preserve its identity. In other cases – but too few – the specific object of association was to rationalize production, to close down the small out-of-date plants and concentrate production on the latest, most efficient units. Potential economies of scale lay behind most merger movements. Here a combine could have teeth, whereas a cartel or a price fixing association often hampered such technical progress by having to fix prices to keep the most inefficient member of the group solvent.

The large combine in 'horizontal integration' had much greater power than the trade association. Imperial Tobacco had over half the total tobacco sales in Britain after 1901; Lever over 60 per cent of soap production and sales in Britain in the 1910's. In more specialized lines, particularly intermediary products, it could be even higher. Hence, potential dangers to the public existed, but examining the history of many attempts by combines to raise prices significantly for a significant time (two important qualifications) is to cut down the power of the bogy. Unless the home market was extraordinarily protected by tariffs, and the capital cost of building a plant exceedingly high, then potential competition remained resilient. When Lever raised prices in the 1920's one of the biggest American producers, Procter and Gamble, bought their way into the British market by purchasing Thomas Hedley's of Newcastle, and the Co-operative Wholesale Society began to make soap on a scale comparable to Lever. If entry into an industry is not particularly expensive in capital investment, a period of high prices may bring a very large number of newcomers mushrooming into existence. Sometimes the flank of a combine holding up prices was turned by a substitute product being developed in these circumstances of hot-house stimulus to innovation, brought by high profit margins. But until 1948 Britain did not have a Monopolies Commission to reinforce these natural restraints with public surveillance.

The second form that combines took was in developing 'vertical integration' as a natural consolidation to the first neutralization of competition in the main stage of manufacture. Whereas the horizontal amalgamation was usually a product of depressed times, the vertical thrust could be encouraged in periods of great expansion when severe competition developed for raw material supplies, bidding up prices, or for transport raising shipping freights, or for sales outlets, raising distributors', merchants' and shopkeepers' margins. When boom conditions widened profit margins in the commercial functions on each side of the manufacturer, creating the fear of being held up to ransom, he was tempted to break into this trade himself and cut out the profits he was paying to others.

Restrictive licensing limited the expansion of retail outlets for brewers. When they had great opportunities for economies of scale, faced rising demand and could gain plentiful capital from incorporation after 1880, they started a race to purchase public houses. They integrated forwards to control marketing. Equally they moved back to some extent, into malting and hop-growing very often, to allow them to avoid the profits paid to their raw material suppliers. The margarine war after 1900 led Jurgens and Vandenbergs, Lever's great rivals in this trade, to buying their way into British multiple shop companies. Here they were anxious, on the whole, to prevent the multiple shops selling margarine too cheaply, because this made life impossible for the independent grocers, to whom the margarine manufacturers sold most of their product. Originally they had begun to buy their way into multiple shops because these were the only firms with the speed and efficiency in selling to handle a highly perishable commodity like margarine effectively on a large scale. The same rivals, finally brought together in 1929 as Unilever, had waged a similar battle over raw material supplies. European consumption of edible oils and fats was mounting much more quickly than production after 1870. The continental margarine makers first collided with Lever in the 1890's over control of raw materials and oil-milling capacity. Because of growing shortages, increasing competition and rising prices Lever bought direct from Africa to supply his crushing mills. He developed plantations in the Solomon Islands in 1906, moved into the Belgian Congo in 1911, and into Antarctic whaling in 1914-18.

The object of such trends, in principle, was to feed all successive stages of the vertical combine with cost-price raw materials and take all the profits at the last stage of sale. In fact this very often did not work. It was easier to spread profit-making inside a combine in this way, and sometimes very difficult to maintain efficiency in subsidiary companies in a large group if they were not allowed some freedom of action over prices and production and profits. It they could use their plant more efficiently, they might have to seek the extra production outside the group. The object was to keep each in harmony with the whole, broadly speaking; but the quest for maintaining efficiency in the production and selling companies on the periphery of these large groups led to much decentralization of control from the central board of the holding company in the middle, particularly between the wars.

The effects of mergers for the national economy are exceedingly difficult to establish – in terms of a national generalization at least. In some industries increasing size, and by implication fewer firms, was necessary to gain economies of scale. But, by itself, size was no proof of realizing such gains without good management. Cartels in Germany, with the much closer links between industry and the banks, did become the instrument for much technical efficiency in growth industries. Rationalization, closing down inefficient plants, allocating production and investment to the most efficient sectors within the group, realizing economies of scale through long production runs and technical uniformities all brought great gains. But the *fact* of cartelization does not necessarily indicate the realization of such technical efficiencies. In England, too often, the objective was to share markets and set prices which allowed the least efficient firm to make profits and go its old way. Very often Britain seemed to get the worst of both worlds in this respect.

THE GREAT DEPRESSION, 1873–96

There are two problems to consider about the 20-year period, 1875–95, dubbed (before the 1930's) the Great Depression: first to try to see what was happening in the economy, and then to review the explanations for these events put forward by various commentators. Certain factors (and explanations) relate to the trends of just these 20 years, which get reversed after 1895; others continue. Clearly the period was not simply a depression according to the usual meaning of that word, which relates to a short-term phenomenon, a phase in the inventory cycle in foreign trade (the trade cycle proper) or in the investment cycle. The export industries would be depressed for a year or two in the former case, in the latter case over-investment from the boom period would result in over-capacity which might take a few years to work off. But the Great Depression is a phrase used to cover a much longer period of history than that; one not cyclical, in the sense of being recurrent like depression years in foreign trade or the investment industries. Within this longer period, 1875–95, are identifiable trade cycles and investment cycles. Although the boom of 1872 was of unprecedented height, with unprecedented extensions of capacity (particularly in the heavy industries and mining), the trough resulting from this peak fell in 1879, which makes the cyclical explanation difficult to invoke to account for the failure of the economy to reach another equivalent peak of expansion for two more decades. If it was not a depression, without a capital 'D', what was it? What things changed and what things did not change?

The population increase stayed above 10 per cent per decade until 1911, although the birth rate fell sharply after 1900. A very slow decline in the rate of population growth developed after the 14 per cent rise in the decade 1870–80, but this trend continued very slowly until 1911 so that the 20 years 1875–95 were

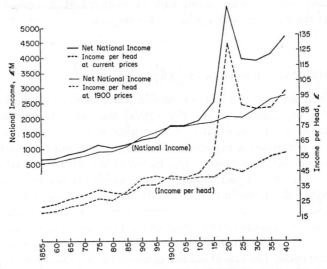

Fig. 19. National income, 1855–1938 (see also Table 9, p. 457). After Mitchell and Deane, 1962, pp. 367–8.

in no way marked out. Only in the period between the wars did population stagnation set a major changed term of reference for the economy. The changes in the structure of the economy, with a rapidly declining share of the national product and labour force going to agriculture also continued. Agriculture had problems of its own, which contributed to the general context in some measure, but the structural changes were of much longer trend than this.

Thirdly, the national income continued to rise throughout

the period, faster than population, faster than in the first half of the century, being supported in real terms by the fall in import prices and the increase in receipts from abroad, particularly from exported capital. Real wages did rise considerably between 1850 and 1910, so that 1875–95 is not out of trend here either, although during this 20 years the rise came more from falling prices than rising money wages. Equally with unemployment; on trend the national rate was 4·6 per cent in the 20 years before 1874, 5·4 per cent from 1875 to 1895, and 4 per cent between 1896 and 1914. Some distinguishing characteristics can be seen (particularly in the capital goods industries) but the swings were not violent, judging by available evidence of national, as distinct from individual-industry experience.

What did change objectively, as far as can be discovered, and why did contemporaries feel that things had taken a turn for the worse? Subjectively it is quite clear that this is a 20-year period of doubts, self-questioning and disenchantment.

On the part of labour some reasons for despondence existed. Checks came to money wages in some years; gains to real wages were more noticeable to the housewife doing her shopping than to her husband getting his pay (perhaps a not unimportant distinction when explaining working-class attitudes, which have reflected the feelings of men more than women). It was also a period of rapid unionization and increasing bitterness in labour relations, as we have seen, with employers also on the defensive.[1] In 1881 a small flurry of publicity was enjoyed by the 'Fair Trade League' – evidence that some of the assumptions of the free trade economy were being publicly questioned. Association by employers had a common theme in that they were all trying in various ways to supersede the national equation of supply and demand by trying to keep up prices, even if it meant restricting supply to do it. As with the labour unions, employers were attempting to opt out of certain aspects of the free market economy. How effective these movements were is another matter but, despite this, they are still important as symptoms of attitudes. Agriculture was involved in problems of rapid adjustment to falling cereal prices, which brought lower profits and

[1] See above, pp. 370–4, 387–91.

lower rents, lower capital values to farmers and landowners in the arable east and south of the country, and an increasing rate of decline of employment in farming.

More generally, certain of the trends of the times were unfavourable to highly articulate sections of the community. When being questioned by the Royal Commission enquiring into the depressed state of the economy in 1886 (the appointment of which was itself significant), Alfred Marshall, the Cambridge economist, acknowledged: 'A depression of prices, a depression of interest, a depression of profits . . . I cannot see any reason for believing that there is any considerable depression in any other respect.' The name 'Great Depression' owed much to the upper and middle class and farming and landowner interests suffering by the fall in profits, interest rates and prices. Published and parliamentary opinion was more a reflection (though not just a reflection) of their interests rather than those of other groups in society. Royal Commissions being appointed was a symptom of the anxieties prevailing in these circles. But was this a storm in an economist's tea cup, or a middle-class tea cup, or was it, as other people have thought, a watershed in the economic evolution of the leading industrial nation, a 'climacteric' in the national economic life as far as rates of industrial growth are concerned? Despite Marshall's opinion, recent calculations have revealed some more deep-seated weaknesses in the pattern of events, though conflicts of opinion about the dating of trends prevent confident assessments at this time about rates of growth in the years 1873-96.

Knowing how committed the British economy was to international trade one might expect some major problems to be centred here. The figures of values in foreign trade, the balance of trade and payments and capital exports – all of which are fairly reliable – do indeed show a marked trend for these 20 years. Export values of the early 1870's were not surpassed until the second half of the 1890's – absolute stagnation developed on trend. Imports were not growing as quickly as previously, but not being stagnant in value a growing deficit emerged on the balance of trade, which was itself deflationary. Some of this movement was occasioned by a price decline (particularly for imports); the decline in the rate of growth in the volume of exports (i.e. at fixed prices) is almost as marked. From expanding at 5 per cent per annum between 1840 and 1870 in volume, the rate fell to 2 per cent per annum in 1870-90, and to 1 per cent per annum between 1890 and 1900. With such a high proportion of output in certain industries destined for exports one could expect this decline in the rates of advance in values and quantities to be reflected in industry as a whole. A very high proportion of investment in manufacturing industry derived directly from profits. As profits were squeezed by declining prices and stagnant volumes in trade (more particularly in textiles) so the funds for investment in export industries under pressure became restricted. At the same time depressed foreign markets diminished the incentives for expansion or re-equipment. It has been argued that these trends relate to changes in the terms of trade, to the purchasing power of the primary-producing economies. But this is not clear-cut, because these were deteriorating (i.e. export prices falling faster than import prices) in the bad years of the 1870's (1874-8), but rising in the 1880's – without much of a trend change in values and volumes.[1] Tariffs abroad had clearly begun to affect the export totals, particularly with the sustained onset of competition from the United States, Germany and France.

The phasing of the movement of capital abroad was not clearcut either. True, capital exports did fall away with the onset of the Great Depression in 1875, but recovered to a new peak in the years 1886-90. Foreign lending then declined to a low level where it remained for the next 15 years and did not recover until after 1905. Relative to the national income the export of

---

[1] The argument runs that the elasticity of demand for primary products was much less than for industrial products. An increase in the supply of primary products thus created a more than proportionate decline in their price, which lowered the foreign exchange earnings of these countries, to the disadvantage of British exports, heavily orientated to such foreign markets. The problems are manifold. The purchasing power of the primary producers cannot be judged in terms of price changes, or demand elasticities alone. Volumes were rising rapidly and a considerable proportion of the decline in prices of imported primary products (valued c.i.f.) is to be accounted for by declining freight rates (overland and ocean) and falls in real costs of production. The fall in shipping costs has to be discounted from the argument.

capital was lower in the generation of the Great Depression than in the 20 years 1855–75 or from 1894 to 1914. The decade when Britain had thrown off the stagnation of values in foreign trade and in falling prices, however, did not see any recovery in the rate of flow of capital abroad. This is important for Professor Rostow's explanation of the causes of the Great Depression. Trends in the volume of foreign trade and prices did get reversed after 1895, when profits also improved, to create an Indian summer for the free trade system as the spate of self-questioning and doubt died down.

Much work has been done recently to try to find out what was happening to production and productivity and capital accumulation – key indicators upon which to gauge the performance of the industrial side of the economy, which provided the engine of growth for the economy as a whole by the 1870's. Some calculations point to the 1870's as a watershed for all these indexes. Indications are that industrial production, which had been growing since the 1820's at about 3 per cent per annum or above (it was 4 per cent between 1820 and 1840), fell to below 2 per cent per annum. Between 1875 and 1894 it was just over 1·5 per cent per annum. Output per man also fell by a similar proportion in the same period – from just over 2 per cent per annum to just under 1 per cent. Meanwhile growth rates and productivity rates in the German and American economies were advancing between two and three times faster than Britain's. The share of the national income going to creating new capital at home fell from above 7·5 per cent per annum before 1870, to just over 4·5 per cent in the decade 1885–94. After recovery for a brief spell during the decade when foreign lending remained low, 1895–1905, the flow of funds into domestic capital fell back again to 4·5 per cent in the final decade before 1914. Other calculations, while not being so definite about a decline in rates of growth after 1870 (in part because of doubtful figures for the pre-1870 period) suggest deceleration after 1895 until the 1920's.[1]

[1] R. C. O. Matthews, 'Some Aspects of Post-War Growth in the British Economy in relation to Historical Experience', *Manchester Statistical Society* (1964).

Thus it appears that these crucial tests for the performance of an industrial economy show that growth rates declined in the late nineteenth century (even if not during the Great Depression years), and did not recover in the decade before 1914, even though foreign trade values did. These were therefore trends beginning, perhaps, with the Great Depression, but not reversing themselves after 1895 as did the trends in foreign trade. Of course, the whole discussion centres on a slowing down of growth rates not an absolute fall in quantities. The figures do not reveal *why* this is happening or *how* it is happening. Economic history consists in giving the explanations which lie behind the statistics; in revealing the dynamics of these processes of change.

Before looking at industrial performance two single-cause explanations for the Great Depression need to be mentioned. The older thesis claimed that falling prices, which had falling profits and interest rates trailing in their wake, were caused by the world economy running short of gold: a monetary cause. The volume of transactions having a gold 'base' originally through the banking systems was growing. Economies like Germany, France, Sweden and the United States adopted gold as the precious metal to back their currencies. The period also saw a lull between major gold rushes, so that new supplies coming onto the market were small compared with the epoch of Californian gold in the 1850's or the South African boom in the 1890's. If the volume of transactions was increasing faster than the quantity of money then prices would fall in terms of gold. This theory was strongly challenged at the time and since. Many vital factors do not fit the thesis.

Bullion dealers reported no shortage of gold: the reserves in the Bank of England stayed high in normal years. The volume of bank deposits rapidly increased (although the reliability of these figures has been challenged). The depressed years 1890–5 did see the onset of the gold-mining boom in South Africa when new supplies were pouring into the world economy. Furthermore – a key fact – interest rates on trend in Lombard Street were low – consols were under 3 per cent per annum yield and the discount rate between 2 and 3·5 per cent per annum. These

depressed interest rates, which were part of the general complaint by owners of capital offering resources for investment,
suggest an exactly contrary thesis to the monetary one – that
excess savings were seeking investment outlets; that money was
over-plentiful in relation to investment opportunities of every
sort. A gold shortage would also not explain the fact that German and American industrial growth rates were higher than
Britain's.

The single-cause explanation that Professor Rostow offered
in place of the gold hypothesis is that the key variable which set
off all the other changes was a change in the direction of the
flow of savings in the 20 years of the Great Depression from
foreign investment to home investment. The argument is that
foreign investment went into projects like railways and public
utilities which threw great demands onto the British iron and
coal industries. It was therefore very expansionist and inflationary on prices by stimulating internal demand relative to the
supply of consumer goods. Until this investment began to result
in lower import prices after 1873 prices therefore rose. The
switch to home investment between 1875 and 1895 was into
projects in home industry which did result quickly in an increase
in consumer goods available – and this domestic investment led
rapidly to greater competition at home, and a fall in profits and
prices. The Depression was thus simply 'what happened when
the railways were built'. Then, the argument goes, foreign investment picked up again and the previous sequence re-emerged.

Several difficulties face this explanation too. The facts of
foreign investment fit the hypothesis well at the start of the
Great Depression; but there is the problem of an immense
surge of foreign investment in the late 1880's – of unprecedented
height – and the problem that foreign investment at the latter
end of the Great Depression did not really expand until 1905 –
10 years after the Great Depression had ended, and trends in
prices, trends in foreign trade had been reversed. The other
difficulty is that the recent indicators of production at home
suggest that this was possibly a time of retardation in the rate
of expansion of the industrial machine; probably of a fall in the
rate of home investment and in the pace of innovation. This

suggests that the thing to be explained is the decline in the overall rate of investment, not just the change in direction of a constant flow of investment. The advances in innovation and technical improvement cited by Professor Rostow are probably

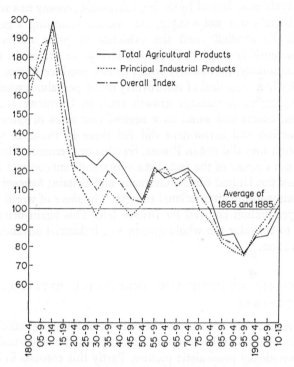

Fig. 20. Rousseaux price indices, 1800–1913 (see also Table 7, p. 455). After Mitchell and Deane, 1962, pp. 471–3.

not sufficient to uphold the argument that this period represented a great leap forward in investment and production at home. Professor Rostow was clearly right that the scale and the nature of investment lay at the back of the trends present through the 'slooms and bumps' of 1875–95. The decline in foreign investment *was* important in many years, even though pinning the whole responsibility onto the decline in foreign lending is inadequate. We are driven back to the whole question of industrial advance and innovation.

Some people have also argued that the 20 years of the Great Depression were really just one downswing of a 'Kondratieff' long cycle experienced by the international economy as a whole; that Britain was not unique, but merely reflecting a general trend. Kondratieff used the evidence of price movements almost entirely – and such secular swings in prices do occur internationally, particularly with primary produce prices. Subsequently a great deal of controversy developed about what was happening to percentage growth rates in Germany and the United States and some have argued that rates of growth in production and investment did fall there in these 20 years, although they did not in Russia, Sweden or Denmark. But this does not dispose of the fact that a very significant contrast exists *between* the United States, Germany and Britain; *between* their responses to the international context. The *share* of world trade and production enjoyed by Britain fell. This again drives us back to consider the whole question of industrial advance and innovation.

ECONOMIC GROWTH AND INDUSTRIAL RETARDATION, 1870–1914

The recent *post mortems* on the failings of industrial efficiency and innovation in the economy after 1870 can be construed into an uncritically pessimistic picture. Partly this consists in comparing each facet of British industry with the world's most eminent exemplar, from whatever country, whether Germany in the case of dye-stuffs or cameras, the United States in the case of machine tools and motor cars, and so forth (rather than making the comparison with – say – Germany for motor cars and cotton, France for coal and agricultural efficiency and the United States for ship-building). Partly it is a question of concentrating on the failings and ignoring the 'growth areas' of the economy. These certainly existed. Ship-building has been mentioned as one area where British world hegemony and technological leadership remained unchallenged. Certain British heavy engineering and armaments firms had an unsurpassed reputation. In much light industry and food processing – from pharmaceutical firms and printing to distilling and brewing – British enterprise, in scale of production and vigorous expansion, had an enviable record. Beecham, Lever in soap making, Cadbury and Fry in chocolates, Guinness and Bass, became household names on the strength of such expansion in exactly these decades.

The same was true of distribution. This generation witnessed the meteoric expansion of the 'multiples'. Men like Thomas Lipton and the Watson brothers (of Maypole Dairies) brought mass retailing into being on a wholly new scale, taking small margins on a vast turnover, exploiting fully the advantages of falling prices and expanding imports. Lipton founded his first shop in 1872: by the time of the firm's incorporation in 1898 there existed 242 branches in the United Kingdom, many factories and overseas agencies. Many lesser Liptons prospered in provincial companies and not only in the food trades. Jesse Boot was transforming the economies of the middle-class chemist as Lipton that of the middle-class grocer. Department stores added a new dimension to middle-class trade. These men were archetypal entrepreneurs in their generation, which casts doubt on any explanation of a 'failure of entrepreneurship' which does not closely relate managerial effectiveness to its precise business context.

Problems remained with these new areas of growth, much of it based on the expansion of working-class purchasing power in Britain encouraged by falling prices. Certain of these industries, such as soap or food processing, were small compared with the giants of textiles, coal or engineering. Few of them contributed significantly to exports. Finally, many of these vigorously expanding sectors, though not all, were scarcely developing technologies which were to prove strategic in terms of the major growth industries of the twentieth century. In this sense a major indigenous electrical engineering industry would have proved a greater long-term asset to the economy than a large, efficient jam-making or chocolate industry, of which the technology was relatively simple. As far as can be measured the 'new' industries were contributing only a small percentage to gross domestic product at the time of the first census of production in 1907.[1]

In trying to sort out the tangle of issues involved in the failure of new industries to come forward in the British economy as fast as they were developing in the United States and Germany, coupled with the relative failure of some traditional industries in Britain to maintain standards of international competitiveness in innovation, one or two preliminary questions have to be asked. In the first place, it is important to determine whether the arguments relate to factors which it was within the power of human agency in Britain to influence or control, or whether explanations lie in changes in the context of the world economy which cannot be seen in the same way as dependent upon or responsive to the situation in Britain. Both have importance, of course, but their significance is different and they often relate to different problems.

Certain issues, often used as 'bogies' in contemporary debates, also relate to false problems. For example, as other countries begin massive production they will inevitably have faster rates of growth initially than those older economies where the volume of production is already running at a high level. This is for purely statistical reasons which have little deep-seated significance. The percentage of world production held by the older industrial economies is bound to decline, for similar reasons, as other nations begin to share in that total. And when much larger economies, which may encompass half a continent such as the United States or Russia, set about the process of industrialization they are going to produce more of everything than a small island. To regret this is sentimentality, rather than concern over a real problem. Furthermore, in the later stages of industrialization the tertiary sector of the economy, providing services, tends to grow at a faster rate than the manufacturing sector. Because productivity increases have tended to be lower in the tertiary sector, such a structural change in a

---

[1] The definition of 'new' industries, with its implied dichotomy with 'old' industry begs many important questions.

maturing economy not uncommonly encourages lower rates of growth.

Other issues lie in the logic of the context facing the British economy in the second half of the nineteenth century. Many problems are just the results of other nations becoming industrialized, over which human agency in Britain can bear no responsibility or incur no blame. Inevitably, British exports in cheap iron or steel and textiles will suffer when other nations learn to make these things efficiently for themselves. One has to accept the fact of tariffs abroad after the 1860's, and the fact that the British resource position was becoming steadily less favourable. Britain's very distorted industrial structure, with a few great export industries prospering in the very special circumstances of the world market in the first half of the nineteenth century, was bound to be very exposed to these changes in the world economy. Indeed, one may be speaking of British success, in part in exporting engineering products, coal and capital to the rest of the world. No nation can keep ahead all the time once other nations begin to industrialize. Problems of transition always face an industrial economy in such a context. To complain about the problems which result from this logic is to lament the inevitable.

None of these complications for the British economy after 1870 need *necessarily* have affected rates of growth or rates of investment or rates of innovation within the British economy. They do not come to the root of the matter which was a failure in innovation and development, widespread and deep-rooted in the British economy. One cannot dismiss the entire sequence, either, just as the inevitable consequence of Britain being first in the field and leave the argument at that point. In the inter-war period after 1920 some of the new industries developing in Britain could stand comparison in efficiency and rates of innovation with anything in the world, in vehicles, electrical equipment, artificial fibres, oil and some others. Overall rates of industrial growth in Britain after 1945 have been more than double those of the pre-1914 period. The inter-war rates, depression and all, were higher than pre-1914. There is thus nothing irreversible or even, perhaps, inevitable in the retardation of innovation and the failure of new industries to come forward rapidly in the late nineteenth century. Indeed, some positive advantages remained in having stolen a march on the rest of the world in industrialization. Britain had advantages of accumulated capital and skills, a trained labour force, established dominance in world commerce and shipping. Why should it have been that after 1870 the established industrial tradition and industrial structure in Britain seems to have become a liability in many ways – that the liabilities were outweighing the assets?

Some people have argued that in the nature of things a technological lag developed in the last quarter of the nineteenth century, a slowing-down in the pace of innovation which made for lags in capital investment and output. The argument goes that the dimensions of a boom depend upon the sort of new innovations which lie behind it and that a shortage of basic innovations at this time did not give the necessary surges in investment. One thesis points to the 1870's as this time of 'climacteric'. By this time, it is argued, the general application of steam power to production and to railways, and iron machinery to factory production had been accomplished. The age of coal and iron had been fulfilled. Then came a lull before equivalently general and basic innovations provided the basis for a new leap forward in productivity and in capital investment. Professor Phelps-Brown has claimed that this turning point should be seen in the 1890's, rather than 1870's, when steam power and steel had become generalized, the previous 20 years seeing the rise of a mass-production steel industry. And then, in the 1890's, came a lull before the new thrust forward from the momentum of new technology in basic new materials, basic new forms of power and prime movers which provided the basis for an entirely new range of industries: electric power and electrical engineering, the internal-combustion engine bringing road investment, the motor car, lorry and aircraft industries in its wake, with petroleum as a prime mover. New forms of instantaneous communication, telegraphy, the telephone and then the radio buttressed this industrial expansion and new materials like aluminium, cellulose-based products, artificial fibres, plastics.

The difficulties, in terms of present statistical series for industrial growth and productivity, both in the 1870-1900 period and before 1870, make it problematical whether these 'climacterics' in innovations are pivotal. The whole assumption that the application of new technology works in such a discontinuous way is open to question. It becomes very difficult to decide what is a basic innovation and what is not. For example, the timing of the birth and growth of the mass-production steel industry does not fit this chronology well. And saying that a lull occurred in the application of new techniques to the economy does not begin to answer the question of *why* this should have been so, and why the record of different countries should be so different. Why were these new sectors and new industries coming forward so much more slowly in Britain and not featuring in exports? Innovation is not the only prime mover of the economy, nor is it an 'unmoved mover'. The flow of innovation itself responds to context.

Evidence from individual industries reveals a pattern which is neither unitary nor simple. At first sight the coal and steel industries do not fit into it. Expansion of production in the coal industry remained at a very high level in the 1870's, in 1880-4, and again after just a few years of slower expansion in 1885-90. Output surged ahead from 110 million tons in 1870, to 180 million tons in 1890, to 290 million tons in 1913. Exports also rose very rapidly, particularly those of Welsh steam coals, as the world's shipping adopted steam power, and coaling stations all over the world were organized by British enterprise, buying from the Rhondda for predominantly British ships. Exports rose from 36 million tons in 1890 to 100 million tons in 1913 – absorbing an increasing proportion of output and a very high fraction of shipping freights in overseas trade. But, in another way, 1880 did see a change of trend in coal mining, for output per man then started on a fairly steep decline at rates faster than those in Germany or the United States. Partly this was a consequence of deeper pits in an older mining area with coal faces further from the shafts needing a higher proportion of workers in the labour force who were not hewers. But, in both Germany and the United States, these inherent progressive disadvantages in an extractive industry were being increasingly counteracted by mechanical cutting, concrete and steel and the use of electric traction below ground. One quarter of American coal was being

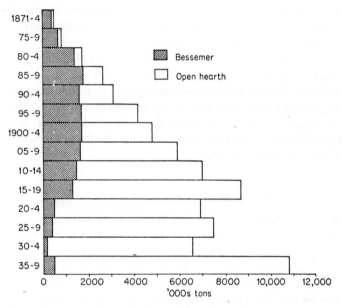

Fig. 21. Steel output in the United Kingdom (ingots and castings) (see also Table 32, p. 484). After Mitchell and Deane, 1962, pp. 136–7.

cut mechanically in 1910, but only a negligible fraction of British coal. For one reason or another, not all of them due to the lower efficiency of the British miner and coal owner, output per head in British coal mining was one half that of American pits by 1914.

The steel industry was the other main capital goods industry which saw enormous expansion through the period of the Great Depression. Sir Henry Bessemer's invention of the converter, in

1856, proved to be the innovation bringing the first mass-production technique to the industry. Bessemer was still the scientific amateur but a professional inventor. The 1860's and the great boom of 1870–2 saw very great investment in this process in the British steel industry. Then came an improved technique in the Siemens-Martin open-hearth furnace invented in 1866. This invention ran more in the new tradition of the times. Wilhelm Siemens was German by birth and had received a full scientific education as a metallurgist in Germany before coming to England and blossoming into the honoured English industrialist, Sir William Siemens. Pierre Martin was a French metallurgist. Production of steel quadrupled in the 20 years of the Great Depression as railways converted from rolled iron to steel rails and the mild steel plate and girder became the basic constructural units in ship-building. One cannot easily phase the growth and innovations of the steel industry into a Great Depression pattern. But here again problems occurred of lags in innovation.

Both Bessemer's and Siemen's inventions suffered from the disadvantage that low-grade iron ore containing phosphorus could not be employed, while the bulk of available British, German, Lorraine and Luxembourg ores were fairly low grade and phosphoric. This problem was solved in 1879 by a Welsh amateur chemist, Sydney Gilchrist Thomas, who was lucky to get in just ahead of the many professional metallurgists in continental steel works who were hard at work to solve the same problem. Thomas, who was a clerk in a police court, heard a lecturer at an evening school remark casually that anyone who could make cheap steel from phosphoric ore would earn a fortune. The subsequent record of innovation in British steel-making was not so good. In 1913 less than one-third of Britain's steel output of 7·5 million tons was made by the Thomas 'basic' process, and two-thirds still by the 'acid' process using pure ore, which was partly responsible for the fact that a third of the iron ore used in Britain was imported.[1] Siemens-Martin furnaces produced better steel more cheaply than Bessemer converters.

[1] See Appendix, Tables 31 and 32, pp. 483–4. Imports of iron ore were valued at half as much again as home-produced ore.

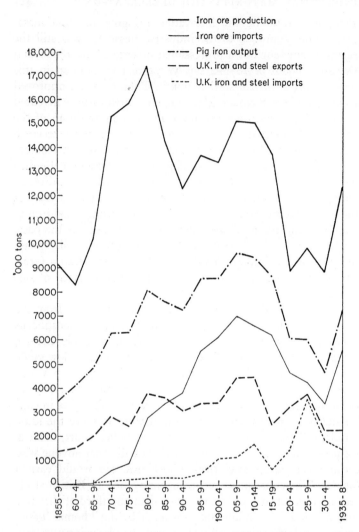

Fig. 22. Iron and steel production in the United Kingdom, 1855–1938 (see also Table 31, p. 483). After Mitchell and Deane, 1962, pp. 129–35, 142–3, 146–8.

Germany had virtually abandoned Bessemer production and was mainly using phosphoric ore by the basic process in Siemens' open-hearth furnaces. Mr D. Burns is very scathing in his analysis of the failure of British Bessemer steel producers to improve their techniques. One of the problems was that originally in the 1860's they had been over-aggressive, over-enthusiastic for innovation and were weighed down with many millions of pounds tied up in expensive converters.

The results of these advances in coal production and steel production upon the pattern of exports was soon clear. Between 1880 and 1900 British exports of iron, steel, machinery and coal doubled, to reach £95 million. The value of total textile exports fell absolutely during the same 20 years from £105 million to £97 million. The contrast in fortune between these two sides of industry was remarkable. In textiles the complete check to expansion in exports meant a virtual closing up of new investment, for well over three-quarters of production was being exported. As the pioneer industry of Britain's industrial supremacy in the world, as the largest single industry in the economy and its greatest single exporter, the fortunes of the textile industry, particularly the cotton branch of it, are crucial in considering the problem of innovation. The main contrast in investment for new innovation here was the widespread adoption of ring-spinning in the cotton industry of the United States, Switzerland and Germany – a simpler, faster and cheaper technique – and the failure of Lancashire to begin to desert the old mule-spinning techniques until after 1900. It was then the same story a little later on with the improved automatic looms and with Japanese competition. The new machinery was easily available to Lancashire at the time: Lancashire machine-making firms such as Platts of Oldham were supplying a booming export market in this technology but failing to find customers on their own doorstep.

The response of the cotton industry to increased competition and tariffs in the sophisticated export markets was not so much to change products or improve design or to cut costs by radical innovation and reorganization. Rather it was to maintain largely traditional-style products and technology and to switch

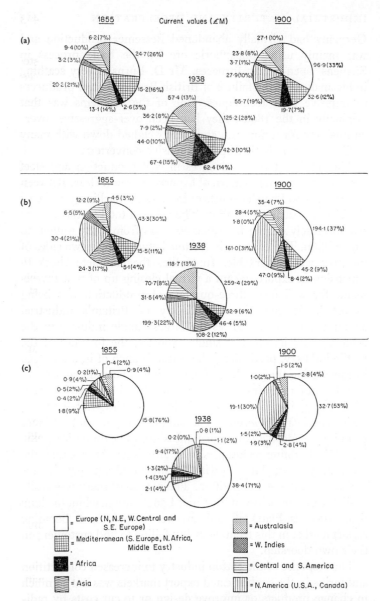

Fig. 23. (a) Direction of exports. (b) Direction of imports. (c) Direction of re-exports (see also Fig. 3, p. 101). Figures in £m. with percentage of total market in brackets. After Mitchell and Deane, 1962, pp. 313–14.

increasingly to traditional-style markets in India, the Far East and the Empire. The great investment in new mills in Lancashire between 1895 and 1914, based upon the renewed expansion of exports, was in largely traditional technology. This was the real indictment of Lancashire; more so than the failure to innovate and re-equip when markets were stagnant between 1875 and 1895. When an industry is growing rapidly a rising percentage of its machinery represents new capacity which can take advantage of all potential technical advances: the 'age structure' of machines installed gets younger. Rapid growth, therefore, can bring self-reinforcing advantages of being able to adopt the latest machines without the need for difficult decisions on scrapping outmoded but unworn-out equipment. Such opportunities were not seized by the British textile industry in the years of prosperity before 1914.

It is difficult to assert conclusively whether this sort of failure to innovate was typical of the times, or to measure it. One cannot quantify innovations satisfactorily. Undoubtedly, however, such failure was widespread and undoubtedly the more aggressive adoption of new techniques would have led to greater industrial investment and possibly to better records in exports. A few examples can be mentioned. Most of the new equipment in dairying – the factory processing of butter, dried and condensed milk and margarine – had Danish, Dutch, Swedish or French patents and was usually imported. In milling, Hungary and the United States were 20 years ahead of Britain in the technology of gradual-reduction systems and roller milling. In agricultural machinery, the most widely adopted of the reapers and binders at this time were American. Many innovations, such as the sewing machine and the typewriter, pioneered in the United States now began to invade the British markets, organized by American firms, and with this came an invasion of predominantly American commercial techniques, particularly advertising. The British glass-making industry lagged behind in the adoption of the Siemens 'tank furnace' and came under very heavy pressure from cheaper Belgian products. The flow of patents in shoe-making was mainly from the United States, so were the new developments in machine tools.

The most important, or the most noticeable, rival was Germany. E. E. Williams published a book entitled *Made in Germany* in 1896, raising the alarm about this commercial invasion of the British market by a more sophisticated technical rival. In metals technology and in mining technology the lead had passed to Germany in Europe by 1900 – not only in production, but also in the advance in techniques which was the more significant. This was also clear in electrical engineering of all kinds, the most important because the largest of the new industries, some precision engineering in instruments, optics and in much of the rising chemical industry. The British government found to its alarm in 1914 that all the magnetos in use in the country came from Stuttgart in Germany, as did all the khaki dye for troop uniforms. The clearest case of all was illustrated by the latter import. Britain had virtually missed out on the new technology of coal chemistry, the raw material of which formed the tap root of British industrial prosperity and resources. Nor could this be explained by the absence of a market for the products in Britain, or a less favourable demand structure, because Britain possessed the largest textile industry in the world which offered the largest dye-stuffs market in the world, a fact which was demonstrated by the extent of dyes being imported.

Although the first aniline dye, mauve, was discovered by a British chemist, W. H. Perkin, in 1856, he had been taught by a German professor, Hoffmann, at the Royal College of Chemistry, and all the major industrial developments of this new range of products based on coal distillation was subsequently German. The irony of it was that Germany imported much of her raw coal-tar from England, where it was a waste product of the coal gas and coking industries. This was a much more significant failing in innovation than the fact that Britain had little to do with innovations in petroleum technology at this time. Many British manufacturing enterprises in chemicals (apart from the older bleaching companies) were branches of German firms or controlled by German-born industrialists like Sir Ludwig Mond. Germany had picked up virtually all the European export trades in many 'fine' chemicals. Where chemistry was concerned Britain was virtually an under-developed country open to the economic invasion and exploitation of a higher culture. What British chemists there were, and there were very few indeed, had mainly gone to Germany for training or had found training under the few German chemists in England. Many professors of chemistry and chemistry masters in schools, where there were any, were German. When the great fermentators of London and Burton-on-Trent accepted the fact that they ought to know about the chemistry of fermentation in the 1870's, they were driven inevitably to Germans or to German-trained chemists.

In the whole range of the new electrical industries, probably the most important single group of the new industries, the large low-cost firms tended to be either American or German. This was true in generating plant as well as traction, in telephones and in telegraph. In electric traction the main London underground railway lines between 1900 and 1914 were built by American expertise with much American plant and more foreign investment than British. Much of the manufacturing capacity established in these industries in Britain, when it did develop, was composed of subsidiary companies of German or American firms like Siemens or Westinghouse. This failure of new sectors to come forward rapidly at this time to take the place of traditional staple industries under challenge from abroad proved one of the most strategic weaknesses of the time and one of the most potentially damaging for the future. The fact that these industries were small meant that these failures did not, at the time, affect total industrial growth rates very much.

It is difficult to perceive a unitary explanation underlying all these trends. Some common features exist in the external context and at home, but not all industries were experiencing the same pressures and the same opportunities so that the reasons for the different responses vary. In particular the diagnosis differs between the response of the older staple industries and the rising new ones.

One reason was a failing in management. With the main

pattern in British manufacturing industry still being the family firm or partnership, or the public company where the family held most of the ordinary shares that gave control, family failings were often at the bottom of the trouble in industries such as textiles. By the second or third generation of owners sometimes the mill was mainly thought of as the provider of revenue for the landed gentlemen in the style of an estate rather than as the centre of ambitions of the industrialist. Pulling out profits to maximize the owner's status as a landed gentleman or to invest in gilt-edged stock could starve the business of capital for re-equipment, as well as managerial drive at the top. It was much more convenient, easier and cheaper in the short run, to repair and replace machines than to scrap and to innovate. Moving out of the old multi-storied mills to more efficient buildings could be difficult and expensive. This attitude has been the curse of British management. Why scrap a perfectly good machine that was superbly made, lovingly maintained and for which the machine-makers still possessed a complete stock of all its parts? At least six engines in breweries which were installed before 1800 still worked a century later. How long these machines lasted was one of the finest tributes to British engineers and one of the worst indictments of British industrialists. Even where the maker's name-plate and the basic frame was the only part of the machine not to have been replaced the issue is the same. Repair and replace was the general rule rather than root-and-branch re-equipping and this goes far to explain the failure to adopt new technology in older industries. Accounting and depreciation policies encouraged the practice. The contrast with traditional American attitudes is quite clear. And looking ahead to the twentieth century, British industrialists were without that immense stimulus to re-equipment given to German, Belgian and French industrialists in northern France by having plant physically destroyed in war or dismantled for reparations after war.

The burden of ageing buildings, and obsolescent equipment did prove a real liability of being first in the field. When others begin to industrialize they can come in at the latest stage of technology available. But it still comes back to a management and ownership problem in the end – the failure to take positive steps to overcome these liabilities. The real explanation was that traditional attitudes had got built in with the machines.

Adaptation to changing markets and new technology was in some cases made more difficult by the institutional pattern established in an industry at an earlier stage of industrial evolution. By 1880, the cotton industry was mainly divided into separate spinning firms, weaving firms and finishing firms in contrast to its developing structure between 1820 and 1850. The man with initiative in export markets was often not the industrialist at all but the merchant and the agency house facing foreign markets directly. Such a development admirably suited the logic of the mid-nineteenth century. But this structure made it more difficult to get changes of product in response to changes in markets than with the few integrated firms like Horrocks in textiles, where there was unified entrepreneurial control over all the basic processes of production. The greater the technical content of exports, particularly in the engineering industries with the need for expert servicing, the greater the premium on the presence of the manufacturer in export markets, or his direct control of facilities. And it needed more ruthless management and greater capital resources to break through such an institutional barrier to progress. In some cases, too, there was less demand for the new industries' products because of an over-provision in the old.

Such institutional difficulties have a financial aspect to them also. When the tradition of the family firm had growing disadvantages the fact that by the 1870's the British banking system was turning its back on the function of making long-term loans to industrialists made it more difficult for large capitals to be assembled quickly by new firms. The Stock Exchange, too, was not an institution which made it easy for the small rising firm in the provinces to collect public capital quickly or cheaply. The able, ambitious man, frustrated from rising to positions of power within a family firm, could perhaps more easily have found the finance for launching his own company had banking traditions been closer to those in France and Germany. In later times the problem of financing the development of new innovations and small firms needing to cover large development costs and wanting to expand more quickly than is possible out of profits much exercised public policy. The large, wealthy, secure, nationally-known, established firms in the economy quite certainly found no difficulty in raising capital publicly, as many did. No national shortage of capital at all existed. Rates of interest remained low. Of course in times of falling profit margins and stagnant sales abroad financing massive re-equipment out of profits was difficult, if not impossible. It was made more difficult if much capital was being withdrawn from firms for non-business spending.

Structural disadvantages of being in the lead of industrialization were compounded by the degree of interrelatedness in different parts of the economy. Over-investment in basic social overhead capital at an earlier stage of technology does create very high costs for reinvestment in later technology and at the same time reduces the incentives to do so. Yet the multiplier effects of such reinvestment can be of major importance for the growth of new industrial sectors. The most important illustration of this was probably the provision of gas lighting in all English towns and steam locomotives reducing investment in the electrical industries. Over-investment in railways and local transport had a similar effect upon the structure of demand facing the motor car industry. Again the issue is not just one of capital costs but also of incentives, skills, motivations, almost emotional commitment to the traditional 'classical' technology. Some initial decisions for any economy are virtually once and for all, being then beyond the decision-making powers of a single firm, or industry, or the manufacturing sector as a whole to change. Rail gauge was a prime example of such a rigidity imposed upon the economy. The narrow gauge of most English railways (4 ft $8\frac{1}{2}$ in) imposed a limitation on the system which had to be accepted. Although change was theoretically possible it was never an operationally practical decision.

Arguments about second and third generation attitudes in management and the burden of an ageing technology cannot, however, apply to rising new sectors of industry where basic innovations were first being applied in this period by first-generation pioneers. Here another basic argument has been put forward, that the preconditions of the process of innovation were themselves changing rapidly at this time; that innovation was becoming more a result of the deliberate and systematic application of scientific knowledge to production. One of the most significant aspects of Germany's advance was exactly the importance of academically-trained scientists in rising industries, a close institutional connection developing between applied science in higher education and research in industry. And innovation in Britain was seen to lag most exactly in the industries most dependent upon applied science: chemicals, dye-stuffs, the electrical industries. This was yet another example of how an earlier industrial tradition, with innovation born of the gifted mechanic, the brilliant amateur, the practical man with no systematic education in science or technology was becoming a liability.

Educational policy raises the question of state responsibility or at least of general social attitudes. A small band of people had been campaigning since the mid-century in the cause of scientific education. Lyon Playfair, a shrewd Scot, sounded the alarm ironically enough in his *Lectures on the Great Exhibition* in 1852. 'Industry must in future be supported,' he wrote, 'not by a competition of local advantage but by a competition of intellect.' Even a Royal Commission noted solemnly in 1864: 'Nor would it be wise in a country whose continued prosperity so greatly depends upon its ability to maintain its pre-eminence in manufactures to neglect the application of natural science to the industrial arts . . .' In 1872 only 12 persons were reading for the natural sciences' tripos at Cambridge, most of them training to be doctors of medicine. Yet by then 11 technical universities and 20 other universities existed in Germany. The first grant of public money to support scientific education in Britain came in 1890; but by 1901 still only £25,000 per annum was going from the Exchequer into British universities. Even if the resources being devoted to pure science in England were not as small in comparison with other advanced countries as has been suggested, the application of science to industry and its adoption by industry greatly lagged.

Certainly this proved one of the fields where the English traditions of parsimony in public spending, putting *laissez-faire* limits to public responsibility, proved most damaging. The only widespread educational response coming in the wake of industry had come in the first half of the nineteenth century in the mechanics' institutes founded by George Birkbeck in 1824. These were self-financing. Within 20 years they had grown into a national system of 200 institutes with over 50,000 members. But they trained only the non-commissioned officers of industry, the literate artisan anxious to improve himself into the foreman or master-fitter status. In no sense were they the context from which might spring a technical university system, as in continental countries. They flourished at a lower technical, and one might add social, level altogether, and even the mechanics' institute movement withered away after 1850. Some have widened the educational arguments still further. An organized system of national elementary education was very late in coming. It did not teach science and was not designed to lead the more intelligent pupils through to the higher educational levels which also did not exist on a large scale in the public sector. This changed after 1900 as so many things in the British educational world.

In the private sector of education, following the regeneration of Rugby and the great proliferation of public schools in this tradition after 1840, an increasing proportion of the youth of the upper ranks of society came within the system of values inculcated there and at the ancient universities. In their own way these also had their backs turned toward the industrial economy, more particularly as far as applied science is concerned. Matthew Arnold, who had a great plan for scientific education at Oxford, complained that what he called the 'professional half' of the English middle classes – the clergymen, lawyers and doctors – had been given an education designed originally for the aristocracy, the landed men of leisure, the amateur public administrators and statesmen; while what he called the 'commercial and industrial half' of the middle classes were now receiving an inferior copy of this. Too often the mill proved too bleak a destiny for those passing through the system, which was reinforced by the dominance of classics, theology and a tradition of mathematics unconnected with science or a career in applied science at Oxford and Cambridge. Extraordinary isolated exceptions, such as Lord Kelvin, proved the rule. The ideals of the cultivated man of leisure, the professions, or of the public service (either in the Empire or at home) led the positions of social status for which a liberal education at this time was deemed to be a preparation. When the civil service was thrown open to competitive examination after 1870 this career quickly joined the club of high-status occupations. It is strange to contemplate the situation of a country officially committed to a free-enterprise system, and its appropriate economic and political attitudes, with its economy becoming more and more dependent upon its business efficiency in a competitive world, yet with the educational system of the upper and middle classes possessing a value system that elevated service to the state and the liberal professions in status and depressed the status of becoming involved in trade or more particularly manufacturing industry. Finance escaped the prejudice to a large degree.

This issue must not be pressed too far. In many individual instances this sequence was not played out. And only a very small percentage of the children in the country saw the inside of a public school or a university. This tradition was not so true of Scottish schools and universities nor of the civic universities in England and Wales forming towards the end of the century. But given the structure of ownership in British manufacturing industry and mining, the educational system and the values current within it could have had an importance much wider than the numbers touched by it suggest. In the United States and in Germany the educational system did not encourage a comparable retreat from business. In Germany an efficient, nation-wide system of higher education and national primary education was state-run. In the United States well over 70 universities were flourishing as early as 1870, closely related to the local business and farming and political communities from which many had been endowed, and the educational traditions of postgraduate science organization in Germany were quickly adopted in the United States.[1] In the United States, too, a career in business brought top status to the top families and the standard of recruitment and efficiency in the American civil service is said to have suffered accordingly. When historians praise the administrative revolution which gave Britain the finest civil service in the world at the end of the nineteenth century, one must be aware that the coin had a reverse side to it.

In what was to become one of the most powerful engines of growth in the next generation, the motor car industry, in inventions, patents, innovation and the commercial expansion of the industry up to 1914 Britain made a relatively poor showing in comparison with the United States and France. The extent and structure of demand was doubtless less favourable in Britain than in North America, though this was scarcely true in comparison with France. Yet one-third of the motor cars existing in Britain in 1914 were imported, most of them American Fords, which showed that the market existed, even if not on such a scale as in the United States. Nor can it be said that there was any lack of technical skills in this industry in Britain. Over 200 tiny firms flourished, many producing very highly sophisticated, very expensive products. It was a first-generation industry, with no problem of ageing mills built in the early nineteenth century or ailing family dynasties. Most of the heads of firms in the British car industry were highly competent engineers. Paradoxically, many problems sprang from the latter fact. Engineers were taking decisions as the heads of firms on technical more than market criteria, certainly not on mass-market criteria. Few firms in the British motor car industry in this period were cost-conscious. Status was given by the technical sophistication of the product regardless of price. This encouraged the production of very expensive objects at very high cost to the select few who could afford them in the first place and afford to run them and maintain them. The techniques of production engineering, of 'Taylorism', in cutting the costs of manufacture were conspicuous by their absence. Henry Ford always kept his technical criteria conditioned by his market

[1] Massachusetts Institute of Technology was founded in 1861.

ambitions. He *reduced* technical standards where necessary to follow the logic of mass marketing, which meant a minimal initial capital cost and minimal maintenance costs. The British motor car industry resembled the later Italian industry without Fiat, and the 'Rolls-Royce attitude' so widely prevalent did not provide the specifications for building a great industry upon a mass market.[1] Although the structure of the electrical industries and railways evolved partly in response to a particular market demand, some at least of the absence of standardization, the absence of national planning and technical uniformities in these industries also derived from the fact that decision-makers were engineers wedded to particular technical criteria and not to the economies of scale which could be derived from standardization and technical uniformities. The influence of the consulting engineer as a powerful 'third party' in decision-making over technical criteria institutionalized this status.

To sum up. Out of the welter of argument which exists about the problems of inefficiency in British business at the end of the nineteenth century, one must seek to discover the relevant evidence. Many of the international comparisons which have been drawn are irrelevant to the essential issue of inefficiency; others are not. The fact that textile industries abroad were catching up on Lancashire is by itself irrelevant because this lay in the logic of the developing situation, and not Lancashire's choice. The fact that there was more than twice as much capital and horse-power per worker in American industry is not irrelevant. In 1907 came the first census of production. One of

[1] This had cultural as well as economic aspects. The following dialogue was reported to a United States Congressional Committee about the attempt of an American engineer and international patent lawyer to sell the Delco self-starter to the head of a famous British motor car firm, who said ' "You know, it will cost £20 or £30 more. Why should we put it on the car?" Mr Hunt, "Well, if you have this starter on the car, when the car stops the owner won't have to get out and crank the engine; he can put his foot on the pedal and start it." The man said, "You know, the people who use our car have their own chauffeurs: they wouldn't dream of driving a car themselves, you see." ... Hunt was baffled but not beaten, and so he said, "I'll tell you, you will sell a lot more cars if they have this starter on, because with this starter on the car, women can drive." The man said, "Women drive, God forbid!" ' (Quoted G. E. Folk, *Patents and Industrial Progress* (New York, 1942), pp. 247–8.)

the themes of the enquiry was productivity. The results showed that the value added to the cost of materials by a worker in specified manufacturing industries in Britain was on average £100. The American average was nearly £500 – a contrast which provides a simple test of relative levels of productivity in the two economies. The reasons behind this relevant international comparison are the important ones to elucidate. Equally, the failure of Britain's industrial structure to change with the times before 1914, compared with other countries or compared with the British record between the wars, was highly significant.

One general hypothesis has been put forward in elegant and sophisticated terms by Professor Habakkuk to explain the higher incentives to invest in labour-saving equipment in the United States than in Britain, viz. the higher level of wages in North America. Although this thesis has much relevance and import-ance to commend it, certain problems still remain. In certain of the rising new industries an equivalent differential existed between the progress of innovation in Britain and in Germany where a reverse wage-differential existed to create a higher relative stimulus for labour-saving equipment in Britain than on the continent. Wage rates had also been higher in the United States than in Britain since the seventeenth century. Equally, in the generation which saw a significant gap open between the performance of the British economy and that of the United States and Germany in certain strategic industries (1870–1914) the level of wage costs was pressing harder upon British industrialists than in previous periods. Prices were falling, profit margins were being squeezed, productivity increases were slow-ing down yet money wage rates did not decline significantly. Invoking the hypothesis of lower money wages in British in-dustry therefore does not seem to explain fully the growing gap in performance with Germany or the growing failure of innova-tion in Britain compared with the early nineteenth century. The problems defy a single unitary explanation, but in their diversity relate to the whole dynamics of industrial growth rates. They cannot be explained just in simple terms of economic hypotheses such as wage rates, shifting terms of trade, or deteriorating natural resources.

Reading list

CHANGES IN THE FIRM (INCORPORATION, COMBINATIONS, AMALGAMATIONS)

CAIRNCROSS, A. K. 'The English capital market before 1914', *Economica*, new series, 1958, **25**, no. 98.

CAIRNCROSS, A. K. *Home and Foreign Investment, 1870–1913: studies in capital accumulation*, Cambridge, 1953.

COOK, P. L. & COHEN, R. *Effects of Mergers: six studies*, London, 1958 (Cambridge Studies in Industry).

COOKE, C. A. *Corporation, Trust and Company: an essay in legal history*, Manchester, 1950 [1951].

DAVIS, L. 'The capital markets and industrial concentration: the US and UK, a comparative study', *Economic History Review*, 1966, **19**, no. 2.

EVANS, G. H. *British Corporation Finance, 1775–1850: a study of preference shares*, Baltimore, 1936.

HALL, A. R. 'A note on the English capital market as a source of funds for home industry before 1914', *Economica*, new series, 1957, **24**, no. 93; 1958, **25**, no. 100.

HUNT, B. C. *Development of the Business Corporation in England, 1800–1867*, Cambridge (Mass.), 1936 (Harvard Economic Studies, vol. 52).

JEFFERYS, J. B. 'The denomination and character of shares, 1855–1885', *Economic History Review*, 1946, **16**, no. 1; reprinted in E. M. Carus-Wilson (ed.), *Essays in Economic History*, vol. 1, London, 1954.

LAVINGTON, F. *The English Capital Market*, London, 1921.

MACROSTY, H. W. *The Trust Movement in British Industry: a study of business organization*, London, 1901.

SAVILLE, J. 'Sleeping partnership and limited liability, 1850–1856', *Economic History Review*, 2nd series, 1956, **8**, no. 3.

SHANNON, H. A. 'The coming of general limited liability', *Economic History* (supplement to the *Economic Journal*), 1931, **2**; reprinted in E. M. Carus-Wilson (ed.), *Essays in Economic History*, vol. 1, London, 1954.

SHANNON, H. A. 'The limited companies of 1866–1883', *Economic History Review*, 1933, **4**, no. 3; reprinted in E. M. Carus-Wilson (ed.), *Essays in Economic History*, vol. 1, London, 1954.

WILSON, C. H. *History of Unilever: a study of economic growth and social change*, 2 vols, London, 1954.

THE GREAT DEPRESSION, 1873–96

BEALES, H. L. 'The Great Depression in industry and trade', *Economic History Review*, 1934, **5**, no. 1.

COPPOCK, D. J. 'Mr Saville on the Great Depression: a reply', *Manchester School of Economic and Social Studies*, 1963, **31**, no. 3.

MUSSON, A. E. 'The Great Depression in Britain, 1873–1896: a reappraisal', *Journal of Economic History*, 1959, **19**, no. 2.

ROSTOW, W. W. *British Economy of the 19th Century: essays*, Oxford, 1948.

SAUL, S. B. *The Myth of the Great Depression, 1873–1896*, London, 1969.

SAVILLE, J. 'Mr Coppock on the Great Depression', *Manchester School of Economic and Social Studies*, 1963, **31**, no. 1.

ECONOMIC GROWTH AND INDUSTRIAL RETARDATION, 1870–1914

(i) *General studies*

ALDCROFT, D. H. (ed.) *The Development of British Industry and Foreign Competition, 1875–1914: studies in industrial enterprise*, London, 1968.

ASHWORTH, W. 'Changes in industrial structure, 1870–1914', *Yorkshire Bulletin of Economic and Social Research*, 1965, **17**, no. 1.

ASHWORTH, W. 'The late Victorian economy', *Economica*, new series, 1966, **33**, no. 129.

COPPOCK, D. J. 'British industrial growth during the "Great Depression", 1873–1896: a pessimist's view', *Economic History Review*, 2nd series, 1964, **17**, no. 2.

HABAKKUK, H. J. *American and British Technology in the 19th Century: the search for labour-saving inventions*, Cambridge, 1962.

MATTHEWS, R. C. O. 'Postwar growth in the British economy in relation to historical experience', *Manchester Statistical Society Paper*, 1964.

MUSSON, A. E. 'British industrial growth during the "Great Depression", 1873–1896: some comments', *Economic History Review*, 2nd series, 1963, **15**, no. 3.

RICHARDSON, H. W. 'Retardation in Britain's industrial growth, 1870–1913', *Scottish Journal of Political Economy*, 1965, **12**, no. 2.

ROBINSON, E. A. G. 'Changing structure of the British economy', *Economic Journal*, 1954, **64**, no. 255.

SAVILLE, J. 'Some retarding factors in the British economy before 1914', *Yorkshire Bulletin of Economic and Social Research*, 1961, **13**, no. 1.

SAYERS, R. S. *A History of Economic Change in England, 1880–1939*, Oxford, 1967.

WILSON, C. H. 'Economy and society in late Victorian Britain', *Economic History Review*, 2nd series, 1965, **18**, no. 1.

(ii) *Special topics*

ALDCROFT, D. H. 'The entrepreneur and the British economy, 1870–1914', *Economic History Review*, 2nd series, 1964, **17**, no. 1.

ASHBY, E., *Technology and the Academics* [rev. ed.], London–New York, 1963.

BEER, J. J. *The Emergence of the German Dye Industry*, Urbana (Ill.), 1959 [chapter on Britain] (Illinois Studies in the Social Sciences, vol. 44).

BROWN, E. H. PHELPS & HANDFIELD JONES, S. J. 'The climacteric of the 1890s: a study in the expanding economy', *Oxford Economic Papers*, new series, 1952, **4**, no. 3.

BURN, D. L. *The Economic History of Steel-making, 1867–1939: a study in competition*, Cambridge, 1940.

BURN, D. L. 'The genesis of American engineering competition, 1850–1870', *Economic History* (supplement to the *Economic Journal*), 1931, **2**.

BURNHAM, T. H. & HOSKIN, G. O. *Iron and Steel in Britain, 1870–1930*, London, 1943.

CARDWELL, D. S. L. *The Organisation of Science in England: a retrospect*, London, 1957.

CARR, J. C. & TAPLIN, W. *A History of the British Steel Industry*, Oxford, 1962.

COPPOCK, D. J. 'The climacteric of the 1890s: a critical note', *Manchester School of Economic and Social Studies*, 1956, **24**, no. 1.

FRANKEL, M. 'Obsolescence and technological change in a maturing economy', *American Economic Review*, 1955, **45**, no. 3.

JEFFERYS, J. B. *Retail Trading in Britain, 1850–1950*, Cambridge, 1954 (National Institute of Economic and Social Research: Economic and Social Studies, no. 13).

JERVIS, F. J. R. 'The handicap of Britain's early start', *Manchester School of Economic and Social Studies*, 1947, **15**, no. 1.

LEWIS, W. A. & O'LEARY, P. J. 'Secular swings in production and trade, 1870–1913', *Manchester School of Economic and Social Studies*, 1955, **23**, no. 2.

MATHIAS, P. *Retailing Revolution*, London, 1967.

POUNDS, N. J. G. & PARKER, W. N. *Coal and Steel in Western Europe: the influence of resources and techniques on production*, London, 1957.

SAUL, S. B. 'The American impact on Britain, 1895–1914', *Business History*, 1960–1, **3**, no. 1.

SAUL, S. B. 'The motor industry in Britain to 1914', *Business History*, 1962, **5**, no. 1.

SCOTT, J. D. *Siemens Brothers, 1858–1958*, London, 1958.

TAYLOR, A. J. 'Labour productivity and technical innovation in the British coal industry, 1850–1914', *Economic History Review*, 2nd series, 1961, **14**, no. 1.

TEMIN, P. 'The decline of the British iron and steel industry', in H. Rosovsky (ed.), *Industrialisation in Two Systems: essays in honor of A. Gerschenkron*, New York, 1966.

VAIZEY, J. *The Brewing Industry, 1886–1951: an economic study*, London, 1960.

16 Epilogue: the inter-war years

The ideograph of Britain's economic position between the two world wars, 20 years of economic history, is simple: 'Mutinies at demobilization in 1918 set the tone for the hostility, violence and disorder which characterized the years of peace to come. Short-lived feverish booms and endemic depression in the basic industries revived all the aggressive traditions in labour disputes experienced in the pre-war years. Violence after 1926 gave way to apathy only when all the main organized political parties had failed to overcome the problems of unemployment. Politics were dominated, and it seems defeated, by economic problems. Political crisis and ineptitude in policy measures enlarged the dimensions of industrial depression until distress became mitigated only by the onset of a crisis in foreign affairs which led, reluctantly, to rearmament after 1936.'

In fact, to write off the entire inter-war period as a period of depression begs as many questions as writing off the 1840's as 'the Hungry Forties' for English economic history in the nineteenth century. For the one event to dominate the historical consciousness of the whole period is quite uncritical. The 1840's was also the decade of free trade legislation, booming foreign trade in some years and the greatest boom years of the railway age. Similarly, the inter-war years could be seen also as the time when a new industrial structure was being established which provided the real basis for the export booms and the rising prosperity of the second half of the twentieth century. So much depends upon whether the spot-light is turned upon Jarrow or on Slough; on Merthyr Tydfil or on Oxford; on Greenock and Birkenhead or on Coventry, Weston-super-Mare and the environs of London. This was a period of such rapidly changing fortunes, of such structural change within the industrial sector of the economy, that national averages conceal more truth than

431

they usually do, and evidence taken from just one part of the country, or one industry (particularly one suffering most prominently) must not be equated with national conclusions without qualification. Many recent national leaders, particularly in the trade unions, had their outlook fashioned by their experience between the wars, often in the worst-affected industries and areas. Invoking the memories of the thirties, even (in the specific sense of the word) the myth of the thirties, has often proved a useful political weapon for post-war politicians. In fact the national income rose by 37·5 per cent between 1913 and 1937, and the national income per head by over 23 per cent – at a faster rate, that is to say, than in the decades before the First World War. And progress was faster between 1929 and 1937 (which includes the slump years) than in the 1920's.

This is, of course, not to deny the presence of failure. The memories of the inter-war years as those of economic disaster and social tragedy relate most closely to the nineteenth-century giants of British industry: textiles, coal, ship-building – exactly the industries where Britain's world dominance had been greatest, which had expanded to the position of being the major industries (with engineering) of the country as far as numbers of employees, capital and their stake in the total export trade were concerned. One of the greatest dynamic forces behind the expansion of the economy in the nineteenth century had been exactly the expanding exports of just a handful of major industries. By 1918 it had become clear that, in relation to changes in world markets, Britain now suffered from a quite distorted industrial structure, with the few giant industries so heavily committed to exports becoming increasingly the dinosaurs of the economy, too large for the opportunities available to sustain them in world trade, and weighed down by the conservatism born of success in a previous age.

Undoubtedly the greatest problem of all centred on the coal industry, if only because it was the largest. Moreover, the coal industry had been sick from the opening of the 1920's – while the world economy was still expanding; before the world-wide slump of 1930 had seriously contracted the volume and the values of international trade. Coal output in 1913 was about

290 million tons, produced by about 1 million miners. Of this, a little more than one-third was flowing abroad. In the last five years of the 1920's exports had declined to about 50 million tons – virtually halved – and total production had fallen almost equivalently. But the major problem was revealed by the existence of over 200,000 more miners on the payroll in 1924 than in 1912, so that productivity had declined sharply. On the

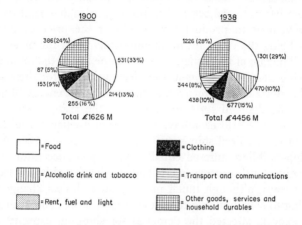

Fig. 24. Consumers' expenditure, at current prices, 1900 and 1938. After Mitchell and Deane, 1962, pp. 370–1.

demand side, undoubtedly, export problems, plus the slumps in export prices, were at the root of the difficulties – the industry's major problem in the short run. But institutional problems were the long-run enemies on the supply side.

Successive attempts to agree on national solutions to cut down the size of the industry, adopt national planning for wages, output and efficiency objectives proved abortive, ending in the great strike of 1926 which proved unsuccessful for everyone, and put back the clock on national planning – the only thing that could save the industry – for 20 years. It is impossible to calculate the national harm done by the state of labour relations in the coal industry between the wars, which embittered the entire trade union–management struggle. After the final cataclysm of 1926, when the General Strike collapsed and the miners fought on alone, which embittered trade union relations almost as much, at least people started leaving the industry. Output fell to about 200 million tons in 1932–3 (with home demand keeping up surprisingly well considering the state of the economy at the time) and only slowly recovered to 225 million tons in 1939.[1] But the main trend was the continuing contraction in numbers employed – an attrition of 400,000 miners left only 750,000 still in the pits in 1939 – a substantial improvement in productivity bought at the price of mining areas being the worst hit in unemployment and the most militant. The fate of the fathers there gave the mines the reputation of being destroyers of men, too bleak a destiny for their sons. Coal exports did not recover, as new sources of energy dragged down the demand for coal relative to the rising total power needs of the world economy. This was particularly true in the case of the oil-fired ship.

Ship-building suffered equally. This most successful of the later nineteenth-century giants had also hardened its arteries in many ways, although much more rapid technical change was coming to ship-building than to cotton or steel. The decline in coal exports affected the demands for shipping capacity very much; when world trade slumped the effect on shipping freights, and demand for new ships, was severe. British ship-builders faced the largest drop in demand for new shipping capacity because British shipping still possessed the largest single share of world shipping freights. British ship-owners still bought British but in the inter-war years Britain lost more of the world's shipping orders than would have been the case if British yards had maintained internationally competitive standards. Japan became one important competitor in ship-building; Sweden and Holland developed more efficient shipyards (although much smaller yards) even without the cost advantages of much lower wages. It was said that Dutch shipyards could build more cheaply, even though importing all their materials from Britain. Next to the coal industry, ship-building possessed some of the most embittered – and unenlightened – labour relations in the

[1] See Appendix, Table 29, p. 481, and Fig. 9, p. 268.

country. The ship-building industry's problems were reflected at once back to the iron, steel and coal industry.

The third failing giant was the textile industry, particularly its largest section – cotton. The long-term troubles of this industry continued throughout the inter-war period, although now there was considerable absolute decline in output, rather than just the retardation in the rate of growth of output which had characterized the last quarter of the nineteenth century. Yarn output had been about 2,000 million lb in cotton in 1912–1913. It was down to 1,000 million lb by 1930, at the trough of the depression year, and recovered to 1,400 million lb in the temporary trade revival of 1937. Over four-fifths of output was being exported in 1914, when textiles still absorbed two-fifths of all exports. Hence, once more, failing exports created the most important single source of trouble for the cotton industry. Exports of piece-goods in cotton fell to less than a third of their pre-war total – from 6,500 million square yards in 1912, to 2,000 million square yards in 1937.

To some extent these export problems were an inevitable reaction to changing world conditions. World trade was stagnating relative to nineteenth-century trends, and to post-1945 trends, with a rising proportion of capital goods and durable consumer goods and a declining proportion of textiles, as more and more countries developed their own textile industries. Japan now became the aggressive exporter in the Far East, to those markets which had become increasingly vital to Lancashire's fortunes before 1914. And even India became a direct threat to Lancashire by erecting tariff barriers against both Japanese and British competition in textiles and developing an export trade to Britain (when British administrators still ruled in Delhi). In the inter-war years sophisticated markets were growing faster than the less developed national economies, and the United States and Germany were taking advantage of this trend more than Britain. In countries such as Argentina aggressive American exporters cracked open traditional British preserves in export lines, such as locomotives and other capital equipment. The structure of Britain's export trade, both in its pattern of goods and its geographical pattern of markets, was least favourable in relation to these changing currents of world trade. The implications of the rise of the United States to a position of world importance industrially were still being worked out. Britain was still failing to hold her share in world trade, quite apart from the general contraction of world trade as a whole after 1929.

British exporters suffered, in common with others selling manufactured goods, from the reaction of the slump in world trade upon the 'primary producers'. These countries were hit relatively harder by the fall in demand occasioned by the declining purchasing power of the wealthier industrial nations, and their prices (of raw materials and agricultural produce) fell more alarmingly than the prices of manufactured goods. In turn, therefore, their own powers of purchasing from the industrial economies fell off, to the detriment of the export industries in those countries. This further increased the local incidence of economic distress. In other ways the industrial nations profited much by the greater relative decline in the prices of the raw products they mainly imported. The terms of trade for Britain moved between one-third and a quarter in her favour because of this relative price movement between exports and imports. The balance of payments position, suffering from the fall in shipping earnings, the sale of some, but not many, foreign assets during the war and the decline of lending abroad (apart from great investments in oil regions) – which reduced income from foreign investment – was bolstered up immensely by favourable terms of trade. Lower import prices meant a fall in costs of living at home, a fall in industrial costs and a release of purchasing power at home. Only the export industries facing the primary producing economies suffered in return.

It will be seen from this review that export industries suffered distress for different reasons, but had two common threads through their difficulties. They experienced a reaction to world economic problems; but a reaction heightened by a failure to adapt quickly to changing world requirements and competitive standards. Thus one prime issue in the economic problems of the period was the structural distortion having developed by 1918, heightened by the failure of new industries to grow rapidly in the generation before 1918, and the forcible adaptation of this outmoded industrial structure under pressure of adverse world conditions. Such a process continued after 1945.

The social tragedy of the inter-war years very largely related to the extreme localization of industry coming with this traditional industrial structure. The great industries under pressure were highly concentrated. The fate of a locality, if not a region, might be made or broken by a single industry, sometimes a single firm. Closing Palmer's shipyard put most of Jarrow out of work, when every shopkeeper except the pawnbroker lost business. The same was true when Vickers ran out of orders at Barrow-in-Furness. When a particular market was lost to Welsh steam coal particular pits in the Rhondda were laid off. National averages of unemployment had no meaning in such localities. In the worst years, 1930–2, it could be up to 50–60 per cent in the worst places, when the national average was just over 20 per cent. For the period as a whole unemployment rates seldom fell below 10 per cent: in the coal industry they averaged about 20 per cent.

Localization meant that there was very often no adequate source of alternative employment. Local employers, even if socially responsible, were quite powerless to cope with problems on this scale. There was no significant national redeployment of resources, led by public initiative and control, to bring large-scale employment to the depressed areas, even though much attention was given to the problem, which was obvious to all observers, and many small schemes were tried. Equally, it was proved by default that mobility of labour did not occur on a sufficient scale fast enough to become an alternative means of redressing the problems of structural unbalance. Miners' sons would not go into the pits so regularly. When a fitter's son at Birkenhead left school he might well refuse to follow his father into Cammell Laird's yard (and there might well be no job for him there). But, for a variety of social and technical arguments, no mass migration occurred of miners or shipyard fitters themselves. Just as the problem of moving alternative employment on a large scale into these areas, the problem of moving large numbers of families out of them depended upon much greater public initiative, resources and public planning than existed at the time. By and large the wage-earners at the heads of these stricken families drew the dole and hoped that next month something might turn up.

The industrial growth that did occur sprang from new conditions. Much of it featured light industry, based on electric power, growing more markedly in the midlands and the south, on the outskirts of London (the metropolitan area being the most rapidly and extensively growing industrial area of all at the time). Other towns like Slough, Reading and Bristol also expanded very much through industrial suburbs and trading estates. The new localization forces were quite different from the old. They were not based much on the wealth of immediately local raw materials or power, or even pools of skilled labour. The most significant new industry of all, motor cars, which was really a whole complex of component industries, grew in Oxford, London, Coventry, Luton and Birmingham, far from steel furnaces; the aircraft industry at places like Bristol, Gloucester and Southampton. By and large the new industries were not vast users of traditional raw materials, except thin sheet steel, or of traditional power. The establishment of the national grid and the public authority of the Central Electricity Board – finally – in 1926 had much to do with this new wave of industrial sitings. Britain was characteristically slower than other European nations in imposing order by public decree over the chaotic local variations of voltages and frequencies which had characterized the spread of electric power up to the 1930's. This held up the whole diffusion of economic activity based on the new power.

Even so, in 1930, a car journey between south Wales and Slough could take one from extremes of depression, economic stagnation and social apathy to almost boom conditions of industrial expansion (even though industries of very small size compared with coal and cotton and ship-building), new markets, urban growth, rising consumption standards and social innovations. Two groups of industries stood out above the others in this industrial renaissance, judged by the number of workers: the new transport industries, bicycles, aircraft and the various branches of the motor industry; and all the forms of electrical engineering from generating plant to electric light-bulbs and radios. Employing far fewer workers, but with very much capital employed, oil and chemicals were expanding rapidly. But by far the largest industry to contribute to expansion was building. In the 1920's, and after 1933, much industrial construction took place and 1·5 million houses were built in the 1920's and 3 million in the 1930's (which put the stock of houses up by nearly 30 per cent). Certainly this was the greatest area of investment so that there is some justification in seeing building as the greatest of the new industries, even though its methods were still primitive and it could not be called a strategic area of industrial advance. Over half these new houses had some public money behind them (a significant fact) but the semi-detached house financed by a building society, the lower middle-class answer to the council estate, became the other characteristic instrument of the housing boom.

One further sector of heavy industry was supported by this new industrial growth – in substitution for contracting traditional markets – the steel industry. Despite great fluctuations in output arising from strikes and the depression years 1930–2 (output dropped, for example, from 9 million tons in 1920 to 3·5 million in 1921), on trend Britain was producing about twice as much steel in the later 1930's (c. 13 million tons) as in the 1920's. The great increases had come in the demand for sheet steel for vehicles.

When expanding and contracting industries are weighted into a general index of industrial production this almost doubled during the inter-war period (1918 – 73; 1919 – 81; 1924 – 100; 1938 – 146). Ship-building, mining and quarrying, leather, textiles, all shrank. Vehicles output multiplied sixfold (which meant very little by itself because so few were being produced to start with in 1918). The output of electrical engineering, paper and printing, building and construction, non-ferrous metals, precision instruments, building materials, gas, water and electricity supply all more than doubled.

Standards in the new industries compared with those of any other advanced country – in technical innovations, the efficient application of science to technology, professional management and capital investment. The general very low national average for net capital investment masked great strides taken here. Much new enterprise was in the hands of large-scale international business – much of it American, as in motor cars, oil, electrical engineering – but some expansion was flowing the other way across the Atlantic, as with Shell, Unilever and Courtaulds. Courtaulds became the largest artificial fibre manufacturer in the United States and Lever Brothers one of the largest soap-makers, as proof of these standards. Britain became the largest exporter of motor cars in 1938 (even if they mainly went to protected Empire markets). Even so, these industries were resurgent upon the home market in every case. Ten per cent or less of the output of vehicles, electrical goods, artificial fibres was exported. Of 400,000 vehicles produced in 1939 only 45,000 were exported. Only 9·1 million lb rayon yarn went abroad in 1934 from a total production of 108 million lb. Here was the foundation for the extraordinary surge in exports after 1945; but from 1920 to 1939 the export trader was no longer a source of dynamic for the British economy. Arthur Lewis claims that he was rather a source of stagnation.

Keynes, D. H. Robertson and other economists argued with varying force at the time that only vigorous action by governments could solve the problem created by the decline in the success of the export system and the industries which lay behind it. The question is many-sided, with the policy recommendations always dependent on the diagnosis for the disease. Some points are clear. The structural changes taking place demanded massive government intervention if social tragedy was to be avoided: yet the post-1945 powers governing location of industry did not then exist. The problem of the major industries, which had of necessity to contract, rationalize and re-equip, could only have been solved by a large degree of central planning, unofficial nationalization to some degree (such as was recommended by several investigations into the coal industry) and large injections of capital. But all these problems were shelved, partly for straight political reasons, partly because a series of head-on clashes between labour and capital had made both sides quite intransigent about agreeing to change. Working agreements over prices and competitive rules grew up between the four main railway companies, working under semi-public 'informal' control; there were a few publicly-subsidized schemes to reduce surplus spindles in textiles, and capacity in shipping. In agriculture, also undergoing deep sectional depression through the collapse of wheat prices again in 1921, a small scheme to subsidize sugar-beet production began in 1925 – a radical new departure but on a very modest scale. This did at least help the arable districts of the eastern side of the country, mainly afflicted by depression (as after 1872). But in coal no attempt was made to grasp the nettle of reorganization. The only large-scale expenditure devoted explicitly to the internal economic problems was unemployment pay.

Reactions to the decline in world trade were characteristically defensive on the part of most governments, and the resurgence of policies of economic nationalism, where states attempted to protect their home markets, increased the dimensions of the decline in international commerce. To be controllable the international difficulties would have demanded international agencies and international co-ordination of monetary policies on a scale inconceivable before 1945. One can doubt whether the International Monetary Fund and the other bodies could cope effectively with problems on the scale of the 1930's even now. In the 1920's European states attempted to bolster activity by competitive devaluation. British trade was severely affected by this sort of currency manipulation until the world staggered back onto the gold standard in 1925. The return to gold with the pound at pre-war parity in that year, coming at a time already of depression, was an added burden for exporters. It meant savage deflation, to the extent of 10 per cent, said Keynes, with a sharp rise in costs of British goods abroad, an equivalent fall in the sterling price of imports. This policy was defended on the grounds that Britain's international commercial and financial position demanded a stable pound fixed to gold to inspire confidence abroad. 1925 was a forlorn gesture to return to the pre-1914 world. To what extent the needs of the City proved actively prejudicial to industrial fortunes is still debated. At all events, the plan was short-lived. A run on sterling balances in the depression of 1931 forced Britain off the gold standard once more in the course of severe financial crisis which was world-wide. In 1932 came the first major break with free-trade policy in the establishment of general protective duties and – almost incidental to this – Imperial preference. In fact, a few protective tariffs in what were called 'key industries', such as dye-stuffs, cutlery, vehicles and some precision instruments, had continued since the duties were imposed during the 1914–18 war, primarily to defend these points of growth against the resurgence of German competition.

A further main policy debate developed round another aspect of government action, and here the new economics, the Keynesian revolution, came into the battle. Structural unbalance was not the only economic problem. Possibly half the unemployment rates could be laid at this door. In conditions of widespread deflation, rates of investment as a whole were lagging behind savings and only government action could re-inflate demand and employment by expanding investment. Keynes argued unceasingly for this sort of government action throughout the 1920's. His *General Theory of Employment, Interest and Money*, published in 1936, became the testament of the new economics. 'The one thing that cannot be saved,' he wrote, 'is savings.' Yet government policy, followed by all the main parties, worked in exactly the opposite direction and fed the forces leading to stagnation at home. Here internal policy acted in a similar way to external policy, being beggar-my-neighbour in result. 'Competitive economy campaigns' reduced purchasing power, by cutting the wages of civil servants, school teachers and the armed forces. There was even pressure to impose more taxes to pay for unemployment benefits. Government investment in road building and other public works was also threatened by the compulsion felt about balancing the budget. The budget remained balanced, in deference to the 'Treasury View', again linked to the need for stable currency and confidence abroad. Treasury opinion remained that of orthodox national accounting

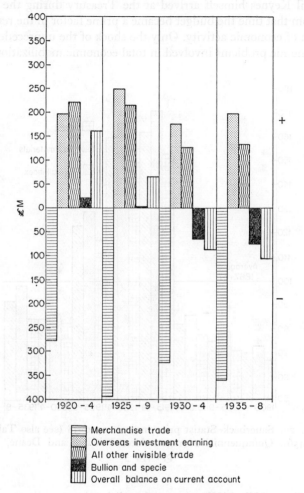

Merchandise trade
Overseas investment earning
All other invisible trade
Bullion and specie
Overall balance on current account

£M

1920–4   1925–9   1930–4   1935–8

Fig. 25. United Kingdom balance of payments, 1920–38 (see Table 18, p. 469). After Mitchell and Deane, 1962, p. 335.

until Keynes himself arrived at the Treasury during the war. From that time the budget became a prime factor in the regulation of economic activity. Only the shock of the unprecedented economic problems involved in total economic mobilization for

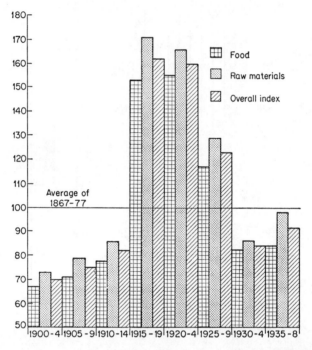

Fig. 26. Sauerbeck–Statist price indices, 1900–38 (see also Table 8, p. 456). Quinquennial averages. After Mitchell and Deane, 1962, pp. 474–5.

the Second World War shattered traditional assumptions enough for the older orthodoxies to be dismantled in the minds of men. Keynes himself was convinced that opposition to new ideas came from the strength of what Professor Galbraith has since called 'the conventional wisdom' not from any sinister interest. 'Soon or late,' he wrote, 'it is ideas, not vested interests, which are dangerous for good or evil.'

Reading list

ALDCROFT, D. H. 'Economic growth in Britain in the inter-war years: a reassessment', *Economic History Review*, 2nd series, 1967, **20**, no. 2.

ALDCROFT, D. H. 'Economic progress in Britain in the 1920s', *Scottish Journal of Political Economy*, 1966, **13**, no. 3.

ANDREWS, P. W. S. & BRUNNER, E. *The Life of Lord Nuffield: a study in enterprise and benevolence*, Oxford, 1955.

BOWLEY, A. L. *Some Economic Consequences of the Great War*, London, 1930.

BRITISH ASSOCIATION, *Britain in Depression*, London, 1935.

BRITISH ASSOCIATION, *Britain in Recovery*, London, 1938.

DOWIE, J. A. 'Growth in the inter-war period: some more arithmetic', *Economic History Review*, 2nd series, 1968, **21**, no 1.

HUME, L. J. 'The gold standard and deflation: issues and attitudes in the 1920s', *Economica*, new series, 1963, **30**, no. 119.

KAHN, A. E. *Great Britain and the World Economy*, New York, 1946.

KEYNES, J. M. [LORD]. *Essays in Persuasion*, reissued London, 1951.

KEYNES, J. M. [LORD]. *Economic Consequences of the Peace*, London, 1920.

LEWIS, W. A. *Economic Survey 1919–1939*, reissued London, 1963, ch. 5.

LOMAX, K. S. 'Growth and productivity in the UK', *Productivity Measurement Review*, 1964.

LOMAX, K. S. 'Production and productivity movement in the UK since 1900', *Journal of Royal Statistical Society*, series A, 1959, 122, pt. 2.

MATTHEWS, R. C. O. 'Some aspects of post-war growth in the British economy in relation to historical experience', Manchester Statistical Society Paper, 1964.

ORWELL, G. *The Road to Wigan Pier* [1937], new ed., London, 1965.

POLLARD, S. *The Development of the British Economy 1914–1950*, London, 1962.

RICHARDSON, H. W. *Economic Recovery in Britain, 1932–1939*, London, 1967.

RICHARDSON, H. W. 'The new industries between the wars', *Oxford Economic Papers*, new series, 1961, **13**, no. 3.

RICHARDSON, H. W. 'Over-commitment in Britain before 1930', *Oxford Economic Papers*, new series, 1965, **17,** no. 2.

RICHARDSON, H. W. 'The basis of economic recovery in the 1930s', *Economic History Review*, 1962, **15,** no. 2.

SAYERS, R. S. 'The springs of technical progress in Britain, 1919–1939', *Economic Journal*, 1950, **60,** no. 238.

STURMEY, S. G. *British Shipping and World Competition*, London, 1962.

Appendix

Tables 1–5: Population and urbanization

TABLE I: *Population growth in Great Britain and the United Kingdom, 1801–1931*

	Total number of persons (millions)			Rate of growth of population in decades ending with year shown		
Year	U.K.	G.B.	Ireland	U.K.	G.B.	Ireland
1801	15·90	10·69	5·22	–	–	–
1811	18·10	12·15	5·96	13·8	13·7	14·2
1821	21·01	14·21	6·80	16·0	16·9	14·2
1831	24·14	16·37	7·77	14·9	15·2	14·2
1841	26·75	18·55	8·20	10·8	13·4	5·6
1851	27·39	20·88	6·51	2·4	12·5	−20·3
1861	28·98	23·19	5·79	5·8	11·1	−11·1
1871	31·56	26·16	5·40	8·9	12·7	−6·7
1881	34·94	29·79	5·15	10·7	13·9	−4·7
1891	37·80	33·12	4·68	8·2	11·2	−9·1
1901	41·54	37·09	4·45	9·9	12·0	−5·0
1911	45·30	40·92	4·38	9·1	10·3	−1·5
1921	47·17	42·81	4·35	4·2	4·6	−0·6
1931	46·17*	44·83	4·18†	−2·3*	4·7	−0·4†

* Excluding Eire. With the whole of Ireland still included total population would be 49·01 m. and the decennial increase 3·9%.
† Including Eire.

See also Fig. 6, p. 247.

SOURCE: Mitchell and Deane, 1962, pp. 8–10.

TABLE 2: *Age distribution in the United Kingdom*

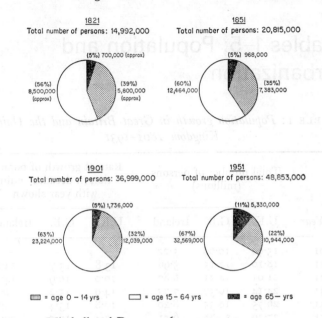

SOURCE: Mitchell and Deane, 1962, pp. 12–13.

TABLE 3: *Growth of Towns*

Town	1801	1821	1841	1861	1881	1901	1921	1931
Bath	33	47	53	53	52	50	69	69
Birmingham*	71	102	202	351	546	760	919	1,003
Blackpool	–	1	2	4	14	47	100	102
Bolton	18	32	51	70	105	168	179	177
Bradford	13	26	67	106	183	280	286	298
Bristol	61	85	124	154	207	329	377	397
Cardiff	2	4	10	33	83	164	200	224
Exeter	17	23	31	34	38	47	60	66
Glasgow*	77	147	287	443	653	904	1,034	1,088
Halifax	12	17	28	37	74	105	99	98
Kings Lynn	10	12	16	16	19	20	20	21
Liverpool*	82	138	299	472	627	685	803	856
Manchester*	75	135	252	399	502	645	730	766
Middlesbrough	–	–	6	19	55	91	131	138
Northampton	7	11	21	33	52	87	91	92
Norwich	36	50	62	75	88	112	121	126
Oxford	12	16	24	28	35	49	57	81
Sheffield	46	65	111	185	285	381	491	512
Southampton	8	13	28	47	60	105	161	176
York	17	22	29	40	50	78	84	94
Greater London	1,117	1,600	2,239	3,227	4,770	6,586	7,488	8,216

* Including environs.

Figures of population in thousands.

SOURCE: Mitchell and Deane, 1962, pp. 19, 24–7.

TABLE 4: *Migration between the United Kingdom and extra-European countries*

Year	U.K. citizens outwards	U.K. citizens inwards	Aliens and unknown out	Aliens and unknown in	Net Balance ($\rightarrow$ out $\leftarrow$ in)
1820–9	216		Included		
1830–9	668		in		
1840–9	1,495		first		
1850–9	2,440		column		
1860–9	1,465	300	376	Included in	1,541 $\rightarrow$
1870–9	1,653	744	496	second col.	1,405 $\rightarrow$
1880–9	2,568	767	1,002	302	2,501 $\rightarrow$
1890–9	1,792	1,027	888	540	1,113 $\rightarrow$
1900–9	2,613	1,295	1,791	992	2,117 $\rightarrow$
1910–19	2,483	1,418	1,043	806	1,302 $\rightarrow$
1920–9	2,833	1,673	1,127	819	1,468 $\rightarrow$
1930–8	1,631	1,764	642	597	$\leftarrow$ 88

Aliens and U.K. citizens distinguished only after 1853.

Figures in '000s.

See also Fig. 7, p. 248.

SOURCE: Mitchell and Deane, 1962, pp. 47–9.

TABLE 5: *United Kingdom standard of living*

(Consumption *per capita*, 1800–1939)

Year	Sugar (lb)	Tea (lb)	Tobacco (lb)	Beer (gallon)
1800–9	19·12	1·42	1·11	25·2
1810–19	18·06	1·29	1·01	22·5
1820–9	17·83	1·27	0·79	20·2
1830–9	17·59	1·37	0·86	—*
1840–9	18·45	1·54	0·91	—
1850–9	30·30	2·24	1·11	—
1860–9	38·84	3·13	1·27	—
1870–9	53·90	4·27	1·41	—
1880–9	68·09	4·86	1·47	36·5
1890–9	78·69	5·58	1·69	39·3
1900–9	77·99	6·15	1·97	37·4
1910–19	72·92	6·93	2·34	29·1
1920–9	78·22	8·94	2·99	20·0
1930–9	97·57	9·52	3·50	14·7

Annual averages per decade.

* No excise figures 1830–80 in the absence of a beer tax.

See also Fig. 18, p. 379.

SOURCE: Mitchell and Deane, 1962, pp. 355–8.

Tables 6-8: Prices
(See also Table 23, pp. 474-5.)

TABLE 6: *Schumpeter–Gilboy price indices, 1696–1823*

Year	Consumers' goods	Consumers' goods other than cereals	Producers' goods
1696–9	126	118	106
1700–4	101	101	102
1705–9	95	92	98
1710–14	112	105	100
1715–19	98	97	90
1720–4	95	94	89
1725–9	100	94	93
1730–4	89	88	91
1735–9	90	86	83
1740–4	97	91	94
1745–9	92	92	88
1750–4	92	87	85
1755–9	100	92	96
1760–4	98	93	102
1765–9	106	94	97
1770–4	112	99	97
1775–9	113	101	103
1780–4	119	108	114
1785–9	119	108	110
1790–4	126	114	114
1795–9	151	134	132
1800–4	186	156	153 (1800–1 only)
1805–9	195	162	–
1810–14	220	182	–
1815–19	188	170	–
1820–3	139	133	–

1701 = 100.

See also Fig. 1, p. 69.

SOURCE: Mitchell and Deane, 1962, pp. 468–9.

TABLE 7: *Rousseaux price indices, 1800–1913*

Year	Total agricultural products	Principal industrial products	Overall index
1800–4	175	159	167
1805–9	168	187	178
1810–14	199	190	195
1815–19	168	142	155
1820–4	127	118	122
1825–9	128	107	118
1830–4	123	96	110
1835–9	130	110	120
1840–4	125	103	114
1845–9	114	96	105
1850–4	105	103	104
1855–9	122	119	120
1860–4	116	122	119
1865–9	119	112	116
1870–4	122	118	120
1875–9	116	100	108
1880–4	106	93	100
1885–9	86	82	84
1890–4	87	78	82
1895–9	77	75	76
1900–4	85	88	86
1905–9	86	96	91
1910–13	99	106	103

Average of 1865 and 1885 = 100.

Figures averaged for each quinquennium.

See also Fig. 20, p. 403.

SOURCE: Mitchell and Deane, 1962, pp. 471–3.

TABLE 8: *Sauerbeck–Statist price indices, 1900–1938*

Year	Food	Raw materials	Overall index
1900–4	67	73	70
1905–9	71	79	75
1910–14	78	86	82
1915–19	153	171	162
1920–4	155	166	160
1925–9	117	129	123
1930–4	82	86	84
1935–8	84	98	91

Average of 1867–77 = 100.

Figures averaged for each quinquennium.

See also Fig. 26, p. 444.

SOURCE: Mitchell and Deane, 1962, pp. 474–5.

Tables 9–11: National income

(See also Table 26, p. 478.)

TABLE 9: *National income, 1855–1938*

Year	Net national income at current prices		Net national income at 1900 prices	
	Total (£m.)	*Per head (£)*	*Total (£m.)*	*Per head (£)*
1855	636	22·9	508	18·3
1860	694	24·1	559	19·4
1865	822	27·5	662	22·1
1870	936	29·9	774	24·8
1875	1,113	33·9	912	27·8
1880	1,076	31·1	932	26·9
1885	1,115	31·0	1,115	31·0
1890	1,385	36·9	1,416	37·8
1895	1,447	36·9	1,587	40·5
1900	1,750	42·5	1,750	42·5
1905	1,776	41·3	1,757	40·9
1910	1,984	44·2	1,881	41·9
1915	2,591	56·3	1,916	41·7
1920	5,664	129·6	2,079	47·6
1925	3,980	88·2	2,070	45·9
1930	3,957	86·2	2,294	50·0
1935	4,109	87·6	2,616	55·8
1938	4,671	98·3	2,725	57·4

Figures taken at quinquennial years.

See also Fig. 19, p. 396.

SOURCE: Mitchell and Deane, 1962, pp. 367–8.

TABLE 10: *Disposition of gross national product, 1860–1939*
(current prices)

Date	Gross national product (£m.)	Consumers' expenditure (%)	Public authority (%)	Gross domestic fixed capital (%)	Net foreign invest-ment* (%)
1860–4	890	85·1	5·5	7·1	2·3
1865–9	1,037	84·3	4·9	7·1	3·7
1870–4	1,278	82·5	4·4	7·4	5·7
1875–9	1,317	84·4	4·8	8·7	2·1
1880–4	1,381	83·7	5·3	6·9	4·1
1885–9	1,403	83·3	5·7	5·3	5·7
1890–4	1,552	83·9	5·9	6·1	4·1
1895–9	1,711	83·3	6·8	7·6	2·4
1900–4	2,084	80·0	8·7	9·2	2·0
1905–9	2,212	80·6	7·0	6·6	5·8
1910–14	2,482	79·4	7·4	5·5	7·8
1915–19		No figures given			
1920–4	5,307	79·2	9·1	8·6	3·0
1925–9	4,918	81·0	8·6	8·8	1·7
1930–4	4,624	83·2	9·3	8·1	—0·6
1935–9	5,545	77·6	13·0	10·6	—1·2

* Net of foreign investment in the U.K.

SOURCE: Deane and Cole, 1967, pp. 332–3.

TABLE 11: *Rates of growth in the United Kingdom*

20-year periods	Average % increase p.a.
1860–80	2·3
1865–85	2·4
1870–90	2·4
1875–95	2·5
1880–1900	2·4
1885–1905	1·9
1900–20	1·3
1905–25	0·1
1910–30	0·1
1925–45	1·8
1930–50	1·3
1935–55	1·4

Each period averaged 1855/64–1875/85 *et seq.*

SOURCE: Deane and Cole, 1967, p. 284.

Tables 12–13: Public revenue

TABLE 12: Public revenue, 1700–1939

Year	Customs and excise		Land and assessed taxes		Property and income tax		Death duties		Rest		Total	
	£m.	%	£m.	%	£m.	%	£m.	%	£m.	%	£m.	%
1700–9	2·9	57	1·8	35	—	—	—	—	0·4	8	5·1	100
1710–19	3·5	61	1·7	30	—	—	—	—	0·5	9	5·7	100
1720–9	4·3	70	1·4	23	—	—	—	—	0·4	7	6·1	100
1730–9	4·4	76	1·1	19	—	—	—	—	0·3	5	5·8	100
1740–9	4·3	65	2·0	30	—	—	—	—	0·3	5	6·6	100
1750–9	5·3	72	1·8	24	—	—	—	—	0·3	4	7·4	100
1760–9	7·1	70	2·2	22	—	—	—	—	0·8	8	10·1	100
1770–9	7·8	70	2·0	18	—	—	—	—	1·3	12	11·1	100
1780–9	9·9	68	2·7	18	—	—	—	—	2·0	14	14·6	100
1790–9	13·7	65	3·6	17	0·2‡	1	—	—	3·5	17	21·0	100
1800–9	29·6	59	4·9	10	5·6	11	—	—	10·2	20	50·3	100
1810–19	40·8	58	8·0	11	11·1	16	—	—	10·3	15	70·2	100
1820–9	41·2	71	6·5	11	—	—	—	—	10·5	18	58·2	100
1830–9	38·2	74	4·7	9	—	—	—	—	8·7	17	51·6	100
1840–9	37·3	68	4·4	8	3·3§	6	—	—	10·1	18	55·1	100
1850–9	39·3	63	3·6	6	8·8	14	—	—	10·5	17	62·2	100
1860–9	42·4	62	3·3	5	8·6	12	—	—	14·4	21	68·7	100
1870–9	46·1	61	2·7	4	6·7	9	5·4*	7	14·1	19	75·0	100
1880–9	45·8	53	2·9	3	12·3	14	7·3	9	17·8	21	86·1	100
1890–9	51·5	49	2·5	2	15·2	15	12·0	12	23·1	22	104·3	100
1900–9	68·0	45	2·6	2	31·1	21	18·0	12	30·9	20	150·6	100
1910–19	95·0	26	2·6	1	102·7	28	27·8	8	135·8†	37	364·1	100
1920–9	271·2	28	1·7	0	283·3	29	60·1	6	357·5†	37	973·8	100
1930–9	290·8	34	0·6	0	261·8	30	81·4	9	231·6†	27	866·2	100

Great Britain 1700–1800 } figures for central government only.
United Kingdom 1801–1939 }

* Previously included under Stamp Duty.
† Principal constituent items: surtax, motor vehicle duties, post office, telegraph, telephone, stamp duties, corporation profits tax.
‡ Introduced 1799.
§ Re-introduced 1843.

SOURCE: Mitchell and Deane, 1962, pp. 386–8, 392–5.

TABLE 13: *Net public expenditure, 1700–1939*

Year	National debt* (cumulative) £m.	Total debt charges £m.	%	Military expenditure £m.	%	Civil government £m.	%	(Education) £m.	%	Total £m.	%
1700–9	19·1	1·3	21	4·0	66	0·7	12	—	—	6·1	100
1710–19	41·6	2·7	35	4·2	55	0·8	10	—	—	7·7	100
1720–9	52·1	2·8	47	2·1	36	1·0	17	—	—	5·9	100
1730–9	46·9	2·1	39	2·3	43	0·9	17	—	—	5·4	100
1740–9	77·8	2·4	25	6·2	65	0·9	9	—	—	9·5	100
1750–9	91·3	2·9	33	4·9	55	1·1	12	—	—	8·9	100
1760–9	130·3	4·5	33	8·1	59	1·1	8	—	—	13·7	100
1770–9	153·4	4·8	38	6·3	49	1·2	9	—	—	12·8	100
1780–9	244·3	8·4	39	11·5	53	1·4	7	—	—	21·6	100
1790–9	426·6	11·6	35	19·4	58	1·9	6	—	—	33·4	100
1800–9	599·0	20·0	33	35·3	59	4·6	6	(0·1)	0	60·6	100
1810–19	844·3	28·5	35	47·0	58	5·5	7	(0·2)	0	81·3	100
1820–9	801·3	30·4	59	15·7	30	5·6	11	(0·1)	0	51·8	100
1830–9	788·2	28·9	58	13·1	26	4·9	10	(0·1)	0	49·7	100
1840–9	794·3	29·2	57	15·1	30	6·1	12	(0·3)	1	51·0	100
1850–9	808·8	28·4	47	21·9	37	7·9	13	(0·7)	1	59·6	100
1860–9	751·0	26·6	41	26·7	41	10·7	16	(1·3)	2	64·6	100
1870–9	736·1	26·2	40	24·3	37	13·5	20	(2·6)	4	66·1	100
1880–9	623·8	27·6	36	28·0	37	18·7	24	(4·9)	6	76·7	100
1890–9	598·7	23·6	26	36·4	40	20·2	22	(9·2)	10	89·2	100
1900–9	716·1	23·2	16	79·1	55	30·2	21	(14·9)	10	143·6	100
1910–19	7,460·4	76·7	8	876·1	87	55·1	5	(20·7)	2	1,018·5	100
1920–9	7,608·3	319·3	37	165·0	19	334·6	39	(51·9)	6	867·4	100
1930–9	8,287·6	245·6	32	122·6	16	369·5	46	(55·9)	7	762·2	100

Figures for Great Britain 1700–1800, United Kingdom, 1801–1939.
Figures for central government only. All figures, except col. 1, annual average per decade.
* Figures are total gross outstanding liabilities (i.e. funded, unfunded debt and outstanding investment borrowing) for final year of each decade.

SOURCE: Mitchell and Deane, 1962, pp. 389–91, 396–9, 401–3.

Tables 14–19: Trade and the balance of payments

TABLE 14: *Principal imports, 1700–1830 (official values)*

Year	Corn £'000	Corn %	Groceries £'000	Groceries %	Textile raw materials £'000	Textile raw materials %	Other raw materials £'000	Other raw materials %	Other imports £'000	Other imports %	Total imports £'000	Total imports %
1700–9	—	0	1,209	25	852	18	281	6	2,451	51	4,783	100
1710–19	—	0	1,657	29	1,042	19	282	5	2,604	47	5,585	100
1720–9	67	1	2,073	31	1,065	17	337	5	3,264	46	6,806	100
1730–9	9	0	2,269	29	1,048	14	401	5	4,021	52	7,748	100
1740–9	11	0	2,263	31	1,075	15	370	5	3,429	49	7,290	100
1750–9	40	0	2,641	32	1,356	16	471	6	3,817	46	8,325	100
1760–9	226	2	3,863	36	1,671	16	608	6	4,351	40	10,719	100
1770–9	421	3	3,918	32	1,967	16	702	6	5,096	43	12,104	100
1780–9	422	3	4,295	31	2,497	18	716	5	5,890	43	13,820	100
1790–9	1,168	5	7,633	35	3,227	15	965	4	8,804	41	21,797	100
1800–9	1,430	5	12,110	42	5,451	19	1,607	6	8,158	28	28,740	100
1810–19	1,476	5	12,912	41	8,079	26	2,476	8	6,697	20	31,640	100
1820–9	1,269	3	13,379	35	12,537	33	3,724	10	7,401	19	38,310	100

Figs. England and Wales to 1790 } annual averages per decade.
Great Britain, 1792–1829 }

Groupings for categories listed:
Corn: all grains and flour.
Groceries: coffee, sugar, tea, wine, tobacco.
Textile raw materials: raw cotton, wool, silk, flax, hemp, linen, yarn, dyewoods, dye-stuffs.
Other raw materials: timber, hides, skins, oils, seeds, iron.

Official values were based on fixed prices, mainly those of 1696. These figures therefore represent changing volumes in trade, not current values. They cannot be used in balance of payments calculations. Corn imports in particular, vary in price and in current values much more than is indicated here.

See also Fig. 11, p. 309.

SOURCE: Mitchell and Deane, 1962, pp. 279–81, 285–9.

TABLE 15: *Principal exports, 1700–1830 (official values)*

Year	Total textile exports £'000	%	Total cotton £'000	%	Total woollen, worsted £'000	%	Iron, steel manufacture £'000	%	Non-ferrous metals £'000	%	Total exports British products £'000	%	Total re-exports
1700–9	3,190	72	13	0	3,095	70	71	2	231	5	4,495	100	1,656
1710–19	3,344	70	8	0	3,222	67	100	2	279	6	4,841	100	2,150
1720–9	3,247	66	16	0	3,116	64	133	3	249	5	4,937	100	2,840
1730–9	3,727	65	15	0	3,581	63	189	3	338	6	5,858	100	3,200
1740–9	3,677	56	11	0	3,453	53	301	5	427	7	6,556	100	3,572
1750–9	4,764	54	88	1	4,239	48	424	5	441	5	8,760	100	3,504
1760–9	5,340	53	227	2	4,448	44	594	6	582	6	10,043	100	4,790
1770–9	4,865	52	248	3	3,991	43	677	7	629	7	9,287	100	5,136
1780–9	4,921	48	756	7	3,518	35	659	6	731	7	10,200	100	4,262
1790–9	9,015	52	2,631	15	5,234	30	1,215	7	1,160	7	17,520	100	9,350
1800–9	17,090	67	9,995	39	5,982	24	1,323	5	1,011	4	25,380	100	12,150
1810–19	25,940	74	18,712	53	5,617	16	1,579	4	954	3	35,050	100	11,680
1820–9	37,178	80	28,800	62	5,553	12	2,042	4	1,113	2	46,530	100	9,980

Figs. England and Wales to 1791 ⎱ annual averages per decade.
Great Britain, 1791–1829 ⎰

Groupings for categories listed:
Total textiles: cotton, woollens, worsteds, linen, silk.
Iron, steel manufactures: iron and steel, hardware, cutlery, machinery.

Official values: See note to Table 14.

See also Fig. 10, p. 307.

SOURCE: Mitchell and Deane, 1962, pp. 279–81, 293–5.

TABLE 16: *Imports to the United Kingdom, 1854–1938*

Year	Grain and flour £m.	%	Groceries £m.	%	Meat, dairy produce £m.	%	Textile raw materials £m.	%	Other raw materials £m.	%	Manufactured goods £m.	%	Total imports £m.
1855–9	19·6	12	24·7	15	5·0	3	50·4	30	26·3	16	2·8	2	169·5
1860–9	31·9	12	33·9	13	12·0	5	90·7	35	32·1	12	5·0	2	260·9
1870–9	52·0	14	49·4	14	23·4	7	95·8	27	44·2	12	9·9	3	360·6
1880–9	55·1	14	44·7	11	36·8	9	94·9	24	45·5	12	12·3	3	393·6
1890–9	55·1	13	42·1	10	51·7	12	89·8	21	52·0	12	15·7	4	435·8
1900–9	66·1	12	40·0	7	73·2	13	107·2	19	77·4	14	31·7	6	570·4
1910–19	105·6	11	70·3	7	116·9	12	178·7	19	149·8	16	52·1	6	937·5
1920–9	116·2	9	101·2	8	165·7	13	210·6	17	202·7	16	68·3	5	1,259·2
1930–8	63·5	8	68·4	8	116·7	13	92·9	11	150·8	18	58·1	7	836·1

Computed values 1854–70, declared values 1871–1938.
Annual averages per decade.

Groupings for categories listed:
  Groceries: coffee, sugar, tea, wine, tobacco.
  Meat/dairy produce: includes animals.
  Textile raw materials: cotton, wool, silk, yarn, flax, hemp, jute, dyewoods.
  Other raw materials: oils etc, rubber, hides and skins, paper materials, petroleum.
  Manufactured products: iron and steel, machinery, non-ferrous metal products.

SOURCE: Mitchell and Deane, 1962, pp. 299–301.

TABLE 17: *Exports from the United Kingdom, 1830–1938 (current prices)*

Year	Textiles (total) £m.	%	Cottons £m.	%	Iron and steel etc. £m.	%	Machinery £m.	%	Coal £m.	%	Vehicles etc. £m.	%	Total £m.
1830–9	31·7	72	20·9	48	5·0	11	0·3	1	0·3	1	—		44·0
1840–9	38·6	70	25·0	45	8·2	15	0·8	1	0·9	2	—		55·4
1850–9	59·9	60	35·6	36	17·9	18	2·4	2	2·3	2	—		100·1
1860–9	98·5	62	57·6	36	24·0	15	4·6	3	4·5	3	—		159·7
1870–9	118·6	55	71·5	33	34·9	16	7·7	4	8·8	4	—		218·1
1880–9	114·1	49	73·3	32	35·3	15	11·8	5	10·5	5	—		230·3
1890–9	104·3	44	67·2	28	32·5	14	16·1	7	17·5	7	1·1	0	237·1
1900–9	126·2	38	86·4	26	45·7	14	23·8	7	32·9	10	8·4	3	333·3
1910–19	200·5	40	135·0	25	62·9	12	27·0	5	50·0	10	9·1	2	504·6
1920–9	287·7	36	192·5	24	96·5	12	58·1	7	65·2	8	29·4	4	791·4
1930–8	106·0	24	62·9	14	54·1	12	41·8	10	37·7	9	22·4	5	438·8

Annual averages per decade.

Groupings for categories listed:

Textiles (total): cotton, woollens, linen, silk, hats, haberdashery, apparel etc.
Iron and steel: iron and steel, hardware, cutlery, non-ferrous metals and manufactures.
Vehicles etc.: vehicles, aircraft, new ships and boats.

See also Fig. 12, p. 311.

SOURCE: Mitchell and Deane, 1962, pp. 303–6.

TABLE 18: *United Kingdom balance of payments, 1920–38*

Year	Merchandise trade (£m.)	Overseas investment earnings (£m.)	All other invisible trade (£m.)	Bullion and specie (£m.)	Overall balance on current account (£m.)
1920–4	−279	+199	+221	+21	+162
1925–9	−395	+250	+213	+1	+68
1930–4	−324	+174	+127	−66	−89
1935–8	−360	+199	+133	−77	−105

+ excess of receipts. − excess of payment.

Annual averages per quinquennium.

For balance of payments figures 1796–1913 see Table VII on p. 305.

See also Fig. 25, p. 443.

SOURCE: Mitchell and Deane, 1962, p. 335.

TABLE 19: *Geographical distribution of foreign investments by the United Kingdom*

(in millions of U.S. dollars to nearest $50 m.)

Area	1914	1938
Europe	1,050	1,750
North America – TOTAL	7,050	5,450
U.S.A.	4,250	2,750
Canada	2,800	2,700
Latin America – TOTAL	3,700	4,900
Mexico	500	900
Cuba	150	150
Argentina	1,550	1,950
Brazil	700	800
Chile	300	400
Peru	150	100
Uruguay	200	150
Rest	100	450

Area	1914	1938
Oceania – TOTAL	2,200	
Australia	1,700	2,650
New Zealand	300	700
Rest	(200)	
Asia – TOTAL	3,550	
Turkey	100	200
India and Ceylon	1,850	3,050
Straits Settlements	150	
Dutch East Indies	200	200
China	600	850
Japan	500	250
Rest	(150)	50
Iran		100
Siam		100
Malaya		400
Philippines		50
Asia and Oceania – TOTAL		8,600
Africa – TOTAL	2,450	2,150
Egypt	(200)	200
British W. Africa	200	200
South Africa	1,550⎫	1,250
Rhodesia	250⎭	
British E. and Central Africa	150	150
Rest of British Africa		150
Belgian Congo		50
Rest	100	
Portuguese Africa		100
World	20,000	22,900

See also Fig. 15, p. 327.

SOURCE: W. Woodruff, *Impact of Western Man*, 1967, pp. 154, 156.

Tables 20–25: Agriculture

TABLE 20: *Wheat and wheat flour trade in Great Britain,*
1700–1800

Year	Imports	Exports
1700–9	negligible	104·8
1710–19	negligible	108·8
1720–9	11·5	116·0
	(all in 1728 and 1729)	
1730–9	–	296·9
1740–9	1·3	290·7
	(in 1740 and 1741)	
1750–9	16·2	329·0
	(in 1757–8)	
1760–9	96·7	235·2
	(mostly in 1767–8)	
1770–9	130·0	86·9
1780–9	152·9	129·5
1790–9	404·7	83·2

Average per annum per decade, in 'ooos of quarters.

N.B. Averaging figures over decades masks sharp fluctuations in individual years.

See also Fig. 2, p. 70.

SOURCE: Mitchell and Deane, 1962, pp. 94–5.

TABLE 21: *Imports of wheat, barley and oats to the United Kingdom, 1800–1938*

Year	Wheat and flour	Barley and meal	Oats and meal
1800–9	1,989	137	1,470
1810–19	2,617	570	1,188
1820–9	1,631	606	2,206
1830–9	3,743	659	1,494
1840–9	10,676	2,182	1,834
1850–9	19,326	3,585	3,523
1860–9	33,692	6,894	6,990
1870–9	50,406	11,088	11,937
1880–9	70,282	14,849	14,162
1890–9	85,890	19,921	15,436
1900–9	102,551	19,840	16,379
1910–19	104,502	16,036	14,485
1920–9	108,699	14,970	8,018
1930–8	110,091	16,190	4,687

Net imports. Average per decade. Amounts in '000 cwt.

No re-export figures for barley and oats after 1839.

Southern Ireland treated as foreign from 1 April 1923.

SOURCE: Mitchell and Deane, 1962, pp. 97–9.

TABLE 22: *Sources of wheat imports to the United Kingdom, 1830–1938*

Year	N. Europe	%	N. America	%	India	%	Australia	%	S. America	%
1830–9	1,767	88	241	12	—	0	—	0	—	0
1840–9	3,905	87	568	13	—	0	—	0	—	0
1850–9	6,200	73	2,262	27	—	0	—	0	—	0
1860–9	14,189	61	8,967	39	—	0	—	0	—	0
1870–9	14,341	35	23,853	58	1,541	4	1,110	3	—	0
1880–9	11,988	23	29,135	55	8,735	16	2,855	5	307	1
1890–9	13,700	22	33,181	53	7,538	12	2,104	3	6,276	10
1900–9	13,187	16	34,098	40	12,604	15	6,809	8	18,252	21
1910–19	6,922	8	52,822	57	11,587	13	9,301	10	11,448	12
1920–9	698	1	60,043	60	4,223	4	13,583	14	21,196	21
1930–8	9,279	10	43,998	46	2,008	2	22,867	24	17,924	18

Average per annum per decade. Amounts in 'ooo cwt.

SOURCE: Mitchell and Deane, 1962, pp. 100–2.

TABLE 23: *Wheat prices, 1700–1938*

Year	Wheat prices (shillings per quarter)	Bread prices: London (pence per 4 lb loaf)
1700–4	29·80	4·8
1705–9	38·02	5·7
1710–14	40·21	5·7
1715–19	34·64	4·9
1720–4	30·05	4·8
1725–9	37·29	5·7
1730–4	25·68	4·5
1735–9	29·79	5·3
1740–4	26·81	4·6
1745–9	27·32	4·9
1750–4	31·25	5·1
1755–9	36·54	5·6
1760–4	32·95	4·9
1765–9	43·43	6·6
1770–4	50·20	6·8
1775–9	42·80	6·3
1780–4	47·32	6·7
1785–9	44·92	6·1
1790–4	49·57	6·6
1795–9	65·67	8·8
1800–4	84·85	11·7
1805–9	84·57	12·2
1810–14	102·47	14·6
1815–19	99·95	12·8
1820–4	57·15	10·0
1825–9	62·47	9·9
1830–4	57·67	9·4
1835–9	55·78	8·7
1840–4	57·87	8·7
1845–9	54·00	8·4
1850–4	49·03	7·8
1855–9	57·61	9·1
1860–4	49·78	8·2
1865–9	53·62	8·7
1870–4	55·00	8·4
1875–9	47·67	7·3
1880–4	42·40	7·0
1885–9	31·58	6·0
1890–4	29·67	5·9

Year	Wheat prices (shillings per quarter)	Bread prices: London (pence per 4 lb loaf)
1895–9	27·82	5·4
1900–4	27·37	5·3
1905–9	31·48	5·7
1910–14	32·93	5·8
1915–19	66·58	9·1
1920–4	44·30	10·1
1925–9	11·18	
1930–4	5·97	7·3
1935–8	7·11	8·3

Winchester College prices per Winchester Quarter to 1770.

Official average prices per Imperial Quarter after 1770.

Average per annum per quinquennium.

SOURCE: Mitchell and Deane, 1962, pp. 487–9, 497–8.

TABLE 24: *Crop acreage in Great Britain*
(figures in thousand acres)

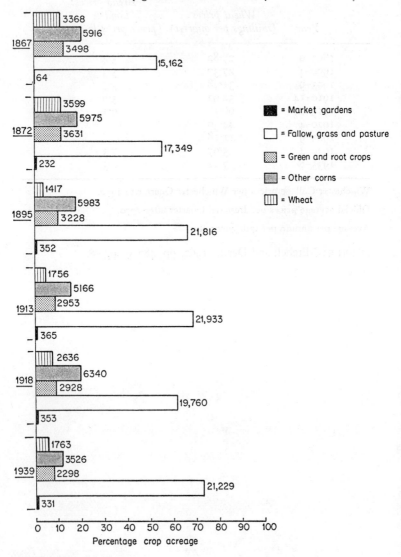

See also Fig. 16, p. 344.

SOURCE: Mitchell and Deane, 1962, pp. 78–9.

TABLE 25: *Numbers of animals in Great Britain (in thousands)*

Year	Cattle	Sheep	Pigs	Horses
1867	4,993	28,919	2,967	*
1872	5,625	27,922	2,772	1,258
1895	6,354	25,792	2,884	1,545
1913	6,964	23,931	2,234	1,324
1918	7,410	23,353	1,825	1,337
1939	8,119	25,993	3,767	987

Annual agricultural statistics begin only in 1867.

* No figures available.

SOURCE: Mitchell and Deane, 1962, pp. 82–3.

Tables 26–38: Production and industry

TABLE 26: *National income: shares of national income by industrial sectors*

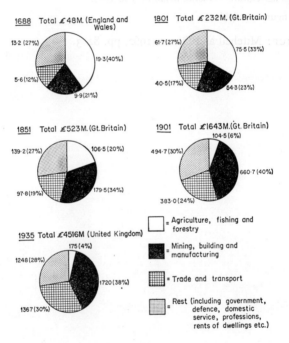

1688 Total £48M. (England and Wales)
13·2 (27%)
19·3 (40%)
5·6 (12%)
9·9 (21%)

1801 Total £232M. (Gt. Britain)
61·7 (27%)
75·5 (33%)
40·5 (17%)
54·3 (23%)

1851 Total £523M. (Gt. Britain)
139·2 (27%)
106·5 (20%)
97·8 (19%)
179·5 (34%)

1901 Total £1643M. (Gt. Britain)
104·5 (6%)
494·7 (30%)
660·7 (40%)
383·0 (24%)

1935 Total £4516M (United Kingdom)
175 (4%)
1248 (28%)
1720 (38%)
1367 (30%)

☐ = Agriculture, fishing and forestry

■ = Mining, building and manufacturing

▦ = Trade and transport

▨ = Rest (including government, defence, domestic service, professions, rents of dwellings etc.)

Figures in £m. with percentages of total.

SOURCE: Mitchell and Deane, 1962, p. 366.

478

TABLE 27: *Coal exported and shipped coastwise from Newcastle and Sunderland, 1700–1830*

Year	Coal coastwise from N.E. field ports	Coal exports from N.E. field ports	Coal to London by sea
1700–9	496		418
1710–19	445		504
1720–9	713		596
1730–9	752	Included in	607
1740–9	756	first column	612
1750–9	1,237		647
1760–9	1,366		742
1770–9	1,492		833
1780–9	1,767		904
1790–9	1,848	140	1,051
1800–9	2,232	121	1,229
1810–19	2,654	113	1,433
1820–9	2,844	181	1,827

Average per annum per decade in '000 tons.

SOURCE: Mitchell and Deane, 1962, pp. 108–14.

TABLE 28: *Coal consumption*

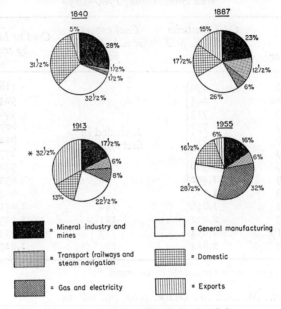

= Mineral industry and mines

= General manufacturing

= Transport (railways and steam navigation)

= Domestic

= Gas and electricity

= Exports

✱ Includes coal sent to bunkering stations for shipping

SOURCE: Deane and Cole, 1967, p. 219.

TABLE 29: *Coal output, exports and labour employed, 1800–1938*

Year	Total U.K. output	Total exports	%	Total employment*	Output per man (tons)
1800	11·0	0·2	2		
1816	15·9	0·4	2·5		
1820	17·4	0·2	1·4		
1850	49·4	3·3	6·8		
1855–9	66·7	5·99	9	–	–
1860–4	84·9	7·83	9	307·5†	276
1865–9	103·0	9·86	10	332·3	310
1870–4	121·3	12·31	10	438·6	277
1875–9	133·6	15·06	11	499·4	268
1880–4	156·4	20·12	13	504·1	313
1885–9	165·2	24·24	15	539·6	306
1890–4	180·3	29·35	16	674·4	267
1895–9	201·9	35·25	17	704·8	286
1900–4	226·8	44·07	19	820·3	277
1905–9	256·1	60·46	24	936·6	273
1910–14	270·0	62·71	23	1,093·5	247
1915–19	243·1	36·78	15	1,034·6	235
1920–4	237·1	50·98	22	1,189·1	199
1925–9	223·2	46·58	20	1,013·5	220
1930–4	220·0	43·05	20	839·2	263
1935–8	229·6	38·11	17	779·8	294

Amounts in million tons, average per annum per quinquennium.

* In '000s.
† In 1864. Output per man based on 92·8m. production for 1864.

See also Fig. 9, p. 268.

SOURCE: Mitchell and Deane, 1962, pp. 115–21.

TABLE 30: *Iron and steel imports and exports, 1700–1860*

Year	Total iron imports ('000 tons)	Total iron and steel exports ('000 tons)
1700–9	16	1·6
1710–19	17	2·0
1720–9	20	2·9
1730–9	29	4·0
1740–9	26	6·8
1750–9	35	9·3
1760–9	45	13·3
1770–9	49	14·6
1780–9	47	14·3
1790–9	53	27·2
1800–9	33	33·3
1810–19	18	47
1820–9	15	77
1830–9	19	180
1840–9	26	458
1850–9	44	1,225

Figures in annual averages per decade.

1700–89, England and Wales; 1792–1814, Great Britain; 1815–60, United Kingdom.

1700–1815: Imports mainly bar iron.

1815–55: Import figures represent bar iron only.

SOURCE: Mitchell and Deane, 1962, pp. 140–1.

TABLE 31: *United Kingdom iron and steel production, exports and imports, 1855–1938*

Year	Iron ore production ('000 tons)	Iron ore imports ('000 tons)	Pig iron output ('000 tons)	U.K. iron and steel exports ('000 tons)	U.K. iron and steel imports ('000 tons)
1855–9	9,106	22	3,526	1,411	50
1860–4	8,391	44	4,152	1,536	75
1865–9	10,255	93	4,905	2,027	108
1870–4	15,342	611	6,378	2,965	184
1875–9	15,892	906	6,381	2,442	221
1880–4	17,405	2,858	8,164	3,901	353
1885–9	14,352	3,412	7,661	3,763	373
1890–4	12,288	3,983	7,285	3,097	361
1895–9	13,748	5,676	8,638	3,407	523
1900–14	13,444	6,140	8,639	3,430	1,090
1905–19	15,132	7,039	9,699	4,502	1,164
1910–4	15,080	6,623	9,495	4,579*	1,793
1915–9	13,889	6,220	8,701	2,540*	658
1920–4	8,996	4,730	6,060	3,303*	1,476†
1925–9	9,984	4,353	6,042	3,911*	3,317†
1930–4	8,926	3,424	4,729	2,240*	1,922†
1935–8	12,418	5,679	7,350	2,293*	1,503†

Annual average for each quinquennium.

* Old iron excluded from 1909.   † Excludes old rails, includes hollow-ware.

Southern Ireland treated as foreign from 1 April 1923.

See also Fig. 22, p. 412.

SOURCE: Mitchell and Deane, 1962, pp. 129–35, 142–3, 146–8.

TABLE 32: *Steel output in the United Kingdom (ingots and castings)*

Year	Total '000 tons	Bessemer		Open hearth		Acid Process %	Basic Process %
		'000 tons	% total	'000 tons	% total		
1871–4	486	444	91·3	42	8·7	–	–
1875–9	883	742	84	141	16	–	–
1880–4	1,793	1,402	78·1	391	21·9	–	–
1885–9	2,814	1,818	64·6	996	35·4	86 (1889)	14 (1889)
1890–4	3,143	1,637	51·8	1,506	48·2	86	14
1895–9	4,260	1,764	41·4	2,496	58·6	84	16
1900–4	4,955	1,774	36	3,181	64	79	21
1905–9	5,994	1,690	28	4,304	72	72	28
1910–14	7,007	1,529	22	5,478	78	73	27
1915–19	8,938	1,271	14	7,410	82	53	44
1920–4	7,067	556	8	6,414	91	37	62
1925–9	7,647	443	6	7,083	93	33	66
1930–4	6,733	195	3	6,409	95	25	73
1935–9	11,257	564	5	10,391	92	20	77

Annual average for each quinquennium.

From 1915 1–3 per cent of total steel output was produced from electric furnaces.

See also Fig. 21, p. 410.

SOURCE: Mitchell and Deane, 1962, pp. 136–7.

TABLE 33: *Non-ferrous metals, 1700–1938 (figures in '000 tons)*

Year	Copper and brass — Output	Copper and brass — Exports	Copper and brass — Imports (net) ore	Copper and brass — Imports (net) wrought	Lead — Output metallic lead	Lead — Exports lead and shot	Lead — Imports (net) ore	Lead — Imports (net) pig sheet wrought	Tin — Output white tin	Tin — Exports	Tin — Imports ore	Tin — Imports blocks
1700–9		0·1				11·9			1·4	1·1		
1710–19		0·2				12·4			1·3	1·3		
1720–9		0·2				10·2			1·5	1·1		
1730–9		0·5				12·7			1·7	1·4		
1740–9		0·8				12·6			1·7	1·5		
1750–9		1·2				13·3			2·7	1·7		
1760–9		2·3				15·6			2·7	1·9		
1770–9	3·4*	3·4				14·5			2·8	1·9		
1780–9	4·0†	3·6				14·9			3·0	2·1		
1790–9	5·2‡	7·7				13·3			3·2	2·3		
1800–9	6·0	6·9				10·1			2·6	1·6		
1810–19	6·5	4·6				15·5			2·9	1·7		
1820–9	8·8	5·6				11·8		0·2	4·3	1·8		
1830–9	11·4	10·9	13			9·1		0·1	4·3	1·1		
1840–9	11·5	17·6	50	0·4	54·4	13·0		0·8	—	1·6		0·4
1850–9	16·1§	20·5	67	4·3	65·7	19·8		12·5	6·4	1·7		2·1
1860–9	12·5	35·5	108	11·5	68·0	31·0	5·6	34·7	9·0	4·1		3·4
1870–9	5·1	43·0	102	22·2	60·3	39·0	14·5	74·8	9·8	5·9		8·0
1880–9	3·3‖	58·1	179	23·5	42·8	41·3	20·5	103·6	9·2	5·1	1·0	11·5
1890–9		63·8	193	39·7	29·0	46·0	26·0	160·2	6·9	5·6	4·3	13·9
1900–9		56·2	169	69·2	21·3	40·2	21·0	207·8	4·5	7·5	16·6	12·9
1910–9		44·2	98	116·9	15·7	33·1	13·8	195·7	4·6	14·2	33·8	12·4
1920–9		61·2	37	123·3	11·9	17·3	4·7	217·0	2·0	20·8	57·1	7·4
1930–8		49·6	36	225·7	31·7	12·1	0·6	309·1	1·8	17·7	50·0	5·2

* Output of metallic copper 1771–1853 from ore sold publicly in Cornwall and Devon. † 1780–6. ‡ 1796–9.

§ U.K. output of British ore, 1854–5. ‖ 1880–5.

Annual averages per decade given.

SOURCE: Mitchell and Deane, 1962, pp. 153–9.

TABLE 34: *Cotton*

Year	Raw cotton (retained imports, '000 lb)	Exports of piece goods (m. yd)	Exports of thread twist and yarn (m. lb)
1750–9	2,820		
1760–9	3,531		
1770–9	4,797		
1780–9	14,824		
1790–9	28,645		
1800–9	59,554		
1810–19	96,339	227†	14†
1820–9	173,000	320	37
1830–9	302,000*	553	87
1840–9	550,000	978	139
1850–9	795,000	1,855	168
1860–9	803,000	2,375	143
1870–9	1,244,000	3,573	229
1880–9	1,473,000	4,575	267
1890–9	1,556,000	5,057	261
1900–9	1,723,000	5,649	219
1910–19	1,864,000	5,460	202
1920–9	1,498,000	4,239	188
1930–8	1,360,000	1,970	152

* Estimated re-exports for 1834–9.
† 1815–19.

Annual average per decade. See also Fig. 4, p. 130.

SOURCE: Mitchell and Deane, 1962, pp. 177–81.

TABLE 35: *Woollens*

Year	Domestic wool clip U.K. ('000 lb)	Raw wool imports '000 lb (totals less re-exports)	Exports of yarn ('000 lb)	Exports of wool goods	
				By the piece ('000 pieces)	By the yard ('000 yd)
1775–9	80,000	1,569*			
1780–9	90,000	2,815			
1790–9	90,000	3,747			
1800–9	100,000	7,451			
1810–19	100,000	13,181	14†	1,405‡	8,277‡
1820–9	113,000	22,300	157	1,693	6,635
1830–9	120,000	42,800	2,270	2,067	6,955
1840–9	128,000	57,700	7,865		93,316§
1850–9	138,000	84,800	19,170		161,563
1860–9	152,000	138,400	31,517		236,267
1870–9	157,000	192,900	34,284		311,598
1880–9	135,000	252,300	37,808	*Total wool manu-factures ('000 yd)*	270,744
1890–9	142,000	354,700	53,335		193,194
1900–9	135,000	374,000	54,475		171,470
1910–19	130,000 (estimated)	562,400	39,705		170,044
1920–9	109,000 (estimated)	426,200	44,307		183,760‖
1930–9	107,000 (estimated)	598,000	36,107		101,245

* 1772–9.
† 1819 only
‡ 1815–19.
§ Including carpets 1840–1889; excluding carpets and blankets 1890–1919.
‖ After 1920 total is of woollen and worsted tissues only (in sq. yd).

See also Fig. 5, p. 131.

SOURCE: Mitchell and Deane, 1962, pp. 190–1, 195–7.

TABLE 36: *Railways*

Year	Paid up capital and loans (£m.)	Miles of track open	Passengers carried (m.)	Freight carried (m. tons)	Passenger train receipts (£m.)	Freight train receipts (£m.)
1845	88·5	2,441	30·4	—	3·9	2·2
1850	234·9	6,084	67·4	—	6·5	6·2
1855	282·4	7,293	111·4	—	10·0	10·5
1860	327·5	9,069	153·5	88·4	12·2	14·2
1865	429·8	11,451	238·7	112·6	15·5	18·7
1870	502·7	13,562	322·2	—	18·1	23·2
1875	600·0	14,510	490·1	196·2	24·3	32·1
1880	694·6	15,563	596·6	231·7	25·8	34·5
1885	780·3	16,594	678·1	253·6	28·3	35·6
1890	860·2	17,281	796·3	298·8	32·7	40·8
1895	961·8	18,001	903·5	329·5	35·5	42·5
1900	1,136·2	18,680	1,114·6	419·8	43·3	51·8
1905	1,228·8	19,535	1,170·0	455·4	46·6	54·6
1910	1,273·2	19,986	1,276·0	507·9	50·5	59·4
1915	—	—	—	—	—	—
1920	1,299·3	20,312	1,579·0	318·1	109·4	126·9
1925	1,177·4	20,400	1,232·6	316·0	94·1	103·7
1930	1,119·7	20,265	844·3	304·3	76·8	99·3
1935	1,127·1	20,152	856·2	270·9	70·0	86·2
1938	1,125·9	20,007	848·9	264·3	75·3	87·8

Figures for quinquennial years only.

SOURCE: Mitchell and Deane, 1962, pp. 225–7.

TABLE 37: *Shipping, 1790–1938*

Year	Shipping tonnage registered in U.K.		Ships built and first registered in Britain	
	Sailing ships ('000 tons)	Steam ships ('000 tons)	Sailing ships ('000 tons)	Steam ships ('000 tons)
1790–9	1,443	–	79·8	–
1800–9	2,003	–	97·1	–
1810–19	2,379	1	90·8	0·4
1820–9	2,291	17	81·0	3·0
1830–9	2,278	52	105·0	6·2
1840–9	3,009	123	119·6	11·8
1850–9	3,867	319	160·0	46·3
1860–9	4,590	724	206·4	107·9
1870–9	4,240	1,847	129·5	258·6
1880–9	3,435	3,783	122·6	337·2
1890–9	2,784	5,993	104·4	500·9
1900–9	1,710	8,921	37·4	674·2
1910–19	795	10,718*	22·6	724·5
1920–9	536	11,314	21·7	615·5
1930–8	439	10,765	15·7	290·7

1787–1814 figures for British Empire and Great Britain, after 1814 figures for the United Kingdom.

* Motor ships included with steam ships after 1918.

Average per annum per decade.

See also Fig. 13, p. 313.

SOURCE: Mitchell and Deane, 1962, pp. 217–22.

TABLE 38: *Houses built in Great Britain, 1856–1938*

Year	Houses built (in '000)
1856–9	48·9
1860–4	54·8
1865–9	64·3
1870–4	88·5
1875–9	113·5
1880–4	81·7
1885–9	78·0
1890–4	83·2
1895–9	128·2
1900–4	145·3
1905–9	115·8
1910–14	61·9
1915–9	23·9*
1920–4	67·5
1925–9	214·1
1930–4	248·5
1935–8	338·5

* 1915–16 only.

Annual average within each quinquennium.

See also Fig. 17, p. 376.

SOURCE: Mitchell and Deane, 1962, p. 239.

Table 39: Finance

TABLE 39: *Stock of money, means of payment, national income, and velocity of circulation in England and Wales, selected dates, 1688–1913*

Components of money stock and means of payment (£m.)

	1688–9	1750	1775	1800–1	1811	1821	1831	1844	1855	1865	1875	1885	1913
Specie in circulation	10	15	16	20	15	18	30	36	50	70	105	109	145
Bank-notes	2	5	10	25	45	32	29	28·5	26·7	27	32·2	27·7	44·7
Deposits		*	*	5†	15†	25†	40	80·5	145	270	409	458	1,074·5
Total money (M₁)	12	20	26	50	75	75	99	145	221·7	367	546·2	594·7	1,264·2
Other	8	20	37	115†	140†	76	67	75	153	–	32·4	–	–
Means of payment (M₂)	20	40	63	165	215	151	166	220	374·7		578·6		

Components of money stock (percentages)

	1688–9	1750	1775	1800–1	1811	1821	1831	1844	1855	1865	1875	1885	1913
Specie	83·3	75	61·5	40	20	24·0	30·3	25	22·6	19·1	19·2	18·3	11·5
Bank-notes	16·7	25	38·5	50	60	42·7	29·3	20	12·0	7·4	5·9	4·7	3·5
Deposits		*	*	10†	20†	33·3†	40·4	55	65·4	73·5	74·9	77·0	85·0
Total (M₁)	100·0	100·0	100·0	100·0	100·0	100·0	100·0	100·0	100·0	100·0	100·0	100·0	100·0

Components of means of payment (percentages)

	1688-9	1750	1775	1800-1	1811	1821	1831	1844	1855	1865	1875	1885	1913
Specie	50	37·5	25·4	21·1	7·0	11·9	18·1	16·4	13·3		18·1		18·1
Bank-notes }	10	12·5	15·9	15·2	20·9	21·2	17·4	12·9	7·1		5·6		
Deposits }		*	*	3·0	7·0	16·6	24·1	36·6	38·7		70·7		
Other	40	50	58·7	69·7	65·1	50·3	40·4	34·1	40·9		5·6		
Total (M_2)	100·0	100·0	100·0	100·0	100·0	100·0	100·0	100·0	100·0		100·0		
National income (£m.) and velocity of circulation													
National Income (Y)	50·8	100	135	196·7	255·9	247·4	290·7	403·8	474·5	640·7	896·9	928·2	2,265
V_1 (= Y/M_1)	4·2	5·0	5·2	3·9	3·4	3·3	2·9	2·8	2·1	1·7	1·6	1·6	1·8
V_2 (= Y/M_2)	2·5	2·5	2·1	1·2	1·2	1·6	1·75	1·8	1·3	–	1·5	–	–
Per capita income (£)	9·24	16·27	18·17	21·71	24·79	20·50	20·77	24·42	25·2	30·3	37·3	34·1	49·6

* Due to the dubious 'moneyness' of deposits in the eighteenth century, they have been included in 'Other means of payment' rather than in 'Total money'. The figures are for 1750, 5·0; for 1775, 7·0.

† For reasons analogous to that given in note *, only one-fourth of estimated deposits have been included in M_1 in 1800-1, three-sevenths in 1811, and five-sevenths in 1821. The remainders have been included in 'Other'.

‡ The figures for 'Other' (bills of exchange primarily) for 1800-1 and 1811 are especially suspect; they are, however, in accord with contemporary estimates.

SOURCE: R. E. Cameron, Banking in the Early Stages of Industrialisation, 1967, p. 42.

Index